BEST VALUE PROCUREMENT

SECOND EDITION

How to use information systems to minimize risk, increase performance, and predict future success

Dean T. Kashiwagi, Ph.D.

PBSRG

Best Value Procurement – Dean T. Kashiwagi
ISBN # 1-889857-26-2
Copyright 2002 by Dean T. Kashiwagi

Published and distributed by:
Performance Based Studies Research Group
Arizona State University
Tempe, Arizona 85287-0204
(480) 965-4273, Fax (480) 965-4371

For information, please email Dean T. Kashiwagi at: dean.kashiwagi@asu.edu

Acknowledgements

To all those who have given their lives to making this world a better place to live, starting with my wonderful wife Judy and family who is the model and originator of IMT, my mentors and head visionaries Bill Badger and Dave Cotts, my wonderful staff, and the greatest friends anyone could want. To those who have shared the dream:

Mark Bollig
Rich Byfield
Ron Campbell
Jamie Ho
Chris Kinimaka
Gordon Matsuoka
Edward Maxey
Steve Mayle

Steve Miwa
Miguel Ramos
John Savicky
Charlie Serikawa
Mike Steele
Thom Tisthammer
Flash Wilkerson

Preface

Two issues bother me here at the end of a fifty-year career in facility management and heavy construction, in both the public and private sectors. I have been a common laborer on a road construction project; an on-site manager of large and small horizontal and vertical construction projects; the responsible officer for construction, operations and maintenance of all Army logistics facilities in Europe; a design and operations and maintenance manager of major facilities as well as an author, educator, consultant and major policy maker for an international facility management organization. Despite looking at the construction and facility management professions and organizations from all of these perspectives, I have never understood the following:

1. Why, at the end of major construction projects, is everyone unhappy with each other party, often leading to lawsuits?
2. Why, at a time when we are increasingly relying on outsourcing, are we still using contracting vehicles and methods which:
   - Are based on being an adversary with our contractors.
   - Require legions of inspectors and checkers to ensure contract compliance.
   - Have inadequate ways to select the right contractor for the right job every time because we conduct some bizarre "beauty contest" for contractor selection using references which, if checked out, are seldom accurate?

The answers, I am convinced, are contained in performance based contracting, specifically the Performance Information Procurement System (PIPS) as developed by Dr. Dean Kashiwagi at Arizona State University.

I literally had a "Eureka" moment the first time I heard Dr. Dean at a seminar we both attended in Atlanta a few years ago. I was searching for an answer to the questions stated above. PIPS theoretically addressed every one of my concerns and put me, as the owner's rep, and my contractor working together to bring a superior product to our customer and to meet that customer's requirements every time.

Subsequently, as I have observed Dr. Dean, PIPS, and those who have used PIPS, I have become more convinced than ever that he has given us the opportunity to absolutely revolutionize our industries and the way that we practice construction and facility management. When I talked to fellow FM's who have used PIPS and they told me that they could do the same amount of work with one-quarter of the workforce and still absolutely delight their customers, I was enthused. But when I talked to a contractor who told me he wished that he could compete only on projects using PIPS to aid in the selection process because he 1) was allowed to use his expertise to really give the end-user a superior project while 2) being able to protect his profit margin because he was allowed to efficiently and effectively run his project, then I knew that we were really onto something big.

This book tells you the what, when, how, and why of performance based contracting. Read it carefully. But it takes more than just reading. I hope this book will be a call to action for you to implement performance based contracting. Personally, I would use Dr. Dean's associates the first time that I implemented PIPS; but whether you do or not, do not delay. Performance based contracting is the wave of the future. Not just a fad, but a best practice for the facility management and construction professions.

Dave Cotts, PE, CFM, IFMA Fellow
Former IFMA President
Facility Manager for the World Bank

Table of Contents

Chapter 4 – Construction Industry Structure and Participants

Chapter 5 – Alternate Delivery Processes & Successful Business Practices

Chapter 6 – Applying IMT and the KSM to Construction Delivery

Chapter 7 –Performance Information Procurement System (PIPS)

Chapter 8 – Six Sigma Applications in Construction

Chapter 9 – Getting Started

Chapter 10 – Modified Displaced Ideal Model (MDIM)

Chapter 11 – How to Select A General Contractor

Chapter 12 – Designers: Problems, Selection, and Design

Chapter 12 – Designers: Problems, Selection, and Design, cont'd.

Chapter 13 – Movement to "Best Value" Using the FAR

Chapter 14 – PIPS Core Group: Information Workers

Chapter 15 – Maintenance and Repair Example: Roofing

Chapter 16 – Manufacturer's Use of PIPS: Alpha Program

Chapter 16 – Manufacturer's Use of PIPS: Alpha Program, cont'd.

Chapter 17 – Hail Resistance of the Alpha SPF Roof System

Chapter 18 – Manufacturer's Simplified Use of Performance Information

Chapter 19 – United Airlines Case Study

Chapter 20 – State of Utah Case Study

Chapter 21 – State of Hawaii Case Study

Chapter 22 – University of Hawaii Case Study

Chapter 23 –State of Georgia Case Study

Chapter 24 – Dallas Independent School District Case Study

Chapter 25 – State of Washington Case Study: How to Implement An Information Environment in the Low-Bid Quadrant

Chapter 26 – The Last Frontier

Commonly Used Figures/Tables

Frequently Used Attachments

1
Introduction
"Seeking Simplicity"

Introduction

Ever since I can remember, I have had a strong desire to know why things happen. I wanted to understand the world in "simple" understandable terms - not lengthy, complicated explanations. I wanted to know in whom I could place absolute trust on. I wanted to know who actually understood what I was going through, and I desired to have a better understanding of why I felt so confused in life.

I contemplated other seemingly unknowns, such as: why the earth was–round, why I was who I was, why I was born in Hawaii, and why I was doing what I was doing. I wanted to understand my life. I wanted to know what was going to happen so I wouldn't have to worry. I wanted to be happy, and I wanted to understand why these questions constantly bothered me, causing worry and concern.

Little did I know there were others who were searching for the same answers. Years later, when attempting to solve the problems in the construction industry, I found myself asking these questions again. Why did things seem so confusing in the construction industry? With all our technology, expertise, and experience, we still couldn't minimize nonperformance. Why is a construction manager hired to manage a contractor? Why is a professional designer directing a contractor how to do construction? Why do contractors continue to do more work for less money? Why is the industry increasing project management, increasing construction management, and decreasing the training of crafts people that actually do the work?

This book solves the problems of the construction industry by going outside the knowledge base of construction. It is not an evolution of thought. It is a revolutionary change in thinking.

My Personal Background

My name is Dean T. Kashiwagi and I was born on the island of Oahu in the State of Hawaii during the early 1950's. Fifty years later, I am the Director of The Performance Based Studies Research Group (PBSRG) at Arizona State University (ASU). My questioning of life led me to formulate the Information Measurement Theory (IMT). IMT is a simple explanation of reality, which unravels the secrets and complexities that have been studied for years by scientists, engineers, and physicists. IMT has baffled many experts, but is readily accepted by those who are logical, quick processing, and gravitate toward simple explanations and solutions to problems.

Initially, I developed and tested IMT within my immediate family, which consists of my wife and eight children. This will be discussed in another book, "The Decision." IMT was then applied to solving nonperformance problems in the construction industry. IMT has progressed to unravel the complexities of bureaucratic organizations. Because IMT applies rather simple concepts to simplify seemingly complex problems, it can be used to simplify any relationship, event or complexity. It also requires no technical background.

The answers, or solutions, to complexity lie within simplicity and "accepting reality for what it is". Thanks to IMT, the answer becomes a product of the most efficient use of artificial intelligence and information. The answer allows managers to immediately focus on overall objectives and the most important factors governing performance, value, and success, instead of spending years learning technical details first. The solution is recursive in nature, meaning that the concept is a part of the solution. The solution lies in accepting reality and not making decisions. It minimizes the need of technical expertise in many decisions by identifying that technical expertise is not really required to solve the problem. The answer minimizes subjective bias, decision-making, and risk.

The journey began in Hawaii in the 1950's, before it became a state. My parents were both of second-generation Japanese descent. Their parents (or my grandparents) were both farmers, who moved to Hawaii seeking a better life. Both of my parents worked in the fields in their youth. They both went on to college to become professionals.

My father graduated from the University of Hawaii with a Bachelor of Science in Civil Engineering. He was a registered civil and structural engineer, and worked for a private design firm before switching to the City and County of Honolulu where he worked for the majority of his life. My father designed bridges as well as other structures. He was very conservative, very strict, hard working, slow to change, and did not adapt well to new ideas. He became the "standards" expert for the City and County of Honolulu.

My mother graduated from the University of Hawaii, with a Bachelor of Science and a Master of Science in Chemistry. She was hard working and was very impressed with those who had great wealth, position, and freedom. She continually searched for what brought a "better life." My perception is that she believed wealth brought freedom and happiness.

Among my parents' greatest disappointments in life were an unsuccessful attempt to start a poultry farm on Kauai, my mother's failure to obtain her PhD in Chemistry, and a failed diamond venture. These events showed me my parents' dissatisfaction with their current careers and their desire to change their status in life. However, they were not really "poor". They started in modest but comfortable areas of Kaimuki and Waialae

Kahala, but the majority of their professional life was spent in the extremely affluent areas of Ala Moana Yacht Harbor Towers, Waialae Iki Ridge, and Iolani Towers.

My parents were constantly worried about finances and their ability to support themselves in their retirement years. They were consumed with making money. They were actually an upper class couple, but were caught in a "poverty" frame of mind. They were consumed with the need to have money instead of adding value to life. Ironically, my dad contracted cancer at an early age and passed away soon after retirement. This made me seriously ponder the effectiveness and value of his life. Did he really maximize the value in his life? Would I suffer the same unfortunate fate as my father: to work, and work, and then die? Would I be so consumed with the worry of money and financial support that I would fail to realize what brought true "happiness" and success in life?

My parents did not travel in their early years. Most of their experiences were limited to the small islands of Hawaii. However, later in their lives, they traveled to North and South America, Asia, and Europe. Ironically, the most important part of the trip was showing everyone a thousand slides of what they saw and did. It was almost as if they went on the trips for the recounting of the tales. They did not seem to enjoy the actual experience as much. They were always looking for something more. It reminded me of the story of "Chicken Little."

As my teenage years came along, I realized my parents' strengths did not include parenting skills. They had no time in their youth to learn and optimize family relationships. Their entire life had been filled with hard work and very little free time. As a result, in our household, communication between parents and teenage children was limited to directions on chores and concerns about grades in school. There was no emphasis on the experience of life. In their minds, "life" was working hard to survive. I later realized that they lacked the information and experience needed to cope with children in an age of relative prosperity and freedom. I also realized that they were continually sorting out concepts of "happiness" in their own lives.

My parents had periods of miscommunication on major decisions such as investments, child rearing, family rules, and a schedule that at times held "a family with two working parents hostage." Their communication skills on family issues were not well developed. I sensed constant frustration, a lack of understanding, and a lack of agreement on what to do. As a youngster, I constantly asked my parents questions that they were not able to answer. I did not realize until later in life that my parents did not know the answers to my questions. It never dawned on me that someone walking ahead of me in life, who had gone through life's critical stages (education, marriage, professional achievement, and children), could not explain "what was going on". At that point in my life, I was unknowingly at the beginning stages of unraveling some of the secrets of life, not realizing that this lack of understanding felt by my parents may be a commonly shared trait among people.

Without a clear direction and understanding of what was going on, my parents were very "control" oriented. Herein lay one of the future tenants of IMT. Those who lack understanding, try to control the situation. Since I was the youngest of three children, I rarely made decisions. Rather I was told what to do and when to do it. This environment brought out a sense of rebellion in me. It also left me in a state of confusion, unable to make decisions and focus.

My Japanese culture had the following features:

1. Tradition oriented.
2. Rule oriented.
3. Severe working ethic.
4. Extreme prejudice based on race and culture.
5. Disdain for things that came easy or without a lot of hard work.
6. Great respect for education.
7. Group oriented.
8. Very conservative.
9. Practiced a concept of "shame" and withholding of information.

My parents had the utmost concern for how others perceived their status, professional success, and our family. What other people thought about us was more important than what was actually happening in our lives. It was almost like our family was wearing a mask, disguising who we really were. I lived most of my life in a very upscale neighborhood and had a relatively leisurely life, but did not have a lot of money to spend. My parents were "wealthy," but I was not. My parents were always encouraging us to work more and study more. It was a part of the never-ending work ethic of the Japanese culture.

Since I am of Japanese descent and was raised in a Japanese-like culture, I realized that these factors described a part of my personality or "operating system." I also realized that there were differences between individuals who were raised in "our" culture. I thought and acted differently from my parents. I was also different from my brother and sister. I quickly realized the following about myself:

1. I continuously asked questions.
2. If someone had a "logical answer" that I could understand, I was satisfied for a short period of time, until I came up with my next question.
3. An answer to a question only led me to another question, and all questions led to the same question, "Why does this life go on the way it does?"
4. I am left handed, right-brained, logical, and generally unemotional. For instance, I remember attending my grandparents funeral and wondering why everyone was so sad. I put on a sad look because I thought that it was my responsibility to look sad as well.
5. I had constraints. Although I perceived some benefit in the concepts that I was taught, I was not always able to apply those concepts.
6. I did not put a lot of time and effort into concepts that others thought were valuable, if I could not personally understand or apply the concepts.
7. I was a very private person who was not especially comfortable with large groups.

8. I wanted clear directions and reasoning or proofs, on everything that people wanted me to do.

9. I had a difficult time adapting to change. I did not like new things. It was an uncomfortable feeling. However, I knew change was important, and I began forcing myself to change.

10. I did not like being at places, or with people, when there was not a clearly defined purpose for my attendance. I did not feel comfortable being with people who really didn't care if I was "there or not." That feeling has continued to this day. I was definitely not a "group oriented" person.

11. I was always impressed with people who had natural talent.

12. I did not place much value on awards or possessions. It was the "achieving" that was important to me. I felt uncomfortable with awards, as though they were meaningless or "after-the-fact." This feeling frames my attitude about professional licenses, tenure, and PhD and master degrees. In my experience, the only people who really worshipped these things were those who either didn't deserve them or didn't have them.

13. I was a very hard worker who enjoyed everything except yard work. (Having asthma from grass and dust was a major reason for not enjoying that).

14. I was fair and honest. I felt uncomfortable about doing "wrong" things, even if it seemed as if everyone else considered it "justifiable" and "a part of life."

15. I did not like rules that didn't make sense. I wanted to do things the fastest, most efficient way.

Some of the memorable questions that I can remember asking my parents included:

1. What is the most important thing in life?
2. What actions make someone the happiest?
3. What is right in life, what is wrong, and what makes it right or wrong?
4. Why do people get married?
5. How does one know whom to marry?
6. Does it make a difference who you marry?
7. How does one know how many children to have?
8. Why do parents have children, if children cause problems for the parents?
9. Why was I Japanese?
10. Why was I the youngest child?
11. Why do you treat me, and my brother, and my sister differently?
12. If I listen to your directions, what liability will you take, if something goes wrong?
13. Why should I be liable for actions, if I was following someone else's directions, traditions, or laws?
14. What is our relationship as a parent and child?
15. Does God exist? If he does, why can I not see him? And why does everyone have a different idea of what or who God is?
16. Why should I go to church if you do not go?
17. How can someone teach me about God, if they have never seen him?
18. Why should I go to school and believe that "energy or matter cannot be created" and then go to Church and learn that "God can create something from nothing?"

19. Why should someone study, study, and study some more so that he can get a job to work, work, and work some more so that he can sustain himself until he dies?
20. Why do you instruct me over and over to be logical and then turn around and tell me "we do it because that is how everyone does it?"
21. Why should someone work at a job, if they do not like what they are doing?
22. When will I ever have control over my own life?
23. What is the purpose of life? What am I looking for?

As you can well imagine, I drove my parents "crazy." I was not the "favorite" person to end up next to at the dinner table. I was told that I talked too much and there were no answers to my questions. The experiences of my young adulthood manifested my frustration at not being able to understand what was going on, as well as a constant search for more information and answers. It included the following:

1. Being a "beach bum" and having hair down to my shoulders. (At my 30th class reunion in 2000, most of my classmates didn't know who I was. I looked that different).
2. Dropping out of college.
3. Working as a yard worker, newspaper delivery boy, roofer, janitor, and lab animal cage cleaner.
4. Going on a church mission to Japan for a couple of years.

The experience of the two-year church mission gave me the time to meditate, observe people, and think about the questions in my life. I began to perceive many of the answers to my questions. I began to create logical diagrams to explain reality (the precursor to the Information Measurement Theory or IMT). I started to see differences between people, situations, and things. I started to see relationships in life. The experience started me on a long road to defining reality, finding out who I was, and changing my life to become as happy as I could be. Amazingly, at the age of 40 and after fourteen years in the Air Force, the experience became my job, the answer became my life, and my life became the Information Measurement Theory (IMT) and the Performance Information Procurement System (PIPS).

The newfound understanding motivated me to change, but I still didn't understand where I was going. However, I became very persistent, forcing myself into situations that would bring change. As I had more experiences, I realized that when I lacked information, I reverted to the actions of my parents and my upbringing. As I began to change, I became more open to new ideas. The major events and accomplishments of my life include:

1. Going to school full time, working forty hours a week, being married and having two children, and donating seven hours a week to church work.
2. Graduating with an undergraduate degree in civil engineering, and becoming a Distinguished Graduate in the ROTC program.
3. Starting my career with $2,000, (having no debt) with little external help.
4. Getting married and having eight children (not all at the same time, and yes, my wife had the children).

5. Joining the Air Force and traveling around the world to many different countries.
6. Obtaining my master's degree and doctoral degree in Industrial Engineering at Arizona State University, on full scholarships with the United States Air Force (USAF).
7. Retiring from the USAF and becoming the Director of the Performance Based Studies Research Group (PBSRG) at Arizona State University.
8. Developing an "artificial intelligent" procurement system called Performance Information Procurement System (PIPS) that transforms data into information and replaces the "biased" processing of the human mind.
9. Developing the "Information Measurement Theory" (IMT), which breaks down the complexities of reality into simple concepts.

Combining observations that I made in life, the mathematics of "fuzzy logic," and the ideas of the greatest minds in the history of man (Einstein, Hawking, Deming, Kosko, etc...), I stumbled across the solution to "why" and "how" everything happens. It was the solution that many of these great minds were searching for. It answers the questions "how" and "when" and allows a relatively accurate prediction of the outcomes of events without having all information. The solution uses the advice of Stephen Hawking, the concept of "fuzzy logic", and advanced computer technology to solve the "problem" (Hawking 1988). It allows the implementation of all of Deming's continuous improvement principles (Deming 1982). As Feynman and Hawking so aptly put it, it is a solution that scientists, philosophers, and the "simple" person can understand (Feynman 1994, Hawking 1988). It uses the philosophy of the Far Eastern cultures. As Bruce Lee proposed in his movie, "Enter the Dragon:"

1. There is no enemy.
2. There is no fight.
3. I hit by not hitting.

The event of life is us. We must think by not thinking. There is no opponent. The opponent is our own self. It is called the "Information Measurement Theory" or "IMT." It defines the difference between leadership and management, and identifies an information technology that can assist someone to be a leader even though they do not have leadership skills. The following chapters will introduce the concepts of IMT and reinforce them with concepts from the greatest minds and studies of our time.

Objectives of the Book

There are two major objectives of this book. The first objective is to explain Information Measurement Theory (IMT). The second objective will be to explain the Performance Information Procurement System (PIPS). The application of the IMT concepts will be incorporated into the PIPS process and will address the following issues:

1. Identification of the "best value" in construction services.
2. How to sustain continuous improvement in the construction industry.
3. How to have a "successful" and "sustainable" training programs.

4. How to optimize decision-making and management operations.
5. How to receive a "fair" profit and reduce life cycle costs.
6. How to have "total competition," but yet have entry barriers that assure that the facility owner is minimizing his or her risk.
7. How contractors can maximize profit while ensuring that the owner gets "best value?"
8. How to predict construction "performance" before it happens.
9. How to minimize litigation and increase partnering with very little management.

As you read through the book, if you come across concepts that you do not understand, please feel free to email me at dean.kashiwagi@asu.edu. Your comments will also be taken into consideration in future revisions. I will also, from time to time, give presentations. You can find where I will be by going to the website www.pbsrg.com.

References

Deming, E.W. (1982). *Out of the Crisis*. Cambridge: Massachusetts Institute of Technology.

Feynman, R.P. (1994). *Six Easy Pieces: Essentials of Physics*. California: Addison-Wesley Publishing Company.

Hawking, S. (1988). *A Brief History of Time – The Updated and Expanded Tenth Anniversary Edition*. New York: Bantam Books.

2

Information Measurement Theory (IMT)

Information Theory

In 1948, Claude Shannon was credited with discovering 'Information Theory' (Waldrop 2001). He stated that all communication systems are fundamentally the same. They all have a speed, measured in terms of binary digits per second. Above the speed, the information cannot be perfectly transmitted. Below the speed, perfect transmission of information is possible, regardless of the signal strength or the static of the environment. Shannon then proposed that 'perfect information' could be passed in all mediums. He realized that the *constraint of communicating (or moving information) was the transmission speed of the medium and not the noise of the environment.* Shannon's work became the foundation of digital technology.

Information Measurement Theory (IMT) applies the theoretical constraint identified by 'information theory' to the process of understanding information. IMT identifies that an individual who lacks processing speed creates the perception that there is a lack of information, when in actuality all of the information always exists. In addition, the author suggests that, when an individual is constrained by a slow processing speed, he or she is unable to see readily available information, and is forced to use his or her database of past experience, or incomplete information, to form expectations of future outcomes. The use of an individual's personal experience to draw conclusions is the application of the person's subjective bias, or more commonly known as decision-making. IMT identifies bias as the major obstacle to perfectly understanding reality.

Traditional thinking uses the following methodology:

1. When confusion exists, identify data that can be used to understand the event.
2. If the data is insufficient, do not use the data.
3. Use expertise (someone's personal bias or decision making) to solve the problem.

In this chapter, the author proposes that a faster, more efficient processor, which will generate more accurate information, can replace the "expert" human processor. Since this information will be used without bias, the decision should be acceptable to more parties. Therefore, the author asserts that the purpose of information-based systems is not only to communicate information, but also to "create" information that can be understood by people with different processing speeds. The motivation behind the employment of this technology is to:

1.   Optimize the use of resources.

2.   Deliver higher value.
3.   Minimize risk.

Information Measurement Theory

The author developed the Information Measurement Theory (IMT) during the last twenty years. IMT was first published in 1991 at Arizona State University as the structure for optimizing the effectiveness of information by creating "easy to understand" information environments (See Attachment 2.1). The purpose of IMT is to:

1.   Minimize subjective decision-making.
2.   Minimize the amount of data required to accurately transfer information.
3.   Identify the relationship between information usage, processing speed, and performance.
4.   Identify a structure that minimizes the requirement for management.
5.   Optimize processes by identifying and removing entities which add no value or bring risk.

IMT can be defined as: *"A deductive, logical explanation of an event. It includes the use of relative and related data to create information that predicts the future outcome of the event."*

There are two major methods of problem solving accepted by the scientific arena: inductive logic and deductive logic (Davies 1992). Inductive logic, also known as the scientific method, follows the subsequent steps:

1.   Establishing a hypothesis that defines an outcome.
2.   Devising an experiment that tests the hypothesis.
3.   Conducting the experiment to discover previously unknown information.
4.   Identifying whether or not the hypothesis has been validated.
5.   Determining under what conditions the test results are repeatable.

Deductive logic is defined as: "The redefining or reordering of existing information to define an outcome" (Davies 1992). Deductive logic differs from inductive logic in the following ways:

1.   There is no new information or theories included in the explanation.
2.   There is no required experimentation.
3.   It is *faster, simpler, and more economical* than the inductive or scientific method.
4.   It requires less technical or specialized information, which is not understood by the average person.

Deduction simplifies complex situations, allowing individuals to understand what is going on with minimal information. Deduction allows those without a tremendous amount of education and technical training to understand. Furthermore, the author advises that the term "existing information" varies depending on the individual. If an individual is more perceptive, they will tend to practice more deductive logic than an individual that perceives less information.

Laws of Physics

The first concept of IMT pertains to the laws of physics that define the physical environment. Laws of physics predict the future outcome of an event, in any state and at any time. Gravity and combustion are examples of these laws.

By definition, the number of laws of physics never changes, but rather stays constant over time. As time progresses, scientists continue to discover more of these existing physical laws. For example, the law of gravity existed before it was "discovered".

It is also possible that science may unknowingly identify a law incorrectly during one period of time, and discover at a later time that the law had been defined incorrectly or incompletely. It is important to understand that laws are not created, but discovered. Hawking's "No Boundary Theory" demonstrates this concept (1988). Hawking states that time and space are boundless. Anywhere that someone has attempted to identify a boundary, the same conditions have been found to exist outside of that boundary. Therefore, *at any one time or at any one location, 100% of the laws of physics exist (Figure 2.1).*

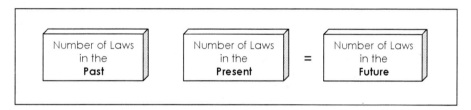

Figure 2.1: Laws of Physics

Description of an Event

The second concept of IMT describes an event. *IMT defines an event as "anything that happens that takes time."* An event has initial conditions, changing conditions throughout the occurrence, and final conditions. The number of laws stays consistent throughout the event (Figure 2.2).

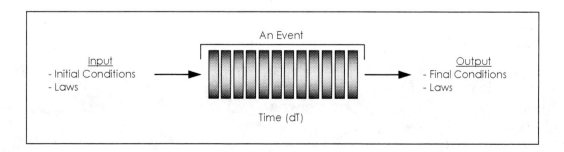

2-3

The following are characteristics of events:

1. Every event has a unique set of initial conditions and a unique set of final conditions.
2. The number of the laws of physics remains constant throughout the event.
3. Two individuals with different levels of perception may look at the same event, and perceive two different outcomes. However, the event happens only one way and will have only one outcome.
4. No event has ever taken place where the outcome is unaffected by the initial conditions or previous state. Nor has any segment of the event been found that is unaffected by the previous segment.
5. All events and all segments of events are bound by cause and effect.
6. Every event is constrained by initial conditions and laws, and its outcome is predictable if all information is perceived.
7. The more information that is perceived of the initial conditions and laws, the more accurate the prediction of the final outcome.
8. The shorter the event, the less information is required to accurately predict the final outcome.
9. The change in the conditions of the event can be identified in terms of differential.
10. Randomness and probability are methods of estimating the final outcome when there is a lack of information about the initial conditions (and the laws of physics governing those conditions). True randomness does not exist (Bennett 1998). The fact that we do not have the methods or means to accurately measure two linearly related characteristics of particles at the same time is the only reason the Hisenberg Theory is valid (Feynman 1994). Einstein was criticized for refusing to accept the premise of randomness (Penrose 1989), but today, science understands that the inability to measure randomness creates the illusion of its existence. No actual random number, event, or object exists (Davies 1992). Einstein was correct. There is no true randomness. It is a perception caused by a lack of perceived information.
11. Every person and every factor impacts an event to a relative degree. IMT does not attempt to explain why a person is in an event, but it does state that the person is a part of the event and will impact that event. Because each individual is predictable or constrained (constraints make everyone unique) an individual's decision-making patterns and future actions are predictable. Therefore, when "all" information is perceived, any event can be predicted.
12. When all information is not perceived, an event will still have only one outcome. However, the outcome cannot be predicted.
13. Characteristics describe people. People can be differentiated by differences in characteristics.
14. Longer or more complex events require more facts about the initial conditions and laws in order to predict the outcome.
15. This identifies that differentiating between two very similar entities, requires more information.

16.   No event exists independently from other events. Every occurrence is relative and related to every other occurrence to a relative degree.

Perception of Information

One of the most difficult factors to predict is the future action of an individual or an organization. Every individual is different (location in time and space being the most obvious). Each person exists in an environment that contains "all" information, even though the person cannot perceive all of that information. To change, individuals must perceive information that was not perceived before, process the information, and, if they understand the information, apply it. The application of newly perceived information

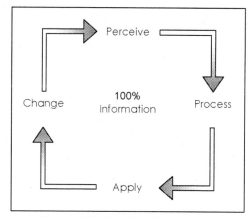

Figure 2.3: Cycle of Learning

causes change, and, by observation, change leads to the perception of more information. This is called the cycle of learning (Figure 2.3).

The study of mathematics is an example of this learning cycle. A person first learns to add and then to subtract. The person then learns to multiply and divide. This cycle of learning continues as individuals are taught to perceive and understand algebra, geometry, trigonometry, and calculus.

By observation, the *more repetitions of the learning cycle that are experienced, the faster the cycle's speed becomes*. By deduction, those with higher processing speeds have faster change rates, perceive more information, and are more skilled. The following are deductive conclusions:

1.   The application of information and the ability to change can be measured more easily than the perception rate and/or processing speed.
2.   There is not enough information on identifying a person's processing speed or level of perception, and therefore there is no consensus. Everyone uses their subjectivity to identify a person's level of perception and processing speed.
3.   The more information perceived, the faster the rate of change. Those who are resistant to change have difficulty perceiving new information.
4.   Those who change slowly are not as open to new ideas.

Figure 2.4 shows three different individuals (labeled Type A, B, and C), which represent people who utilize different amounts of information. The Type A person uses a high level of information, Type B uses an intermediate amount of information, and the Type C individual uses very little information.

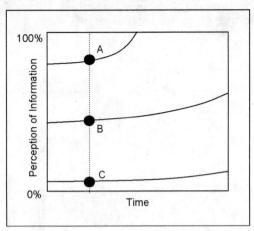

Figure 2.4: Rate of Change

The "Type A" person (or entity) is labeled as one who has a high level of perception and processing speed. According to the Rate of Change model (Figure 2.4), the "Type A" person will perceive more information, process it faster, apply a greater number of correct principles, and change faster than the "Type C" entity. This is represented by a steeper curve (change rate over time).

Within any environment, there are individuals at different relative levels. No person is more important, or better, than any other person. Every person is a part of (and essential for) the event. The event cannot happen without any one of its parts. Therefore there are no people who are more important or not right for the event. The level of a person at a specific time is defined by the following:

1. An environment that represents the level of information of the person.
2. All of the individuals in the event.
3. A combination of factors (i.e. genetics, occupation, financial status, birth date, etc.), which can be related to a relative level of perception, processing, and amount of information.

This can be deduced using the following assumptions:

1. A person can be defined by a combination of factors and values.
2. The person's environment can be defined by the same combination of factors and values.
3. The person's environment, the person, and the description of the environment are three different views of the same event.
4. The event has a specific level of information as defined by Figure 2.4.

IMT does not address the "which-came-first-the-chicken-or-the-egg?" argument. The environment describes the person or entity, and the environment cannot be described without the person. There is no differential between the entity and the environment of the entity at a particular location and at a specific point in time. Therefore, the environment or event is the person.

Every person possesses a unique level of perception and information (Hawking 1988). The restriction here is not whether the information exists, but the individual's ability to perceive and their processing speed. IMT identifies differentials (criteria) between individuals. No two individuals have the same combination of values. Figure 2.5 is an example of the differences between two people.

The combined values for all of the different factors create an individual's unique identity. Each of the aforementioned factors has a relationship to the level of perceived information, the ability to process information, and the opportunity to access information.

CRITERIA	INDIVIDUAL 1	INDIVIDUAL 2
Education level:	21 Years	13 Years
Financial status:	$100K/Year	$27K/Year
Location:	North America	Asia
Time of birth:	5/5/1965	5/5/1950
Type of government in environment:	Democracy	Communism
Family size:	8	2
Birth order:	Last	First
Genetic makeup:	Unique	Unique
Occupation type:	Engineer	Farmer

Figure 2.5: Differences in Individuals

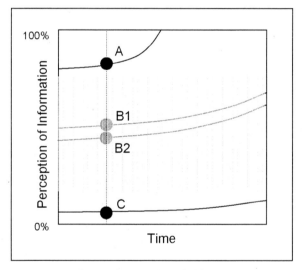

Figure 2.6: Rate of Change
of Similar Individuals

Figure 2.6 shows two individuals (B1 and B2) who are very similar in terms of processing speed, amount of information perceived, and rate of change. To differentiate and predict the difference in a future time period requires a lot more information than to differentiate between A and C. This data may not be easily and economically acquired. Within our current methodologies and measuring tools, this necessitates extensive statistical analysis with large amounts of data from a representative, random sampling. Often, this becomes too costly and impractical.

To avoid extensive statistical sampling, IMT focuses on the two extremes, where deductive logic can be applied instead of the more costly inductive logic. Therefore, IMT concepts are identified from the comparison of characteristics of a Type A individual (that perceives a relatively large amount of information), and characteristics of a Type C individual (that perceives a relatively small amount of information). This is the foundation of the Kashiwagi Solution Model or KSM, which will be discussed in the next chapter.

Conclusion

IMT states that laws define all events, and all event outcomes are predictable. Events happen one way, but may be perceived as happening in various ways by individuals with different processing speeds. Randomness exists due to a person's inability to perceive "all" information; it is a methodology of understanding what is going on, by analyzing large samples of data in the absence of all information. When an individual obtains "all" information, they will be able to perfectly predict a person's actions or an event. However, the author does realize that "all" information is never perceived for an individual or an event.

Chapter 2 Review

1. Define IMT.
2. Does the number of laws: Increase over time, decrease over time, or stay constant over time?
3. Does not having enough information on the input of an event change the output of the event?
4. How many ways can an event happen?
5. Can an event have two outcomes?
6. Are all events and individuals predictable?
7. Is there any event that is random? Why or why not?
8. What happens to the speed of the learning cycle as individuals go through more cycles of change?
9. Are any two individuals exactly the same? Why or why not?
10. Who is more important in an event, a scientist or a janitor? Why?
11. Is it better to live in Afghanistan or America?
12. Are wars necessary in the History of Mankind? Explain.
13. What would qualify as a "wrong" event in the "History of Mankind?"
14. Should individuals be treated the same or differently? Why or why not?
15. Illustrate the number of Laws of Physics over time.
16. Illustrate an Event.
17. Illustrate the cycle of learning.
18. Illustrate the rate of change figure.
19. Why is the person the same as their environment? Give an example.
20. What happens to time if you have more information?
21. What is the relationship between the level of information and decision-making?

References

Bennett, D.J. (1998). *Randomness*. Massachusetts: Harvard University Press.

Davies, P. (1992). *The Mind of God*. New York: Simon & Schuster.

Feynman, R.P. (1994). *Six Easy Pieces: Essentials of Physics*. California: Addison-Wesley Publishing Company.

Hawking, S. (1988). *A Brief History of Time – The Updated and Expanded Tenth Anniversary Edition*. New York: Bantam Books.

Penrose, R. (1989). *The Emperor's New Mind: Concerning Computers, Minds and the Laws of Physics*. Oxford: Oxford University Press.

Waldrop, M.M. (2001 July/August). Claude Shannon: Reluctant Father of the Digital Age. *An MIT Enterprise Technology Review*, pp.64-71.

Attachments

Attachment 2.1: IMT Theorems of IMT

Attachment 2.1: IMT Theorems of IMT

The following theorems provide the framework of IMT:

Theorem 1: Laws are accurate explanations of reality, which allows a person to predict the future outcome of a physical event in any environment at any time.

Theorem 2: Physical laws supersede both time and space. Every physical law exists in every space. Each space has the same number of physical laws at all times.

Theorem 3: Physical laws are discovered, not created. Laws exist before they are discovered and are merely perceived by the first individual who can quantify the event and implement the quantification to accurately and consistently predict the outcome of the occurrence.

Theorem 4: Information is defined as: Using a set of laws and conditions that describe the event at a point in time, along with useful data, to accurately describe an environment. All information can consistently predict the future outcome of an event.

Theorem 5: All information exists at all times. Information must be perceived.

Theorem 6: "More" information is better than "some" information, and "some" information is better than no information.

Theorem 7: The IMT's objective is to predict the outcome of an event, not to judge whether an event is right or wrong, good or bad.

Theorem 8: Anything that happens is an event.

Theorem 9: There are no actual random events or patterns. No random pattern has ever been created.

Theorem 10: Every event represents cause and effect (input/output).

Theorem 11: There is a reason or cause for every event.

Theorem 12: Since everything occurs for a reason, if an event does not happen, there is no reason for the event. There is also a reason or cause for every part of an event. If no reason exists, there is no input or first state for that event and the event does not occur.

Theorem 13: All components of an event are required for the event to transpire.

Theorem 14: There is no evidence that leads to the conclusion that a "different" event can replace an "existing" event in the larger event of the "History of Man."

Theorem 15: Any event happens the same way in all space and over all time. Caution must be taken to ensure that the event is the "same event."

Theorem 16: There is no "new space." All space exists prior to discovery.

Theorem 17: All events are predictable. Therefore, Theorem 2 must include not only physical laws, but also all laws, that govern human behavior.

Theorem 18: All individuals possess a certain level of perception (understand a percentage of the existing physical laws), which allows each of them to predict certain outcomes of events in their lives, with a particular level of accuracy.

Theorem 19: A person's perception represent who the person is.

Theorem 20: A person's ability to predict is relative to their understanding of the event.

Theorem 21: The intensity of emotion, or the degree to which an individual becomes upset, is an indicator of their lack of understanding, but not always an indicator of their understanding.

Theorem 22: The more information perceived by an individual, the shorter an event seems. The less information perceived by an individual, the longer an event seems.

Theorem 23: Longer events must be shortened in order to formulate more efficient decisions.

Theorem 24: If the event duration dT is zero, only one set of conditions exists. The input is the output.

Theorem 25: The shorter the event, the fewer decisions must be made. If the event time is zero, there are no decisions to make because nothing changes.

Theorem 26: Each event can be subdivided into many "finite element" events that have only one input and one output. The input of the first and the output of the last finite elements are the event's input and output.

Theorem 27: Since each finite element has only one input and one output, each event, which is comprised of many finite elements, has only one input and one output. Holding dT constant, each event has only one input and one output. If an event has a different output, then it must have a different input. Therefore, given "all" information about the input, each event becomes predictable: one output for one input.

Theorem 28: Not perceiving the information about the input does not change the output of the event. It simply impacts an individual's ability to predict the output. However, if a person perceives more information, he or she could change the event (in which case the person would be a different individual and the event would be different).

Theorem 29: A person faces a decision when he or she does not perceive all information. The individual must then make a decision on which outcome he or she thinks is the best choice.

Theorem 30: If all of the information exists and someone perceives all of it, the person does not need to make any decisions because the outcome cannot be changed.

Theorem 31: There is no "chance" or unpredictable event.

Theorem 32: There is no randomness. Randomness, probability and statistics are used to understand what is currently happening in the absence of complete information.

Theorem 33: The cycle of change requires the perception of information, the processing of the information, and the application of the information. By nature, it is a cyclical process.

Theorem 34: The rate of change increases as the individual or entity repeats successive cycles of change, learns more information, and is able to process and apply the information quicker. A greater rate of change requires a greater level of perception.

Theorem 35: A person's rate of change correlates to his or her ability to perceive, process, and apply new information. The "more intelligent" person changes at a faster rate and is able to more consistently predict the outcome of events. The "less intelligent" person changes at a slower rate.

Theorem 36: Individuals who change at a very slow rate are "less perceptive," have more difficulty identifying differences, and feel very uncomfortable with a changing environment.

Theorem 37: All individuals have a change rate. No individual stays the same, even if the person's change rate is very slow. It is impossible not to accumulate information over time.

Theorem 38: All individuals are changing in a positive direction. All individuals are improving their perception of more information.

Theorem 39: All individuals are constrained by their capability to perceive and can only change at a predictable rate.

Theorem 40: An individual is fully responsible and has full control over his or her own actions, decisions, and future environment. This will be discussed more in the next chapter on KSMs.

Theorem 41: A person or entity's environment represents that person or entity and can be used to predict a future state or outcome of the person or entity.

Theorem 42: If the environment represents the person, measuring the person or the environment can identify the performance of an individual.

Theorem 43: An "information" person does not have a position of right or wrong within an event.

Theorem 44: An "information" person does not use personal bias, because the "information" person has no position or bias.

Theorem 45: An "information" person makes no decision. The "information" person uses information to predict the future outcome, and the future outcome becomes the course of action.

Theorem 46: An "information" person allows the information to dictate the future outcome.

Theorem 47: Individuals who do not perceive a lot of information find it harder to believe that everyone is different, because they lack the information to tell the difference.

Theorem 48: If performance is predictable, the environment is the person, and performance is the person's capability to apply information, then every individual is "doing what he or she can" or "doing the best that he or she can." Therefore, every person is constrained by his or her capability to perceive.

Theorem 49: What you see is what you get. There are no such persons as "hypocrites," "underachievers," or "overachievers." These are terms used by individuals who do not have enough information to identify people's real position.

3

Kashiwagi Solution Model (KSM)

Introduction

The Kashiwagi Solution Model (KSM) uses the principles of Information Measurement Theory (IMT) (Chapter 2) to show the relationship between different factors. KSMs are based on the theory that everything is relative and related.

A KSM consists of two main components: the left side (LS) triangle and the right side (RS) triangle as shown in Figure 3.1. Each side represents opposite sides of a factor. For example, if the left side (LS) factor was "Unemotional", the right side (RS) factor would be "Emotional". The horizontal width of the shape identifies the amount of the factor. Combining the two triangles forms a two-way KSM for a related factor.

The objectives of KSMs include:

1. Determining if a characteristic belongs to the left side or right side.
2. Evaluating whether one entity has more information than another entity.
3. Identifying the relationship between different factors and the level of information.

KSMs cannot accurately identify the amount of differential between two very similar entities. The primary concern here is which side a characteristic belongs to. The slope of the lines separating the sides is not critical to the above three objectives. To identify the slope, extensive statistical data must be collected and analyzed (the cost of which is prohibitive).

KSMs effectively identify relationships between different factors, and minimize subjectivity by referencing "common knowledge" or documented findings to ascertain the location of the characteristics.

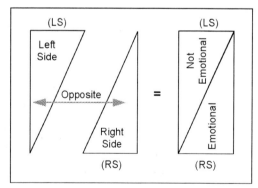

Figure 3.1: A Two-Way Kashiwagi Solution Model (KSM)

Information & the KSM

Figure 3.2 shows the Rate of Change Chart (described in Chapter 2) with a two-way Kashiwagi Solution Model (KSM). The figure illustrates that for a particular time period (t), the Type A person has more information than the Type C person (identified by the dark lines on the 'Information' triangle). As defined by the Rate of Change chart, information is located on the left hand side. Therefore, the Type A has more information than the Type C. The KSM does not quantify how much more information, but merely illustrates that Type A has more information (the slope of the dividing line is

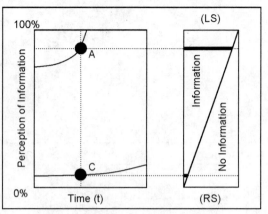

Figure 3.2: Rate of Change and a Kashiwagi Solution Model

unimportant). 'No Information' is found on the opposite side of the 'Information' triangle. The KSM chart might also be interpreted as indicating that a Type C individual has more instances of 'no information' than the Type A person.

Decision Making & the KSM

A decision-maker can be defined as 'an individual who does not have enough information to identify or predict the future outcome' (Chapter 2, Theorem 16). When a person makes a decision, he or she perceives that there are multiple possible final conditions to the initial conditions of the current event due to a lack of information (see Figure 3.3). The person then makes a subjective decision, filling in the lack of information with their limited experience. When the actual final conditions do not match their expectations, they are displeased or surprised at what happened.

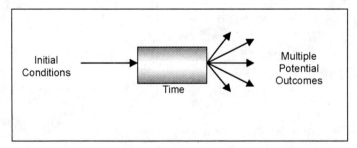

Figure 3.3: Individuals who lack information perceive many outcomes to an event

However, in the previous chapter we learned that all events are predictable, if we had all the information. Stated differently, the individual would not have made a decision, if they had had all the information. This is because every event is constrained by the initial conditions. Therefore, an individual or group will only make decisions in matters where they lack sufficient information. Intelligent individuals (or groups) attempt to get as much information as possible to minimize the need for subjective decision-making. An example of decision-making is discussed below:

Two people are flying from New York to Arizona. The first person must 'decide' what clothes to bring. Since Arizona is known for being sunny and hot, the first person decided to pack plenty of shirts and shorts. The second person checks the weather on the Internet and discovers that there is a severe rainstorm in Arizona that is expected to last for a week. The second person does not bring shorts, but packs warmer clothes including a jacket and warm trousers.

Just because the first person did not know about the weather in Arizona did not change the fact that it was raining there. By obtaining additional information, the second person did not have to decide whether or not to bring shorts because that person already knew what weather to expect.

Figure 3.4 shows the decision-making KSM. Decisions are made when information cannot be perceived. Successful people constantly minimize risk, by collecting and using information. The more information that is available, the easier it is to predict the outcome and minimize decision making. Some individuals describe the impact of information as making the decision easier. However, if someone has "all" information no decision is necessary, because all things are constrained by the previous conditions. The following are observations of decision-making:

1. If someone is making decisions for every second of the day, the person perceives very little information about what is going on around them.
2. The more information a person perceives, the fewer decisions a person will make.
3. Decisions are made only when there is a doubt about the future conditions.
4. People who perceive and understand the constraints of an event (information) know the requirements of an event. They make very few decisions about the personnel who can work within the event. On the other hand, those without information, will be nervous, micromanage, and have false expectations for the event.

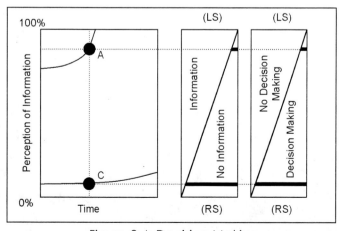

Figure 3.4: Decision Making

Efficiency & the KSM

People who have more information about the constraints of an event (including the laws) are able to predict the future outcome of that event much more accurately, and will act in accordance with the constraints. These people are successful because they are efficient. Efficient people make fewer decisions (Figure 3.5). They expend the minimum amount of resources to meet the accurate expectations.

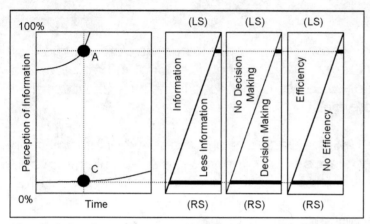

Figure 3.5: Information, Decision Making, and Efficiency

Figure 3.5 shows that a Type C person:

1. Uses less information. (RS)
2. Makes more decisions. (RS)
3. Is less efficient. (RS)

The KSM rule establishes that the Type C person's dominant characteristics are found on the right-hand side and the individual's less dominant characteristics are located on the left-hand side. All of the left-hand characteristics relate to the amount of information perceived, processed, and applied. All of the right-hand characteristics correlate to people or entities possessing less information.

Therefore, KSMs can identify if an individual or entity's characteristics are more like a Type A or Type C individual or entity. Since all factors are relative and related, each KSM can be associated with the amount of information the individual uses as well as with other related characteristics. Scientific findings or deductive logic must then support the location of the characteristic (whether it is on the left side or right side).

Experience, Emotion, Events & the KSM

The following characteristics will be discussed (see Figure 3.6):

1. Experience. (LS)
2. False expectations. (RS)
3. Control over others. (RS)
4. Emotion (excitement, anger, fear, being offended, criticism). (RS)
5. Positions on events as either good or bad. (RS)

As people gain more experience, they perceive more information (experience is information) and realize that all people are constrained by their capabilities. Not all people are equal in capability. Some people are more capable than others, and some will never be capable of doing what is "falsely" expected of them. Successful leaders identify the capability of their people and build their business plans based on their people's capabilities (Walsh 1998). *False expectations lead to failure.*

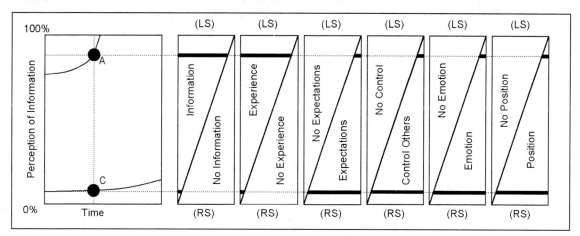

Figure 3.6: Experience, Expectation, Control, Emotion and Position

For instance, a person cannot expect a group of farmers to build a nuclear submarine. This example may seem exaggerated; however, the important point is that a person's "false" expectations demonstrate their lack of information (since they could not realize that his or her expectations simply could not be met).

If a person is doing his or her best (Chapter 2, Theorem 48), that individual's decision-making patterns and actions are constrained and become predictable. Therefore, when other people do not have enough information on a person, they may come to one of the following conclusions:

1. The person is under or overachieving.
2. The person was not given a 'fair' chance.
3. If given a chance, the person will achieve.
4. The person is not trying their best.
5. The person is a hypocrite because they know better.

These are all subjective expectations based upon a person's limited subjective experience and the lack of sufficient information. The following confirm this deductive concept:

1. The more information people have, the more accurate their predictions are.
2. The more a person knows about someone, the more accurately he or she can predict that individual's future actions.
3. People can predict the future decisions and actions of their family members more accurately than those of strangers.
4. Most people feel they can impact the actions of their spouses more before they are married than after 20 years of marriage.
5. Parents can often predict the future actions of their children.
6. Every individual can predict his or her own future actions more accurately than anyone else.

The author proposes that the future decisions and actions of people are no more difficult to predict than physical phenomena that operate on the laws of physics. Furthermore, the author asserts that all actions are predictable if all of the information is perceived by examining extremes in the KSMs, it becomes apparent that a person who does not perceive and utilize a high degree of information possesses certain characteristics.

One of these characteristics is to control people, or the attempt to force someone to do something that they may be incapable of doing. Someone with a high degree of information allows the people with whom he or she is working with to dictate the level of information and control they need. This is the action of a facilitator. The facilitator passes along only as much information as the people who are being facilitated feel comfortable with. The facilitator distributes more information to those who are faster at processing, and less to those who are slower. While a controller tries to dominate, manipulate, and control everyone, a facilitator treats everyone differently based on each person's capability to perceive and use information. A facilitator rarely makes someone feel uncomfortable.

Human emotions are also related to a lack of information. Whether someone is excited, angry, worried, offended, or feeling criticized; all of these actions are related to a lack of perception. For instance, if a person is driving on the freeway and a big truck cuts the person off, nearly causing the person to swerve off the road, the person may get angry. However, if the person later finds out that the driver who cut him off was rushing two of his children, who had just been stabbed by an intruder, to the hospital, the emotion would quickly subside. The anger (emotion) is associated with a lack of information.

As described in Chapter 2, an event can happen only one way (Chapter 2, Theorem 18,19,20). *Since everyone is part of the event, there is no one in the event that is more important* than anyone else (there are no good or bad people since all individuals are needed in the event). A "Type A" will always stress this point. *Any attempt to label people or events as "good" or "bad" is a position based on the lack of information.* For example, which person more important, a scientist or a janitor? Obviously the answer is neither, because they are both equally important since they are both part of the event. (This is not to say a janitor and a scientist are both equally in demand.) Drugs are another example. Some people may believe that all drugs are "bad", while other people may say that they are "good" for various medical reasons. Neither person is right or wrong; it is all a part of the event. Ironically, deductive logic identifies that all people are:

1. Required for the event (Chapter 2, Theorem 13).
2. Important in the event.
3. Should be respected in the event.
4. Doing the best they can be doing (Chapter 2, Theorem 48).

Apparent Irony

Once it is understood that everyone is constrained by their capability, it is easy to recognize that those who lack processing speed are those who are more likely to commit crimes, get hurt, take more resources to do the same job, be unhealthy, and do things that are detrimental to themselves and others.

Due to everyone's lack of information, it is very easy to fall into the practice of false expectations and taking positions. For instance, some may feel that a person who processes information very quickly may commit white-collar crime. This idea leads to the conclusion that some criminal minds are fast processors. However, in order to reach that conclusion, the following factors must be disregarded (Figure 3.7):

1. Type A persons (fast processors) believe in "win-win."
2. Type A persons are just as concerned about the welfare of others as their own.
3. Type A persons are leaders and not managers.
4. Type A persons are facilitators who pass on information.
5. Type A persons create wealth instead of spending wealth.
6. Type A persons are efficient.

White-collar criminals do not exhibit the above characteristics. They are the opposite. However, people with incomplete information, may incorrectly perceive that people in white-collar positions are fast processors. This is similar to thinking all people who have wealth are Type A. Wealth is only one factor. Judging a person on only one factor is considered "negative" discrimination and can often lead to false conclusions (IFSW 2002).

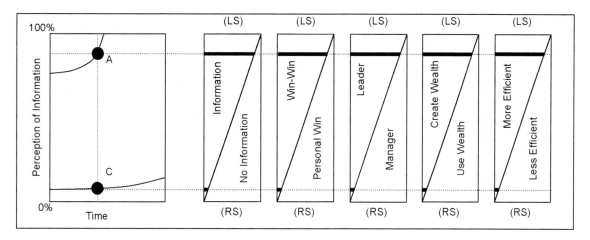

Figure 3.7: White Collared Criminal Minds Are Not Type A persons

Understanding Our Environment Using KSMs

Figure 3.8 uses KSMs to explain the irony of the Japanese culture and people. Many people hold the perception that because the Japanese people are wealthy, they must be in a Type A environment. Readers may quickly identify the relationship between the Japanese culture and the author's heritage (third generation Japanese). Figure 3.8 identifies dominant traits of the Japanese culture:

1. No range or variety of environment. (RS)
2. No ability to change. (RS)
3. Tradition. (RS)
4. No freedom. (RS)
5. Worry. (RS)
6. No creativity. (RS)

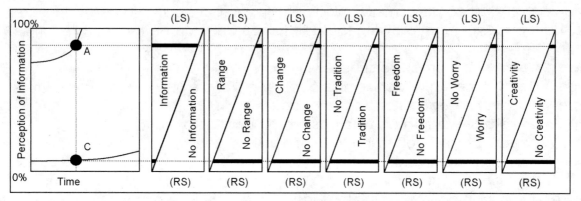

Figure 3.8: Understanding Your Environment

The following are characteristics of the Japanese environment (World Factbook 2002, Zielenziger 2001, Chicago Tribune 1999, Hadfield 1999, The Guardian 2000, Smith 2001, Seeman 1985):

1. Japan is dominated by people of pure Japanese descent. 99.5% of all people who permanently live in Japan are pure Japanese.
2. Japan is very traditional.
   a. Intermarriages have not been well accepted.
   b. It is not well accepted for Japanese to act as foreigners act.
   c. Japanese who serve foreign assignments often "cleanse" themselves of their foreign habits before returning to Japan.
3. Japanese are very suspicious of earning money without hard work.
4. Japanese are not very active in the stock market.
5. Japanese are producers, not spenders, thus, becoming the richest per capita people in the world. This has caused trade deficits wherever they go.
6. Japanese have not had a successful record as investors or spenders. They do not buy value. Their bad debts have caused a worldwide economic problem.
7. The Japanese culture has always had a very hard work ethic.
8. Japanese also experience a high level of worry, leading to a high suicide rate.
9. Japan depends on the creativity of foreign countries. Their "in-house" developed research is not as successful as the United States. They are much more successful at taking ideas developed abroad and refining them.
10. A year ago, the Japanese prime minister, laid out the recovery plan for Japan. It included:

    a. Allowing more foreigners to live in Japan.
    b. Not being so "Japanese."
    c. Having more lawyers in the country, this would lead to more debate, differential, and new ideas.

At first, many people believe that Japan is a Type A environment, since the people are very wealthy. However, when analyzing multiple characteristics, Japan appears more like a Type C environment than a Type A.

Having grown up as a third generation Japanese descendent, the author's personal experience mirrored the above environment. By analyzing his own cultural background, he and his spouse were able to make substantial changes in their lives and the lives of their eight children. They have not been able to totally overcome all of these traits. The Japanese cultural traits are:

1. Much stronger in the author's life than in the life of his children.
2. Much stronger in the older children than the younger children.

Understanding Individuals Using KSMs

Understanding IMT and KSMs can allow a person to understand different individuals. By asking questions, one can quickly discover if individuals are more like Type A or Type C people (remembering that neither person is better or worse). One of the first questions the author uses in interviews is, "Do you feel that if given the chance to do whatever you want, you could do more than you have achieved before?" Other questions with the same purpose include:

1. Do you feel that you were being controlled at your last job?
2. What external constraints were being put on you?
3. What has stopped you from achieving in the past?
4. Given a chance, could you make a difference?
5. What are your weaknesses?
6. How do you plan to overcome them?
7. What will you do differently on this job?
8. How could you have done better on your last job?

KSMs identify the perception of being controlled by others as a Type C behavior. The Type A individual (with a high level of information) perceives himself or herself as having more freedom and more control over personal destiny and as being more proactive.

Those who perceive that they are being controlled tend to be more:

1. Bureaucratic.
2. Worried about what could go wrong.
3. Reluctant to pass along and use information.
4. Uncomfortable without external rules.

5. Resistant to change and unwilling to take the liability that may come with change.
6. Concerned with their own position rather than the organization.

Every person has the above traits to a relative degree, some more than others. These traits are neither good nor bad. They simply assist in describing and predicting the future actions of people.

Conclusion

The use of the KSMs confirms the IMT theories proposed in Chapter 2. In addition, KSMs provide a simplistic method of identifying which characteristics have a positive correlation to the use of information. Coupled with the Rate of Change chart, the KSMs also propose that by increasing the amount of information required, entities can be identified which are more efficient and bring less risk. KSMs can allow an individual to understand different characteristics in relationship with information, which can assist an organization in becoming less bureaucratic, more efficient, and minimize false expectations.

Chapter 3 Review

1. What does KSM stand for?
2. What is the purpose of a KSM?
3. Which individual is more emotional, a Type A person or a Type C person?
4. Label each of the following characteristics as LS or RS:

       a.   Information
       b.   Decision making
       c.   Control of others
       d.   Anger
       e.   Tradition
       f.   Worry
       g.   Expectations
       h.   Criticism
       i.   Inspection
       j.   Performance
       k.   Profit
       l.   Value
       m.   Treating everyone the same
       n.   Working harder
       o.   Efficiency
       p.   Facilitation
       q.   Management

References

Chicago Tribune. (1999, May 2). Japanese Loosen Corporate Culture. *The Honolulu Advertiser*: Business, pp. H1, H4.

Hadfield, P. (1999, December 27). Many Japanese Immune to Sticker Shock. *USA Today*, p.5B.

IFSW. (2002, July 10-12). Ethics in Social Work Statement of Principles. *International Federation of Social Workers* (IFSW). Retrieved from http://www.ifsw.org/GM-2002/GM-Ethics-draft.html

Seeman, R. (1985, June). Liberalization for Foreign Lawyers in Japan. *The Japan Lawletter*. Retrieved from http://www.japanlaw.com/lawletter/june85/deg.htm

Smith, R. (2001, 20 September). Rescue Plan for Japan's Banks. *BBC News Online: Business*. Retrieved from http://news.bbc.co.uk/1/low/business/1555248.stm

The Guardian. (2000, January 19). Japanese Urged to Stop Being so 'Typically' Japanese. *Honolulu Star-Bulletin*.

Walsh, B. (1998). *Finding the Winning Edge*. Champaign, IL: Sports Publishing Inc.

World Factbook 2002, The. (2002, January 1). The World Factbook 2002: Japan. Retrieved March 19, 2003, from http://www.cia.gov/cia/publications/factbook/geos/ja.html

Zielenziger, M. (2001, September 7). Koizumi's economic fix for Japan criticized. *Detroit Free Press*, pp. 1C, 4C.

4

Construction Industry Structure and Participants

Introduction

This chapter introduces the Construction Industry Structure (CIS) model. The model is based upon two components of industry stability: competition and performance. When used in conjunction with the IMT, the KSM, and successful business practices, the CIS model becomes a very effective problem-solving tool.

IMT proposes that everything is related and relative. There are many factors in the construction industry: facility users, owners, budgets, designers, contractors, manufacturers, environmental conditions, construction skill levels, construction managers, differing project conditions, unknown and unforeseen events, and different expectations. *Because of the infinite number of factors, the industry appears complex and difficult to optimize.*

For the past ten years, the International Council for Building Research Studies and Documentation (CIB) has been unsuccessful in finding a mechanism to optimize construction performance in Europe, the Middle East, Asia, Australia, and Africa (CIB-Programme Committee 2003). The CIB has moved from one potential solution to another, among them: continuous improvement, total quality management, partnering, business process re-engineering, and lean construction. The CIB and other construction organizations have not been able to fix the inherent problems of construction nonperformance.

Major problems include: 1) The inability to finish on time, on budget, and meet the expectations of the building owner/user, 2) A shortage of competent entry-level personnel, 3) The diminishing value and profit of high-quality construction services, and 4) The declining quality of construction (Rosenbaum 2001, Green 2001, Post 1998)(see Chapter 6). These issues led to the CIB's latest effort: identifying the construction industry's value.

The construction industry in the U.S. has fared no better. According to the Engineering News Record: "Although owners were satisfied with their construction quality, many would not hire the contractor again" (Post 1998). No contractor sector: general, mechanical, or electrical, received a 'hire back' rating based upon a performance of 70 percent or more. Of these contractors, 42 percent did not finish on time, 33 percent were over budget, and 13 percent had litigation pending against them. The gravity of the situation can be quickly recognized when the construction nonperformance rate is compared with the rate of nonperformance in the manufacturing sector, which is less than 1%. Cost overruns, quality issues, and late completions, have made the construction industry in the United States very unpredictable (Post 2001, Post 1998).

Solution by Simplicity

A complex environment is always confusing. By stepping back from the confusion, the event becomes more simplistic. Construction is a "zero sum game." The input is fixed, since there is a certain amount of resources in terms of time and money. The farther away from the problem one moves, the more non-subjective the analysis becomes. If the analyzer is a participant, the lack of all of the information and the subjective bias of the individual, renders the problems more complex.

Any component of the system that is being used either adds or does not add value. If the component does not add value, it is using resources and not producing. Any component that is inefficient in the system, is forcing another component to make up for the inefficiency. However, due to the confusion, the rest of the components do not realize there is a nonproductive or inefficient element or elements in the system. Therefore, the system is unstable or unsustainable. Industry stability is defined as:

1. Ability to consistently provide a high performance product or service.
2. Continually improving the performance of the product or service.

The author has modified the Herbiniak and Joyce industrial engineering model (Herbiniak and Joyce 1985) to develop the Construction Industry Stability (CIS) model. The author has identified the following requirements of an effective model:

1. Simplistic. The model must break down the problems in terms of functions of management, inspection, quality control, high performance, profit, and risk of the different construction industry participants. Profit and the minimization of risk are the basic building blocks of business.
2. Non-technical. Any model that requires technical expertise cannot be understood by the customer of the construction industry. In other words, the model should not require the skills of technically qualified individuals for interpretation.
3. Identification of non-value added elements. The model should allow users to identify non-value added elements through deduction and commonly known business practices.
4. Identification of political concepts. Political concepts are identified by the author as concepts that do not lead to optimization, higher value, higher performance and efficiency. This model will identify where political concepts are the most sustainable.

The current status of the construction industry identifies that it is neither efficient nor capable of improving value. The purpose of the CIS model is to assist the participants to increase the industry's stability. In conjunction with IMT and the KSM, the CIS and related models simplify the problems of the construction industry, and shows how an information environment will optimize value for the owner and profit for the vendors.

The CIS model will also identify how the industry (building owner/user, designer, contractors, and manufacturers) can become more efficient.

CIS Model

The construction industry is described by two characteristics: competition and performance (Figure 4.1). The CIS model divides the industry into four quadrants:

1. Quadrant I - Low-Bid or Price-Based Sector: This sector is described by high competition and marginal performance.
2. Quadrant II - Best-Value Sector: This sector is described by high competition and performance.
3. Quadrant III - Negotiated-Bid Sector: This sector is described by high performance and low competition.
4. Quadrant IV – Unstable Sector: This sector is described by low performance and low competition.

Figure 4.1: The Construction Industry Structure (CIS) model

Quadrant I: Low-Bid or Price-Based Environment

In the low-bid or price-based environment, the owner employs a design-bid-build process. This process awards the contract to the lowest bidding construction contractor. Traditionally, this is the most common method of awarding contracts. Quadrant I has the following characteristics:

1. The process is managed or controlled by the owner's representative (design professional).
2. The design professional has stated to the owner that construction is a commodity. The designer then directs the awarding of the contract to the lowest price, minimizing the risk of low quality by using their professional expertise.

3. The design professional uses minimum standards to specify the commodity. The minimum standards have very little correlation with performance.
4. Contractors are directed to bid the lowest possible price. The participants who can control performance and quality (construction contractor) are not quality controlling their work. The owner's design professional manages and inspects the work.
5. There is no construction performance information on products, systems, contractors, designers or individuals. With an absence of performance information, politics and marketing becomes a powerful force.

The author will explain the above in the following order:

1. The impact of minimum standards.
2. The impact of the low-bid process.
3. The importance placed on management.
4. Subjectivity, relationships, and a lack of information lead to poor quality.

Minimum Standards

Minimum standards are meant to ensure that a contractor performs to a minimum level of performance. Many owners, designers, engineers, and consultants feel that minimum standards are necessary in order to prevent non-performance. The minimum standard means that the lowest level of performance is acceptable. Minimum means low (Szigeti 2002, Sharp 2002).

There is no documentation that shows minimum standards lead to higher performance. To the contrary, minimum standards offer low performing contractors, materials, and construction systems, the opportunity to compete against high performing alternatives, with a better chance of getting the bid due to their lower price. *Minimum standards provide the contractor who feels comfortable with minimal quality the advantage.*

When coupled with an award based on the lowest price, standards (which are always the lowest acceptable performance and quality) lead to lower performance and lower quality. Standards become useful only when procuring a true "commodity" (no risk, all alternatives are the same, can be bought in volume). In a construction environment, which is fraught with risk, standards should be used by contractors and manufacturers to ensure quality, and not by the owner/user's representative to ensure "equality."

To make it worse, standards are not set based upon performance information (Sharp 2002, Graham 2002). As discussed throughout this book, there is no performance information being kept in the construction industry. Therefore standards cannot meet the owner/user's performance expectations, and do not ensure performance. Many experts no longer have the necessary performance information to support their subjective decision-making. Instead they rely on their own personal experiences to attempt to define what performance is. The owner/user has no method to identify the delivered performance, but must trust in the design consultant's expertise. This has resulted in the following (Sharp 2002, Construction Claims Monthly 2002, Steyaert 1997, Graham 2002, Winston 2001, Horn 2002):

1. Minimum standards set by the lowest common denominator (lowest number in each physical characteristic).
2. Minimum standards on products set by individual testing procedures on different physical characteristics; the summation of which rarely has any correlation with the actual performance of any existing product or system.
3. A lack of actual performance information.
4. Contractors and manufacturers lowering their performance to meet the minimum standards.
5. A lack of liability for nonperformance. Once the owner/user's professional sets the minimum standard (which has no correlation with performance), the user's professional must prove when a product does not meet the minimum standard and who is to blame. Due to the number of participants (designers, contractors, subcontractors, manufacturers, and material suppliers), this becomes a difficult task, and fosters an environment of no liability.
6. Standards and standard setting becoming more important than the performance of construction systems. Otherwise, performance information would be used instead of standards.
7. Standards causing risk, instead of minimizing risk. Other products of standards are low performance, minimum liability, and lower profits.

How Standards Are Set

"However, through NRCA's involvement, it has realized the values established in many of these standards are not necessarily based on what is required to achieve satisfactory field performance (Graham 2002)."

"At press time, an ASTM International standard for TPO's is on its way to reaching a consensus. However, ASTM standards often are viewed as reflecting the lowest common denominator for many products unless they are proven commodity products...The standard that finally is issued for TPOs may reflect the consensus of manufacturers' minimum requirements for a laboratory-tested roof membrane; it is most unlikely the standard can ensure a product's performance in the field." (Sharp 2002)

A group called the American Society for Testing and Materials (ASTM) identifies construction materials that need standards. The author attended an ASTM standard setting meeting in 1997. The following steps occur when creating a standard:

1. A committee is formed to work on the standard. The committee is composed of industry professionals, manufacturers' representatives, and government personnel.
2. The committee meets and identifies physical characteristics and accompanying ASTM tests which can measure the physical properties.
3. Each manufacturer then tests their materials, bringing back the test results. There is no standard testing procedure governing how many tests, which test results are valid, and what number to report (low, high, medium, or average).

4. The committee reconvenes, and goes over the test numbers from all of the manufacturers.
5. The committee then considers the numbers for all criteria, for each manufacturer.
6. The predominate choice is the lowest number. (The author questioned the validity of picking the lowest number at the 1997 meeting, and there was no clear answer).
7. The ASTM standard for a product, usually does not match up with a specific product. Using the standard, any product in that product group meets the standards.

Figure 4.2 illustrates how a standard is created. A group of manufacturers test their products and submit their results. In most cases, the ASTM standard selects the lowest possible value for each test. This becomes the new "standard".

PHYSICAL PROPERTY	TEST METHOD	MANUFACTURER'S DATA						PROPOSED REQUIREMENT
		A	B	C	D	E	F	
Initial Elongation % (break)	D412	150%	100-200%	200%	100-150%	140-250%	140-160%	100% Min.
Initial Tensile Strength (max stress)	D412	400	150-600	450	300-400	400-625	500-600	150 psi Min.
Final Elongation % Weathering	D412	n/a	100% min	200%	125%	N/a	140-160%	100% Min.
Permeance	E96, B	3.7	n/a	3.5	2.9	N/a	2.6-3.0	2.5 U.S. perms Min
Weathering (5000 hours)	G53	No cracking	No cracking	No cracking	No cracking		No cracking	No cracking
Adhesion	C794	2 pli	6-10 pli	3 pli	n/a	N/a	n/a	2 pli min.
Tear Resistance	D624	20-30 lb/in	n/a	30 lb/in	n/a	33-53 lb/in	n/a	20 lb/in
Low Temperature Flexibility	D522	n/a	n/a	Passes	Passes	N/a	Passes	Passes
Viscosity	D2196	30,000-50,000	8,000-25,000	115-130 KU	< 60,000	Varies	35,000-40,000	35,000-50,000cps
Volume Solids	D2697	62%	80%	57-66%	62%	66%	62%	57-80%
Weight Solids	D1644	0.77	0.66	70-77%	0.75	0.74	0.71	As listed by Mfg.

Figure 4.2: Example of How a Standard is Created

From this example, it is clear to see that the standard is not set based on performance information. The standard has no correlation to how well this product will last. These standards motivate manufacturers to lower the quality of their product to meet the bare minimum requirement. By doing this, they can save money and compete with other manufacturers products. For example, manufacturer F (Figure 4.2) will reformulate their product to have a tensile strength of 150psi instead of 500psi.

Standards motivate minimum performance and a lack of liability. Standards cause risk. Standards have very little correlation with actual performance. Standards penalize high performance manufacturers and contractors, and create an environment of confusion. Confusion requires two major players: consultants and litigation lawyers.

Source of Contractor Motivation to Lower Performance

Figure 4.3 shows four contractors with four different levels of performance, expertise, quality and ability to perform. However, many owner representatives such as designers, engineers, or consultants cannot recognize or explain the differences between performance levels. Instead they treat the contractors as commodities (they believe that they all perform at the same level). Contractor 1 gets no credit for being able to perform at a very high level.

The owner's representative sets a minimum level of acceptable performance, which is subjective and therefore requires interpretation and regulation (Figure 4.4a). The standard is set to prevent risk of a very low performing contractor. Figure 4.4b shows how the higher-performing contractors lower their levels of performance in order to meet the minimum level as closely as possible. The message is clear. The owner is telling the contractor, "<u>Give me the cheapest possible job at the lowest possible price.</u>"

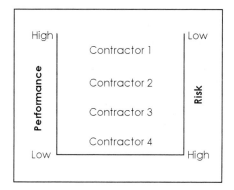

Figure 4.3: Performing Contractors

By considering contractors as commodities (no performance differential) <u>a contractor's sole objective is to lower cost to get the project.</u> The building owner/user's representative is actually the source of the low level of construction performance. The professional hired to minimize risk, has used a mechanism that actually increases risk.

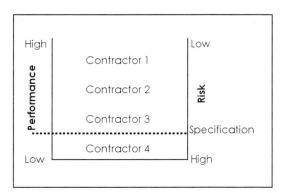

Figure 4.4a: Minimum Standard

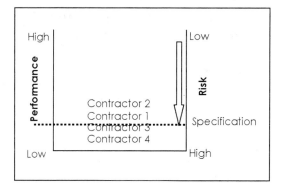

Figure 4.4b: Impact of Minimum Standards

Low-bid Award

The design-bid-build delivery process traditionally awards to the lowest priced contractor. The rationale involves:

1. The designer identifies the commodity by identifying products, means and methods, and design.

2. All contractors are treated as a commodity, they are all the same, and therefore the best value is the lowest price.
3. The owner's professional has to minimize the risk caused by the specification and impact of the low price award through management and inspection.

The problems with the low-bid process are that:

1. Minimum standards motivate the contractor to lower performance levels. No two contractors offer the same performance. The higher performer, who is on time, on budget, and who meets quality expectations, usually has more experience and employs better craftspeople. However, the high performer receives no credit for good performance. Instead, this contractor must reduce quality in order to compete with the lowest price options.
2. The process places the owner and the contractors on opposite sides, each with different objectives (to be covered in detail in the following section).
3. Means and methods specifications in combination with owner management and inspection allow inexperienced contractors to bid. Where, if they were not directed in detail in what to do, they could not bid or compete on the project. The document that is meant to minimize risk, ironically attracts the risk, motivates contractors who bring risk to the owner, and puts experienced contractors and craftspeople in a disadvantageous position.
4. The professional who tells the contractors what to do, then manages and inspects to minimize risk, has actually become the "magnet" for nonperforming contractors. If the nonperforming contractors did not have the means and method specifications from the professional, they could not even bid, due to their lack of experience with the project.
5. Management and inspection force the owner's representatives to make subjective decisions on acceptability. When decisions are made by the owner, liability shifts from the contractor to the owner.

Best Interest of the Owner vs. Best Interest of the Contractor

The low bid process puts the owner and contractor in an adversarial position. Figure 4.5 shows that on the left hand side, the owner sets a minimum standard, but expects higher performance. The owner feels that the minimum standard is required to ensure they are not being cheated by low bidding contractors. Because of the low bid award, the contractors and manufacturers, transform the minimum into a maximum, so profit can be made in three ways:

1. Lowering the level of performance from what they have offered in the past.
2. Offering something that does not meet the intent of the specifications but because of a lack of information and inconsistent standards, is accepted as meeting minimum specifications.
3. Identifying errors in the requirement, bidding the project low, with the knowledge that in the low bid system, the owner will have to cut a change order to get the required work done. Change orders are advantageous to the contractor because

at the time of the change order, there is no competition, and the risk is extremely high to the owner.

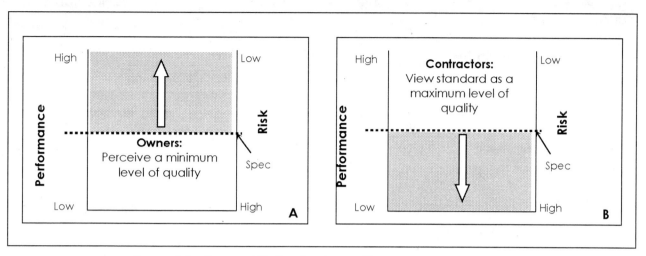

Figure 4.5: Owners VS. Contactors: Difference in Objectives

The contractor is in business to make a profit. A contractor who does not make a profit brings risk to the owner, because the lack of profit may force the contractor to go out of business. A contractor who goes out of business brings the biggest risk to the owner in the long run. This voids warranties, causes liens, does not cover improper work, and makes the owner's representative or professional look unprofessional because the construction is a failure.

The contractor is in business to make a profit and can increase profits by dropping the performance as low as is acceptable. The contractor will not use their profit to pay for the additional quality and performance. If the owner/user decides to use a professional to manage, control, and minimize the risk of nonperformance, they are attempting to do something that has been proven to be a very unsuccessful business practice. It is illogical, it is inefficient, and it has never worked.

The difference in objectives creates a gap. There is no overlap. The owner/user has created a new function to close this gap. It is called partnering. Partnering is another function in the Low Bid Environment (Quadrant I); it has the following features:

1. It costs money. Partnering experts charge for this function.
2. It forces the two parties to talk and solve problems.
3. It forces a "deal" to make between the parties if the problem is to be solved.

If the parties do not make a deal, then the partnering fails, and the result is nonperforming construction and litigation. If the partnering works, then no one revisits the issues. The partnering may work for a while, but then break down due to "poor business practices."

The author proposes that partnering is a function that borders on collusion. This is based on deductive logic. If the specification is correct, and it can be enforced, the owner has no need of partnering. If the contractor does not meet the requirements of the specification, the contractor is not paid. Performance bonds are then forced to pay to finish the project. Partnering is only needed when the specification is not correct.

Role of the Designer in the Low-Bid Environment

The design and engineering professional has seen their role change over time in the low bid environment. Historically the following has happened. The designer started out being responsible for the identification of the owner's requirement, and translating the requirement into a construction requirement. This was then turned over to a contractor who constructed the project.

Over time, due to price pressures and to gain control over the construction, designers convinced the owner that they could deliver the construction as a commodity, deliver it at the lowest price, and minimize the risk by managing and inspecting the contractor. This ensured the design and engineering professional a guaranteed cut of all construction funding (6-10 percent). This ensured the survivability of the function.

However, when the process resulted in poor performance (not on time, not on budget, and not meeting the owner/user's quality expectation), the owner/users started scrutinizing what the design and engineering professional were doing. They started minimizing functions and cutting fees. The designers reacted by covering their risk with insurance.

Insurance companies then forced the designers to identify to the owners what they could not do (anything with risk). The impact of the insurance companies was to make the owner take the risk. When the owners were faced with taking the risk, the owners further reduced the function and importance of the designer. Some resulting actions include: moving to alternate delivery systems where the designer works for contractors, bidding design work, hiring designers to inspect designers, and making contractors liable for verifying the design. The real impact on the designer has been:

1. The designer is not spending enough time identifying the owner's requirements and translating the requirement into construction requirements.
2. The designer is being taken out of their core expertise.
3. The design and engineering professional have turned to managing and inspecting construction as their core competency, a function that is inefficient, a function that they are not educated and trained in, and a function that is only justified by the owners either hiring inexperienced contractors, or experienced contractors who are forced in an adversarial position.

The designer is a professional who can add value by returning to their core competency of design, and becoming a knowledge worker by being able to identify performance, and awarding contracts to performing contractors and manufacturers.

The Assignment of Skilled Craftspeople and Construction Managers

Many owners think they are using best-value or performance-based procurement. However, a simple analysis of the environment can quickly determine if "best-value" procurement is truly being applied.

Every contractor employs craftspeople with different degrees of training (Figure 4.6). Some workers are very highly trained, some have been slightly trained, and some workers are rather inexperienced. The following discussion will identify two relationships:

1. How the successful contractor assigns the personnel.
2. What controls the number of craftspeople in each group?

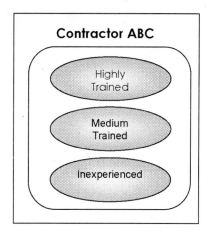

Figure 4.6: Three different crews working for a contractor

Figure 4.7 shows Contractor ABC servicing three different owners. The first owner outsources construction. The outsourcing owner understands that they do not have the technical expertise or the capability to efficiently get construction done. They pass the function and the risk to the contractor.

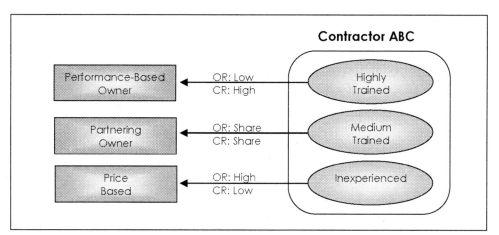

Figure 4.7: Contractor Assignment of Craftspeople
(OR= owner risk, CR=contractor risk)

The second owner is a partnering owner. They have some knowledge of construction and feel comfortable sharing the risk with the contractor.

The third owner, hires a professional designer/engineer that will represent them. This owner will award to the lowest-priced contractor and have the professional identify what, how, where, and when the construction will be done. The professional will then manage and inspect the contractor. This owner has hired the professional to minimize the risk. Whatever risk is not minimized by the professional, resides with the owner. No risk is passed to the contractor.

The contractor's objective is to make a profit. There is nothing technical about making a profit. A contractor can only supply personnel who the owner pays for. The contractor is not in business to take a loss. The contractor must use their personnel efficiently. The contractor will not send their highly paid (expert craftspeople) to a job where:

1. They have to take directions (from someone who does not have the expertise).
2. They will have to do the work twice because they were directed to do something that won't work
3. They will have to sit around due to mismanagement by the owner/user's professional representative.

Contractors have liability and risk. The liability is covered by bonding and insurance, but the risk must be minimized by expertise. The contractor makes their profit by lowering the risk that they are given. If they are given no risk, they will make a profit by using the least experienced personnel.

Contractor ABC will send their most experienced craftspeople to the outsourcing owner. They are given liability and risk, and need to minimize the risk to make a profit. It is also the most efficient use of skilled craftspeople because they have complete control over the project. Highly skilled personnel have the following characteristics:

1. They quickly analyze the problem and identify the best solution.
2. Plan their solution to be the most efficient use of resources.
3. Do the work right the first time.
4. Take complete responsibility for their work.
5. Do not like listening or working with people who do not know what they are talking about.

Contractor ABC will send the medium trained personnel to the partnering owner due to the following:

1. The owner's representatives want to discuss the problem and solution and come to an agreement.
2. The owner wants to share the risk.
3. The owner wants everyone to be a team player, open to everyone else's ideas.
4. If the owner wants to partner, the owner is accepting the liability. A party is never at risk when they do not have the liability, regardless of what is perceived.
5. The owner may send their highly trained personnel to the partnering owner if they are not servicing any outsourcing customers. However, highly trained personnel do not survive long in a partnering relationship where they have to listen and accept concepts from inexperienced participants.

Contractor ABC will send the most inexperienced personnel to the owner/user who uses a professional to minimize the risk. This owner is asking for the most inexperienced personnel who are the cheapest. This owner is telling the contractor, "Don't worry about risk; I have a professional who will manage and inspect to minimize the risk."

Contractor ABC increases their profits by sending the most inexperienced construction personnel to the low bid owner. If the most highly trained personnel were sent to the owner, they would do the following:

1. Review the design and construction requirements.
2. Identify what is wrong; optimize the design for construction efficiency and performance.
3. Do the work quickly and with high quality.

However, this does not make the contractor profit. They have to bid low to get the work. Instead the contractor will send the most inexperienced to the project. They will do the following:

1. Start construction.
2. Get into the construction as far as they can before they identify a problem.
3. Turn over the problem to the owner's representative.

Once the owner's professional representative solves the problem, the following situation exists:

1. The project completion time is at risk.
2. The owner is upset because of the "unforeseen" problem and the increase in project cost.
3. Everyone involved is trying to place the blame somewhere else.
4. There is no competition, and it is perceived that the contractor is going to overcharge for the change order.
5. The owner wants to pay as little as possible for the change. The representative will pay time and materials and overhead and profit.

The contractor's objective is to make a profit. It now is beneficial for them to finish the work as slow as possible. It behooves the contractor to put the personnel on the project who will take the longest time to complete (inexperienced personnel). It is also to the advantage of the contractor if the solution is not completely correct. The owner will end up paying more for less. The contractor will end up making a profit if they understand the issue of risk. By tracking their time and interruptions, a contractor can make the low bid award into a profitable business.

Assessing the contractor crews' performance levels is the easiest way to identify the type of system an owner is truly running. When an owner claims to use best-value procurement, but the contractors are not performing to their expectations, the owner is using either a partnering or low bid approach. Changing the name of the procurement system will not change the result. Previous graphs show how contractors send their most experienced crews to the jobs where they have maximum risk. Although an owner may claim to use best-value procurement, by performing functions of management, inspection, and control, the owner is actually creating a low-bid environment. A true best-value system is characterized by the presence of high-performing contractors and the absence of owner management and control functions.

Management and Control by the Owner's Representatives

Management and control functions by the owner's representative are only done in Quadrant I. Figure 4.8 shows the major functions in Quadrant I, which are controlled by the owner's professional representative:

1. Writing the specifications.
2. Managing the contractor.
3. Inspecting the contractor.

The owner's representatives control all of the functions in Quadrant I but they have been unable to control construction performance. The result of this quadrant has been:

1. The owner's representative makes the construction decisions.
2. High performing contractors are motivated to lower their quality.
3. The owner's representative controls and directs the contractor.
4. The design becomes a regulatory document (instead of a document of intent). If it is not in the specification, the contractor wants a change order.
5. The contractor is motivated to find items needed in the construction but not included in the regulatory document (change orders).
6. This environment involves redundant functions that make it inefficient.

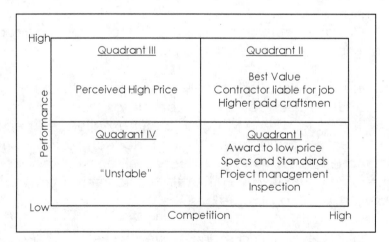

Figure 4.8: Major Functions of Quadrant I

The author advises that all participants "lose" in Quadrant I. There is no precedence of one party successfully controlling another party in any relationship. In this relationship the owner's professional representative has no direct control, but must control through a contractual relationship.

The contractor is forced to do more work for less profit. This is called leveraging volume. To do more work, the contractor must hire more workers and cannot afford to adequately train these workers. This forces the contractor to manage additional workers (with less experience) using fewer managers who understand performing construction. The contractor's highly qualified personnel are always subject to offers from other contractors who need qualified personnel on projects that pay more.

Designers initially thought of themselves as the master builders or "controllers" of construction. This is a false perception, as the designers needed high quality contractors and craftspeople to deliver performing construction. The design-bid-build process maximizes their services because the resulting lower quality construction requires even more design effort than before. However, as performance has declined, the demand for the services of professionals (who were supposed to ensure performance) has also declined. Owners now ask, "If poor construction performance is the inevitable result, why pay someone to ensure poor performance?" With this view, owners are gradually returning control to the contractors and minimizing designer's functions. The design and engineering professionals are currently seeking ways to identify their value. To add value, they must realize that their core competency is design, and not construction. In the current construction environment, designers and engineers are accountable for construction without sufficient education, training, or control. Another negative result is that the owner is not recognizing that the designer needs more resources to do proper planning, programming, and design. Proper design will minimize confusion and assist performing contractors (Angelo 2002, Dodson 2002, Butler 2002, Post 2000, Gray 1999, Sawyer 2001, Maryland Society 2003).

In the end, the owner is the real loser. The owner is actually paying for functions that are not required and not paying enough for functions that are required. It is the classic "Emperor with no clothes." The designers and consultants have convinced owners that the procurement of construction is a risky and difficult process that requires their technical expertise. What the owner didn't realize is that if they hired performing contractors, the process is simplistic. (Krizan 1998)

Politics in Quadrant I

The author suggests that "politics" is the opposite of information. Politics has the following characteristics:

1. Win-lose.
2. Puts interest of a component ahead of the whole industry.
3. Not supported by information.
4. Based on decisions.
5. Stops change.
6. Is inefficient. Resources are being used for functions that add no value to the performance of construction.

Consider the following:

1. Manufacturers, design firms and contractors spend more money on marketing (dinners, vacations, golf trips, sponsoring booths at conferences, sports activities, and so forth) than they do on training, analyzing, and improving performance.
2. The major objective of contractors and design consultants at conferences is not to learn how to become more efficient, but to network with owners.
3. Sales personnel earn as much or more than engineers, designers, or craftspeople.
4. Sales personnel receive more freedom and funding than engineers.

The construction industry is like a huge pond in a forest populated with monkeys. The pond (industry) is filled with very large fish that eat smaller fish. When the forest suffers a drought, the water level drops and the big fish devour the smaller fish. As the water level gets dangerously low, the larger fish can no longer move around. However, they spend their remaining energy devouring the smaller fish, which have now become more mobile in the shallow water. As the pond dries, monkeys from the surrounding forest invade the pond and pick out the larger fishes' eyes. The larger fish in the construction pond are the participants who are fighting to survive in the low bid environment. As the owners continue to lower the price of construction, the large fish (status quo design firms and contractors) attack every other fish in the lake of construction where the zero sum resources are getting lower and lower. The monkeys are problem solvers from outside of the construction industry. They are logical, understand proper business practices, and will outsource construction to performers. The performing construction of the future will come from a whole new generation of thinkers if the low bid environment continues.

Capability of the Construction Industry to Sustain Itself in Quadrant I

One of the construction industry's largest problems is a shortage of qualified personnel. This problem can be analyzed using the following characteristics in the low-bid environment:

1. High volume of work. Low profit forces contractors to manage a higher work volume, compelling contractors to lower their work quality. A higher volume of work requires more craftspeople; but a shortage of competent craftspeople leads to lower quality work. Contractors are leveraging volume, obtaining more work by offering construction at a lower price. This works in the commodity manufacturing sectors, where automation has been implemented, but cannot work in a non-commodity environment (Grogan 2002, ENR Staff Writer 2002).
2. Lower Profit. Profit margins are lower when contractors do more work for a lower unit price (Horn 2002).
3. Lack of quality control. Quality control is not required in an environment of low price and inspection (Post 2001).
4. Management and inspection by third parties hired by the owner becomes the most important function. It is an "overhead" or non-operational function. It has no true responsibility; it is inefficient.

5. Training is not a requirement. Craftsperson training is needed, but not required. Low profit margins and no credit for performance prohibit contractors from implementing effective training programs (Korman 1997, Krizan 1997, Tompkins 2001, Korman 2002, Burrough 1995, Feyek 2002, Rosenbaum 2001).

As identified by these characteristics, construction personnel must do the following in order to be the most successful:

1. Work more for less money.
2. Have no pride or value.
3. Perform without incentive or reward.
4. Do the lowest possible quality of work.
5. Compete with low performers.
6. Be comfortable with having an inspector or project manager constantly directing their work.

An intelligent, continuously improving, quality oriented person does not gravitate toward this type of environment. Figure 4.9 demonstrates how, in a Quadrant II environment, the industry can much more successfully attract professional personnel, high quality craftspeople, making the industry considerably more sustainable.

Figure 4.9 – Characteristics of Quadrant II

Quadrant II: Best-Value Environment

Quadrant II, the "Best-Value" environment, is a high competition, high performance environment in which users consider both performance and price. The terms 'performance' and 'value' are often used interchangeably. However, value is the owner's end objective. If the owner has an unrestricted budget, performance is the only concern. The "best-value" differs from the other quadrants because it:

1. Compares price and performance to ascertain value.
2. Uses performance information.

3. Maximizes competition by allowing the contractors and vendors to use standards to ensure performance.
4. Allows the contractor to accept and reduce risk. Shifting the risk to the contractor diminishes the owner's need to manage or inspect the contractor.
5. Allows the performing contractor to control the construction project.
6. Forces quality control.
7. Forces continuous improvement.
8. Minimizes decision-making.
9. Forces decision making by the participant who has liability and the most information.
10. Forces continuous improvement by continuously tracking the performance of all contractors.
11. It is continually trying to make the entire delivery system more efficient.

Quadrant II is the smallest and least understood environment. Although many owners endeavor to avoid "Quadrant I performance," misunderstanding Quadrant II requirements often places the owner back in Quadrant I where low price is considered the best value. One of the problems is that the design and engineering professional, which the owner has depended on in Quadrant I, does not understand how to run Quadrant II. They have therefore taken the same toolbox of tools from Quadrant I: standards, means and methods, construction management, inspection, and low price awards. Instead of taking the owner into Quadrant II, they have returned to Quadrant I with new names for slightly changed processes.

The only way the requirements of Quadrant II can be met is by the owner/user's representative being a knowledge worker or information worker. There is no education or training for the knowledge worker. The knowledge worker must have the following characteristics:

1. Uses performance information.
2. Does not use subjective information (expertise).
3. Minimizes management and control.
4. Identifies performance instead of managing performance.
5. Selects best value.
6. Minimizes the amount of information during construction.
7. Minimizes directions.

Quadrant III: Negotiated-Bid Environment

High performance and low competition represent Quadrant III and summarize negotiated-bid contracts. Typically, users pre-qualify contractors and subjectively select the best value using minimal performance information. Next, owners build relationships with contractors by sole-sourcing projects to them.

This quadrant is difficult to sustain in the competitive worldwide economy due to its lack of competition and to the perception that a better value, at a lower price, is obtainable through added competition.

The major difference between Quadrant II and Quadrant III is the trust requirement in Quadrant III. Quadrant II does not require trust and personal relationships. Rather, it forces contractors to perform to their own expectations based upon past performance, motivation to improve, and the use of the best-qualified personnel on each project. Although that may seem to be a personal relationship founded on trust, the contractor is actually at risk based on their performance.

Quadrant III is being minimized due to the price pressures of the worldwide competitive marketplace. Building owners/users are being pressured to lower the prices of their products and services. The cost of facilities and the maintenance of the facilities is one of their major costs.

Quadrant IV: Unstable Market

Quadrant IV is unstable. The following are features of Quadrant IV:

1. There is no identification of performance. Level of performance does not have a consistent relationship with doing work or making a profit.
2. Contractors with less performance can get paid more.
3. No one has a competitive advantage.
4. The environment is highly political.
5. There is no real competition. There are bidders, but through political means, a contractor has the advantage.
6. Performers have a difficult time competing.

When the low bid environment forces the unreasonable cutting of prices, contractors seek an edge through political means. One of the methods is to get the job at any cost and make profit on the project by extensive change orders. Another method is to have a personal relationship with the owner's design/engineering representative. Another method is to minimize competition by specifications or requirements. When nonperforming contractors can gain the competitive advantage, the environment is close to Quadrant I.

Conclusion

The Construction Structure Industry (CSI) model shows that the industry is not very stable. The majority of the sectors is not efficient, cannot produce performing construction for a sustained period of time, and cannot identify the value of construction. In Quadrant I, the traditional sector, the low bid, minimum standards, delivering construction as a commodity, the adversarial relationships, and the management and control of contractors by the owner's professional representative, has made the industry very inefficient and incapable of producing performing construction over a sustained period of time. Owners/users in Quadrant I want better value and performance.

Quadrant III, the negotiated bid quadrant, is fast disappearing due to the price pressures of the worldwide competitive marketplace on building owners/users to minimize their costs and become efficient. Owners/users understand that more competition will bring a better price.

Both Quadrant I and III owners/users want best value. Best value can only be achieved when the delivery process becomes efficient. Efficiency is achieved when resources to deliver the construction services are optimized, both on the owner's side and the contractor's side. This includes a minimization of effort to deliver and a win-win between the owner who wants best value, and the contractor who is motivated by profit. The most efficient construction environment is composed of the designer designing and the contractor constructing. The selection of the contractor must be done based on performance and price. Contractors must quality control their own work and be motivated to perform without external management. This environment requires a knowledge worker. This environment must minimize both project and construction management. The only way to achieve this is by using an information-based environment. If the process is efficient, it will contain the best business practices. In the next chapter, these business practices will be discussed.

There is a correlation between performance information and performance responsibility, the minimization of risk and the minimization of the passing of information, and Outsourcing construction. The next chapter will identify successful business practices, which will help frame Quadrant I.

Chapter 4 Review

1. What are the two main components of a stable industry?
2. Draw the CIS model and label all components and quadrants.
3. What quadrant is the construction industry currently in? Why?
4. Which is the best quadrant?
5. Identify five factors of the Quadrant I environment.
6. Which Quadrant has more inspection?
7. Which Quadrant has more quality control?
8. Who is responsible for the majority of functions in the Quadrant I environment?
9. Who is responsible for the majority of functions in the Quadrant II environment?
10. Does hiring additional designers or management firms increase the possibility of procuring a high performing project? Why?
11. How do we set a perfect standard?
12. Do minimum standards (specifications) create a conflict of interest between the owner and contractor? Why?
13. Do minimum standards (specifications) raise or lower the performance of contractors? Why?

14. If a contractor has 3 different levels of performing crews (high performing, medium, and low performing) whom does he or she assign to a low-bid owner? Why?

15. If a contractor has 3 different levels of performing crews (high performing, medium, and low performing) whom does he or she assign to a partnering owner? Why?

16. If a contractor has 3 different levels of performing crews (high performing, medium, and low performing) whom does he or she assign to a performance-based owner? Why?

17. What is the easiest way in which an owner can determine if they are truly running a performance-based system?

18. How are standards a source of Risk?

19. How can designers be a source of risk?

20. What is a performance specification?

References

Angelo, W.J. (2002, August 12). Team Should Be Contractor Lead. *Engineering News Record (ENR)*, 249 [7], pg. 47.

Burrough, D.J. (1995, September 1). Builders Dispute ASU Study. *The Business Journal*, pgs. 21, 30.

Butler, J. (2002, March 18). Construction Quality Stinks. *Engineering News Record (ENR)*, 248 [10], pg. 99.

CIB-Programme Committee. (2003). Re-Valuing Construction. *CIB 2003 – International Council for Research and Innovation in Building and Construction*, Manchester, UK. Retrieved 5 August 2003, from http://www.revaluing-construction.com/

Construction Claims Monthly Staff Writer. (2002, October). Assessing Risk in the Contract Documents. *Construction Claims Monthly*, 32 [9], pp. 1,7.

Dodson, M. (1995, May 1). Selling Quality. *Western Roofing*, pg. 4.

ENR Staff Writer. (2002, 26 August). Volume or Value. *Engineering News Record (ENR)*. 249 [9], p. 76.

Fayek, A., & Nkuah, M. (2002, January). Analysis of Change Order Markup Allowances on Stipulated Price Building Contracts. *Cost Engineering*, 44 [1], pp. 28-31.

Graham, M. (2002, September). NRCA's performance standards initiative. *Professional Roofing*, 32 [9], p. 80.

Gray, J.A. (1999, April-May). Design-Build in the Public Sector? *Military Engineer*, [598], pp. 67-68.

Green, S.D. (2001). "Towards a Critical Research Agenda in Construction Management". *Proceedings of CIB World Building Congress, Performance in Product and Practice*, Wellington, New Zealand. Retrieved from http://www.personal.rdg.ac.uk/~kcsgrest/critical-research-agenda.htm

Grogan, T. (2002, December 23). Strong Volume, Weak Prices. *Engineering News Record (ENR)*. 249 [26], p. 22-24.

Herbiniak & Joyce. (1985). Organizational Adaptation: Strategic Choice and Environmental Determinism. *Administrative Science Quarterly*, pp. 336-349.

Horn, J.V. (2002, 1 August). Parking Equipment Manufacturers Must Lower Quality to Meet Price Requirements. *Parking Today*. 7 [8], pp. 28-31.

Korman, R. (1997, June 9). Training Goals Divide Industry. *Engineering News Record (ENR)*, 238 [23], pp. 8-9.

Korman, R., Illia, T., & Barnes, J. (2002, October 28). Investigators Show the Routine Errors behind Jobsite Deaths. *Engineering News Record (ENR)*, 249 [18], pp. 24-25,27,28.

Krizan, W.G., Winston, S., & Korman, R. (1997, January 27). Training, Cooperation May Produce a 'New Industry'. *Engineering News Record (ENR)*, 238 [4], pp. 84, 87-88.

Krizan, W.G., & Winston, S. (1998, January 26). Scarcity of Skilled Workers Will Put Brakes On Growth. *Engineering News Record (ENR)*, 240 [4], pp. 95, 98, 101.

Maryland Society Staff Writer. A Design Professional: Through Qualifications Based Selection. Maryland Society: American Institute of Architects. Retrieved June 3, 2003, from http://www.msaia.org/qbs_info.htm

Post, N.M. (1998). Building Teams Get High Marks. *Engineering News-Record (ENR),* 240 [19], 32.

Post, N.M. (2000, May 1). No Stamp of Approval On Building Plans: Contractors sound off over difficulties with bid documents. *Engineering News Record (ENR)*, 244 [17], pp. 34-37, 39, 42, 45-46.

Post, N.M. (2001, May 14). Bumpier Road to Finish Line. Engineering News Record, 246 [19], pg. 56-63.

Rosenbaum, D. (2001, July 30). No fix for craft labor shortage. *Engineering News Record (ENR)*, 247 [5], p. 14.

Sawyer, T. (2001, June 11). A Whirlwind of Change is Transforming Plan Rooms. *Engineering News Record (ENR)*, 246 [23], pp. 31, 32, 34.

Sharp, S.A. (2002, June). What are the Standards? *Professional Roofing*, 36 [6], 39-40.

Steyaert, J. (1997, December 1). White paper past performance. Retrieved from http://www.acqsolinc.com/pastperfdoc/pastperfwp.html

Szigeti, F., & Davis, G. (2002, January/February). User Needs Quality and Assessment. *Facility Management Journal*, pp. 19-27.

Tompkins, S. (2001, November). Construction Industry Faces Potential Labor Crisis. *Cost Engineering*, 43 [11], p. 36.

Winston, S. (2001, October 29). Building GSA still backs performance standards. *Engineering News Record (ENR)*, 247 [18], p. 9.

5

Alternate Delivery Processes and Successful Business and Management Practices

Introduction

The construction industry's performance has been under discussion for some time. Although many approaches have been proposed, there is very little documented changes, results, or success (Post 1998, Jaggar 2002, Hindle 2002).

There are Performing and nonperforming contractors. Simply put, Performing contractors perform and nonperforming contractors have a difficult time performing. Performing contractors have two kinds of personnel, those that know how to perform and those who have a difficult time performing. Performing contractor personnel know how to identify and minimize risk and use insurance and bonding to minimize liability. If owners and owners' representatives do not use procurement processes that identify and select performing personnel from performing contractors, they will retain the risk of nonperformance (Figure 5.1). If either of the requirements is not met, performing personnel and performing contractor, they will retain risk.

Using the concepts of IMT and KSMs, nonperforming contractors have nonperforming personnel who do not perform because of the way they do their job. They have less perception, less experience, more problems, make more decisions, need more management and direction, do not quality control their own work but force the owner's representative to inspect and make the decision, and produce marginal work, which is often times not on time, not on budget, and does not meet the expectations of the owner. This should not be a surprise to owners. This is not a technical issue. The issue at hand is plain and simple: It is having confidence that the person hired for the job, can do what he was hired to do. Risk management, meeting quality expectations on time and without change orders, is a shortcoming of contractors (Murray 2002). The Engineering News Record identifies that although satisfied with the construction quality, many owners would not hire the contractor again (Post 1998).

Procurement processes that do not differentiate by performance and then motivate performing contractors to send their best personnel, will retain risk for the owner. If the risk of construction nonperformance is transferred to the contractors, contractors that cannot minimize the risk will not bid. In order for this to happen, the following is required:

1. The risk must be transferred to the contractor. The contractor therefore must control their project. They must be severely penalized if they do not perform. The owner must not help the contractor do their job.
2. The contractors must perceive that the risk is being transferred. This is not an issue of fairness. The function of construction, the management of construction, the coordination of construction, the planning of construction, and the inspection of construction, must be transferred to the contractor.
3. Contractor's performance must be considered in the procurement or selection process.
4. Contractors who perform must have a competitive advantage.
5. Contractors who do not perform must have a competitive disadvantage.
6. The process must center on the pride and motivation of the contractor to perform. The motivation for performance comes directly from the contractor and not the process itself (IMT, KSM).

The less subjective or more accurately the process follows the above, the less risk the owner has. These points have no correlation with any specific type of delivery process. These points deal with the selection of a contractor, not the function of a contractor. As soon as an owner starts to solve the problem of construction nonperformance by changing the function of what a contractor does, they will find out that they have just exacerbated the problem. The author proposes that the origin of many of the processes have been just that, an attempt by the owner to minimize risk of nonperformance by changing the function of the contractor.

There have been many modifications in the construction delivery processes to increase construction performance. This chapter discusses the differences between the various construction delivery systems. These delivery systems include:

1. Design-bid-build
2. Construction Management
3. Design-build
4. Construction Management at Risk (CM@Risk)
5. Indefinite Delivery, Indefinite Quantity (IDIQ)
6. Job Order Contracting (JOC)
7. Time and materials
8. Performance contracting
9. Best value procurement (The Performance Information Procurement System is a type of best value procurement that forces a full information environment).

Indefinite delivery, indefinite quantity (IDIQ), job order contracting, and time and material contracts have been around for the last 10 years (Badger and Kashiwagi 1991). Design-build and construction management-at-risk are two processes that have had better results than the design-bid-build results (Konchar and Sanvido 1998). Performance contracting and best value contracts are the latest processes tested in the construction industry.

The building owners have been dissatisfied with the traditional design-bid-build process (Chapter 4). To overcome the finger pointing between the contractor and the designer, the building owner came up with the design-build concept. One party (a general contractor) can be hired at the beginning of the process and handle both the design and the construction, minimizing the amount of change orders. However, to select the design-build contractor so early in the process forces the owners to select a contractor based on a specific product and price.

Once the contract is awarded, any changes to the design product become change orders. As most owners do not know what they want, this becomes a problem. The Owner loses flexibility, the contractor is being forced to change the design, and everyone distrusts everyone else because everyone has different expectations. A common result is that the owner hires another designer to watch the design-builder.

The Owner has realized that design-build does not solve the problem with meeting their high expectations. They want more control over the design, but are still convinced that the contractor can help the designer. A process is created where the designer is hired to design. The owner then hires the contractor before the design is complete, to assist the designer in making the design constructible. The contractor is then called a construction manager at risk with a guaranteed maximum price (GMP). The process does not motivate the designer or the contractor to act in the best interest of the owner.

IMT and KSMs identify that this motivation cannot come from a process or through management. It must come from inside a person. It is their mode of operation, which is identifiable, predictable, and can be documented. Any process that tries to motivate individuals to perform instead of finding individuals to perform will be less successful in delivering performance. The more successful processes will have overcome the following:

1. Logic and deduction.
2. All past events in the history of mankind.
3. All the evidences from psychology and psychiatry.
4. All successful business practices.

This has been one of the reasons the construction industry has been so slow to change. Even if something has been unsuccessful 99 times out of 99 times, the industry feels that on the 100th time, it has a good probability of being successful.

This chapter will discuss the various alternative delivery processes and show that they do not follow successful business practices, which are built upon the above stated requirements. However, they can all be successful if the owner understands the problem is not in the grouping of functions, but in proper selection (using performance information) and outsourcing (minimizing management, control, and inspection).

Design-Bid-Build Process

Figure 5.1 shows the construction industry in terms of competition and performance. In Quadrant I, competition is high and performance is low, representing the results of the traditional Design-Bid-Build (DBB) process. *A designer is hired to design the project.* The designer designs the construction requirement as a *commodity* and *awards to the lowest bidding contractor.* Under the assumption that all of the options are the same (commodity), the lowest bidder is the best value.

Figure 5.1: Construction Industry Structure

The impact of the design-bid-build process in Quadrant I is described in Chapter 4. The design usually includes:

1. General conditions, which are contractual terms that identify punitive actions if the contract terms are not met.
2. Construction requirements that meet the owner's intent.
3. Means, methods, and materials.
4. Drawings.
5. Specifications.

The DBB process in Quadrant I also requires *construction management and inspection* which is usually provided by the design/engineering firm. The design and specifications are a *regulatory document* which, when combined with the contractors forced to bid the lowest possible price, encourages the contractors to submit change orders and deliver the lowest possible performance. The construction manager and inspector are required to be experts in construction in the DBB process.

Contractors identify the reason for construction nonperformance as the low-bid environment (Erdmann 2002). Due to the poor construction performance of the DBB process, the designers' value has been questioned, leading to reduced fees and design functions (Post 2001). This results in more incomplete designs, which may lead to more risk from change orders and lower performance. Oblivious to this cycle, owners continue to look for the lowest design costs.

This trend was highlighted by the Arizona Business Journal (Burrough 1995), which concluded that more than forty percent of all design projects were won through bidding or price competition. Up five percent from the previous year, eighty percent of all design firms surveyed said that they participated in some type of bidding or price competition. In addition, more than ninety percent of architect engineer (A&E) firms surveyed believed fee competition was on the rise. In a market environment of increasing fee competition, A&E firm compensation is likely to decrease. The DBB process awarding to the lowest bidder (Quadrant I) results in an adversarial environment for designers, contractors, and owners, and has had a very poor performance record.

Price pressure of the worldwide competitive marketplace demands competition in all services. Quadrant II (Figure 5.1) is a performance and value based quadrant in which competition is based upon price and performance. In this quadrant, competition among high performers drives continuous improvement. Quadrant II requires minimal management by the owner. Partnering is a perception instead of a function. Quadrant II is a true outsourcing Quadrant. The requirement for performance also compels the contractors to be performers, to quality control their own work, to be efficient, and to train their personnel.

Movement into Quadrant II requires the following process attributes:

1. Construction performance information.
2. Competition based on performance and price.
3. Owner gets best value and contractors maximize profit.
4. Designer liability and risk are minimized.
5. Contractors are motivated to continuously improve.
6. Owners accept liability for their actions.
7. The risk of construction nonperformance is transferred to the contractor.

The construction industry's designers and contractors have proposed several processes to move construction into Quadrant II including:

For capital investment projects

1. Construction management
2. Design-build
3. Construction management at risk

For maintenance and repair projects

1. Indefinite delivery, indefinite quantity (IDIQ)
2. Job order contracting (JOC)
3. Time and materials

Analysis of the CIS chart in Figure 5.1 identifies the difference between Quadrant I and II as a level of performance and not the functions of the contractor. In Quadrant II, the high level of performance requires identification. The high competition of performance requires the identification of the difference between competitors. Performance information (on time, on budget without increase in cost change orders, meeting quality expectations) must be used. If there is no performance information, it is not Quadrant II. If the performance information is not used, the process is not in Quadrant II.

The performance information must be used at the beginning of construction or during the selection. If it is not, the process is not Quadrant II. The use of performance information in the selection process does not differentiate any of the above listed alternate delivery processes. Therefore, all the above processes can be moved to Quadrant II or remain in Quadrant I. Interestingly, the design-bid-build process can also be moved to Quadrant II. *It is not the design-bid-build process that causes problems; it is the concept of treating construction as a commodity and awarding to the low price option.*

Construction Management

Construction management (CM) is when a professional designer, engineer, or consultant group represents the owner and manages the contractor who is hired by the owner. CM of a low-bid contractor has not greatly improved performance of construction in Quadrant I. The additional management of a non-performing contractor does not increase performance; neither does it minimize the owner's risk, as the construction manager always passes the risk to the owner. *Added management does not create a win-win environment.*

CM has no real responsibility. If construction goes bad, they report to the owner that the contractor is not performing. If there is something wrong with the design, the CM can blame the designer. The CM has no real risk. When groups have no risk, but are making decisions and directing others, they form a bureaucratic relationship between organizations.

In order to justify their value to the owner, the CM is motivated to identify what the contractor is doing wrong and requires that the contractor do nonproductive functions such as additional paperwork and passing information which is not needed. This is verified by the poor performance of the low-bid environment and by the movement to other alternative delivery processes (Edrich 2002).

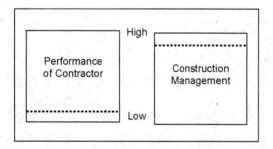

Figure 5.2a: Perceived need for CM

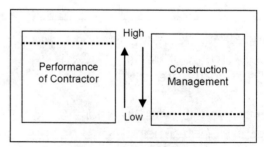

Figure 5.2b: Effect on the need for construction management by hiring a performing contractor

Owners who use CM, perceive the need for CM due to the low performance of contractors (Figure 5.2a). However, if the owner initially hires a performing contractor, the need for a construction management team decreases (Figure 5.2b). The owner who uses CM is bureaucratic, has a poor performing contractor base, and has a very inefficient delivery system. *Construction management is used in Quadrant I but never in Quadrant II.* Construction management should be used only when the political risk is high, the contractor is a nonperforming contractor, or the construction risk is very high (not enough funding, not enough time, or the contractor cannot meet the owner's expectations), and not to use construction management will be an opportunity for someone who knows nothing about construction to criticize the owner's project management group. *Construction managers have had minimal impact on construction performance.*

Design-Build Process

In the Design-Build (DB) process, the owner hires a single entity called a Design-Build firm, which is typically a partnership between a contractor and a designer. The contractor is the lead entity due to their bonding and insurance capability which is needed to legally meet the requirements of the construction contracts. The advantage of the DB process is the *reduction of delivery time* due to the capability of simultaneous design and construction work. Also, procurement of services is done in just one time. Other advantages include: *one point of contact* for the owner to deal with and the fact that the *selection can be based upon factors other than price in most government projects* (Crane 1999, Stortstrom 1999, Eickmann 1999, Grammer 1999, Carpenter 2003, Gray 1999, Edrich 2002, Krizan 1998).

Disadvantages of the design-build process include (Grammer 1999, Crane 1999, Krizan 1998):

1. *High bid preparation costs.* Many owners don't know how to differentiate between designers, and therefore ask for partial designs, design and construction detailed cost estimates, and extensive presentations. Not only are the designers involved, but now the contractors are also involved.
2. *Biased selection.* The selection may be more biased due to the lack of performance information.
3. *Inflexibility.* The owners must select using performance and price and do not know how to differentiate performance. They usually do not use performance information. Therefore they lock in the delivered construction product requirement. The process becomes very inflexible for the owner. Any change to this leads to change orders.
4. *No motivation to act in the best interest of the owner.* The DB process gives no motivation for the design build contractor to act in the best interest of the owner.

DB teams are usually required to prepare costly preliminary designs. Due to the heavy investment required by each DB team, users often pre-qualify DB teams to a maximum of five bidders. The pre-qualified DB teams then propose a preliminary design and price. After a team is selected, the process becomes fairly inflexible, unless the owner decides to increase the budget.

Due to the lack of information, inflexibility in the DB contractor's option once awarded a contract, and perceived lack of checks and balances in the process, owners sometimes hire additional consultants to regulate the design build team. The DB process motivates partnering between the contractor and designer but not always between the DB team and the owner. Design liability is minimized by the DB team relationship. The process transfers the risk of nonperformance to the contractor only if the user can clearly indicate the requirement was present at the beginning of the project and has not been changed. The owner's propensity to change his or her mind in the course of design is the biggest problem in the design phase. Change of the owner's requirement now raises the cost due to accelerated and simultaneous construction. A risk of the design-build process is that the contractor makes a preliminary cost estimate before a completed design is done, and then attempts to meet the owner's expectations within the cost constraint. This will lead to the same problems experienced in the design-bid-build, low bid award process (Angelo 2002, Ricketts 1999, Krizan 1998, Samad 2002).

The DB process should only be used when:

1. The owner has a good idea of what they want.
2. Construction is required in a very short time period.
3. The owner has performance information on alternatives and major components and can use the performance information.
4. There is no other way to select based on performance and price and move the construction into Quadrant II.

Construction Management At Risk

The construction management at risk (CM @ Risk) project delivery method is similar to that of Design-bid-build. However, under CM @ Risk, the owner hires the contractor early in the design phase to assist the designer. Although it is a very subjective decision, the contractor is chosen on a performance basis. The contractor is responsible for providing value engineering and constructability reviews during the design phase of the project. The contractor then takes control of the project once the design is complete, and a guaranteed maximum price is set.

Major advantages of this process are the following:

1. The designer is hired by the owner giving the owner time to make design changes, which do not raise the construction price.
2. The contractor can be selected on performance and price.
3. The designer is involved very early in the design to assist the contractor.
4. The process is more like the traditional process than design-build, making traditional owners more comfortable with CM@Risk.
5. The two points of contact offer some check and balances for traditional building owners.

The contractor is hired later in the process, allowing more competition between contractors. The later the contractor selection, the more information is available, optimizing the selection of the contractor.

The disadvantages of this process include:

1. There are two points of contact (designer and contractor).
2. An absence of competition after the initial selection is made.
3. Minimal incentive added by the process to make the contractor perform in the owner's best interest.

CM @ Risk may not be as widely used as design-build because there are still two points of contact and the requirements to minimize design liability and increase contractor profit are incongruent. *CM@Risk is a term in contradiction* because unless it is done in Quadrant II, the *CM@Risk is not at risk.* The guaranteed not to exceed price (GNP) or guaranteed maximum price (GMP) has the same connotation as a low bid contractor who is awarded a DBB contract. If the contractor bids too low, they will use change orders to recoup their money or reduce quality. The GMP is a misnomer and gives the owner a sense of false security. *GMP is a Quadrant I term.* If CM@Risk is done in Quadrant II, it has very few advantages over Quadrant II DBB. If the owner is in Quadrant II, the choices are DB or DBB.

CM @ Risk should be used when:

1. Time period is sufficient. Otherwise Design-build is the method of choice.
2. When Quadrant II design-bid-build cannot be achieved.
3. When the owner does not know exactly what they want to be built.
4. In Quadrant I, when performance information is not used in selection, but selection can be made on factors other than price.

Therefore, although CM@Risk will be more successful in Quadrant II, it rarely will deliver better performance than DB or DBB in Quadrant II. The advantages of CM@Risk are possessed more in DB or DBB in Quadrant II.

Indefinite Delivery, Indefinite Quantity (IDIQ)

IDIQ is a contracting mechanism for awarding a contract to a contractor for a well-defined, repeated repair and maintenance function, usually at a fixed price. Contractors bid the work on a unit price. Once a contractor wins a contract by having the lowest bid, the contractor can be issued repeated work on the unit price if they perform. IDIQ has the following advantages (Anderson 2003):

1. Minimizes procurement functions. After a contract is awarded based on a unit price, the construction can be procured through a work order instead of being bid out.

2. Faster delivery. Bypasses the procurement functions of design, advertising, bidding, and award.
3. Motivates contractor to act in the best interest of the owner. If the contractor doesn't perform, the owner does not have to give the contractor any more work.

Disadvantages of IDIQ include:

1. Lack of competition after first award.
2. May not bring best value to the owner.
3. Does not encourage the contractor to raise their level of performance. The giving of more work does not raise the level of performance; however, it does encourage the contractor to not respond.

IDIQ has evolved, and currently owners may pre-qualify a minimum number of contractors, and then bid each work order. This evolution is attributable to the owner's mistrust of the IDIQ contractor in Quadrant I. It minimizes whatever advantages the system has over the traditional DBB or DB processes. This distrust originates from a lack of performance information and the lack of information on best value.

Strengths of the IDIQ process involve the *ability to minimize procurement actions*. Instead of multiple procurements, there is just one procurement. IDIQ is strengthened by moving into Quadrant II and using performance information. Procurement actions are simplified even more due to the minimization of change orders, negotiations, construction problems, and the legal paperwork to protect the owner.

However, if the owner moves into Quadrant II with DBB, the owner can get better results because the minimized procurement requirements allow more competition. Whenever there is more competition it brings better value to the owner. The advantage of the reduced procurement functions of IDIQ is nullified by the minimized procurement requirements in Quadrant II. However, if the owner cannot minimize their procurement functions, IDIQ is the clear choice of delivery of maintenance and repair or renovation construction in Quadrant II. If the owner is in Quadrant I IDIQ becomes a "lose-lose" proposition, as motivation is to minimize price, profit, value, and quality. However, when compared with DBB in Quadrant I it delivers construction faster with similar quality.

Job Order Contracting (JOC)

Job Order Contracting (JOC) is an IDIQ contract with different types of repair and maintenance work. The contractors bid on a unit-price-book by estimating the type of work (combinations of functions with unit prices) that will be required by the user over the length of the contract, usually one to three years with an option to extend (Anderson 2003, Schreyer 2003).

The contractors bid by estimating the type and amount of work, using prices from the unit price book, and then adding overhead and profit as a coefficient. *The owner usually accepts the lowest coefficient.*

Once the contract is awarded, the owner pinpoints a requirement and has the JOC contractor scope and price the work. The owner reviews and approves the estimate and directs the contractor to do the work.

JOC is an IDIQ contract; because it requires management at site, there is a minimum amount of guaranteed work. The advantage of JOC is similar to IDIQ. The JOC contractor is required to maintain an on-site staff that manages the contract. A guaranteed minimum amount of work motivates the contractor to perform, and first-rate performance can earn the contractor additional job orders.

The weakness of JOC lies in the owner's misunderstanding of the process, which results from a lack of information about construction and may lead the owner to mistrust the contractor. The majority of JOC's are awarded to the lowest bidder. Many contracts fail due to the contractor's low profit margins. Also, owners may not issue enough work orders to cover the contractor's overhead and profit expectation. If they do not receive enough work, contractors may inflate work units and charge higher prices on unlisted items. As a result, owners hire consultants to manage the JOC or award multiple JOC's, making the contractors bid against each other on work orders. These actions minimize the effectiveness of JOC.

Time and Materials Contracting

The simplest type of contract is the time and materials contract. The owner directs the contractor to do work and pays for overhead and profit, time and materials. The process limits procurement actions, encourages the contractor to do good work in order to obtain more work, and allows the contractor to maintain a higher profit margin. Two disadvantages of this process are that the owner's representative must manage the contract, and it is very difficult to determine a contractor's performance. This process is optimized if it is moved to Quadrant II. If it is a Quadrant II process, it becomes like a design-build process (Carpenter 2003).

Performance Contracting

Performance contracting is defined as the process whereby contractors bid on an owner's performance requirement such as building, roofing system, or maintenance and repair items. There are no detailed directives or means and methods specifying how work has to be accomplished. One objective of performance contracting is to procure performance. This means completing the job on time and on budget while meeting quality expectations. Another objective is the minimization of management of the contractor and the contract, and the transfer of performance risk to the contractor. "...[Performance contracting] is designed to ensure that contractors are given freedom to determine how to meet the Government's performance objectives, that appropriate performance quality levels are achieved, and that payment is made only for services that meet these levels"(OFPP/OMB 1998). Performance contracting is the outsourcing of functions.

One of the major obstacles to using performance contracting is the lack of performance information and the lack of a consistent methodology and structure to compare performance and price. Thus, performance contracting has stayed in Quadrant I, and has been relatively ineffective.

Best Value Selection

The United States federal government, one of the largest owners of facilities procuring construction, has had difficulty procuring performance construction through the low-bid design-bid, specification procedure. The federal government, through the Federal Acquisition Regulation (FAR), allows best value awards to move to a performance-based environment (considering performance and price).

However, the inability of procurement agents to compare value has restricted the use and diminished the effectiveness of best value processes. Best value procurement allows the owner to consider factors other than price, such as past performance and a contractor's value, when selecting a contractor. Many procurement agents have difficulty using the best value process because determining a contractor's value can be highly subjective. Procurement agents also have difficulty using performance information, since the information gathered on a unique project may not apply towards another project. Many construction and procurement personnel still think that the best value is the lowest initial price (Winston 1999).

The transition from the price-based bid to a performance-based bid has been difficult due to the following (Mather and Costello 2001, Muzio 2002):

1. Inability to change the current bureaucracy, where a lack of performance information leads to a low price award. A low price award always requires a minimum specification or means and methods directive.
2. Difficulty in identifying performance due to a lack of performance information.
3. Inability to minimize subjectivity in the selection.
4. Inability to minimize the risk of nonperformance (on-time, on-budget, meeting quality expectations).
5. Inability to influence the contractor's performance based on the potential of future work.

Although the U.S. Federal government recommends using best value and performance contracting for construction, the process of moving from a Quadrant I to a Quadrant II has been unsuccessful due to a lack of understanding about performance and lack of knowledge on how to use performance information without bias.

If best value can be implemented, performance contracting can ensure that best value is optimized. All alternate delivery processes can be used with best value selection (using performance information) and performance contracting (identifying the requirement and allowing the contractor to perform).

Performance Information Procurement System (PIPS)

PIPS is an information based procurement system that uses best value selection and a performance contracting approach. It minimizes management and inspection, the liability and risk of the designer and owner, maximizes the profit of the contractor, uses partnering as a perception but not a function, and transfers the risk to the contractor. It motivates contractors to improve on every project and do their own quality control. PIPS has a methodology to find the best available value and motivates the contractor to assign the best performers to the project. PIPS uses performance information to select the best value contractor, and then uses the rating on the best value on the project to alter the contractor's future competitiveness and performance. PIPS is fully discussed in Chapters 7.

Comparison of Procurement Processes

Table 5-1 compares the different procurement processes as they are currently practiced, using the seven requirements necessary to move into a performance environment. Process ratings include "2" if the process always involves the criteria, "1" if the process possibly includes the criteria due to the owner's representative understanding Quadrant II concepts, and "0" if the process cannot incorporate the criteria.

Table 5-1: Comparison of Procurement Processes

NO.	CRITERIA	PROCESS									
		DBB	DB	CM@R	CM	IDIQ	T&M	JOC	PC	BV	PIPS
1	True competition for construction services after design.	0	1	1	0	0	0	0	1	1	2
2	Profit is maximized for the contractors.	0	1	1	0	0	0	0	1	1	2
3	Design liability is minimized.	0	1	1	0	0	0	0	0	0	2
4	Contractors are motivated to continuously improve.	0	0	0	0	0	0	0	0	0	2
5	Forces owner to be liable for their actions.	1	0	0	1	0	1	0	1	1	2
6	Forces partnering.	0	1	1	0	0	0	0	0	0	2
7	Transfers the risk of nonperformance to the contractor.	0	1	1	0	0	0	2	1	1	2
	Total	1	5	5	1	0	1	2	4	4	14

Another comparison of procurement processes was made by using successful business practices of seven noted business experts (Table 5-2):

1. Buckingham and Coffman, authors of "Break All the Rules"
2. Phillip Crosby, author of "Quality is Free" and "Quality is Still Free"
3. Edward Deming, originator of continuous improvement and author of "Out of Crisis"
4. Peter Drucker, management guru and author of "Post Capitalist Society"
5. Paul Friga and Ethan Rasiel, authors of the "McKinsey Mind"
6. Jack Trout author of "New Positioning"
7. Jack Welch, former CEO of GE and coauthor of "Straight from the Gut"
8. James Womack, coauthor of "The Machine That Changed the World"

Table 5-2: Successful Business Practices (identified by the above experts)

NO	SUCCESSFUL BUSINESS PRACTICES	B. & Coffman	Crosby	Deming	Drucker	Rasiel	Trout	Welch	Womack
1	Use only the best past performers	X						X	
2	Structure of interactions based on logical goals/expectations	X				X	X		
3	Minimize control, direction, inspection (management)	X	X	X					X
4	Quality is achievable, measurable, and profitable		X						
5	Assist others to be successful		X						
6	Faith in system that works/minimize experts		X						X
7	Quality means customer satisfaction		X	X					X
8	Transactions should be rated relatively (benchmarking)		X						
9	Quality environment is set by the user		X						
10	Zero defects		X						X
11	Quality is measured by the price of nonperformance		X						
12	Continuous Improvement			X					
13	Do not award on price			X					
14	Break down barriers (team orientation)			X				X	X
15	Minimize minimum standards			X					
16	Knowledge worker have responsibility and liability				X				
17	Identify key factors					X			
18	Look for direction instead of precision					X			
19	Worker or contractor minimize risk					X			
20	Structure should be setup to listen and not dictate					X			
21	Minimize information, maximize responsibility					X	X		X
22	Understand goals in clear terms (performance)						X		
23	Simplicity is sophistication					X	X		
24	Minimize functions of insecure who cloud the issues						X	X	X
25	Information reduces uncertainty						X		
26	Competition is required							X	
27	Pay the best more, because they minimize total cost			X				X	
28	Change requirements to change the workers							X	
29	Differentiate people in A, B, C classes							X	
30	Proactive and preventative approach								X
31	Fix problems by finding the cause								X
32	Increase performance instead of dropping price								X
33	Feedback loop for incremental improvement								X

Table 5-3 lists the procurement processes that contain the successful business practices. The rating scheme is "2" for the practice embedded in the process structure, "1" if the practice can be used in the process, and "0" if the practice cannot be used in the process.

Table 5-4 lists the relative success of the processes based on their characteristics of successful business practices.

Table 5-3: Characteristics of Procurement Processes Using
Selected Criteria From Table 5-2

PROCESS	SUCCESSFUL BUSINESS PRACTICES																				Totals
	1	2	3	4	7	8	12	13	14	15	17	18	19	20	21	22	25	26	32	33	
DBB	0	0	0	0	0	0	0	0	0	0	0	0	0	0	0	0	0	0	0	0	0
DB	1	1	1	1	1	1	1	1	1	1	1	1	1	1	1	1	1	1	1	1	20
CM@R	1	1	1	1	1	1	0	1	1	1	1	1	1	1	1	1	1	1	0	1	18
CM	1	0	0	0	0	0	0	1	0	0	0	0	0	0	0	0	0	0	0	0	2
IDIQ	1	1	1	1	1	0	1	1	1	0	1	1	1	1	1	1	1	1	1	1	18
T&M	1	1	1	1	1	1	1	1	1	1	0	1	1	1	1	1	1	1	1	1	19
JOC	1	1	1	1	1	1	1	1	1	1	0	1	1	1	1	2	1	1	1	2	21
PC	1	1	1	1	1	1	1	1	1	1	1	1	1	1	1	1	1	1	1	1	20
BV	1	1	1	1	1	1	1	1	1	1	1	1	1	1	1	1	1	1	1	1	20
PIPS	2	2	2	2	2	2	2	2	2	2	2	2	2	2	2	2	2	2	2	2	40

Table 5-4: Relative Success of the Processes

PROCESS	TOTAL
Design-Bid-Build	0
Construction Management	2
Construction Management at Risk	18
Indefinite Delivery, Indefinite Quantity	18
Time and Materials	19
Design-Build	20
Performance Contracting	20
Best Value	20
Job Order Contracting	21
Performance Information Systems	40

Creating "Win-Win" Relationships

A key component for creating a "win-win" relationship is determining and understanding the performance level of both contractor and owner. Figure 5.3 shows contractors and owners at three different performance levels. Although not always correct, the most likely assumption is that the best relationship is the Contractor 1: Owner 1 scheme, meaning a high performing owner partnered with a high performing contractor. In actuality, "win-win" relationships depend upon the performance level of both parties.

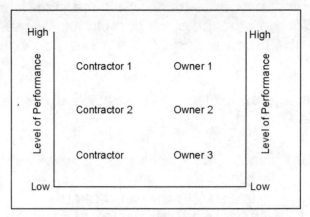

Figure 5.3: Contractor/Owner
Relationships

The ideal relationship involves a partnership where there is minimal differential between the two parties. If a high performance owner wants a "win-win" relationship, they should partner with a high performing contractor. By the same token, if a low performing owner wants a "win-win" relationship, they should partner with a low performing contractor. Once again, the most important idea is the lack of differential between the two parties (see Figure 5.4).

Figure 5.5 portrays a relationship in which a low performing owner attempts to partner with a high performing contractor, forming a match with a substantial amount of differential between the two parties. Certain goals of the low performing owner contradict those of the high performing contractor. A high performing contractor is usually motivated by performance rather than price, while a low performing owner is typically motivated by the lowest initial cost. Ultimately, this type of relationship fails because differences in the parties' objectives force the need for additional resources such as time, money, and manpower, resulting in a "lose-lose" relationship. For this reason, some owners should not expect to partner with high performing contractors.

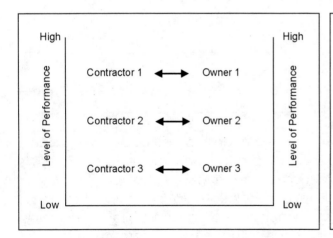

Figure 5.4: "Win-Win" Relationships

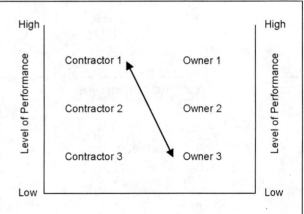

Figure 5.5: "Lose-Lose" Relationships

If the process is a Quadrant II process, partnering is a perception of what is going on, however it is not a function that must be implemented. Participants partner in Quadrant II because they think alike. If functional partnering is required, the process is a Quadrant I process.

Experts and Expert Systems

Most information systems are complex and difficult to implement. These systems require extensive programming knowledge and the decision-making skills of experts (INFO WEEK 2003). Any effort to implement a new system requiring more work or expertise is doomed to failure. *The PIPS process works because it reduces the amount of work and decision-making while continuing to minimize risk.* This concept can be understood in two ways.

First, if expertise is required, the user does not have enough information to make a decision. Remember, with enough information, decision-making is minimized. "Experts" are substitutes for the process of using information. PIPS, decreases the need for an expert by using performance information to make decisions. The information environment generated by PIPS forces the expert to work for the contractor, who should be the expert. At this point, the responsibility and liability for performance belongs to the expert. Issues of responsibility and liability are confused when the expert works for the owner or buyer. If the contractor, who should be the expert, does not perform, the contractor can blame the expert who managed, inspected, and directed the contractor while acting as the owner's representative. This is a root source of the construction industry's problems (Manning 2001, Horn 2002).

Second, if construction delivery is treated as a supply chain, the management and control of one component over another must be minimized. Components in a supply chain are identified by their different core competencies. If one component can perform its own core competency as well as another component's, the first component absorbs the second.

Experts belong to the component with the responsibility, liability, and risk, allowing them to utilize technical data to make decision and minimize their risk. Hence, experts should work with the contractor and not for the owner. Experts working for the buyer or owner become an obstacle to performance and the root source of nonperformance. Any supply chain with experts working for the buyer or end user is paramount to placing experts at the end of a manufacturing line. They are a manifestation of an inefficient delivery system.

Outsourcing

The objective of outsourcing is to transfer functions that are not among the company's core competencies. In other words, the functions that are not core competencies of one company can be performed more efficiently by another company (who already performs those functions as their core competencies).

Successful outsourcing is the ability to find companies who are efficient and performance oriented to a specific task, particularly, completing work on time and on budget while satisfying quality expectations. Successful outsourcing is accomplished by providing the experts with the requirements and allowing them to perform, transferring the risk to the expert.

Unsuccessful outsourcing occurs when companies outsource functions to non-performing companies, causing them to manage and control their functions. All components of a company who manage an outsourced function should be eliminated since these components offer no value.

Instead of hiring another expert to manage and control the outsourced function, the user needs a process to determine the requirement, identify a performing vendor (expert), and communicate the requirement to the vendor.

Industry consensus contends that poor construction is the fault of non-performing contractors (Butler 2002). However, research confirms the reason for poor construction is the owners' inability to competently outsource (Elliott 2001). Owners outsource construction to contractors and then hire managers to oversee the outsourced construction, and since these "experts" representing the owner manage them, contractors are not compelled to accept risk. These "experts" shift all of the risk back to the owner. When the construction is late, exceeds budget, and does not fulfill quality expectations, the managing "expert" is blamed, although the expert rarely accepts any liability.

The low-bid system forces the owner to hire managers to extract performance out of low-bid, non-expert contractors. This is the most inefficient way to outsource work because it forces the contractor to use the most inexperienced, inexpensive personnel. The system increases the risk of nonperformance and makes it useful to justify the need for a managing "expert." Instead of paying a managing "expert" 10% to manage the contractor, the owner can pay a performing contractor (performing expert) 5% more upfront and receive high-performance results at a savings of 5% of the delivery cost. The odd man out in optimizing efficiency is the managing "expert." Owners need to save on cost without increasing risk. They need to dispose of experts who manage, and hire experts who perform.

Conclusions

Tables 5-1, 5-2, 5-3, and 5-4 coupled with the documented performance of the delivery processes lead to the following conclusions:

1. The design-bid-build process, which uses specifications and low-bid, is not congruent to successful business practices. This process creates an adversarial environment and results in non-performing construction.
2. Construction management, the first reaction of facility owners to combat the construction nonperformance, is an ineffective method of increasing construction performance.
3. Facility owners use alternate delivery mechanisms (design-build and construction management @ risk) to increase construction performance. These processes work much better as shown by the higher use of correct business practices. However, in the long run, these processes do not motivate all parties to continuously improve.
4. Facility owners are using IDIQ, JOC, and time and materials to minimize bureaucratic actions, that is, repetitive procurement time and control. This in itself improves performance. However, these three processes still do not fully utilize all of the recognized successful business practices.
5. Performance contracting and best value contracting are procurement methods that compare performance and price, but still lack some of the characteristics required to force a performance environment.
6. An information-based or performance contracting process has the best probability of increasing construction performance. This is shown in later chapters and confirmed by the results of over 350 tests.

The author asserts that the cause of construction nonperformance is not a construction issue but a business issue. Every other industry has improved performance by using performance information and correct business practices (Tulacz 1997).

Chapter 5 Review

1. What are the advantages / disadvantages with the design-bid-build process?
2. What are the advantages / disadvantages with the design-build process?
3. What are the advantages / disadvantages with the CM@Risk process?
4. What obstacles do owners face when attempting to implement best-value procurement systems?
5. Why is a "win-win" relationship created when a high performing owner hires a high performing contractor?
6. Is a "win-win" relationship created when a low performing owner hires a high performing contractor?
7. Is a "win-win" relationship created when a low performing owner hires a low performing contractor?
8. What three factors must an information system (expert system) have to be successful and sustainable over a period of time?
9. Are experts necessary? If so, should they represent the owner or contractor?
10. What does outsourcing mean?
11. Is the majority of construction currently being outsourced? Why?
12. Should owners have to inspect, manage, and direct contractors on how to do their work?
13. List 10 features of a successful delivery system.

References

Anderson, N.R., Asmar, C., Des Sureau, E.P., Kane, J.W., & Skolnick, S. (2003). Job Order Contracting. *Washington Building Congress Bulletin.* Retrieved from http://www.jocinfo.com/default.htm.

Angelo, W.J. (2002, August 12). Team Should Be Contractor Lead. *Engineering News Record (ENR),* 249 [7], p. 47.

Badger, W.W., & Kashiwagi, D.T. (1991). Job Order Contracting: A New Contracting Technique for Maintenance and Repair Construction Projects. *Cost Engineering,* pp. 21-24.

Buckingham, M., & Coffman, C. (1999). *Break All the Rules.* New York: Simon and Schuster.

Burrough, D.J. (1995, Sep). Builders Dispute ASU Study. *The Business Journal,* pp. 21, 30.

Butler, J. (2002, Mar). Construction Quality Stinks. *Engineering News Record (ENR),* 248 [10], p. 99.

Carpenter, D. (2003). General Contracting. David L Carpenter, Inc: Fine Carpentry. Retrieved July 1, 2003, from http://www.davidlcarpenter.com/general_contracting.htm

Crane, J. (1999, April-May). Who Says You Can't Use Design-Build? *Military Engineer,* [598], pp. 46-48.

Crosby, P. (1980). *Quality is Free.* New York, New York: McGraw-Hill.

Deming, E. (1982). *Out of the Crisis,* Massachusetts Institute of Technology, Cambridge, Mass.

Drucker, P. (1994). *Post Capitalist Society.* New York, New York: , HarperCollins.

Elliott, V. (2001, September/October). Performance-based outsourcing. *Facility Management Journal,* pp. 15-16, 18, 20.

Edrich, J., Richard, B., and Bruce, S. (2002, August). Weighing the Options. *Civil Engineering,* 72 [8], pp. 48-51.

Eickmann, K.E. (1999). Secrets of Design-Build? *Military Engineer,* [598], pp. 53-54.

Erdmann, R. (2002). *The Relationship Between the Design-Bid-Build (DBB) System and Construction Nonperformance.* Unpublished Masters Thesis, Arizona State University, Tempe, AZ.

Friga, P.N., & Rasiel, E.M. (2002). *The McKinsey Mind.* New York: McGraw-Hill.

Grammer, M.E. (1999). Design-Build in the Corps of Engineers? *Military Engineer,* [598], pp. 59-61.

Gray, J.A. (1999, April-May). Design-Build in the Public Sector? *Military Engineer,* [598], pp. 67-68.

Hindle, B., & Mbuthia, G. (2002). From Procurement System to Delivery System, An Important Step in the Process of Construction Business Development. *CIBW92 Procurement Systems Symposium: Procurement Systems & Technology Transfer,* pp. 169-178.

Horn, J.V. (2002, 1 August). Parking Equipment Manufacturers Must Lower Quality to Meet Price Requirements. *Parking Today,* 7 [8], pp. 28-31.

Info. Week Staff Writer. (2003, March 3). Supply on Demand: Vendors are Ramping Up their Supply Chain Software to Give Vital Real-Time Information. *Information Week,* [929], pp. 47, 48, 52, 54, 56, 58.

Jaggar, D.M., Ross, A., Love, P.E.D., & Smith, J. (2002). Towards Achieving More Effective Construction Procurement Through Information. *CIBW92 Procurement Systems Symposium: Procurement Systems & Technology Transfer*, pp. 179-193.

Jones, D.T., Roos, D., & Womack, J.P. (1991). *The Machine that Changed the World*. New York: Harper Perennial.

Konchar, M. & Sanvido, V. (1998, November/December). Comparison of U.S. Project Delivery Systems. *Journal of Construction Engineering and Management*, pp. 435-444.

Krizan, W.G. (1998, June 15). Big Tests Ahead for Design-Build. *Engineering News Record (ENR)*, 240 [24], pgs. 47, 49-50.

Manning, A. (2001, February 14). Their Message: Don't Trust Experts. USA Today, p. 10D.

Mather, C. & Costello, A. (2001). An Innovative Approach to Performance-Based Acquisition: Using a SOO. *Acquisition Directions Advisory, Acquisition Solutions, Chantilly, Virginia*, May, pp. 1-10.

Murray, M.D., Tookey, J.E., Langford, D.A., & Hardcastle, C. (2002). Construction Procurement Systems, Don't Forget Murphy's Law! *CIBW92 Procurement Systems Symposium: Procurement Systems & Technology Transfer*, pp. 147-167.

Muzio, D. (2001 & 2002). Personal conversation with FPPO deputy on the FAR and movement toward best value procurement of construction, October, 25 2001 and February, 7 2002.

OFPP/OMB. (1998). Statutory and FAR Requirements; OFPP Policy Letter 92-5 Retrieved from http://www.arentfox.com/quickGuide/businessLines/govcont/govcontRelatedArticles /statfarreq/statfarreq.html

Post, N.M. (1998). Building Teams Get High Marks. *Engineering News-Record (ENR)*, 240 [19], p. 32.

Post, N.M. (2001, May 14). Bumpier Road to Finish Line. *Engineering News Record (ENR)*, 246 [19], pp. 56-63.

Ricketts, M.L. (1999, April-May). Design-Build not Draw-Build. *Military Engineer*, [598], pp. 65-66.

Samad, S. (2002). Managing Change Orders. *Cost Engineering*, 44 [10], p. 13.

Schreyer, P.R., & Mellon, H.H. (2003). Partner Postner & Rubin, The Gordian Group. Job Order Contracting. Consulting Specifying Engineer. Retrieved July 2, 2003, from http://www.jocinfo.com/default.htm

Stortstrom, G. (1999, April-May). Advantages of Design-Build? *Military Engineer*, [598], pp. 51-52.

Trout, J., & Rivkin, S. (1986). *The New Positioning*. New York: McGraw Hill.

Tulacz, G., Krizan, W., & Tanner, V. (1997, November 24). The Top Owners. *Engineering News Record (ENR)*, 239 [21], pp. 30-32.

Welch, J. (2001). *Straight from the Gut*. New York, NY: Warner Books, Inc.

Winston, S. (1999, October 4). Pentagon Pumps Up Performance. *Engineering News Record (ENR)*, 243 [14], p. 10.

6

Applying IMT and the KSM to Construction Delivery

Consultant Emile Troup: 'Do you think the quality in building construction is improving?'
Design Professional: 'Yes.'
Troup: 'Really?'
Design Professional: 'Of course. It has to be improving. It can't get any worse'" (Post 2001).

Introduction

The previous five chapters discuss IMT, KSMs, industry structural stability, six sigma, and best business practices. These concepts have been combined to address the following issues in the delivery of construction:

1. Can the design-bid-build delivery process work?
2. Why do volume-based contractors have a problem with quality?
3. Why does the low-bid process minimize performance?
4. Why do contractors fail to "minimize the owner's risk" as an objective?
5. Why do most project managers thrive in a complex environment?
6. Why do low-bid contractors prefer working with project managers who know construction?
7. Why do large organizations dislike information-based or performance-based procurement?
8. Why do many users who apply performance-based procurement still have poor performance?
9. How does an information environment self-regulate performance?
10. How can designers, engineers, project managers, and construction managers effectively and successfully add value?

The first seven issues relate to the low-bid environment. The last three issues relate to an information-based environment.

Design-Bid-Build and Low-Bid Environments

Many individuals in facility management and in the construction industry still believe the design-bid-build (DBB) process adds value. In general, the DBB process follows these steps (Ricketts 1999):

1. The owner's representatives write a specification that tells the contractor what to do.
2. The owner selects the lowest-priced bidder who is qualified and fulfills the minimum requirements (meaning the bidder is licensed, bonded, and has submitted a cost proposal).
3. The owner's representative manages and inspects the construction, makes corrections, and determines if the contractor has followed the specifications.
4. Project completion is normally considered when the project is substantially completed. Substantial completion precedes the identification of punch list items. In most cases, the completion of punch list items does not affect the contractor's ability to finish on schedule. This means that an owner may think construction is completed on time, when in actuality the contractor is still performing work.

The low-bid process encourages the following characteristics:

1. Subjective decision-making by the owner (or owners representative) to identify minimum standards, requirements, and qualified contractors.
2. Experts managing, controlling, and inspecting the contractor.
3. Acceptance of the lowest-priced qualified bidder.
4. Contractors are motivated to make change orders to increase profit.
5. Contractors are motivated to do the lowest quality work, use the cheapest possible material, and hire the cheapest labor and management available.
6. Contractors provide the lowest possible performance.
7. Contractors are motivated to leverage volume and to complete more work for less profit.

Figure 6.1 shows the KSMs for this type of procurement. Obviously, high management, minimum performance, motivational differences between the owner and the contractor, a high volume of work, a poorly trained work force, and the most inexpensive materials are all factors closely related to nonperformance. These factors are depicted on the right-hand side of the KSM and violate every successful business practice (Chapter 5).

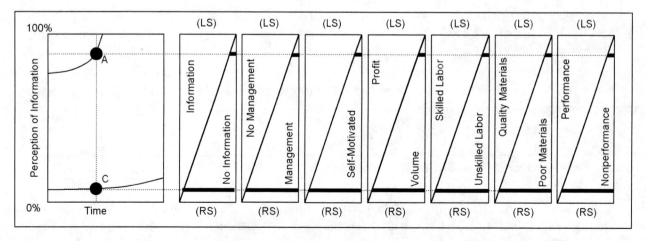

Figure 6.1: Low-Bid Procurement KSM

"It's an old story for seasoned facility executives. Given a choice between two assets to be purchased, management would rather go with the one that costs less. The problem with that approach is obvious: When utility and maintenance costs are factored in, the lower-priced item may cost more in the long run. But convincing management that the more expensive item is a better value can be impossible" (Casavant 2002).

"Roofers know that the facility executive is not really looking for the best solution, but rather the cheapest price. When price is the overriding criterion, cheap is better and more likely to win the job for the contractor. That is what they will deliver—maybe not all the bidders, but at least one. And when low price is the goal, the low bid will win" (Warseck 2002).

"'The shortage of skilled labor means more supervision in the field. Formerly, a supervisor was able to handle a crew of 20, 25 or 30. Now there are seven or eight workers to one supervisor,' says Donald M. Marks, concrete contractor" (Post 2001).

"'We have a process that's generating problems of scheduling and budget,' says Robert C. Hixon Jr. director of GSA's Center of Construction and Project Management" (Post 2001).

"A contractor with successful tender is selected under various criteria but the low bid system is the most commonly accepted. However, this system is not broadly recognized as an appropriate solution for choosing a contractor" (Hung 2002).

"Addison was the project's low bidder at $14.6 million; over $1.1 million lower than the next lowest bid. Addison has filed $1.1 million in claims for delay of work resulting from state-implemented design changes. 'Already $1 million over budget… [the project] is hundreds of items away from completion. Doing a low-bid process has caused a lot of problems,' says Daniel O'Brien, state public works director in Carson City" (Illia 2001).

From the author's experience in over 350 test cases, the following are causes for the continued use of the low-bid system:

1. <u>Inability to justify the higher price:</u> It is very difficult to convince management that a higher initial price may be a better value than a lower price. Quality is seen as an immeasurable factor, and it is nearly impossible to justify. The technical engineering personnel cannot define performance in non-technical terms.
2. <u>Procurement of construction as a "complex" task:</u> Owners are told that the procurement of construction is such a complex task, that the need of experts is necessary to protect the owner. Each "expert" justifies his or her job by identifying the inefficiencies of another party. However, *the owner does not understand that some parties perform without needing an expert to tell them what to do.* The owner's expert is truly valuable only when the owner hires a non-performing contractor. In the subsequent quote, John R. Butler points out a contractor's inefficiencies, justifying additional and improved inspection and management:

"'General contractors are not performing their duty to provide quality construction,' says John R. Butler, Jr. Georgia State Financing and Investment Commission…. 'Almost every project that we build has construction defects. Some are fairly major, such as in a multistory building where a contractor failed to install 98% of the brick ties needed to keep exterior brick from falling onto the sidewalk. At a parking structure, a contractor left out or misplaced much of the reinforcing steel needed in columns and post-tensioned beams. And at a major new laboratory that we wanted to use to aid in anthrax research, we cannot because the cracked, ostensibly airtight walls cannot contain airborne bacteria and viruses…. We seem to have forgotten one simple fact. The constructor whether a general contractor, construction manager at-risk or a design-builder, has complete responsibility for the proper and timely completion and installation of the work…'" (Butler 2002).

"Most constructors have become obsessed with winning the game rather than building the job" (Post 2001).

Any party that increases the management and inspection functions has a broken system. There is no real liability in a state of confusion. Most participants in the low-bid process possess very little risk except the owner. In most cases, the owner does not know this because he or she depends on an expert that is perceived to be minimizing the owner's risk. The low-bid system holds no one responsible for nonperformance. The designer dictates the requirement, the owner corrects the design, the contractor bids low and then submits change orders, and the designer, construction manager, or inspector, directs, manages, and inspects the contractor to ensure compliance. Any problems that may arise will result in finger pointing between all of the parties. Eventually, in most cases, the owner is accountable for the risk of nonperformance. Therefore, any party that is comfortable with the low-bid system is not acting in the owner's best interest.

"Officials are analyzing the $91-million change order filed by Honeywell, that involves more than 300 items… The changes involve hardware and software issues that have yet to be resolved" (Angelo 2002).

"$2.8-million pedestrian 'bridge of glass'…additional change orders have pushed cost overruns to $850,000 and the overall project cost to $3.7 million" (ENR Staff Writer 2002a).

"Winning $167.8-million bid… change orders brought the contract value to $220 million by 1999" (ENR Staff Writer 2002b).

"An audit by the U.S. Dept. of Transportation's inspector general says costs on a Virginia interchange project have jumped 180% since 1994, to $676.5 million" (ENR Staff Writer 2002c).

"It's not uncommon for a constructor to agree to an unreasonable schedule to secure a contract. In many instances, 'nobody [on the team] thinks the schedule can be made…but does anybody say it? No. Because you want the job,' says engineer Daniel

A. Couco, a managing principal of LZA Technology/ Thornton-Tomasetti Group Inc. New York City" (Post 2001).

Bureaucracies are found in both the public and private sectors, and are easily identified. As the old adage states, "Birds of a feather flock together." *Bureaucratic organizations* are uncomfortable with performance because they are usually comprised of *people who do not perform or do not operate in the best interest of the company.* Those individuals feel that protecting their jobs assumes precedence over doing what is best for the organization, and they feel comfortable in an environment of confusion. Bureaucracies cater to the non-performers under the guise of fairness. Bureaucracies retain no performance information about themselves or about the contractors they work with. Those that do track performance rarely use the information to impact the contractor's future competitiveness. These "birds" commonly invoke the following phrases to avoid engaging in information-based systems such as PIPS:

1. "The quality and performance of our contractor is fine."
2. "No one else has used your system successfully, and we don't want to be the first to find out."
3. "We can't implement your process within our current regulations."
4. "We are already doing what you are proposing to do."
5. "Why are you doing this? Are you getting paid by someone?"

A performance-based information system is useful only when the owner is savvy enough to optimize an operation by minimizing the overhead of delivery, maximizing the value of any purchase, and locating a sufficient number of performing vendors to support himself or herself as a performance-based owner. Identifying a performance-based owner is the first requirement. The owner must retain a core team (see Chapter 14) and group of performance-based vendors who operate in his or her best interest. Implementation of an information-based system should be a slow process. High performance will occur immediately when the system is implemented (see Chapter 19 Results); however, the owner must show great patience not to move too quickly. The risk to PIPS is not related to construction performance, but is political.

One of the most important objectives when implementing an information-based system is assisting owners and industry participants with overcoming the obstacles to implementing an information-based system. Large contractors, design firms, construction organizations, and owner representatives feel successful in the design-bid-build, low-bid process. Journals, construction conference papers, and daily news publications reviewed by PBSRG describe the low-bid process as a broken system that has rendered the construction industry unstable, unable to continuously improve performance, and unable to provide performing construction on a continuous basis.

Construction Industry as a Broken Industry

The current construction industry, which is structured by the DBB/LB delivery process, is an inefficient and broken system.

"'The old design-bid-build method...has done great damage to the industry. We must continue to support delivery systems that foster more relationship building rather than just getting to the lowest bid,' says Leslie C. Battersby, Project Manager of Blach Construction Co. Santa Clara, California" (Angelo 2001).

The Quadrant I environment results in poor performance; it forces the contractors to do more work and accept less compensation. Consequently, contractors have attracted fewer skilled personnel, their training programs are barely in existence, and the number of skilled designers, manager, and craftspeople in the industry has declined. The industry now requires more management and additional overseers, even though common sense dictates the need for more skilled craftspeople and construction superintendents.

"'But it is still the mason in the field who causes the whole project to go sour...Further complicating the situation is a critical shortage of qualified designers and construction workers in an era of extremely high production,' says Kimball J. Beasley, a principal of the New York City office of Wiss, Hanney, Elstner Associates Inc" (Post 2001).

Rules, Minimum Standards, Inspection, and the KSM

Figure 6.2 displays rules on the right side (RS) of the KSM. Rules slow people from changing and direct people to respond the same way for similar events. Rules are necessary for people who may have less information and provide people with guidance on how to perform their jobs. The Type C entity follows more rules, makes more decisions, and uses less information.

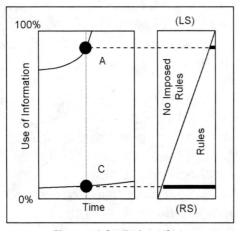
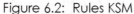
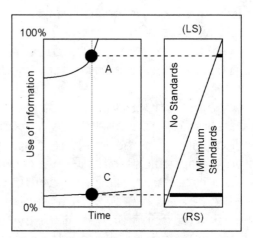

Figure 6.2: Rules KSM   Figure 6.3: Minimum Standards KSM

The KSM model places minimum standards on the right-hand side (Figure 6.3). As explained in Chapters 4 and 5, minimum standards, or specifications, promote low performance. When applying a minimum standard, a user's representative must make subjective decisions about whether or not an alternative meets the minimum standards and whether or not the work is acceptable. Minimum standards force decision-making by the owner or owner's representative and have very little correlation to performance.

Figure 6.4 shows user inspection on the right side (RS) of the KSM. This concurs with decision-making, as inspectors must now decide if the minimum quality of the contractor meets the specified minimum standard. The contractor now holds the inspector responsible for delivering the construction to the owner's quality expectations. In turn, the inspector must decide how logical and politically correct it is to require the contractor to redo substandard work. The inspector must intercept the contractor as soon as work becomes unacceptable, otherwise the contractor can claim the inspector observed problems but said nothing. If a problem occurs later in the project, the

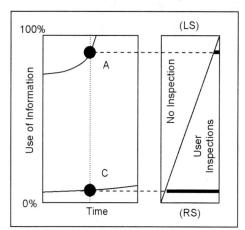

Figure 6.4: User Inspection KSM

contractor may also claim that the work was done correctly, since the inspector approved the work. Any decision made by the inspector on behalf of the owner is a risky proposition for the owner.

"'A death of unskilled labor means a need for more supervision,' says Donald M. Marks" (Post 2001).

"'The overall quality of construction has deteriorated somewhat in the past 10 years and greatly in the past 25... The weak links in the construction process are poor design, lack of caring by contractors and their personnel, little or no inspection, and lack of qualified inspectors...Material shortages can play a part in deterioration of quality when an inferior product is substituted for a product that cannot be obtained in time to meet the construction schedule,' from Henry Deutch, HHD Consultants Inc., Kissimmee, Fla." (Post 2001).

"'[W]e are finding that engineering students are not getting 10 job interviews, they are getting 10 job offers,' says Robert C. Doeer, manager of steel operations for director A.J. McNulty & Co. Inc. Maspeth, N.Y." (Post 2001).

Management, Control, Volume, Profit, and the KSM

Management and control (RS) are required to ensure the outcome of any decision (see Figure 6.5). The previous factors define the low-bid award process in construction, since users force the use of subjective minimum standards when making a selection. The user then inspects and manages the contractor to assure their work is performed as specified.

IMT proposes that high performing contractors with highly trained craftspeople do high performance work without the need of minimum standards. These contractors are experts and need very little instruction on how to do their work. High performers are not low-price oriented and require little or no inspection since they apply quality control to their own work. They minimize the risk of nonperformance because they know how to do their work.

"'If workers are not properly qualified; if the construction schedule is unreasonable; if the construction documents are incomplete, inaccurate or ambiguous; if there is a lack of qualified oversight and inspection how can there not be quality problems on the job-site?' asks Consultant Emile W.J. Troup" (Post 2001).

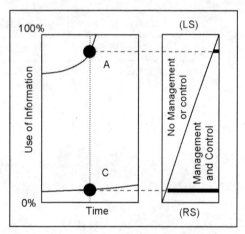

Figure 6.5: User Management and Control KSM

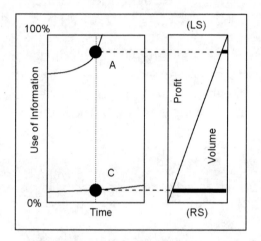

Figure 6.6: Profit and Volume KSM

Figure 6.6 shows volume on the right side (RS) of the KSM. Traditionally, projects are awarded to the lowest priced contractor. Hypothetically, if two contractors can perform the exact same work and offer the exact same quality, the contractor with the lowest cost is willing to reduce their profit margin so that the overall cost is lower than the competition.

Due to this price-based process and lower profit margins, contractors must do as much work as possible in order to stay in business. By definition, performing contractors are not volume-based contractors; they do not depend on a high volume of work to make ends meet.

Quality contractors earn more profit because they are more efficient, are not price-based, perform work properly the first time, and are requested by owners who want work done right.

Skilled Craftspeople, Training, and the KSM

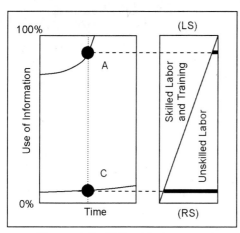

Figure 6.7: Skilled Labor and Training KSM

On the left side (LS) of the KSM, in Figure 6.7, are contractors with skilled craftspeople and training programs. Logic dictates that contractors must pay skilled employees more than they pay unskilled labor. In the low-bid, volume-based arena, each contractor's objective is to submit the lowest priced proposal in order to receive the award of the project. Contractors that participate in this arena are forced to work at low profit margins. The cost of paying for skilled employees and training programs reduces profit margins even further, forcing many contractors to hire unskilled laborers who have had very little training.

Contractors in the volume-based arena who pay for skilled labor and training programs jeopardize the viability of their businesses since they may not receive the award of the project because they cannot submit the lowest bid.

"Good contractors do have costs that other contractors will not, including training, insurance and workers compensation, salaries to keep superior mechanics in an employee-driven job market, and equipment. All these things add up, but without them, the contractor cannot provide superior work. In addition, it takes time to do the details that make the difference between long roof life and a short-term disaster" (Warseck 2002).

"'Many nonunion employers remain reluctant to invest in long-term training because workers could use their skills to win higher paying jobs at competing firms giving competitors a "free ride" on their training dollar. Open shop contractors tend to pay only for training that has a short-term payoff,' says Peter Philips, professor of economics at the University of Utah" (Korman 1997).

"We think the federal government can achieve some of its desired social objectives without the union-nonunion controversy by falling into line with big private users of construction services that will hire only contractors that train craft workers in a significant fashion...people become more employable and productive by receiving meaningful training in worthwhile skills" (ENR Staff Writer 1998).

"The availability and the quality of skilled staff is the key to whether the industry will be able to grow...virtually every construction industry survey shows that craft labor shortages were the overriding issue in 1997 and the problem shows absolutely no sign of abating...Higher skilled workers in technical crafts are hardest to find" (Krizan 1998).

'"Today, we do not have craftsmen, we do not have apprentices, we have poor people,' says Franklin J. Yancey, a former senior vice president and now a consultant at Kellogg Brown & Root, Houston" (Rosenbaum 2001).

"'Craft manpower availability and training remains the top problem for the nation's largest owners, followed only by their own ability to assess and manage projects... The Roundtable wants the industry to train more people and is developing model pre-qualification language that would allow only contractors that train to a certain level to be eligible to participate on projects,' according to J. Kent Underwood, chairman of the business roundtable's construction committee and manager of construction management" (Krizan 1997).

"A shortage of experienced senior people... The average staff-level turnover rate among contractors was 14.1% this year, according to a survey of contractor benefit released by PAS Inc., a Saline, Mich. Based management consulting firm specializing in the construction industry" (Tulacz 2001).

Performance Information, Bureaucracy, and the KSM

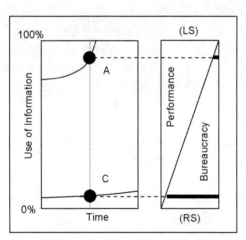

Figure 6.8: Bureaucracy KSM

The Type A organization is very efficient, requires less effort, management, and responsibility, and results in high performance and value. The Type C organization uses rules and minimum standards, forces contractors to compete based on price, and aims to control the contractor, which has led to a high management requirement and minimal performance.

As performance decreases, the Type C person creates additional rules and standards, attempts to secure an even lower price, and expects better performance. In reality, the Type C person no longer knows what he or she is buying because the contractors must lower their quality and performance.

The Type C person becomes bureaucratic in this ineffective situation, forcing contractors to work for minimal prices while seizing the opportunity to highlight the contractors' poor performance simply to justify his or her value. This justification hinges on the idea that performance would surely be much worse without the Type C individual's presence. However, the absence of the Type C person forces the owner to purchase a performing contractor, which is ultimately a more economical choice for all parties involved (see Figure 6.8).

How can designers, engineers, project managers and construction managers effectively and successfully add value?

Figure 6.9 exhibits KSMs with the following characteristics:

1. No performance information (RS)
2. Low-price award (RS)
3. User decision-making (RS)
4. Means and methods directions and minimum standards (RS)
5. Management by user's professional (RS)
6. Decision-making of user's professional (RS)
7. No responsibility for nonperformance (RS)
8. No performance (RS)

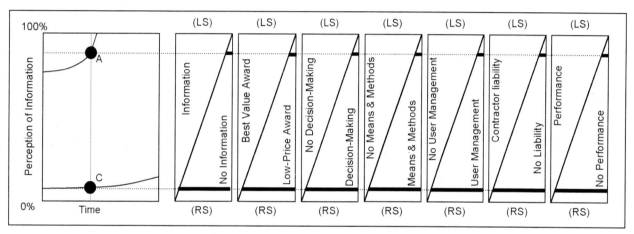

Figure 6.9: How can designers, engineers, project managers and
construction managers effectively and successfully add value?

By definition, the Type A person uses performance information. Thus, information is on the left side (LS) of the KSM. Currently, very little performance information is documented and available in the construction industry.

Decision-making is the act of using one's experience (limited information) to predict a future outcome. By definition, decision-making is on the right side (RS) of the KSM.

Minimum standards are to allow "or equal" products or systems to be priced. Therefore, minimum standards are on the right side (RS) of the KSM. When someone in the delivery process makes a decision, this subjective decision must be explained, and requires the management of the decision maker to minimize the risk of failing to meet expectations.

One party making decisions and giving directions and another party doing the work creates confusion about who is responsible for nonperformance. Therefore, responsibility is on the left-hand side of the KSM and non-responsibility on the right. When nonperformance impacts compensation, accountability for performance forces the person to accept appropriate responsibility. Therefore, the responsibility to identify and minimize risk is located on the left side. When a contractor or designer identifies and minimizes the risk of nonperformance, the result is performance (LS).

The following are characteristics of professionals who work for the user or owner and do not use performance information:

1. *They use no performance information,* thus, they have *no knowledge of risk* or how to minimize the risk.
2. *They make subjective decisions* with *no legal responsibility* for nonperformance unless proven negligent in their duties.
3. They *identify products, means and methods, and minimum standards_*to assure themselves that the lowest bidder is the best value. In actuality, the status quo process delivers the cheapest, lowest quality solution (see Chapters 4 and 5).
4. The professional convinces the owner that the cheaper solution is just as good as the performing solution, and *his or her experience can minimize the risk* that comes with the cheapest solution. However, because the professional has no performance information, it is difficult to minimize risk. The professional's status quo justification is that he or she is saving the owner money by acquiring cheap options and making them work to perform.

   It is important to note that in Figure 6.9, the solid lines represent the extent to which the characteristic is exercised. For example, very rarely does a user's designer or consultant use absolutely any performance information. In most cases, the performance information used is negative information or incomplete information. Whichever the case, some information is used.

Theoretically, professionals with these practices should not be successful in delivering performing construction on time, with no cost generated change orders, meeting quality expectations. Documented studies have verified this hypothesis (Chapter 4 Industry Structure). The construction industry has the following documented problems:

1. Professionals seeking to maintain their professionalism. Professionals' work is minimized and bid on price only. They are becoming nonprofessional (Gawlik 2002, Shearer 2000).
2. Owners are moving away from using the professionals and use performance contracting or other delivery systems where the professional works for the contractor.

   "In Design/build Change orders were low [and the] customer was 'very satisfied,' however Design/Bid/Build had a very high amount of change orders and the customer was only 'satisfied'" (Edrich 2002).

   "'Design-build may not be perfect, but it is definitely more popular than the low-bid procurement approach. On many low-bid awards, the contractor brings a claims consultant to the job trailer on day one to try to recover the money left on the table. In those cases, more attention is given to building a case for a claim than it is to constructing the building. Sources complain that another weak link in the quality chain is inadequate oversight and inspection,' says Daniel A. Cuoco, structural engineer...Troup says it's common to have inspection agents on the site who barely have a high school education" (Post 2001).

"Legislation has been passed, with several provisions in Nevada Revised Statute 338, that enables the Public Works Board to pre-qualify contractors based on past performance" (Illia 2001).

3. Professionals who control the construction industry are losing their control because they are unable to deliver performing construction (Angelo 2003).
4. Insufficient training and skilled craftspeople: with the professionals advising the owners that they are responsible for construction performance, construction skills are treated as a commodity, making training a need, but not a requirement. As a result, contractors are losing their capability to perform. Ironically, professionals are also losing their capability to perform (Rosenbaum 2001a).

"The shortage of skilled craft workers provoked considerable hand-wringing at an Aug. 8-9 meeting in San Francisco of some of the industry's largest constructors and owners of industrial facilities..." (Rosenbaum 2001b).

"Recent research highlights the extent of the need for more skilled workers... showed that 82% of 162 respondents had shortages of skilled craft labor;' 78% thought that the shortages had worsened over the past three years and 73% considered the impact to be moderate to significant" (Rosenbaum 2001b).

In order for designers, engineers, project managers, and construction managers to effectively add value for the owner, they must minimize all of the activities they are accustomed to performing. These professionals should hire a performing contractor instead of the lowest priced contractor and impose fewer minimum standards.

The optimal position for a designer or engineer is employment with a performing contractor rather than with an owner. By working for the contractor, the designer or engineer is at risk for any failures in the specifications. If something goes wrong, the contractor and designer must resolve the problem rather than the owner. This is similar to the design-build procurement process, except that the firm should be one entity rather than a design firm and a contracting firm collaborating on a particular project.

Why do large contractors have a problem with quality?

Figure 6.10 examines the following characteristics:

1. No performance information (RS).
2. Price-based work (RS).
3. Volume-based work (RS).
4. Minimum standards (RS).
5. User management (RS).

6. User inspection (RS).
7. Unskilled labor (RS).
8. Construction quality (LS).

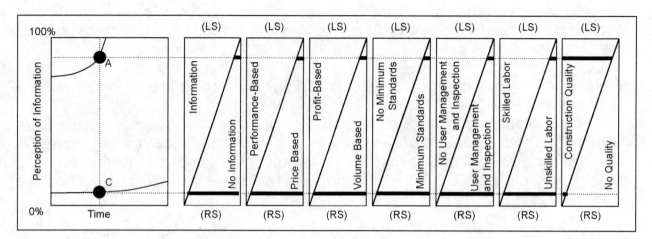

Figure 6.10: How large contractors can improve quality

Type C organizations do not use performance information. If an owner cannot differentiate between contractors, he or she awards based upon lowest price. The owner assumes that all of the contractors offer the same level of quality. Awarding projects based upon price forces contractors to leverage volume instead of making profit.

In price-based work, users issue minimum standards or specifications that direct the contractors on how to do their work. Once the owner tells the contractor how to do the work, the owner must then manage, control, and inspect the contractor to ensure the contractor meets the owner's minimum acceptable quality standard.

Since the contractor works in a price-based arena, the contractor must take all the necessary steps to ensure profit margins and construction costs are as low as possible in order to attain the project. Because of this, the contractor hires the cheapest possible labor, which typically is unskilled labor with little or no training.

Due to these factors, contractors who leverage volume must complete construction faster with lower skilled craftspeople, have less control over their employees, and have difficulty administering their own quality control. To acquire the volume of work, contractors earn smaller profits, provide a lower quality of work, and operate based on price.

As soon as an owner identifies a contractor as a large volume-based contractor, the issue of quality should be a concern. The owner must ensure that the craftspeople on the job are the highest performing craftspeople the contractor employs.

Why does the low-bid process minimize performance?

In a price-based environment, low price is the driving factor since the assumption is that all products are equal. This equality cannot be proved or disproved without performance information. Low price means:

1. Specifications and minimum standards (RS).
2. Decision-making by the owner's representative (RS).
3. Award to the low price bidder (RS).
4. User inspection (RS), management (RS), and control (RS).
5. Poor quality construction (RS).

Contractors no longer consider the owner's risk or the owner's best interest. Instead, contractors think about how to use the cheapest products with the cheapest labor and to install the material as soon as possible in order to maintain the minimal profit margin required by the owner.

"John R. Butler blamed general contractors, construction managers and the like for not 'caring' about their projects, for hiring unskilled workers" (Anderson 2002).

Why do contractors omit "minimizing the owner's risk" as an objective?

The low bid award owner is a Type C owner who does not use performance information. In other words, better performance does not offset a lower price.

It is in the best interest of the owner to induce a performer to do the project right. By definition, this has the best overall or lifecycle cost. If the owner awards the project based on price, then the contractors submit low prices, which are associated with a certain level of quality. When lowest price is the driving factor and no other information is considered, the contractors install the cheapest, easiest system requiring the lowest skill level. There is no other way to do optimal work for very low profit margins and continue to stay in business. This forces the contractor to refrain from minimizing the owner's risk.

"Most constructors have become obsessed with winning the game rather than building the job, charge designers" (Post 2001).

"'Project delivery systems, such as construction management-at-risk and various forms of design-build, have solved some problems and created others, say sources. New and old plagues—adversarial relationships and the low-bid mentality—can combine to make building construction a living hell,' says Kenneth A. Giller, engineer-CM" (Post 2001).

Figure 6.11 shows the factors involved:

1. Price-based (RS).
2. Profit margin (LS).
3. Volume-based (RS).
4. Overall cost (RS).
5. Best interest of the owner (LS).

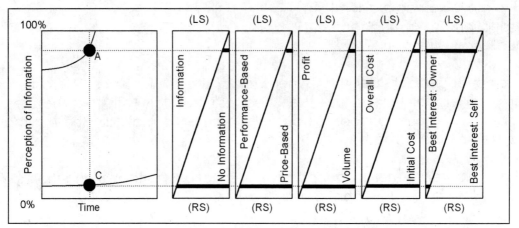

Figure 6.11: Why a contractor should minimize the owner's risk

Why do many project managers thrive in an environment of complexity?

Many project managers seem to be performers in the complex environment of construction. This is a perception based upon a lack of information, since there seems to be no simple answer, no way to fix the problems, and no liability or responsibility for the project performance.

In actuality, by using an information system and requiring construction performance, meaning on-time and on-budget delivery meeting quality expectations, the complexity disappears. Figure 6.12 shows the following characteristics:

1. Ability and understanding to perform (LS).
2. Assignment of responsibility (LS).
3. Acceptance of the responsibility to perform (LS).
4. Need for user management (RS).
5. Performance (LS).

The user's project manager only has responsibilities if the contractor does not know how to perform. If the contractor has the capability to perform, the contractor does not need a project manager. In other terms, if a project manager has a greater number of higher performing contractors, there are fewer problems, and the project manager is able to manage additional jobs. The managing function becomes a simple coordination, facilitation when required, and communication to the end user and the facility manager.

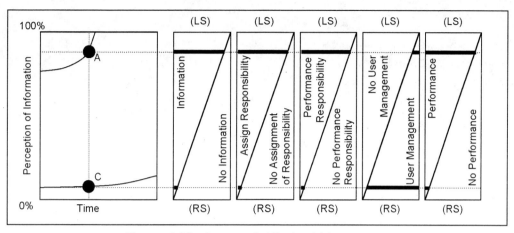

Figure 6.12: Successful Project Mangers

Why do low-bid contractors prefer working with project managers who know construction?

Once the owner's project manager begins managing the project, the owner accepts the risk of nonperformance (since they are making decisions instead of the contractor). The contractor's personnel follow the PM's direction. The owner has purchased manpower and not construction.

The contractor earns more profit when the owner's PM manages because the contractor can use unskilled craftspeople that have little training. These unskilled workers are trained by the owner's PM when the PM directs them on what to do. Invariably, when an unexpected condition arises, the contractor's personnel ask the owner's PM, "*What do you want us to do?*"
"I say that the people who pay the bills need to demand that constructors meet their obligations to install the work right. We need to put the responsibility for proper completion back where it really belongs. So, what am I doing to address this problem? Besides increasing the quality and quantity of inspection preformed by our designers and project managers, I'm trying to put the emphasis back on the constructors" (Butler 2002).

Performing contractors employ trained, skilled craftspeople that know how to do their jobs. However, these contractors require additional compensation (profit) in order to sustain their high level of quality, which they cannot receive in the price-based arena.

Why do organizations with high numbers of project managers and/or consultants dislike information-based performance-based procurement?

The following factors are shown in Figure 6.13:

1. Use of performance information to select and motivate contractors (LS).
2. Complexity of the organization (RS).

3. Number of managers (RS).
4. Decision (RS).
5. Responsibility of performance (LS).
6. Amount of data (details) (RS).
7. Rules (RS).
8. Performance (LS).

The use of performance information and minimized decision-making reduces management and data filtering. It extensively restricts bureaucratic involvement. With performance measured in terms of the final product, the performance information makes a contractor liable for performance.

If the contractor minimizes the risk of nonperformance, no one else should be required to minimize nonperformance. The performance information must be in understandable terms, requiring no translation. The objective is obtaining high performance and not knowledge on the details.

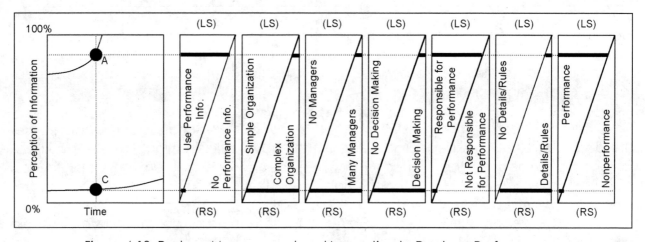

Figure 6.13: Reduce Management and Inspection to Produce Performance

Once the contractor achieves performance, there is minimal need for managers to document, negotiate, make decisions, and make deals with the contractor. The performing contractor is always thinking in the best interest of the owner. Organizations with a large number of project managers do not like information systems because they fear that the system will eliminate jobs, since the performing contractors will do their job correctly.

How does an information environment self-regulate performance?

1. Performance information (LS).
2. Specifications (RS).
3. Minimum standards (RS).
4. Means and methods (RS).
5. Inspection (RS).
6. Owner's regulation (RS).

7. Owner's decision-making (RS).
8. Risk identification and minimization (LS).
9. Performance (LS).
10. Quality control (LS).

An information environment minimizes specifications such as minimum standards, means and methods, and material specification, while forcing the contractors to identify and reduce risk during bidding. A contractor, prioritized as the best value, must minimize all of the recognized risk identified by all contractors for the same price.

Another factor in an information environment is the minimization of the owner's decision-making, which causes the performance information, including the identification and minimization of risk, to become dominant. In other words, if the owner does not make decisions, the contractors' performance dictates who receives the project. In this manner, the contractors regulate the selection and performance level by identifying the differentials and closing the differential by making all contractors perform.

Why do many users who utilize performance-based procurement still have poor performance?

Many owners are creating new "buzzwords" that may sound like they are performing best-value procurement. Nevertheless, if the owner fails to minimize all of the RS functions that go along with low-bid procurement, they are still procuring low-bid construction.

For example, if an owner claims to do performance-based work but actually performs any of the following functions, the owner is still performing low-bid procurement:

1. Using specifications to identify what the contractors should do.
2. Using a two-step process of pre-qualification and low price award.
3. Using project managers and inspectors to ensure contractor performance.
4. Using documents stating a "not-to-exceed guaranteed maximum price".

Using any of the previously determined functions eventually yields nonperformance, and the owner labels the performance-based approach ineffectual. However, the owner fails to understand that a contractor performs because the contractor is capable of identifying and minimizing risk (Type A).

"'Project delivery systems, such as construction management-at-risk and various forms of design-build, have solved some problems and created others, say sources. New and old plagues—adversarial relationships and the low-bid mentality—can combine to make building construction a living hell,' says Kenneth A. Giller, engineer-CM" (Post 2001).

An information-based process draws performers. When performers perform, the result is minimal owner direction, management, and inspection. Identifying the performers is the most important step in the performance-based process. Contract documents have very little impact on a performer. The more the owner relies on these documents, the more price is emphasized, resulting in increased risk. The contract documents simply explain the environment and possess no real ability to minimize risk. These documents are only as effective as the contractor is. Therefore, using performance information and an information system are the most important factors in the process to minimize risk. The documents are of very little importance.

Self-Assessment Using KSMs

KSMs provide a quick method of self-assessment. In an information environment, KSMs ascertain which characteristics to minimize and maximize. The KSMs quickly identify individuals who do not understand the process or individuals who may bring risk to the project. For example, a contractor may ask the project manager to come out and inspect the project. As logical as this may seem, the project manager should decline and ask the performing contractors to make their own decision. The project manager should assist the contractor in performing, but should not make any decisions for the contractor (RS functions). The best advice to the contractor: "If this project was your own house or building, would you accept the things that you are suggesting to me?"

The contribution of KSMs is the ability to logically relate the functions leading to performance and the functions leading to nonperformance. The most important factor is performance, and whether the user is always dictating performance (Deming 1982).

Value, meaning price and performance, is a procurement function. Industry structural analysis (Chapter 4) shows that, in best value procurement, performance always dominates as long as the contractor stays within budget. However, if the contracting officer cannot justify the difference in price due to political pressure, the procurement officer may step in to override the system. Yet, the procurement officer should not try to regulate the system. As difficult as it is, the procurement officer should allow the system and the contractors to regulate themselves. The system structure forces the contractors to remain within budget and the best value.

Information Environment

To establish an information environment, rules, minimum standards, inspection, and control of the contractor must all decrease. Therefore, the owner obtains poor performance if he or she is maximizing these characteristics and not applying performance information. If the owner utilizes information, he or she can minimize the number of people employed to manage and inspect a project.

By definition, a true information environment does the following:

1.   Reduces the amount of data exchanged and managed.
2.   Minimizes decision-making.
3.   Has a structure that is recursive in nature or forces the above without training.
4.   Maximizes the use of resources of all related entities.
5.   Maximizes value and quality.
6.   Creates a "win-win" partnership.

"Architect Michael E. Willis, who is president of the San Francisco based firm, wants to stop the blame game. 'We don't get any points as architects, pointing fingers at the building team... it doesn't make us look smarter'" (Post 2001).

This is contrary to the status quo perception of information systems and technology, where specialists who understand the technology are the managers and decision makers. The author proposes that the true understanding of information identifies the technology as a means and as a commodity, supports the use of information.

High performing contractors perform their own quality control to minimize their risk, regardless of an owner's inspectors. Contractors who leverage volume and low price do the majority of their work in the low-bid arena. These contractors use less quality control, lower skilled craftspeople, and depend upon the owner to control the quality of their work by inspecting to determine if it meets minimum standards.

KSMs identify that owner inspection, control, use of minimum standards, award based on price, and subjective decision-making are related to low quality work. IMT does not state which factor causes or is the major cause of the low quality work. It merely identifies decision-making, rules, use of minimum standards, and owner management as related to poor performance.

Conclusion

The KSMs answer some tough issues the construction industry has not been able to resolve. These issues include:

1. Specifications must not be regulatory documents. They must show intent and minimize the use of minimum standards.
2. Contractors must clarify what they cannot construct. Contractors are responsible for construction. However, they are not responsible for the design. The designer is still responsible for the design.
3. The construction management function is not required.
4. Project management and inspection must be minimized.

Designers, engineers, and consultants should provide the owner with programming and design. They can function as information workers, managing the information environment.

Project managers, construction managers, or construction consultants should work for the contractor. Continuing to work for the owner creates a conflict of interest. In order to demonstrate any benefit, project managers, construction managers, or construction consultants actually need to have non-performing contractors. This is because their motivation conflicts with the performing contractor, and therefore, conflicts with the owner's interest. To justify their position, these managers and consultants must regulate the performing contractor. The attempt to instruct the performing contractor on how to do a job causes further conflict.

KSMs identify which factors relate to an information environment. By definition, an information environment minimizes management, direction, inspection, and control of others. The existence of the above factors classifies the environment as one with minimal and incorrect information. An information environment produces information that all participants can understand and forces the optimization of resources and the value of the event.

KSMs are useful in conjunction with IMT (Chapter 2), industry structure analysis (Chapter 4), and successful business practices (Chapter 5), to optimize the delivery and performance of construction and other services.

Deming's continuous improvement (Deming 1982), Crosby's quality (Crosby 1980), Ohno's lean manufacturing (Ohno 1988, Womack 1990), Buckingham's Break All the Rules philosophies, and Trout's understanding of the perception and performance of people (Buckingham 1999, Trout 1986), can all be implemented in the construction industry. The deductive KSMs identify the problems in the construction industry as business issues that are no different from any other industry. Those that make the issue technical and specific to the construction industry are attempting to justify their own value and not improve the construction industry.

Chapter 6 Review

1. Can the design-bid-build delivery process work?
2. Why do volume-based contractors have a problem with quality?
3. Why does the low-bid process minimize performance?
4. Why do contractors fail to "minimize the owner's risk" as an objective?
5. Why do most project managers thrive in a complex environment?
6. Why do low-bid contractors prefer working with project managers who know construction?
7. Why do large organizations dislike information-based or performance-based procurement?
8. Why do many users who apply performance-based procurement still have poor performance?
9. How does an information environment self-regulate performance?
10. How can designers, engineers, project managers, and construction managers effectively and successfully add value?

References

Anderson, B. (2002, May 20). We Care. *Engineering News Record (ENR)*, 248 [19], p. 7.

Angelo, W. (2003, January 13). Project Management: Keeping Costs Under Control. *Engineering News Record (ENR)*, 250 [1], p. 45.

Angelo, W. (2002, April 1). Central Artery Weighs New Costs. *Engineering News Record (ENR)*, 248 [12], p. 16.

Angelo, W. (2001, June 25). Web voters seek alternatives. *Engineering News Record (ENR)*, 246 [25], p. 107.

Buckingham, M., & Coffman, C. (1999). *First, Break All the Rules.* New York: Simon & Schuster.

Butler, J. (2002, March 18). Construction Quality Stinks. *Engineering News Record (ENR)*, 248 [10], p. 99.

Casavant, D. (2002 December). Mastering a Fundamental Tool: Understanding Net Present Value Can Help Facility Executives Communicate With Top Management. *Building Operation Management*, 49 [12], p. 21.

Crosby, P.B. (1980). *Quality is Free, The Art of Making Quality Certai.* New York: Penguin Group.

Deming, E.W. (1982). *Out of the Crisis.* Cambridge: Massachusetts Institute of Technology.

Edrich, J., Bartels, R., Spiller., & B.J. (2002, August). Weighing the Options. *Civil Engineering*, 72 [8], pp. 48-51.

ENR Staff Writer. (2002, April 8). Glass Span Delay Cracks Budget. *Engineering News Record (ENR)*, 248 [13], p. 16.

ENR Staff Writer. (2002b, May 27). Corps Closes Out Seven Oaks File. *Engineering News Record (ENR)*, 248 [20], p. 14.

ENR Staff Writer. (2002c, December 02). Virginia's Big 'Mixing Bowl' is 180% Over Budget, Late. *Engineering News Record (ENR)*, 249 [23], p. 7.

ENR Staff Writer. (1998, January 26). Training Requirements Can Put Public Back Into Works. *Engineering News Record (ENR)*, 240 [4], p. 148.

Gawlik, K., and Puniani, A. (2002, November 1). A Matter Of Perspective: Roofing Professionals Discuss How To Improve Communication Among Industry Segments. *Professional Roofing*, 32 [11], pp. 20-25.

Hung, T.T. (2002, May). Prequalification and Qualified Tendering Group. *Cost Engineering*, 44 [5], pp. 36-42.

Illia, T. (2001, July 2). Late, Overbudget State Job Sparks Contracting Changes. *Engineering News Record (ENR)*, 247 [1], p. 17.

Korman, R. (1997, June 9). Training Goals Divide Industry. *Engineering News Record (ENR)*, 238 [23], pp. 8-9.

Krizan, W.G., & Winston, S. (1998, January 26). Scarcity of Skilled Workers Will Put Brakes On Growth. *Engineering News Record (ENR)*, 240 [4], pp. 95, 98, 101.

Krizan, W.G., Winston, S., & Korman, R. (1997, January). Training, Cooperation May Produce a 'New Industry'. *Engineering News Record (ENR)*, 238 [4], pp. 84, 87-88.

Ohno, T. (1988). *Toyota Production System: Beyond Large-Scale Production.* Oregon: Productivity Press.

Post, N.M. (2001). Bumpier Road to Finish Line. *Engineering News Record (ENR)*, 246 [19], pp. 56-63.

Shearer, R. (2000, September 4). Hold Architects Accountable. *Engineering News Record (ENR)*, 245 [9], p. 83.

Ricketts, M.L. (1999, April-May). Design-Build not Draw-Build. *Military Engineer*, [598], pp. 65-66.

Rosenbaum, D. (2001a, July 30). No Fix for Craft Labor Shortage. *Engineering News Record (ENR)*, 247 [5], p. 14.

Rosenbaum, D. (2001b, August 20). Craft Labor Shortages Provokes More Studies of Pay and Safety. *Engineering News Record (ENR)*, 246 [5], p. 11.

Trout, J. (1996). *The New Positioning,* New York: McGraw-Hill.

Tulacz, G.J. (2001, December 3). Staff Turnover Plagues Contractors Despite Remedies. *Engineering News Record (ENR)*, 247 [23], pp. 14-15.

Warseck, K. (2002, October). Reroofing: What Do You Get for You Money? *Building Operation Management*, 49 [10], pp. 76,78.

Womack, J.P., Jones, D.T., & Roos, D. (1991). *The Machine that Changed the World. The Story of Lean Production.* New York: HarperPerennial.

Attachments

Attachment 6.1: Non-Performance Articles

Attachment 6.1: Non-Performance Articles

Articles relating to not-on-time (Not-OT), not-on-budget (Not-OB)

1. Costs Climbing in Anchorage
Project: Ted Stevens Anchorage International Airport
Contractor: N/A
Not-OT: The remodel is now about two years behind schedule.
Not-OB: Delays and redesigns have pushed the costs up by $65Million. Original Budget was $230 million.

2. California Court Limits Change Order Claims
Project: Civic Arts Plaza
Contractor: Amelco Electric
Not-OT: N/A
Not-OB: Original budget was $6.2 million, $1 million in change orders. The city then lost 2 legal rounds that gave Amelco another $2.1 million.

3. Jury Awards Fluor $2.8 Million
Project: Criminal Justice Center in Texas
Construction Manager: Fluor Daniel
Not-OT: More than three years late.
Not-OB: The price tag ballooned from $22 million to $45 million

4. Central Artery Segment Design May Have Led to Cost Overrun
Project: Central Artery/Tunnel Massachusetts
Contractor: Bechtel/Parsons Brinckerhoff
Not-OT: N/A
Not-OB: Original budget was $378-million, approximately $49 million in change orders.

5. Dispute Mars Historic Renovation
Project: University of California's Berkeley Campus Building
Contractor: Turner Construction Co.
Not-OT: More than 70 change orders so far... the project is now months behind
Not-OB: Originally estimated to cost $51.2 million, the total was increased to $80.6 million

6. Central Artery Weighs New Costs
Project: Boston's Central Artery/Tunnel
Contractor: Honeywell Technology Solutions Inc.
Not-OT: N/A
Not-OB: The huge job's final tab is now pegged at $14.6 billion, with more than 300 change orders, with cost overruns of $91 million or more.

7. Glass Span Delay Cracks Budget
Project: Tacoma's Interstate Bridge of Glass
Contractor: N/A
Not-OT: After being accelerated to 10-hour-a-day, six-day workweeks, the project is back within 10 days of its original schedule.
Not-OB: $2.8 million original budget. Additional change orders have pushed cost overruns to $850,000 and the overall project cost to $3.7 million.

8. Corps Closes Out Seven Oaks File
Project: Seven Oaks Dam in southern California
Contractor: Odebrecht Construction Inc.
Not-OT: N/A
Not-OB: Original $167.8 million bid, change orders brought the contract value to $220 million.

9. Clark County Brings in Bechtel to help with Troubled Projects
Project: New Courthouse and jail in Las Vegas
Construction Manager: Jacobs Facilities Inc.
Not-OT: Project is a year behind schedule. The courthouse has had 1,100 design changes, including the removal of a planned 18th floor.
Not-OB: Another $33 million is needed to finish the buildings, plus $5 million more to temporarily house inmates.

10. Costs Rise for Bypassing Dam (5/20/2002)
Project: Hoover Dam Bridge
Engineers: HDR Inc. Jacobs Inc., T.Y. Lin International
Not-OT: N/A
Not-OB: Initial $198-million estimate was too low, the bridge has increased by 20% and could run even higher, and is now at $240 million.

11. Liquidated Delay Damages Nixed for Hoover Dam Job (10/28/2002)
Project: Hoover Dam Bridge
Contractors: PCL Construction Services Inc.
Not-OT: 363 days because of delays and defective drawings and specifications.
Not-OB: Submitted a claim for an additional $23.2 million

12. Cracks Plague California Ramp
Project: California concrete bridge girders
Contractor: C.C. Myers Inc.
Not-OT: Bridge opening was pushed back 8 months
Not-OB: Original budget: $12 million. Cost to repair: $10 million.

13. Virginia's Big 'Mixing Bowl' is 180% over Budget, Late
Project: Virginia interchange
Not-OT: The 2007 completion target will not be met.
Not-OB: Costs have jumped 180%...to $676.5 million.

14. Beach Development Awash in Delays
Project: Oceanfront Diplomat Resort Florida
Not-OT: More than a year behind schedule
Not-OB: The original cost was $400 million...costs have ballooned to more than $500 million.

15. CM Says Local Preference Lifts Nevada Building Costs
Project: Nevada Jail and Court
Company: Jacobs Facilities
Not-OT: Three of the four jobs are over budget and behind schedule, with a six-month delay on each job.
Not-OB: Original budget was $120 million to the low bidder... project costs have ballooned to $291.7 million.

16. Late, Overbudget State Job Sparks Contracting Changes
Project: Nevada, Nursing
Contractor: Addison Inc.
Not-OT: Opened 16 months after the planned opening.
Not-OB: Doing a low-bid process has caused a lot of problems…Already $1 million over budget, and "Hundreds of items" away from completion,   says Daniel O'Brien, State Public Works Director.

17. Nevada Removes Contractor
Project: Nevada Veterans nursing Home Healthcare Center
Contractor: Addison Inc.
Not-OT: Contractor removed for delays, cost overruns and alleged construction defects, from 500 design changes.
Not-OB: Original budget at $19.3 million, with $1 million in change orders.

18. Rising Costs, Slipping Schedule Have Tren Urbano in Hot Water
Project: Commuter Rail Line in San Juan, Puerto Rico
Not-OT: Two years.
Not-OB: Costs have risen approximately $260 million, to $1.9 billion.

19. If you build it, they will take advantage
Project: Safeco Field (Mariners)
Not-OT: N/A
Not-OB: Original budget was $517.6 million, with $100 million in cost overruns.

20. Raytheon Raises Cost Estimate to Complete Projects
Project: Two Massachusetts Power Plants
Contractor: Raytheon Co.
Not-OT: Cost will rise because of schedule delays.
Not-OB: Original costs at $325 million and its most recent estimate was $813 million. Up to $1.2 billion in write-offs.

21. Judge's Ruling Hits Tutor-Saliba
Project: Wilshire-Normandie Subway Station
Contractor: Tutor-Saliba Corp.
Not-OT: N/A
Not-OB: The original $79 million contract increased by $20 million in change orders…there were additional claims of about $3 million.

22. Stadium settlement doesn't cover repairs
Project: Aloha Stadium, Honolulu
Contractor: 30 companies, state sued architects, designers, engineers, the construction contractor, steel companies.
Not-OT: N/A
Not-OB: Cost to build stadium (1975): $32 Million.
Cost of repairs: $45 million to $50 million.

23. Stadium cost overruns the rule, but who pays?
Project: 12 Football/Baseball Stadiums
Contractor: Various Contractors
Projected: $3.5 billion
Overruns: $807 million (30% more than original cost)
Final cost: $4.3 billion (with overruns)
Not-OT: N/A
Not-OB: Originaly projected at $3.5 billion, the various projects with cost overruns of $807 million, brought the final cost over $4.3 billion.

24. Hilton Ready to Reopen Waikiki Tower
Project: Waikiki Hotel
Contractor: N/A
Not-OT: Shut down only a year after it was built because of a persistent mold problem.
Not-OB: Original cost was $95 million...A $55 million cleanup.

References

1. McFall, Kathleen. (2003, February 3). Costs Climbing in Anchorage. Engineering News Record, 250 [4], p. 16.
2. ENR Staff Writer. (2002, February 11). California Court Limits Change Order Claims. Engineering News Record, 248 [5], p. 7.
3. ENR Staff Writer. (2002). Jury Awards Fluor $2.8 Million. Engineering News Record, 248 [6], p. 13.
4. Tuchman, Janice L. (2003, February 24). Central Artery Segment Design May Have Led to Cost Overrun. Engineering News Record, 250 [7], p. 12.
5. Rosenbaum, David. (2002, March 4). Dispute Mars Historic Renovation. Engineering News Record, 248 [8], pp. 10-12.
6. Angelo, William (2002, April 1). Central Artery Weighs New Costs. Engineering News Record, 248 [12], p. 16.
7. ENR Staff Writer (2002, April 8). Glass Span Delay Cracks Budget. Engineering News Record, 248 [13], p. 16.
8. ENR Staff Writer (2002, May 27). Corps Closes Out Seven Oaks File. Engineering News Record, 248 [20], p. 14.
9. Illia, Tony (2002, April 22). Clark County Brings In Bechtel to Help with Troubled Projects. Engineering News Record, 248 [15], p. 20.
10. Illia, Tony (2002, May 20). Costs Rise For Bypassing Dam. Engineering News Record, 248 [19], p. 38.
11. Staff Writer. (2002, October). Liquidated Delay Damages Nixed for Hoover Dan Job. Engineering News Record, 249 [18], 18.
12. ENR Staff Writer (2002, December 02). Cracks Plague California Ramp. Engineering News Record, 249 [23], p. 14.
13. ENR Staff Writer (2002, December 02). Virginia's Big 'Mixing Bowl' is 180% Over Budget, Late. Engineering News Record, 249 [23], p. 7.
14. Post, Nadine. (2001, February 5). Beach development awash in delays. Engineering News Record, 246 [5], pp. 56-60.
15. Illia, Tony. (2001, April 2). CM Says Local Preference Lifts Nevada Building Costs. Engineering News Record, 246 [13], p.12.
16. Illia, Tony (2001, July 2). Late, Overbudget State Job Sparks Contracting Changes. Engineering News Record, 247 [1], p. 17.
17. ENR Staff Writer. (2001, August 27). Nevada Removes Contractor. Engineering News Record, 247 [9], p. 15.
18. ENR Staff Writer. (2001, September 17). Rising costs, slipping schedule have tren urbano in hot water. Engineering News Record, 247 [12], p. 15.
19. Bickley, Dan. (1999, July 19). If you build it, they will take advantage. The Arizona Republic, p. C3.
20. Gunsalus, James. (2001, July). Raytheon Raises Cost Estimate to Complete Projects (Update6). Bloomberg.com financial news.
21. Rosta, Paul. (2001, July 16). Judge's Ruling Hits Tutor-Saliba. Engineering News Record, 247 [3], p. 12.
22. Kobayashi, Ken. (1998, June 17). Stadium settlement doesn't cover repairs. The Honolulu Advertiser. p. A1, A10.
23. McKinnon, Shaun. (2001, March 11). Stadium cost overruns the rule, but who pays? The Arizona Republic, p. A2.
24. Reyes, B.J. (2003, August 12). Hilton Ready to Reopen Waikiki Tower. The Mercury News. Date accessed: 9-10-2003. URL: http://www.bayarea.com/mld/bayarea/news/

7

Performance Information Procurement System (PIPS)

Introduction

The Performance Information Procurement System (PIPS) was initially called the Performance Based Procurement System (PBPS). Its name was changed to distinguish it from the myriad of other performance-based procurement systems, which although called performance-based, are actually price-based processes. A PIPS process incorporates all of the characteristics of a win-win relationship. PIPS creates a full information environment, which has resulted in best value for the client and maximized profit for the contractor.

This chapter includes:

1. Historical development
2. Objectives of PIPS
3. PIPS overview
4. Major PIPS steps: setup, collection of past performance information (PPI), bid proposals, selection, pre-award period, and construction and final performance rating.

To run PIPS for the first time, using a quick and easy checklist and instructions, go to Chapter 9, Getting Started.

PIPS is a very simple, non-technical, logical process. However, when clients start to use PIPS after years of using a very inefficient process, simple, logical processes are counterintuitive. The following questions are often asked due to a lack of understanding of the theoretical discussions of IMT in the previous chapters:

1. Why can't we prequalify and then bid the contractors?
2. What use is it to ask contractors for only their best references?
3. Why do we have to use the Displaced Ideal Model (DIM) when we can use easy to understand matrix type comparisons?
4. Won't the contractors charge more for performance?
5. Aren't the project managers the minimizers of risk?
6. Why do we have to rate the performance of subcontractors?
7. Why do we need so many references?

If these questions arise, the reader should review the first six chapters. Clients who run PIPS should not deviate from the steps. Any deviation from the steps as presented will increase the risk of nonperformance. If a client follows the process, the following can be logically expected:

1. Projects which, 96% of the time, have no contractor generated cost change orders, on time, and meet the client's expectations of quality.
2. Minimized construction management (50 – 80%).
3. Higher contractor profit and performance.
4. Transaction first costs will be the same or less.

Historical Development of PIPS

PIPS has undergone the following developmental stages:

1. Formation of the concept (1983 – 1991).
2. Testing of the concept (1994 – 2001).
3. Modification and optimization of the process to meet the demands of different users (2000 – present).
4. Development and documentation of the Information Measurement Theory (IMT) (2000-2001).
5. Documentation and modification of PIPS as a rule-based process that can be run by personnel who are not well versed in IMT (2003 - 2005).
6. Implementation of the PIPS/IMT concepts into the low bid environment to assist Quadrant I users who, for one reason or another, cannot run PIPS (2003-present).

PIPS has been run by the following clients (for an updated list and points of contact see the website www.pbsrg.com):

1. Private entities around the Phoenix metropolitan area (Intel, Motorola, IBM, Honeywell, Boeing, etc....).
2. States of Wyoming, Hawaii, Utah, and Georgia.
3. United Airlines.
4. Federal Aviation Administration (FAA,) US Coast Guard, and the US Army Medical Command.
5. Dallas Independent School District (DISD).
6. Denver Hospital.

Major changes in PIPS over the last ten years include:

1. Using of ten basic criteria for all contractors and personnel.
2. Requiring the contractors to send out their reference forms to the client.
3. Minimizing the amount of verification of reference data.
4. Allowing the procurement agent to make the final selection with the input of the modeling.
5. Allowing the award to the price based bidder if the difference in cost is too hard to justify.

6. Weighting the contractor past performance less than the risk assessment and interview scores unless it is a design-build system such as roofing, painting, and waterproofing.

Objective of PIPS: Sustainability, Minimization of Risk, Reduction of Work

There are three important requirements to make a process sustainable:

1. The process must minimize decision-making.
2. The process must not add any additional work, and must minimize work done by the owner.
3. The process must minimize risk.

If a best value process does not meet these criteria, the author proposes that the system will not be sustainable. Facility and construction managers are constantly being reorganized, reduced, and outsourced. They are forced to do more with less. The only way to effectively do more with less is to reduce their workload. Their work is not physical work, but making decisions. If decision-making is minimized, their workload will be minimized. This may threaten many facility and construction managers. However, efficiency is a requirement of the PIPS environment. Any manager, who is not efficient, does not add value for the owner and will be dispensable.

If a new process does not drastically minimize risk, most managers will not implement. New processes mean change, and the majority of construction managers are adverse to change. The majority of managers will not risk forcing change if it does not bring a huge payback.

In the development of PIPS, these three requirements became guidelines. If any proposed modifications did not match these guidelines, it was not implemented. During the testing and development, functions were continually modified to optimize compliance with these guidelines.

PIPS Process Overview

The PIPS process is comprised of the following seven phases (See Figure 7.1):

1. Setup of the process and education.
2. Selection of test project.
3. Collection of past performance information (PPI).
4. Bidding and analysis of bids.
5. Selection of the best value contractor.
6. Pre-award phase.
7. Construction and rating of construction.

Clients should first identify if they can use the process and if it matches their procurement objectives. The process is then setup. The first time that a client uses PIPS, the author recommends using the assistance of the Performance Based Studies Research Group (PBSRG) or certified PIPS training groups.

The process is very similar to the status quo construction delivery system: Generate a request for proposal (RFP), educate the contractors, collect past performance information, receive and analyze bids, put data into the selection model to prioritize the contractors, select a contractor, force the contractor to minimize the risk through preplanning, award the construction, and then rate the contractor when they are completed.

The major reason for the success of PIPS is that performing contractors are motivated to compete with their best craftspeople and construction managers in the natural selection environment (Fig 7.7). The motivation to perform comes from the contractor's best people. The best way to cultilvate performance is to hire performers and let them do their job. PIPS therefore minimizes owner functions during construction. It rates the contractor's performance at the end of construction to modify the contractor's future competitiveness. PIPS creates a documented, closed-loop information system that becomes self regulating over time (DMAIC) (see Chapter 8 Six Sigma application). The performers will maintain the process, regulate the process, and ensure that the owner is running the process correctly.

PIPS is:

1. Performance information collection and use.
2. A process to compete the contractors based on the ability to perform over a period of times on numerous projects and the ability to minimize risk on a specific client's project.
3. Turning over all risk to the contractor during the pre-award phase forcing the minimization of risk before the construction.
4. Allowing the contractor to monitor their performance based on the minimization of risk.
5. Measuring the contractor's performance in the critical areas and modifying their future performance.

The rest of the chapter will cover the details of PIPS by phases.

Setup and Education Phase

The setup phase is one of the most crucial phases. If it is done correctly, it will minimize problems during the process. The design of PIPS should be done by personnel who understand IMT. When the managers do not understand IMT, they create opportunities in the process for decision-making. This brings risk to the success of the process.

Potential users should:

1. Seek the assistance of Arizona State University. The PIPS/IMT technology is licensed and trademarked.

2. Educate a potential core team in the client's organization.
3. Define the constraints of the user in policies that may require modifications to the PIPS process.
4. Seek a legal review.
5. Identify a prototype project.
6. Identify the performance criteria.
7. Identify the relationship of the criteria in terms of weights.
8. Finish RFP.
9. Advertise the project. The owner needs to convey to the contractors that the process is an information based process that will be awarded to the best performer within the budget and that the owner is intending to use the process and the performance information in the future.

The PIPS Process is shown in Attachment 7.1. Very rarely does the PIPS process get in the way of procurement cycle timing. Once the above functions are completed, the client is ready to move on to the bidding and collection of past performance information.

Performance Based Studies Research Group (PBSRG)

PBSRG was started by Dean Kashiwagi in 1994, and for the past ten years, PBSRG has tested PIPS 380 times, given over 350 presentations on PIPS, and identified and analyzed the source of construction nonperformance. The performance line of PBSRG is listed in Figure 7.2.

The author recommends that clients with major and repeated construction and facility needs, contact PBSRG to assist in the first time testing and implementation of PIPS. PIPS has different paradigms that are counter intuitive. It has been the experience of PBSRG, that project managers revert to their traditional paractice of decision making and directing the contractor while running PIPS. The number one cause for construction nonperformance is the misunderstanding of a client on the sources of construction nonperformance. Over the last ten years, PBSRG has identified the client's misunderstanding of PIPS/IMT as the number one source of risk. With the help of PBSRG, project managers can see how PIPS runs from beginning to end. After the first round of education/test/analysis, the client has the potential to run PIPS on their own. Clients should call previous PIPS users or references on the pbsrg.com website should they need further advice.

The client should identify a core team (see Chapter 14 PIPS Core Group). Success of the implementation depends on having a core group. The implementation has to be done on a test basis, and the core group will be the test implementers.

Client or Owner Policies

The owner policies and regulations are the structure PIPS must work within. *Policies cannot be changed by PIPS.* Policies must be changed by the client. Policies have

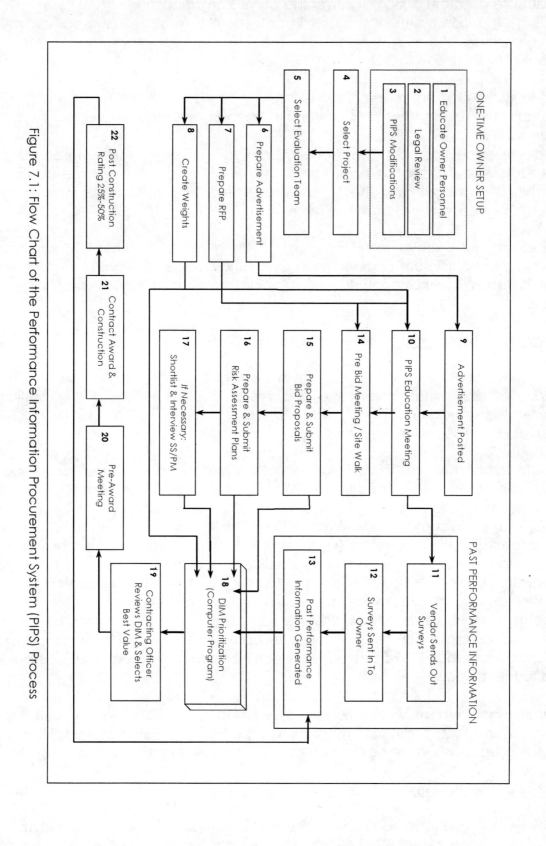

Figure 7.1: Flow Chart of the Performance Information Procurement System (PIPS) Process

Publication Overview

23	Number of refereed journal articles (published and approved)
71	Number of refereed conference papers
4	Number of different refereed journals that were reviewed
3	Number of editorial boards served on
11	Number of published books

Invited Presentations

335	Number of total invited presentations
54	Number of presentations given in 2003 calendar
1506	Number of attendees in 2003
27	Number of presentations given in 2004 calendar
1129	Number of attendees in 2004
4.7	Overall performance of the presentations (maximum is 5.0)
96%	Percent of attendees that would attend another presentation

Grant Overview

111	Number of grants
$4.75 Million	Total amount of research/educational grants
$396K	Average grant per year since 1993 ($K/year)
$375K	Total grants for 2003
$617K	Total grants for 2004

Research Impact

$231 Million	Total cost of procured construction in research
391	Total number of researched procurements
26	Total number of different research partners (public & private)
3	Total number of licenses (DAGS, UH, USCG)
100%	Percent of users that would use PIPS to procure another project
99%	Percent of satisfied customers
99%	Percent of projects completed within budget
98%	Percent of project completed on time
9.7	Average contractor post project evaluation (maximum is 10)
3	Average rating of their current process (maximum is 10)
9	Average rating of the PIPS process (maximum is 10)

Teaching Overview

50	Number of classes taught
4.6	Average course evaluation (maximum is 5.0)
22	Number of chaired master thesis's
1	Number of PHD Students

Figure 7.2: PBSRG Performance Line

nothing to do with PIPS. Owners must decide which existing delivery system will allow PIPS to be implemented successfully. PIPS is inherently a one-phase, no pre-qualification process. However, owners may decide to go with a two-phase, design-build, or pre-qualification and selection process. PIPS can work either way.

PIPS is a selection methodology. It is housed within the policies of the client. For example, the theoretical PIPS encourages hiring the best available performer identified by the selection model. However, under the conditions of the FAR, the contracting officer is directed to make the final decision. PIPS may then be modified to direct the contracting officer to take all the information produced by the selection model, and make the final decision. Policies can be implemented to minimize the risk of the owner. Past history of PIPS identifies that there is no construction risk resulting from PIPS. In other words, performing contractors are not a source of risk. Risk (not on time, not on budget, and not meeting owner's expectations) is caused by three sources:

1. Contractors being surprised, then surprising the owner.
2. The owner having expectations that do not match reality and then being surprised.
3. Unforeseen conditions.

All three of these sources, involve "being surprised." Performing contractors minimize the first two sources. The third source can usually be explained by the designer and owner. The remaining risk can be minimized by using logical policies. For example, when the Dallas Independent School district (DISD) used PIPS for procuring roofing, they added the following policies:

1. No roofing system could receive more than 66% of the roofs being procured at one time.
2. No roofing contractor could receive more than 33% of the roofs being procured at one time.

These policies were implemented so that DISD would not put all their eggs into one basket, and, when the eggs were put into the baskets, the baskets were big enough to hold the eggs without making people nervous and causing political risk.

An issue that has been raised, is that PIPS will award to the same contractor over and over. However, the environment should prevent this from occurring. If one contractor's performance is very high relative to all the others, one of the following should occur:

1. The weights of the performance vs. the price should be changed to make it more competitive.
2. If a project has low risk, the weights on past performance should be minimized, depending more on current ability to do the project.
3. The areas of differential should be weighted less, forcing all contractors to continually improve.

4. If a project is of sufficient risk, and the risk can be defined in terms of past nonperformance and the possible cost of nonperformance, the performing contractor will have an advantage.

Legal and Procurement Review

PIPS should be reviewed by the client's lawyers and procurement officers. If the client can use request for proposals (considering both performance and price), the legal staff will approve PIPS. If design-build can be implemented, PIPS can be used. If performance can be considered, PIPS can usually be used. If the law defines the use of how performance must be used, the low-bid version of PIPS can be used (see Chapter 25). The lawyers and procurement agents will make the decision. The project managers must remember that the lawyers and procurement officers *will be conservative*. This could result in the keeping of the status quo, even though it is only their interpretation of the law that makes PIPS illegal.

There are a number of suggestions that the construction managers need to consider when working with the legal staff. *The lawyers* interpret the laws and regulations. If the lawyer or the procurement agent thinks that PIPS cannot be used, use PIPS in the low bid environment (Chapter 25).

If the legal staff is composed of various lawyers, select the lawyer who is the most open minded, logical, progressive, honest, secure, and hardest working. Pre-qualify the lawyers if you have a choice. Invite the lawyers to participate from the very first meeting to consider PIPS. Find the lawyer who is the most comfortable and knowledgeable with IMT.

Most lawyers will have a defensive posture. It is their environment. Managers should not be discouraged. It is important to do the following:

1. Keep the lawyers updated.
2. Always ask their opinion.
3. Always provide them with alternative solutions.

The procurement or contracts staff is the next important group. They may be difficult to work with for the following reasons:

1. Their whole environment is one of mistrust. Their job is to regulate, control, and penalize. Their job environment is adversarial. Their job is the opposite of PIPS. They will not feel naturally comfortable with PIPS.
2. They lack technical expertise in the services or products they are purchasing. They are always in a position of lacking information. This insecurity is balanced with the power of contractual clauses. The contractual clauses are bureaucratic.
3. PIPS will minimize the amount of their bureaucratic work and some may feel threatened by this.

4. PIPS/IMT changes their environment from one of control to one of facilitation. This is very difficult for most people, and very difficult for procurement agents. This will be a monumental change for procurement agents.

Once again, the same rules that apply to the lawyers apply to the procurement agents. Pick the procurement or contract agents who can understand and feel comfortable with IMT. Once the legal and procurement/contracts department approves the contract delivery system, the project managers can proceed with the PIPS process. If the legal representatives disapprove, the project manager should implement in the low bid environment. The project manager must understand that *modifications to the PIPS process increase the amount of risk of construction nonperformance*.

Selection of the Test Project

Selection of the test project should be done considering the following factors:

1. The political situation.
2. The type of projects that are available.
3. The understanding of the core group.

If the political climate is antagonistic, smaller, maintenance, repair, or system type projects (roofing, painting, waterproofing, mechanical repair, or modification) should be selected. If the core group understands PIPS/IMT well, and has political influence, and the a critical project is at risk, PIPS can be run on the critical project. Tests have shown that PIPS will result in the same or greater performance than the status quo. The more understanding of the core group, the larger projects can be tested. It should be remembered that the only risk when running PIPS is political risk.

Performance Criteria

PIPS selects contractors based on performance and price. Therefore the two main criteria are performance and price. The performance will be made up of the following criteria:

1. Past performance of the general contractor and critical subcomponents: site superintendent, project manager, electrical subcontractor, mechanical subcontractor, waterproofing contractor including roofing and waterproofing, and other critical systems (high cost, high risk items).
2. Current capability to minimize risk on the unique project (which may include criteria such as warranty periods, performance periods of major systems, interviews, and risk assessment plans).

PIPS is a structure for delivering construction. It covers the design, the competitive bidding, the selection of the contractor, the minimization of risk before award, the construction, and the rating of the contractor that affects the contractor's future competitive opportunities. Past performance criteria affect the entire cycle, and not only the selection of the contractor.

The objective of past performance criteria includes:

1. Identify if a contractor has performed in the past.
2. Motivate a contractor to pay attention and perform on the project at hand. The ratings on a project will count toward a minimum of 25% against the future performance rating.

These two objectives must be kept in mind when selecting criteria. Project managers must think ahead to when the project is awarded, constructed, and the contractor is rated. By having the performance criteria on items such as "close out documentation" and "documenting risk information during the project," the contractors are motivated to perform and eliminate the risk of the owner.

Ten years of testing has led to the generic past performance criteria for all contractors. The criteria below were developed from test cases, contractor expert opinions, and analysis of past performance data (Attachment 7.6).

1. Ability to manage the project cost (minimize change orders).
2. Ability to maintain project schedule (completed on time or early).
3. Quality of workmanship.
4. Professionalism and ability to manage, minimization of the client's representative's time, including responses and prompt payment to suppliers and subcontractors.
5. Close out process, meaning no punch list upon turnover and warranties, as-builts, operating manuals, tax clearance, and so forth submitted promptly.
6. Communication, explanation of risk, and documentation (construction interface reporting on time at least 90% of the time, and accurately at least 90% of the time).
7. Ability to follow the user's rules, regulations, and requirements such as those involving housekeeping, safety, and more.
8. Overall customer satisfaction and comfort with rehiring the contractor on the basis of performance.
9. Total number of different jobs surveyed.
10. Total number of different customer responses.

The first eight areas identify if the contractor can perform (performance determined by non-technical terms that the client understands). Criteria 4, 5, 6, and 7, place the contractor who gets the project at risk. Past tests have shown that most past references give a contractor consistent ratings for all the criteria. However, the contractor that gets the project, and who will have their future competitive performance rating affected by the performance on the project, will have to do the tasks in criteria 4, 5, 6 and 7 well. If they do not do it well, they will be downgraded, affecting their future competitive rating. The last two criteria are related to the amount of experience of the contractor. They minimize the risk of the client by giving credit to contractors who have more performing past performance.

Despite the logic of having unique criteria for different types of construction and contractor types, PIPS uses the generic criteria for all types of contractor performance for the following reasons:

1. Minimizes the amount of work managing the performance data.
2. Keeps the database manageable.
3. If the data was different, it would be technical, and performance data should not be technical.

Contractors do not have to be re-surveyed every time a different type of project is done. For example, if the owner is constructing a hospital, the performance criteria would pertain to contractors constructing hospitals. However, if the owner has to build a clean room building next, the owner should not have to recollect performance information on the construction of clean rooms (this would create too much work which goes against the 3 factors of a sustainable system). Tests have shown that when owners altered criteria for different projects, the data collection was not maintainable. Also, bonding, insurance, and license requirements already force a contractor to have the right technical expertise. PIPS also has steps that force the contractor to minimize risk, and, without the proper expertise, the contractor would be unable to be competitive in PIPS.

The PIPS processor considers *the number of jobs and the number of different references* against the subjective performance ratings on a relative basis. The bottom line: a contractor with forty references on forty projects and an average rating of 10 will prevail against a contractor with only two references on two projects and an average rating of 10. The system will minimize the owner's risk. Therefore on risky projects, the owner is telling the contractors, "The contractor who has done this type of work successfully, over and over, will minimize the risk." This approach forces contractors to show both the ability to perform and repeated performance.

When purchasing systems (roofing, painting, waterproofing, mechanical etc...), objective past performance information may also be considered in addition to the subjective criteria. For example, when purchasing roofing systems, the following performance criteria have been used to minimize risk (Chapter 15 discusses the case study of procuring roofing systems):

1. Documented service period of the proposed roofing system.
2. Documented performance of the contractor.
3. Percent of roofs in database that do not leak.
4. Percent of roofs that never leaked.
5. Percent of roofs that still leak.
6. Amount of traffic on the roof system.
7. Size of the roofs installed.

Performance criteria should not be technical. It should be in terms of what owners can verbalize and understand. Any effort to force owners and owner representatives to understand technical terms or capabilities is inefficient if the owner is attempting to outsource. If something is technical, it forces decision-making (which does not abide with the goals of PIPS).

Bidding Phase and Past Performance Information Phase

Once the project is selected, the next two phases are run simultaneously. The past performance information (PPI) and the bidding process begin at the same time. The PIPS process is similar to the regular procurement cycle. The only difference is the educational meeting where the contractors are instructed on how to submit the past performance information.

The next steps in the process are:

1. Prepare the RFP.
2. The RFP should include the owner's definition of performance, which is the weights on the various criteria.
3. Sending out the invitation to bid to the contractors which will have the initial education meeting and the prebid walkthrough date for the project.
4. The holding of the education meeting.
5. The contractors are given directions on how to turn in the past performance numbers.
6. The contractors submit the performance information to the client.
7. The prebid meeting is held.
8. The contractors turn in their bid (legal requirements, risk assessment plan, the team composition, and their bid price.
9. Interviews are conducted on key personnel.
10. The DIM is used to prioritize the contractors.
11. The procurement agent takes the output of the DIM and makes the decision on which contractor to prioritize best value.
12. The best value contractor minimizes the risk during the preaward phase ending with a preaward meeting.
13. The contractor is awarded the project, and enters the construction phase.

Request For Proposal (RFP)

The RFP includes the following:

1. Request for contract documents (bid price sheet, legal requirements of bonding and insurance, and contractor team composition).
2. Usual RFP (design and general conditions for a fully designed project, requirements only for design-build project).
3. Short description of PIPS (Attachment 7.9)
4. Weights defining performance.
5. Request for risk assessment plan.

The differences from the normal RFP are requirements 3 and 5. To assist the contractors in understanding the requirements, the contractor should be given a cover sheet with the requirements to be checked off (Attachment 7.5a). To implement PIPS, the author proposes to change as little as possible. PIPS requires no punitive general conditions. However, there is nothing wrong with leaving the general conditions in place. If PIPS is successful, none of the general conditions will be used. If PIPS is unsuccessful, the owner has a low bid contractor and contract, and the owner can exercise the general conditions. The author proposes to add the following statement to an owner's general conditions:

"The owner, at the owner's discretion, in the best interest of the owner, can modify the general conditions to assist the contractor to be successful."

If the contractor is a non-performer, the general conditions will stand "as is." If the contractor is a performer, and performs, the general conditions will not be used. By placing the above statement into the general conditions, it reinforces to the contractors that the owner will not penalize the performer. It also allows the owner to not make modifications to the general conditions, which is one of the biggest obstacles to implementing PIPS for government organizations.

Weights for the Criteria

The assumption behind PIPS and the prioritization model is that the owner and their project are unique. Performance is always a tradeoff among the different criteria. Value is a tradeoff between the owner's definition of performance and price (Figure 7.3). Weighting the criteria allows the user to describe who they are and their expectations to the contractors. The weights are unique for each owner and each project. They should be weighted as such, and not on anticipated project risks.

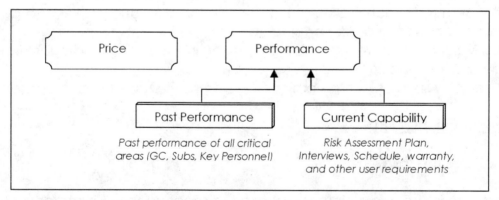

Figure 7.3: Illustration of Weighting Scheme

As an owner makes more tests, the user will use the weights to increase the competitiveness of the contractors. The contractors will identify the risks of the project and minimize the risks. The resulting ratings of the contractor's current capability will minimize the risk of the owner. If an owner wants less experienced contractors to participate, the owner will lessen the weight on past performance, especially on the number of past projects and references. By doing this, and by reusing the contractor performance lines, the owner is actually giving a competitive advantage to less experienced contractors.

A general construction project example can explain how the weights are set. The first decision an owner or the owner's representatives must make involves weighing price and performance. Owners predominantly want to weight price at least 50% and performance 50%. The PIPS model analyzes relative distances (Chapter 10). If there are large differences in performance, the model results will override small differences (less than 10%) in price. If the differences are not major differences, the owner's contract person can override the model's prioritization and award to the second highest performer. Therefore, regardless of the weighting, the following will happen:

1. If the top-performing contractor is minimizing identified risk through high performance, they will be prioritized first even if the weighting favors price.
2. If the top prioritized contractor is too expensive when compared with the next highest performing contractor, and the contracting officer cannot justify the differential, the next performing contractor will be awarded the project.

Regardless of the weighting, the contractor who has the best perceived value will be awarded the contract. The process allows the owner to be totally comfortable with the best value contractor. If the owner is uncomfortable, and is more comfortable with another contractor, they should choose the second rated best value contractor. Value is always a tradeoff of performance and price.

The author recommends the following options for weighting performance and price:

1. <u>Performance based</u>: performance/cost - 70% and 30%.
2. <u>No bias</u>: performance/cost - 50% and 50%. This is a good starting point and follows the IMT of not making a decision, which is more important when information is unknown.
3. <u>Cost conscience</u>: performance/cost – 40% and 60%. Cost is more important, although performance has a significant impact.
4. <u>Very cost conscience</u>: performance/price – 30% and 70%. The contractor does not have to be the low bidder to acquire the project but must be very competitive in price. If the contractor is incapable of identifying and minimizing risk and has poor past performance, that contractor is noncompetitive unless the weight on price is dramatically higher.
5. <u>Price-based</u>: performance/price – 0% and 100%. Contractor must have a past performance rating but not necessarily as a performer. Performance on the job for which the contractor is currently bidding impacts the future performance rating if the contractor is awarded the project.

An owner's second major decision concerns the relative importance of the different performance criteria, which includes:

1. Past performance of critical components (explained later in this chapter).
2. Current construction capability to minimize risk on the unique project, including a risk assessment plan (explained later in this chapter).

The author proposes that current capability to minimize risk on the specific project that will be completed is *much more important* than past performance on projects which are different. Current capability considers:

1. The unique requirements of the construction project being considered.
2. Matching the critical personnel to the project.
3. First person information. The owner sees the potential matches, whereas past performance is determined by other people who may have different perceptions.
4. Comparing the best available values, while past performance is comparing a contractor against who the reference has had experience with.

Owners have concerns that heavily weighting current capability may allow the owner to subjectively bias the selection. If the owner uses bias in PIPS, they will use bias in any selection and delivery system. PIPS is an information environment, and by definition, bias and subjectivity based on non-construction issues are harder to introduce and use in the selection process. Therefore, the author suggests using the following breakdown:

1. Past performance: 30%
2. Current capability: 70%

If the performance rating is 50%, then based upon the above weights, current capability accounts for 50% X 70%, or 35% of the total weight. The next decision is to weight the Past Performance Information (PPI) in areas such as (Figure 7.4):

1. Site superintendent PPI
2. Project manager PPI
3. General contractor PPI
4. Electrical subcontractor PPI
5. Heating, Ventilation, Air Conditioning (HVAC) PPI
6. Plumbing PPI
7. Roofing contractor PPI
8. Waterproofing contractor PPI

The last decision necessitates weighting the current capability areas (proposed weights in parenthesis):

1. Schedule: (10%)
2. Risk assessment plan document: (40%)
3. Interviews with the site superintendent and project manager: (50%)

The schedule can be weighted more heavily, if schedule is an issue. However, contractors will maximize their profit by finishing as soon as possible. If the required construction time is too short, they will take all the time and try to minimize risk by putting more resources on the project. If the required time is too long, they will shorten it, and maximize quality. However, the chance that one contractor will finish far ahead of their competitors is remote.

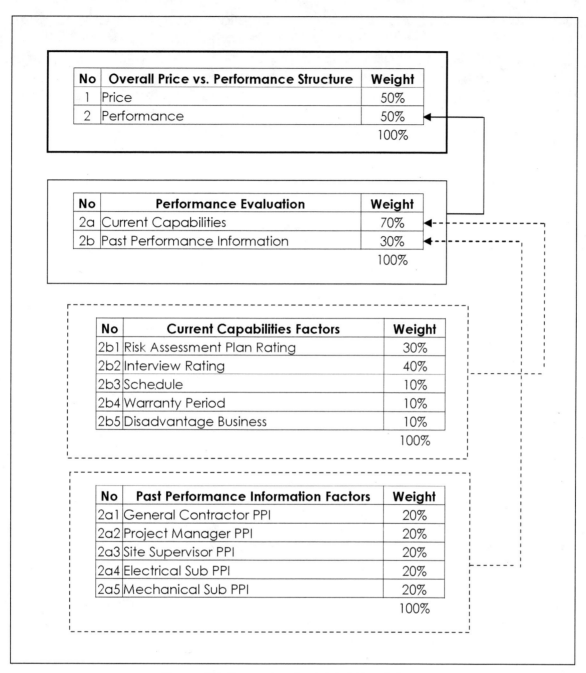

Figure 7.4: Example of a Weighting Scheme

If they do have a solution that will make a significant difference, it will be rated very highly in the risk assessment plan and the best value contractor option does not need the credit in the schedule. If the options are very close, and schedule is the differentiator, a small weight will still make an impact. The owner needs to understand that the model's prioritizing process takes the difference from the best number, the weighting factor, and the information factor (relative difference of the factor with all other factors) into consideration.

The risk assessment plan ratings will knock out anyone who cannot identify risk to the owner, minimize risk, and act in the best interest of the owner. The plans should have an impact on the selection, but is not the most influential factor. To be able to identify and manage risk is a requirement for a performing contractor. However, to have a person on the project that understands and can minimize the risk is even more important. If the key person does not understand, the person will have to be managed. If management of the project team is required by either the contractor or the owner, the system will be inefficient, value is minimized, and risk is increased, because it is not truly a "win-win" situation.

The interview should be rated the heaviest, because it provides the most information. The interview, described later in this chapter, is not a traditional "marketing and sales" interview where senior officers of the contracting company and marketing personnel give a marketing pitch. It is an in-depth look at the site superintendent or project manager's understanding or risk, minimization of risk, experience with like projects, and level of perception and ability to predict the future outcome.

Owners and contractors also worry about bias being introduced in the interview ratings. However, it is no longer in the best interest of the raters, because if the project results in nonperformance, they will be held accountable. Their names will be signed on the interview ratings, assessing the contractor's ability to identify and minimize risk, understand the project, and add value. If someone wanted to introduce bias in the interview rating, they would have to overturn the impact of the risk assessment plan rating and the past performance, while also convincing the other members of the rating team to do the same. Tests have shown that this is too difficult, too easy to identify, and not worth the risk of resulting nonperformance.

Listing of Budget Amount

The author highly encourages the listing of the project budget. If performance and price will be considered, the low bidder will gain points on price. They will not raise their price if given the budget. The higher their price, the less competitive they will become due to the high performance of the competitiors. The high performers will lower their price if they are given more information. High performers always minimize risk. Risk is when there is insufficient information. The less information a performer is given, the higher their price will be. The most critical information for a performer is expectation, budget, and time. If any of the three is missing, the performers will raise their price to cover their risk. By not giving the budget, the following results:

1. High performers are more affected and will raise their prices.
2. High performers are more likely to be over budget due to not knowing the budget.
3. Low performers will have the advantage. They do not minimize risk. They will pass it back to the owner.

Giving ranges of budgets is helpful, but not as effective as giving the budget. If the client feels uncertain about their budget, reduce by 10% and give the remainder as the budget.

Education Meeting

An example of the invitation to the education meeting is shown in Attachment 7.2. All critical contractors (contractors who bring risk and who are required to give references) should be invited to the meeting including the critical subcontractors. The author strongly recommends that the education meeting is mandatory for all contractors desiring to participate. Results of tests show that the subcontractors impact the performance of construction more than the general contractors. If clients do not invite the subcontractors, they will be increasing the risk of nonperformance. The general contractors may often suggest to the client that it is unnecessary to have the subcontractors educated and performance lined. This is in keeping with the status quo and should not surprise the client. They do not see it in their best interest to go to a PIPS system and lose their control over the project. The education meeting should cover the following:

1. Short PIPS explanation.
2. Performance data collection.
3. Introduction to the test project.
4. Schedule.

The objectives of the education meeting is to convey to the contractors the following concepts about PIPS:

1. This is not a price based process. It does not serve the contractor to minimize price at the expense of risk. Low price is a red flag!!!!!!!!!!!!!!
2. The competitive advantage will go to the performers.
3. The performers must minimize the risk of not being on time, not being on budget with change orders, and not meeting the quality expectations of the owner.
4. The client is going to use this information over and over.
5. If the contractor cannot minimize risk, they will be eliminated in the risk assessment and interview phase, or the pre-award phase.
6. If the contractor can compete and win based on performance, they will have to be able to manage their project by documenting and minimizing risk.
7. If they do not perform once, they will probably not have another chance.

PBSRG has presentations that can be given at the education meeting. The instructions are given on how to turn in the reference list and past performance information (Attachment 7.7). A roll is taken, and the contractors are invited to the prebid meeting.

Past Performance Information (PPI)

The objectives of the past performance information phase are to:

1. Communicate to the contractors that the owner will purchase best value based on performance and price, and not only on price.
2. Identify and attract the best performing construction personnel and craftspeople by giving credit to efficiency and performance.
3. Have the contractors identify their best references and collect the performance data from the references to show their best capability.

Past performance information identifies if a contractor has high performing personnel who have performed in past construction projects. Because all construction projects have unique characteristics and requirements, it is obvious that information other than past performance is required to ensure performance on a unique future construction project. Therefore, the past performance information does not have to directly relate to projects very similar to the current project being bid.

The Past Performance Information phase is the second phase in the PIPS process. Although some consider it a qualification phase, it is *not a qualification process*. *No contractor is disqualified or unable to bid* unless they do not meet the legal requirements to bid (insufficient bonding or lack of proper licenses). PIPS does not unfairly penalize contractors for lack of performance. It simply gives credit to contractors who have more experience.

Pre-qualification

PIPS is recommended as a one step process without pre-qualification. However, it can be run as a two-step process if that is the only available legal option. The two-step process uses a pre-qualification step, the advantages of which include:

1. Simplified process. Pre-qualification divides the collection of past performance information and the rating of current capability into two separate activities. This minimizes the possibility of contractors protesting about their past performance during the second phase or selection/award process of the procurement.
2. Minimization of paperwork. Pre-qualification reduces the administrative boilerplate material for each contract, compelling contractors to agree to and comply with the user's requirements.

Pre-qualification forces contractors to meet the following requirements during the pre-qualification stage:

1. Bonding.
2. Licensing.
3. Meeting all user boilerplate requirements.
4. Meeting minority, women-owned and small business requirements.

Identification of Past Performance References

There are various ways to identify past performance of a contractor or individual. Some of these options may include:

1. Surveying all projects done for a particular owner.
2. Selecting a random number of past projects (good and bad).
3. Surveying the last ten projects or the projects completed within the last two years.
4. Surveying only projects that are similar to the type of project being procured.
5. Allowing contractors to select their best references.

The client must remember the three basic rules of PIPS: minimize risk, minimize decision-making, and minimize the amount of work done by the user. The first four options above do not meet these rules (discussed later in this section). However, the last option, allowing contractors to select their best references, satisfies the three basic rules of PIPS. Therefore, based on IMT principles and PIPS test results, the author suggests contractors should be allowed to identify only their best performing projects. Many users may argue against this suggestion for the following reasons:

1. Contractors may submit jobs dissimilar to the type of job being bid.
2. The user may not receive a good representation about how well the contractor actually performs since the contractor chooses the best references and the majority of the contractor's jobs may have been very poor.
3. Contractors may submit jobs completed by previous crews who no longer work for the contractor. The majority of a contractor's current crews may perform poorly.

At first, these arguments may seem reasonable. However, once the PIPS process is understood, it is very easy to understand that the contractor who is selected as the best value can perform and is not affected by the above concerns. PIPS tests have been run allowing the contractor to select their own references. This places the contractor in the following position:

1. If they have never performed (on time (OT), on budget with no cost increase change orders (OB)), or meeting quality expectations of the owner), they will not be able to compete and make a reasonable profit.
2. If they don't have the personnel to perform on the project, they will not be competitive in their ability to identify and minimize risk and add value to the project. To stay in the competition would be costly and not successful.
3. If they buy the project (bid very low and make no profit), poor performance on the project would stop them from being competitive in the future. There would be no reason to work without profit when the result is that you will not get further work.

The difference between PIPS and the design-bid-build or any other process is that PIPS awards to the best value performer. All other processes require minimum qualifications. Minimum qualifications are always subjective, require regulation, are price based, motivate contractors to perform to the lowest possible level, and are time intensive.
By allowing the contractors to choose their references, the owner minimizes the following problems:

1. Deciding if the contractor or owner is at fault if a project did not result in performance.

2. Being accused of picking the wrong projects.
3. Being accused of not being fair with all the contractors.
4. Being questioned that the number of references required is too many or too little.
5. Clarifying any "bad" ratings.
6. Deciding if the reference is valid or not.

The owner instructs the contractors to:

1. Pick only their best references. Submit no references where there is a chance of disagreement on the performance of the contractor.
2. Call the references before submitting them to verify their performance.
3. The contractor should turn in at least one reference. However, because the objective of the process is to minimize risk, the process will give the advantage to those with more references and better performance ratings.
4. Once references are turned in, they will not be discarded. They will be used repeatedly in the future to select projects.

Users must understand that past performance is not the only contributing factor in contractor selection. The PIPS process is similar to understanding salmon as they make their annual trip to their spawning grounds. This will be discussed later in the chapter. The PIPS process puts the contractor at risk. The contractor must make the decisions. *The only avenue for a protest is that the contractor protests that the process is unfair because it gives a competitive advantage to performers and penalizes the non-performers.* PIPS is fair (treats all contractors alike), is impartial (allows the contractors to identify their own past performance), and very forgiving because it allows the contractors to turn in only the projects where all the conditions were optimal.

Contractors have three types of projects: successful projects, unsuccessful projects where the contractor is at fault, and unsuccessful projects where the owner is at fault. If the contractor is forced to submit jobs that may have been unsuccessful, the owner must clarify which party was at fault. Whatever the case may be, this forces the user to do more work and to make subjective decisions. Any time a decision is made, there is risk involved (Figure 7.5).

When selecting the best references, a contractor chooses from a population of:

1. Projects where the contractor performed (high performance (HP)).
2. Projects where something went wrong, and the contractor was responsible for the nonperformance (contractor fault (CF)).
3. Projects where something went wrong, and the owner was responsible due to the owner's direction, management, or inspection (owner fault (OF)).

Contractors whose "high performance projects"/(OF+CF) percentage is high will have the best competitive past performance based on the number of references and the scores of the references. Contractor D in Figure 7.5 will have the competitive edge based on past performance.

The ability to consider the number of past performance jobs and number of references is what makes PIPS different from all other systems. This consideration makes the contractors regulate themselves. For example, if a non-performing contractor wants to gain a competitive advantage using past performance, they are required to:

1. Submit as many references as possible (40 being the maximum that they get credit for).
2. Get high marks showing there is no doubt they have performed and the past owner wants them back.

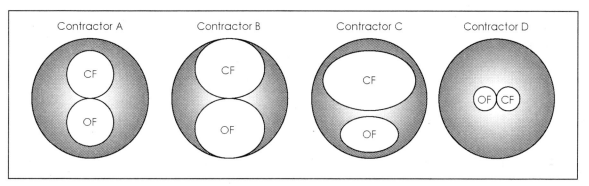

Figure 7.5: Four companies with different amounts of past performance information
Contractors B and C have a high number of poor performing jobs, either due to the contractor's fault (CF) or the owner's fault (OF). They cannot submit the same number of successful references as Contractor D can.

Contractors are carefully instructed to turn in only their best references. If a contractor attempts to turn in a large number of references to gain the competitive advantage, the contractor faces the risk of having lower numbers in all the other categories. Contractors should check with their references before they are submitted as a reference.

The objective of the references is to have the contractor show their optimal performance. If the contractor sends in references with sub optimal performance, they will lose the competitive advantage in past performance. There is no minimum number of references. However, if a contractor has no references, they will be severely penalized. A contractor should attempt to get one reference to turn in performance data. There is a maximum of 40 references that a contractor can turn in. However, many owners allow contractors to turn in more references at a future point in time.

Contractors with a limited number of performing personnel and high performance projects have a decision to make:

1. Do they turn in more references knowing that their average scores may go down? However, staying competitive in past performance will give them a chance in the current capability factors.
2. Do they stay with a low number of references, knowing that the model will identify them as not consistently doing high performance work?

How poorly a contractor does in any criteria depends on the competition. The contractor is placed in a position of making his or her own decisions. The contractor must put the best possible combination together.

Even though a contractor may not be eliminated by poor past performance, they will rarely win the bid. If the nonperforming contractor is able to compete in the project being bid, if they do not have absolutely the best performance numbers, they will not affect the presenter.

If a user's constraints prevent the contractor from selecting their best references, the PIPS process can still be modified to suit any requirement. However, based on the PIPS concepts, the user must keep in mind that the risk of the owner increases as the delivery system efficiency decreases.

In most general construction projects, the subcontractors are ultimately responsible for the quality of the work. A high performing general contractor with poor performing subcontractors may be as risky as a lower performing general contractor with high performing subcontractors. Both are required.

The relationship between the general contractor and the subcontractor is no different than the relationship between the owner and the contractor. This is another "win-lose" relationship, which may cause construction nonperformance and the instability of the industry. Any requirement to manage another party's performance leads to inefficiency, and it would have been better to pay more for performing subcontractors than trying to manage performance from cheaper subcontractors.

For large or complex projects, past performance information should be collected on all of the critical components. For example, on most large general construction projects, past performance is collected on the:

1. General contractor
2. Site Superintendent / Project manager
3. Electrical Subcontractor
4. Mechanical Subcontractor
5. Roofing/Waterproofing Subcontractor

These components may not be critical on every project since every project is unique. One of the benefits of collecting performance information on all critical components is to:

1. Ensure that all critical elements are made of performing groups and individuals, minimizing the risk of nonperformance.
2. When all elements have a performance rating, the owner can give all contractors the same rating at the end of the project. This makes everyone responsible for everyone else's work. It assists the project to have many eyes instead of just the general contractor's eyes.
3. It makes subcontractors motivated to do their work in a timely fashion.
4. It brings together a group of talented people who have pride.

5. The pride and knowledge of the general contractor and their subcontractors and key personnel is a synergistic relationship.

How to Collect Past Performance Information

The collection of past performance information is one of the largest modifications to the PIPS process. During the initial process, the user's representative:

1. Received a reference list (spreadsheet and hard copy) from the contractor (Attachment 7.7).
2. Verified the reference list and allowed contractors to correct the list.
3. Called all references and sent each an evaluation form to the end user.
4. Called each respondent twice if the evaluation form was not returned.
5. Formulated past performance line and provided the contractor with the overall past performance line but not with the individual responses.

This process resulted in an average return of over 70% of the submitted references. However, this also increased the amount of user's time and effort since:

1. Contractors and manufacturers who did not have the proper reference information took an inappropriately large percentage of the project manager's time. This forced the user's representatives to assist non-performers, conflicting with the logic of the process.
2. The time spent on relative non-performers created the perception of bias and unfairness.
3. The numerous iterations of reference lists became confusing and time consuming to manage.
4. The user's project manager became responsible for the references instead of the contractor. Contractors with a poor number of responses questioned whether the survey was sent to and received by the right reference, and whether they had been treated fairly.
5. Contractors claimed that the reference ratings were inaccurate due to the wrong person filling out the reference.

After seven years of testing, the process recommend by the author has changed. The following process has been implemented (See Figure 7.6):

1. At the education meeting or as part of the RFP, a reference rating form is given to the contractor, designer, manufacturer or any other element being rated.
2. Vendors submit a reference list to the user.
3. The vendor fills out the survey evaluation form with the project names, corresponding project number, and the point of contact of the reference, person and contractor being rated, and sends the form and cover letter to their reference.
4. The reference is then directed to send the form directly to the owner's representative running PIPS.
5. The user's project manager enters the reference's ratings.

6. Each vendor is given a copy of their overall performance ratings and which references have responded. The owner can also give the contractors the individual performance ratings.

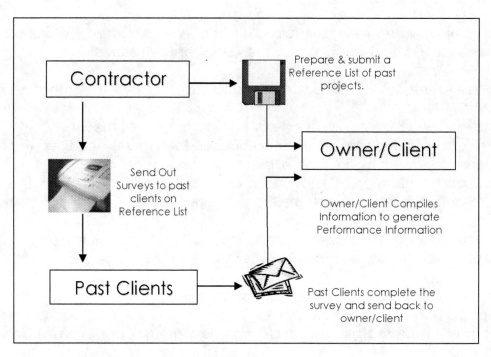

Fiaure 7.6: Collection of Past Performance Information

This has the following impact on the process:

1. Minimizes the project manager's efforts, which is the most time consuming part of the process.
2. Forces contractors to accept responsibility for their references.
3. Compels contractors to know and find out about their performance from their references.
4. Transfers the liability of data collection from the project manager to the contractor.
5. Prevents any discussion of the user's bias entering into the past performance numbers.
6. Defuses contractor protests and arguments about the inequity about the process.
7. Removes the doubt about whether the references were given a chance to vote.

This change is in line with the philosophy and objectives of PIPS and IMT and forces contractors to be aware of their performance. The only way that contractors can improve without outside regulation is by knowing their own performance, and improving their performance to increase their profit margins. Tests show that many contractors do not know their performance, and therefore require regulation by professional managers representing the owners.

The drawback to this process is that it has not been fully tested. Theoretically it should not decrease performance; however, until it is fully tested, it is only a hypothesis.

Therefore, the user has the option to execute the initial process, the proposed process, or any combination of the two processes. The conclusion is simple: if the process is more efficient, more logical, and minimizes management, the resulting value to the owner will be higher, and the profits of the contractor will be higher. An efficient and logical system will place the non-performing contractor at a competitive disadvantage.

The owner's representatives should only verify the references that put the owner at risk. This includes:

1. The winning contractor's team's references.
2. Any team that is close to the winner.
3. Any reference score that has a big impact on the spread of values.

Rating Past Performance of Contractors

The subjective rating of a contractor should range from a high of ten to a low of one. The author proposes that the rating system be very straightforward. The following rules apply:

1. If the owner has no questions about hiring the contractor again based on their performance, the rating should be a 10.
2. If the owner isn't sure about hiring the contractor again, the rating should be a 5 or somewhere in between.
3. If the owner does not want to hire the contractor again based on their performance, the rating should be a 1.

These instructions are given to all past references (Attachment 7.8). The contractor could also explain this verbally to the references. Many references will not give "10s." The contractor is responsible to pick owners that will give "10s" and other very high numbers, which show that the owners would hire the contractor back without any hesitation. This rating system has the following objectives:

1. It places the contractor who takes the job at risk. If the contractor who wins the project does poorly, the contractor must compete with all the other contractors who have high past performance ratings. If all other factors are equal, the contractor will not have a competitive advantage.
2. It makes it easy for the owner to reward the contractor for performance, and punitive for the non-performer. An "I don't know rating needs no justification."
3. It makes the contractor perform where performance is simply defined. For the contractor who wins the project, the contractor close out, weekly risk documentation, and minimizing the need for the client to get involved in the project become critical.

If 1-10 ratings cannot be used, whatever process is used (colors or descriptive words) are transformed into relative numbers and fed into the prioritization and information generation tool.

Pre-Bid Meeting

The client's representative can pass out the RFP at or after the education meeting. The prebid meeting is the next meeting and should be mandatory for general contractors and highly recommended for critical subcontractors. Over time, the high performance subcontractors will start attending the prebid meetings. If it is a very complicated project, which requires substantial work by a critical subcontractor, or where the risk in a certain area is high, it should be mandatory for the critical subcontractor to attend. The prebid meeting should include the following:

1. Brief project description by the designer.
2. Logistics, operational conditions, schedule, and clients in the area should be reviewed.
3. Q&A with the contractors on any information that the contractors may request.
4. A site walk if possible.
5. Quick review of the risk assessment plan requirements, the key personnel interviews, and the preaward phase for the selected contractors.

It is imperative that the contractors understand that the risk is being passed to the contractors to be minimized. The designer and client project manager is not minimizing the construction risk. It is also important that this is not a price based selection, even though price is important, will be considered, and may be the deciding factor if all contractors "look the same."

Capability to Perform the Required Construction

Past performance information reduces the field to performers without using minimum requirements. If contractors' past performance information shows nonperformance, and they wish to compete, they must first prove to themselves that they can perform by performing on projects and submitting new references. However, past performance does not match up performing contractors with their performing personnel and the unique project requirements. *To accomplish this using past performance information requires too much work, too much data, and too much management and maintenance of the information.*

Tests have shown that if past performance information is used without subjective translation, and past performance will be used in the final selection and affect their future competitiveness, contractors will bid a project only if they can provide the expertise and perform to provide a "win-win" (best value for the owner and profit for the contractor).

The combination of past performance, risk asssment, interview, and the responsibility to accept and minimize all the risk is an impossible task for nonperformers. Once the field is reduced to those contractors who can perform on the unique project, PIPS competes the contractors based on their current capability to identify, prioritize, and minimize risk (based on time, expectation, and budget). Only very experienced personnel and contractors will know how to add value based on efficiency, using performing materials and products, and coordination. The ability to minimize risk on the project is made up of the risk assessment plan rating and interview rating (Attachment 7.3). In each area, the criteria are the identification and minimization of risk, and how to add value to the project.

In specialized or one system retrofit areas such as roofing, painting, waterproofing, or mechanical divisions, the proposed value of system, which includes the perceived value of what is being offered, may also be factored into the current performance (see Chapter 15).

It is important to impress upon the contractors that if they do not have performance in past performance, risk assessment plan, and key personnel, the only way to get the project is by bidding low. And bidding low raises the flag of risk, will force the contractor to an even higher level of performance that will have to be documented by the contractor before they are awarded the project, and even then, the procurement agent may override their selection due to a perception that they are a nonperforming low bidder. PIPS makes it very difficult for a nonperforming contractor to make a profit.

It is important for the client to explain that they are interested in minimizing risk of construction nonperformance. The contractor who is prioritized best value must win the bid based on performance. If no one steps out ahead of the pack with exceptional performance, the process will force the client to make a decision based on price. The process controls nonperformance. The process' first objective is not to "totally and accurately identify the best value." It is to minimize the risk of nonperformance. And if no contractor is clearly the best value, the client's representative will select based on the minimization of risk (price based between the highest performers). This also means that a price based contractor, who is not within the highest identified values, will not be selected.

Bidding Phase

There are very few changes in the bid phase from the traditional process. The bid includes:

1. Legal requirements including bonding, insurance, and appropriate signatures.
2. Risk assessment plan without any names.
3. Price.
4. List of critical components including name of site superintendent, project manager, and critical subcontractors. This cannot be altered unless there are unforeseen conditions as determined by the owner.
5. General schedule including total number of construction days (total days).

Attachment 7.5 is an example of a cover sheet that the contractor should turn in with their bid. If any of the information is not submitted, or is incorrect, the bid should be identified as non-responsive.

The biggest difference with PIPS is the time between the bid and the award. Unlike the Quadrant I low bid award, where the low bidder is almost immediately identified, this process takes a couple of weeks to identify the top prioritized contractor, and another one to three weeks for the preaward phase before the contract is actually awarded.

The contractor's bid (risk assessment plan, legal documentations, and price) may be submitted in one package at one time for projects under $1M or with no critical subcontractor work. However, anytime the project exceeds $1M, or critical subcontractors are involved, the bid package should be submitted in two different submittals at least one week apart.

The first submittal will be composed of the legal documentation and the price. The second submittal is composed of the risk assessment plan. This process is required as the owner changes from a low bid award to a performance-based award. In the low bid environment, the subcontractors wait until the very last moment to turn in their bids to the general contractors. The general contractors do not know who their subcontractors are until the very last moment. Tests have shown that the contractors are still continuing this practice as they bid on performance based projects.

If the owner requires the risk assessment plan at the same time as the bid prices, the contractors will submit risk assessment plans with minimized value. For smaller projects or where the general contractor is a subcontractor (mechanical, electrical, or waterproofing contractor), the subcontractor already has the risk information they need.

If the contractors were already performance based, they would partner before the bid, and could easily submit a risk assessment plan. However, in many occasions the price basing of contractors is a difficult habit to overcome.

The bids should be received by a contracting personnel (no members that will be evaluating the proposals should receive the bids). A cover sheet should be removed from the risk assessment plan, and the risk assessment plan should be numbered. The numbered risk assessment plan is then reviewed and rated by the rating group. The risk assessment plan then is given back to the raters when the site superintendent and/or project manager are interviewed and rated.

The contractor is not permitted to switch any critical components without the user's approval. Any switches result in a financial penalty and if done before award, during the interviews, or during the pre-award period, will result in disqualification.

Value Added Features by Critical Subcontractors

There is a problem in the price based environment where a subcontractor may identify value added concepts and pass it along to the general contractor who they are bidding with. The general contractor then passes the ideas to a price based contractor, eliminating any competitive advantage of the performance based contractor.

In the PIPS process, all contractors can submit value added concepts directly to the client's representative before bid day. The concepts are reviewed, and the concepts that are not approved, are published to everyone. As a part of their bid to general contractors, critical subcontractors can now submit the added value of their bid (terms of $$$) plus their price. After being selected, the general contractors who hire the value added subcontractors can incorporate the concepts into their risk assessment plan.

Risk Assessment Plan

The risk assessment plan (RAP) includes five major components:

1. Identification of the risk of the contractor finishing on time, on budget, and meeting quality expectations.
2. Method of risk minimization.
3. Value Engineering (VE).
4. Cost breakout.
5. Construction schedule.

The entire document should be no longer than 2 pages for a design-bid, systems project such as roofing, waterproofing, painting, or modification. It should be no longer than ten pages for a $200M project. This is a high level business plan and should be concise, well organized, and showing an understanding of the magnitude of risk.

The contractors should understand that if all the plans are equal, no contractor has the advantage, and the decision will be based on past performance, interview of key personnel, and price. The review committee should not spend a lot of time on the evaluations. They are not technically based. They are only considering price, time, expectation, and added value. If a contractor submits a very promising risk assessment plan which cannot be accomplished, the contractor will be stopped in the interview. It is not an advantage to write something which cannot be substantiated. That is looked at by the review committee as the biggest form of risk and nonperformance. Also, anything submitted in the risk assessment plan (RAP or interview becomes a part of the contractor's contract.

The RAP should identify how the contractor knows that the risk is a risk, how the risk can be quantified in terms of cost, time, and quality, and how the contractor will minimize the risk. For example:

1. Commissioning is a problem. The contractor identifies that 4 out of 5 similar projects have commissioning problems. The site superintendent proposed has a record of

95% success with commissioning, is the contractor's expert in commissioning, and performed commissioning at five other recent projects.
2. The relative cost of a similar facility is $150/SF. The cost can be reduced by an accelerated schedule. These factors must be applied. The site superintendent has finished five similar projects, with the cost savings of $20/SF.

The RAP should not include technical terms, material technical descriptions, or means and methods unless it significantly affects the performance (time, cost, or quality) in a manner that can be supported by performance information. The risk assessment plan must:

1. Be concise. No more than two pages for retrofit projects under $1M, and two to five pages for larger projects.
2. Be well organized and clear.
3. Have a high-level business approach (VE should save at least five to ten percent of project cost).
4. Have *no names* (no marketing information or brochures).
5. Include a cost breakout showing major areas of relative expense.
6. Include a schedule expressed in time units in general stages.

The RAP should <u>not</u> contain any names or products that may be used to identify the contractor. The risk assessment plan's purpose is to create a blind rating to eliminate personal bias in the raters' scores. *The owner should clearly identify that the risk assessment plan should include no names (personal, company, brand, or construction projects).* The author suggests that risk assessment plans containing names should be identified as non-responsive. The risk assessment plan should contain a cover with the company information that can be removed by the user's representative.

The RAP identifies current capability. The author asserts that current capability is considerably more important than past performance for the following reasons:

1. The risk assessment plan identifies if the contractor has the right people, the right solution, and can do the unique project at a specific time.
2. All construction projects are unique. As similar as projects may seem, there are always major differentials in terms of critical staff, owner's staff and expectations, delivery schedule, extenuating circumstances, complexity, and subcontractor performance.
3. Contractors are asked to submit only their best references.
4. Contractor project manager and site superintendent may be different on the subject project.
5. Type of procurement: low-bid, negotiated, or performance-based. The type of procurement tremendously impacts performance.
6. Weighting the current capability more heavily than past performance compels contractors to submit their best personnel on the project.

Identification of Risk by the Contractor

What is risk? Risk deals with not being on time, within budget, and meeting customer satisfaction. It is when the owner is not satisfied with what was constructed for the amount of money and time spent constructing. In a performance-based environment, performance is minimizing the risk. If the contractor cannot satisfy the owner, the contractor should not accept the work. Risk can be described in other ways:

1. Lack of quality. There is a lack of performance information, specifically, customer satisfaction as well as delivery and quality problems.
2. Not perceiving the owner's expectations.
3. Risk of nonperformance on the job due to the lack of time and/or resources, or to special project constraints.
4. Problems on this type of project that cause other contractors problems.
5. The points to which a performing contractor has to pay particular attention to.
6. Differential with other contractors' proposals including performance periods, serviceability, required maintenance, and so forth.

Every project has risk. The only projects that do not have risk are projects where the owner has unlimited time and unlimited funding. The contractors have to analyze the construction project in terms of expectation, time, and cost. The owner wants the best possible performance (time and quality) within the cost constraint. *The owner wants non-technical information in terms of time, cost, and performance.*

The risk assessment plans will be collaborated by the interviews. The interview will be a time for the client's review team to:

1. Find out details of the risk assessment plan.
2. Determine if the key personnel have a clear understanding of the risk assessment plan.
3. Identify the expertise level of the key personnel based on their ability to predict, communicate, and handle stress.

The more perceptive and experienced contractors will be able to write the risk assessment plan clearly and concisely. There are many different ways to accomplish this. This can include:

1. Using an alternate system.
2. Using designers or manufacturer's representatives to look for alternative systems.
3. Utilizing the best project manager and site superintendent who have had similar projects including number of years, scope, and performance differentials with others in the company, and percent success.
4. Using a different or an innovative schedule.
5. Spending additional money to cover risk.
6. Trading off schedule vs. money vs. quality. The contractor must demonstrate the ability to work within the user's constraints.
7. Gaining more control of the delivery process from the client.

8. Minimizing the redundant paperwork and design requirements placed on the contractor.

An example of this happened on one of the first PIPS general construction projects. The University of Utah housing project (2002 Winter Olympics Housing Project) required the contractors to begin in March 1999 and finish in May 2001. The completion date was predicated as a result of the following University of Utah requirements:

1. Gain income from the housing before the Olympics to help defer the construction cost.
2. Open up needed housing for university students.
3. Correct construction deficiencies identified by the students before the athletes arrived for the Winter Olympics.

These are owner requirements. One of the contractors could not meet the schedule. This contractor proposed the substantial completion of the housing units and other buildings with completion of the landscaping a month later due to winter ending in March or April. The University rejected the bid for failing to meet their requirements. The contractor protested to the state, claimed that no contractor could install the landscaping until all the buildings were constructed and that the harsh Utah winter prevented the landscaping installation by May 2002.

Another contractor proposed to do the landscaping the year before, even though the building construction would not be complete and ready for landscaping. The contractor planned that some of the landscaping would be damaged by both on-going construction and the oncoming winter, and budgeted to have the damaged landscaping replaced. There was no time to do the entire landscaping by the scheduled completion date, but there was time to do replacement of damaged landscape. By allocating additional money for landscaping for damage control and replacement, the contractor could finish the landscaping by May 2002. This example showed how one contractor met the owner's requirements and minimized the user's risk. The other contractor stated that the user's requirement was invalid and could not be met.

In the PIPS environment, the user sets the constraints, and the contractors use their expertise to optimize the cost, the schedule, and the quality to meet the user's requirements. The contractors attempt to meet the user's requirements, but if the requirements are impossible to meet (due to a limitation of budget or time), the contractor will identify how to minimize the risk and still meet as many of the client's requirements as possible. The contractor must also identify the cost of the owner's requirements. This gives the owner the option to modify the intent and scope before the award and construction.

The biggest difference with PIPS is that the contractor and not the client's designer or project manager will minimize the construction risk. As described in Chapter 4: Construction Industry Structure (Figure 4.8) and Chapter Eight: Six Sigma Applications in Construction, the problem is solved by process and not by the client's representative's technical expertise. The process is to let the performing contractor minimize risk with expertise, instead of having engineering and design experts try to direct a price based contractor with minimal construction expertise how to minimize construction risk. Designers and engineers minimize design risk.

Additional Value

Contractors are accustomed to cutting corners in the existing price-based process and are not experienced in adding value (Kwok 1995). When bidding the project, the contractor must bid a base requirement. The base requirement must meet the owner's minimal intent. This is the base price. If the basic bid is not within the project budget, the contractor must identify the factors that drive them overbudget.

If the contractor is above the budget, and there are other contractors below the budget, the contractor above the budget should not be considered unless risk is identified that none of the contractors within budget can minimize. If the risks are identified (which forced the price above the budget), the contractor who is ranked the highest will be forced to minimize the risk identified by all of the contractors. If they cannot, the next highest prioritized option within the budget will be given the opportunity. If none of the other contractors below the budget can minimize the risk, the contractor who had identified the risk, will have the opportunity to either do the project at the increased price (above the budget), or do their proposed method of minimizing the risk and bringing the project within budget.

If the project cost is below the budget, the contractor should look at the work and identify items that would add value to the project. The additional items should have either additional costs or savings. The contractor should explain how much the owner is saving by having it done at the same time.

Contractors should apply the following checklist to ensure that they are communicating their value to the owner:

1. Does the basic bid stand alone? Will it perform to meet the owner's expectations?
2. Did the contractor bid the basic bid within budget? If not, does the contractor anticipate any competitors who can perform within the budget?
3. If the answer to the previous question is yes, the contractor must then identify the risk that will constrain performance. By identifying the risk all contractors will be forced to minimize the risk. By identifying risk, the contractor is regulating the performance of whoever is awarded the project.
4. Did the contractor identify risk; prioritize risk in terms of cost, time, and performance or quality?
5. Did the contractor identify how they know that the risks are valid?
6. Did the contractor define any construction activities or systems that other contractors may not perform because of the skill required or high expense (so the competitors are doing something of lesser quality)?
7. Did the contractor include requirements for the risk assessment plans, particularly identification and minimization of risk, value engineering, cost estimate, and schedule?

8. Did the contractor take a look at value engineering (VE), that is, what the contractor would do if it were the contractor's money? The contractor must remember that VE ideas must be substantial, meaning at least 5% of the project value.

The contractor must also keep in mind, that even though this is not a low bid environment, if there is a large differential in cost, and the contractor has not identified the differential in performance and value, the lower priced option will still get the project. *The contracts officer can always override the final selection model prioritization and select another contractor.* However, this is unlikely if the top prioritized contractor has differentiated their plan.

Rating the Risk Assessment Plan

The review committee is selected at the beginning of the procurement. The committee should be made of two or more individuals, depending on the owner's rules. The user of the building and the building owner's project manager should be on the committee. The risk assessment plan (RAP) review committee should be the same committee to rate the interviews. Members should rate the RAP's individually. Rating committee members should be briefed on how to rate the risk assessment plans. They should have the following explained to them:

1. The definition and purpose of a risk assessment plan.
2. The risk assessment plan should be a concise, well organized business plan.
3. It should include identification of risks, minimization of risks, prioritization of risk, and added value.
4. The RAP should prioritize the risk in terms of cost, time, and expectations.
5. It should be in non-technical terms.
6. It should identify differential.

The committee reviews and rates the risk assessment plans in terms of relativity. The author proposes that the reviewers do the following (Attachment 7.9):

1. Identify if any of the risk assessment plans identify the risk in terms of cost, time, and quality.
2. Identify if any of the contractors have prioritized the risk.
3. Identify if any of the contractors have differentiated themselves.
4. Pick the best RAP.
5. Put the RAPs in three piles: high quality, average, and do not meet requirements.
6. Give the average plans a 5, the good plans relatively higher ratings, and the not so good plans a 1-3 rating.
7. *If the raters cannot tell the difference, give all contractors a 5 rating. If there is a difference, go through the above procedure again.*
8. Do not spend a lot of time on the reviews. The plans should be concise, well organized, and will become a part of the contract. Do not try to make a decision if the contractor will do what is proposed. That will come out in the interview. Both will become part of the contract.

Raters should be told "Do not make decisions." If you don't know, it is all the same. Rate them all 5. there is nothing wrong with not knowing. PIPS has other steps that will take care of risk. Engineers and designers have a difficult time with not making decisions.

The RAP is an opportunity for differentiation. If they are all the same, it is not bad. Make the contractor step out. If the past performance of all the contractors is good, and the RAP is the same, it will go to the interview. The interview is the most revealing. If the interview is the same, than it will go to price. The more everything is the same, the more critical it becomes for the best value to have all good numbers. If any number is out of range, and all the other numbers are about the same, the contractor with any bad numbers will never win.

Handling of the Bid Documents

The PIPS project manager, procurement, or contracts individual should separate the risk assessment plans and the bid documents. They should perform the following:

1. Risk assessment plans should be reviewed for any names or proprietary information. If names are found, the procurement officer should identify the bid as non-responsive.
2. The risk assessment plans should then be marked with a number that corresponds to the contractor's bid. Anyone who knows a contractor's name in connection with a risk assessment plan cannot serve on the rating committee.
3. Each member of the rating committee should sign a form stating that the rater acknowledges no previous knowledge of any of the contractor's bid.

These instructions are very critical to the efficiency of the PIPS program. Past experience shows that if these instructions are not followed, the user's representative is placed under extreme stress and may not want to continue using the PIPS program.

Interviews

Interviews are not mandatory in the PIPS process. In some cases, the amount of risk minimized is not worth the user and contractor's time and effort, since risk is already minimized by the other steps in the PIPS process. However, for major, complex projects, the interview is a key component. The interviews are the most risk-minimizing component of the PIPS process. The factors to consider when deciding whether to interview the contractors are:

1. The number of bidders.
2. The amount of time in the bidding schedule.
3. The number of committee members and the time each member has to participate.
4. The amount of risk involved.
5. The complexity of the project.
6. The number of subcontractors involved.

7. The scope of the project in terms of price and value to the owner.

If there are too many bidders and the owner still wants to interview, a short listing can be created by running the DIM selection model (Chapter 10) and choosing the top five contractors. The top five can then be interviewed, and the interview scores can be input into the model and reprioritized.

The interview is one of the best mechanisms to minimize risk due to the following factors:

1. It is face to face. It is the most accurate method of measuring the differential of perception and expectation between the user's representatives and the critical personnel.
2. It is the best opportunity to implement IMT and identify the processing speed and experience of the critical personnel.
3. It provides a method of comparing the relative experience and capability of the best site superintendents and project managers.
4. It is easy to identify if the site superintendent and project manager is not experienced, performance-based, or customer driven.

A performance-based site superintendent has the following characteristics that becomes apparent during the interview:

1. Responds quickly and without hesitation to any technical or potential problem area.
2. Provides short, non-technical answers.
3. Minimizes the amount of work needed by the user.
4. Prioritizes risk.
5. Has a plan for each type of risk foreseen.
6. Gives the impression that he or she has already built the facility.
7. Is very comfortable being quizzed.
8. Understands that it is part of the job to minimize political risk, risk that is not related to construction performance.

Questions that should be asked in the interview include:

1. What is your background with the current company?
2. Why were you selected for the project?
3. What are the most critical components of the project?
4. What are the largest risks on the project?
5. How do you prioritize the risk?
6. How do you minimize the risk?
7. How do you know that they are risks?
8. How did you choose the subcontractors for this job?
9. How much information will you pass on to the user's representative?
10. What do you expect from the user's representative?
11. How is this project different from previous projects on which you have worked?

12. Are you uncomfortable managing the construction project and having no construction manager from the owner's side?
13. What are your company and individual goals on this project?
14. What will you do differently on this project from previous projects and why?
15. What are your strong points and weak points, and what are you doing to minimize your weak points?

The questions should be the same for all interviewed personnel. However, the owner's representatives should be allowed the freedom to ask further questions that force the interviewers to elaborate on their answers if the interviewers feel the site superintendents and project managers have not answered the question to their satisfaction. A sample question sheet is in Attachment 7.10.

Rating the Interview

Site superintendents and project managers should be interviewed alone. No other company person should be in attendance. The contractor's RAP should be their business plan. The interview serves as an opportunity to assess how well the site superintendent and/or project manager understand the risk assessment plan. It is also an opportunity to see how close their perception mirrors the risk assessment plan. The interview will also show their experience in doing the unique type of construction required. A sample interview-rating sheet is included in the attachments (Attachment 7.4).

The rating should be done in a similar manner to the risk assessment plan. An average site superintendent or project manager should be given a 5. A superior SS/PM should be given a 10. If a SS/PM is not desired, they should be given a 1. Ratings can be given between high, average, and low performers.

Rating members may change their ratings anytime during the interviews of any of the interviewed SS/PMs. If a rating member was not impressed with a specific person, but after interviewing all the SS/PMs feel that the first SS was the best SS by a large differential, the rater can change their score. The author encourages the raters to discuss strong points and weak points of all the SS/PMs interviewed, however should never discuss what ratings will be given.

All ratings should be individually done, and the same disclaimer should be signed off (that there was no collusion by the rater and that the ratings were not discussed with anyone else). The author also proposes that if an interviewer knows one of the SS/PMs, an additional rater be brought aboard if possible.

The PIPS administrator, who is not a rater, should also have the authority to drop specific ratings if the ratings seem out of line with the other ratings (20% differential from the average differential of the other raters).

The interview is the most critical information step. It should be weighted heavily. No contractor should be awarded a project without key personnel with great interview ratings. The best value should also have great risk assessment scores and great past performance. If the best value does not have the best interview score, the best RA plan, and good past performance, this should be identified as risk. If the price differential is great, and a lower value is selected based on price, this decision brings risk. If the price of the contractor is far below the average price of the other top performers, this can be identified as risk. Risk is when the contractor cannot make a decent profit and give the owner best value because their price is too low. When their price is too low, they cannot minimize risk as well. If this is the case, the price based contractor who is selected must have their plan down to the nth degree, because they do not have a lot of leeway for surprises or inefficiencies.

PIPS Modeling to Prioritize Best Value

The project manager inputs the following information into the Displaced Ideal Model (Chapter 10):

1. Prices.
2. Weights.
3. Past performance information.
4. Risk assessment plan ratings.
5. Interview ratings.
6. Other performance factors such as schedule, warranty, etc.

The model is run. If there are many bidders, the model can be run before the interviews take place to prioritize the top five bidders. The model will then be re-run with the interview scores of the five bidders.

The prioritized contractor prices are then compared with the budget. The project manager should do the following:

1. If the top rated contractor is below budget, the author proposes moving forward with the highest performing bidder.
2. If the top rated contractor is over budget, the author suggests selecting the next highest-rated contractor (that is within the budget).
3. If the top rated contractor is within budget, but has proposed a price that is considerably higher (over 10% higher than the next bidder), the author suggests awarding to the next bidder if the performance differential is very small.
4. If the top rated contractor is within budget, but has proposed a price that is considerably higher (over 10% higher than the next bidder), the author suggests awarding to that same bidder if the performance differential is very high. The owner must feel comfortable justifying this decision.
5. If all of the bidders are over budget, the user must subjectively choose the best value based upon factors such as:
    a. How much additional funding can be acquired?
    b. What is the difference in prices and performance?

Figure 7.7 shows the performance ranking of five different contractors. Contractors C and E are the two highest performers, but they are both over the owner's budget. Contractors A, B, and D are all under the budget. In this example, the author suggests that the owner should award to the 3rd contractor, Contractor A, since this contractor is the highest performing proposal within the owner's budget. Even though another proposal offers a better value, it is not the best value for the owner since the owner cannot afford it.

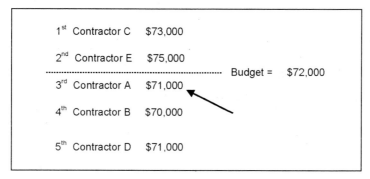

Figure 7.7: The contract should be awarded to Contractor A since this contractor is the highest performing proposal within the budget.

Figure 7.8 shows another example of five different contractors. In this example, the first ranked proposal is eliminated because it is over budget. The second ranked proposal is within budget. However, since this proposal is considerably more than the third ranked contractor (Contractor C, who has only slightly worse performance numbers), the owner should award to the third ranked contractor due to the political risk involved when trying to justify the substantial cost difference in relationship to the slight performance difference.

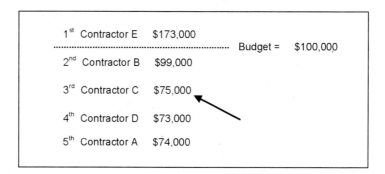

Figure 7.8: The contract should be awarded to Contractor C since the owner cannot justify the added cost of choosing Contractor B

After the best available value is identified, the pre-award period is setup.

Pre-Award Phase

The objective of PIPS is to:

1. Select the best value contractor who can minimimze the construction risk of the client.
2. Assist the best value contractor to minimize their risk of nonperformance.
3. Ensure that the contractor uses the best practices principle of reviewing the project in detail, minimizing any misconceptions and potential problems before construction.
4. Minimizing the need for the client to manage the contractor.

The pre-award phase has the following possibilities:

1. The best value contractor is a price based contractor who brings risk to the owner, and the preaward period will be used to minimize the risk.
2. The best value contractor is a performing contractor who needs to ensure that all risks are minimized to maximize their profit.
3. Forces the designer to address issues which should have been previously minimized.
4. Informs the client and their users of exactly what they are receiving.
5. Minimizes risk due to misunderstanding or not enough communication.

If a price based contractor is selected due to a low price, the contractor brings risk to the project. The contractor will have lower prices. The lower prices mean that the contractor's profit is minimal. They do not have the latitude to address contingency issues or surprises. This contractor must be forced to carefully analyze the project. This type of contractor needs to have a more effective preaward phase. All options must be analyzed. The contractor cannot afford to have problems.

The pre-award period is designed to shift all the construction performance risk to the contractor. If they are a performing contractor, they will know how to minimize the risk. The pre-award phase is very important for the contractor. It is their project to lose or forfeit. The objective of the pre-award period is to allow the contractor to verify that they can perform on the project and meet the users expectations. In traditional construction, too many times the designer, project manager, or contractor will want to dive into the construction, only to find out that better planning would have saved money and time. Diving into a project without having the construction experts review and coordinate with the designers results in confusion, non-performing work, and a lack of responsibility.

The author has seen designers convince an owner to start construction before the design was complete, only to see the designer use the ensuing confusion to absolve the design firm from incomplete work, irresponsible work, and complete lack of responsibility for cost and time control. The following activities should be accomplished by the contractor:

1. Coordinate the design and drawings with all critical participants.

2. Clarify all conflicting drawings and any construction that cannot be constructed. Force the designers to finish their design work.
3. Check the critical lead time items.
4. Identify what is required from the user.
5. Be able to minimize all risk identified in all the risk assessment plans.
6. Ensure that the contractor understands the contractor interface.
7. Introduce the contractor to the key user, owner, and project manager personnel. Confirm and understand their expectations. The contractor should communicate the risks and expectations on the project.

The pre-award phase could last two to three weeks. It should be culminated by a non-technical presentation by the project team to the user, owner, and owner's project manager. All questions by the user should be given to the contractor in advance. The pre-award presentation should be attended by:

1. The owner's project manager.
2. The contractor team and key critical components.
3. The designer.
4. The facility user.
5. The owner.

The project manager and site superintendent should control the meeting. They should review:

1. Construction team and reason for their selection.
2. Risk.
3. Minimization of risk.
4. Prioritization of risk in terms of time, money, and expectations.
5. Schedule.
6. Key roles of critical components.
7. Major systems.
8. Value added items.
9. Requirements and assistance of the user.
10. Construction interface.
11. Contractor/site superintendent/project manager goals.

The minutes of the meeting become a part of the contractor's contract. The author recommends that long lead time shop drawings and submittals be approved during this period. During the construction, the approval and turn around time becomes a serous issue. The general contractor coordinates the design drawings and specifications with all critical subcontractors, and identifies any inconsistencies (or areas of incomplete information) or other methods to increase the value of the construction. The purpose of the pre-award meeting is the finalization of all decision-making before construction, thereby minimizing decisions during construction and allowing the contractor to better plan and schedule the work.

Contractors must understand that they regulate the performance on the project. By identifying risks in risk assessment plans, a contractor forces all other contractors to minimize that risk. The contractor who receives the project is required to minimize all of the risk identified by the competing contractors. If a contractor perceives that another contractor may lower the price by not performing the "same" job, the contractor can force the low bidding contractor to perform the function by listing it in their risk assessment plan. This process quickly forces non-performing contractors to either perform or withdraw.

Contract

The construction contract should include the following:

1. The owner/designer's requirement and intent (design).
2. Design drawings and specifications with modifications.
3. Approved list of submittals.
4. Information interface format and frequency.
5. Contractor's final risk assessment plan.
6. Pre-award meeting minutes.
7. All clarification documentation.
8. Schedule.
9. Cost.
10. User's legal contract documents such as bonding, insurance, and so forth.

To minimize changes in the status quo prescriptive specifications, the contract may include the owner's general conditions with the statement that the owner can modify the general conditions to assist the contractor to perform in the best interest of the owner as determined by the owner's representative.

Construction

During construction, the owner, project manager, and designer's *objective is to assist the contractor to be successful.* If the contractor is a high performer, the work of the owner's representatives is minimized. If the contractor is less performing, the work of the owner's representative is increased. There are two options for the owner's representative:

1. If the contractor does not perform, penalize the contractor financially.
2. If the contractor does not perform, assist the contractor to become better performing.

Option 2 leads to the owner's representatives understanding how to bring change. The PIPS process environment will minimize the amount of work for the owner's representative. By working with the contractors, the owner's representatives will begin to understand that there is a difference among contractors. They will identify how this difference can be identified, and their understanding of IMT will increase.

The objective of PIPS is to deliver performance. Inspectors can still inspect; however, they should be more like facilitators. The contractor should make the majority of the decisions and should ask the opinion of the owner's representatives only when it involves information that the PM has, and which has not been given to the contractor.

Contractor Interface

The traditional approach to construction in Quadrant I is construction management and inspection. In this environment, users have attempted to implement "real time" information systems, where the construction manager (CM) or project manager (PM) can access the contractor's detail scheduling and financial information. The information is used to make decisions, and to manage the contractor.

The Quadrant II environment uses a different approach. Successful management occurs when a performer is hired, and the management of performers is minimized. Successful management is where the majority of time is spent minimizing the risk of non-performers. Performers and non-performers are managed differently. Performers need encouragement and are given the freedom to make their own decisions. Non-performers need to be told what to do because they do not know what to do. Therefore, when managing performers, the amount of information needs to be minimized, and when managing non-performers the amount of information needs to be maximized.

PIPS minimizes the number of non-performers. Therefore, the amount of non-performing contractor management is decreased. The system should be an optimal environment for high performing contractors. The information system environment has the following requirements:

1. Pass as little information as possible.
2. The information needs to be risk information (on time, on budget, change orders, and potential risks in terms of time, money, and performance)
3. The information needs to be kept and updated by the contractor every week.
4. The information needs to be processed in a way to identify the projects that are at risk.
5. The information needs to give a performance line of not only contractors, but also the entire owner's project management group.

The only purpose of the information is to identify and manage risk (not on time, on budget, or meeting the user's expectations). The job of performing construction is the job of the contractors and not the owner's PMs or CMs. Traditional management must be minimized.

The contractor interface (CI) documents (Attachment 25.1):

1. The schedule, and days ahead or behind.
2. The number of contractor generated change orders and dollar amount.

3. A short description of any change orders and who is responsible for the change orders.
4. The number of days that delayed the project due to the client, contractor, and suppliers.
5. A list of risks in terms of time, cost, and expectation (rated from 1 – 10, 10 being the highest.)

There are two numbers to keep track of besides the on-time, no contractor generated cost change orders, and no political problems with the users near the site. The first is the percentage of times the contractor turns in the CI on time at the end of the week. The other number is the percent of times the report is accurate.

The contractor who is awarded the project is at risk. This is because the contractor is evaluated on factors like communication. If the contractor does not respond 90% of the time and 90% correctly on their CI report, the contractor will get a very low score on their communication criteria. If all other contractors have high past performance rating in this area, the contractor may become noncompetitive in future projects. After all of the filters are applied, the chance of construction nonperformance is very minimal; but if a contractor does fail to perform, the post-project rating greatly impacts the possibility of that contractor receiving another job for that user. In other words, if a contractor does not perform, the chance of that contractor receiving another job is highly unlikely. This serves as a potent performance motivator.

The CI can be hooked up to the Information Environment (IE) system described in the Six Sigma chapter and shown in Figure 8.7. The purpose of the IE is to:

1. Give the head of a client's organization the critical risk information of all projects without any effort or participation from within the organization. The contractor who is at risk will submit the information directly to a database by email.
2. The risk information will identify the overall performance of the client's contractors.
3. Identify which projects have the most risk along with the project manager.
4. Motivate the working PMs to minimize the risk on their projects by hiring the best value, minimizing direction to those contractors, and check the lowest performing contractors to ensure their reports are turned in and correct.
5. Without any physical effort, the IE will influence everyone to do their job in an optimal way.

The role of the owner's representative will be more of leadership than management, more of educational than directional, and more of understanding risk than managing performance. This role will pass the risk to the contractor, result in improved performance, and allow the PM more time to continually optimize the process.

End of Project Ratings

All contractors and key personnel on the project are rated with the same rating. This creates a true team environment (everyone is responsible for everyone else on the site). It motivates cooperation and thinking about the group more than about their own company. It also regulates the selection of performing components by the general contractors, and encourages performing subcontractors to work with performing general contractors.

The issue of fairness was raised by a large facility owner's procurement agent. They did not want to penalize a general for a subcontractor's lack of safety practices. They felt more comfortable penalizing just the subcontractor. Doing this causes the following:

1. The general contractor does not feel responsible for the safety practices of the subcontractor.
2. The site superintendent is not concerned about the subcontractors' safety on the site.
3. Finger pointing occurs (the subcontractor blames another contractor for the mistake or accident).
4. The general contractor passes any problems back to the owner.

This is a performance based contract. The general contractor is at risk. They must minimize the risk by hiring performers. Whatever risk remains, must be minimized by proper management and cooperation between the contractors. Risk will not be minimized if the client allows the contractors to point fingers.

Unforeseen Conditions

Unforeseen conditions include:

1. Scope changes by the user.
2. Conditions that clearly could not be predicted.
3. Any conditions covered by insurance.

Updating Performance Information

The most important duty of the PIPS core team is to update and maintain the contractors' and manufacturers' performance information in the PIPS system and in the price based environment. The following data should be compiled:

1. Change order rates with and without PIPS.
2. Customer satisfaction ratings with and without PIPS.
3. Design costs with and without PIPS.
4. Project costs with and without PIPS.
5. Project performance with and without PIPS.

Performance Filters

A considerable difference between the PIPS process and other "best-value" systems is the ability of the process to filter out poorly performing contractors by natural selection. The goals of the PIPS environment are to minimize:

1. The need for experts.
2. The need for minimum standards.
3. The amount of user manpower necessary to run the system.
4. The number of user decisions.
5. The chance of any protests.
6. The amount of user effort.
7. The amount of resources (such as money and time).
8. The owner's risk.

Figure 7.9 and 7.10 show PIPS' "automatic" filters, which create an environment where the low performing contractors become noncompetitive. One of this system's substantial benefits is that the owner does not need to make a subjective decision on whether a contractor should be eliminated, reducing the risk of any protest. The system does not require pre-qualification filters. Contractors make their own decision to drop out due to their inability to compete in this performance environment. A nonperforming contractor can remain in the system, however they will be noncompetitive.

Each filter in the PIPS process acts like a sieve, gradually passing more and more of the risk and liability to the contractor. The chance of selecting a non-performing contractor becomes smaller and smaller. At the end of the process, the best value (or the highest performance for the best price) is comfortable accepting all of the risk for the project. The process filters include:

1. Education and Past Performance Information (PPI).
2. Risk assessment plan and any project manager interviews.
3. Competition based on price and performance.
4. Pre-Award meeting and an understanding of the post-project rating.

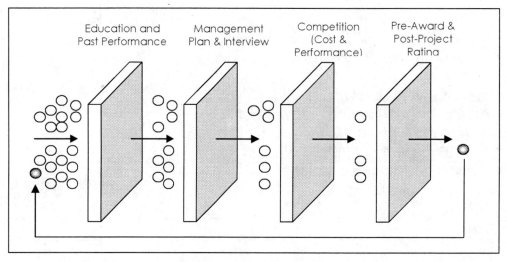

Figure 7.9: Poor performing contractors gradually withdraw from the process due to the various filters, ensuring success.

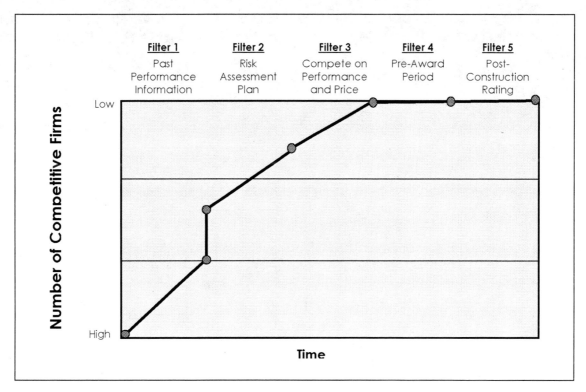

Figure 7.10: PIPS Performance Filters

Similarity to Salmon

The PIPS process can be compared to salmon as they make their annual trip to their spawning grounds. The salmon's journey is an uphill battle, and if performance is defined by reaching the spawning grounds, the performers must be strong, skilled, and lucky. The salmon is always at risk. If they do not reach the spawning grounds, it doesn't matter what the reason was, the end result is that they do not reach the spawning grounds and cannot participate in the reproduction of more salmon.

PIPS is very similar to the journey of the salmon. Like nature, it doesn't care why some contractors don't make it to the final competition. The contractor may have poor past performance, may not have the right personnel, may not be able to construct as efficiently as the next contractor, or may not have the proper experience to identify and minimize risk. PIPS is like a river. At a certain point, there are only so many salmon left. There is one major difference. The owner using PIPS to outsource construction can give the contractors information about the difficulty or risk, how long it will take, the expectation, and the probability of repeat work. This helps contractors to know if they should compete. This makes the overall system efficient, as contractors do not waste effort if they do not see a high probability of success.

PIPS ensures that the contractor performs construction in a logical manner by forcing the contractor to understand the project before it is constructed. It forces the contractor to assign personnel and subcontractors to the project that can perform. Previous PIPS tests identified that poorly performing contractors are uncomfortable participating in this logical approach. Contractors with a nonperformance objective usually feel very uncomfortable and leave the process. However, if a non-performing contractor does receive the project, the project risk is no worse than the risk of a low bid project.

Frequently Made Mistakes

The following is a list of frequent mistakes made by PIPS users:

1. Forming personal relationships with perceived performing contractors. When errors occur, the contractors then force the facilities group to share or accept the brunt of the liability.
2. Making allowances for contractors who have the right intent but do not meet the requirements. This transfers the risk to the owner. Tests show the non-performer consumes a disproportionate percentage of the owner's time. This function of educating and assisting the non-performer belongs to the construction industry.
3. Attempting to give poor performing contractors a chance. This is subjective and causes risk to the owner. The owner makes two decisions. Firstly, the contractor is non-performing, and secondly, the non-performing contractor must be given a chance. Both are poor decisions.
4. Failing to document questions and answers. Documentation of information is the key. The owner should maintain a list of frequently asked questions (FAQ).
5. Failing to document education sessions. Educational sessions should be held quarterly to educate project managers, contractors, and designers on the process.
6. Becoming an expert and modifying the process. PIPS project managers sometimes take credit for the performance and begin changing the process. All changes to the process must satisfy the objectives of PIPS to ensure performance.
7. Changing the structure of PIPS to improve performance. The overall structure of PIPS should not be changed. However, policy changes and changes in weights and in performance criteria can be modified to increase value.
8. Not performing as a core team and not knowing core team performance (Chapter 14).
9. Employing personnel who are not a part of the core team to implement PIPS without proper education. Personnel who are not educated and trained should not participate in PIPS. The PIPS is designed to minimize management and inspection, allowing cradle-to-grave construction management.
10. Attempting to implement the process too quickly which can cause an uneducated team to overlook key steps in the process.
11. Not documenting the results of the PIPS projects in comparison to the user's past procurement using existing methods.
12. Not educating contractors and staff members on a consistent basis.
13. Taking personal credit for the performance of contractors under the system.
14. Not forming an industry support group of performers who can assist in auditing the performance information.
15. Awarding to the price based contractor without minimizing the risk by requiring a very complete preaward meeting final report.

Chapter 7 Review

1. What does PIPS stand for?
2. What is PIPS?
3. What is different about PIPS?
4. Draw the PIPS filter chart.
5. What does the PIPS filter chart show?
6. Does PIPS require contractors to submit all jobs done for the owner? Why?
7. Does PIPS require contractors to submit their last 10 jobs? Why?
8. Does PIPS require contractors to submit jobs similar to the one being bid? Why?
9. Does PIPS require contractors to submit all jobs, and then randomly inspect 5? Why?
10. Does PIPS require contractors to submit their best projects? Why?
11. Illustrate how this requirement gives an advantage to high performing contractors.
12. Can a contractor get past clients to make up good ratings for them? Does it matter? Why?
13. What is an education meeting?
14. How does the data collection process work? (Illustrate)
15. What is the purpose of the risk assessment plan?
16. What should/shouldn't the risk assessment plan contain?
17. What is the pre-award period?
18. What is measured and when?
19. How is value measured?
20. Who regulates the value?

Reference

Kwok, A. (1995, June 3). Audit: City Cleaning Firms Washed Up. *The Arizona Republic,* Valley Section.

Attachments

Attachment 7.1:
> Attachment 7.1a: Design-Build Schedule
> Attachment 7.1b: DBB Schedule (Large or Complex Projects)
> Attachment 7.1c: DBB Schedule (Small or Simple Projects)
> Attachment 7.1d: Fast-Track Schedule

Attachment 7.2: Advertisement / Announcement Example

Attachment 7.3: Risk Assessment Plan Rating Sheet

Attachment 7.4: Interview Rating Sheet

Attachment 7.5: Contract Cover Sheet

Attachment 7.6: Performance Criteria

Attachment 7.7: Data Collection (How to Prepare For a Survey)

Attachment 7.8: Roof Survey Form Example

Attachment 7.9: Example Request for Proposal (RFP)

Attachment 7.10: Sample Interview Question Sheet

Attachment 7.1a: Design-Build Schedule

NO	TASK	DURATION	START	FINISH
1	SETUP PHASE	6 days	11/01/02	11/08/02
2	Advertisement	5 days	11/01/02	11/07/02
3	Registry Meeting	1 day	11/08/02	11/08/02
4	DESIGN BUILD PHASE I QUALIFICATION	23 days	11/11/02	12/11/02
5	Companies prepare reference list	5 days	11/11/02	11/15/02
6	Companies submit lists to the User	1 day	11/18/02	11/18/02
7	Data Collection	10 days	11/19/02	12/02/02
8	Past Performance Line Generated	1 day	12/03/02	12/03/02
9	All data put into modified DIM	1 day	12/04/02	12/04/02
10	Contractors are Prioritized	1 day	12/04/02	12/04/02
11	PO Selects Top 5 Contractors	1 day	12/04/02	12/04/02
12	Pre Bid Meeting Notice	5 days	12/05/02	12/11/02
13	DESIGN BUILD PHASE II SELECTION & AWARD	15 days	12/12/02	01/01/03
14	Pre Bid Meeting	1 day	12/12/02	12/12/02
15	Contractors Prepare Bids	5 days	12/13/02	12/19/02
16	Contractors Prepare Management Plans	5 days	12/13/02	12/19/02
17	Contractors Submit Bids	1 day	12/20/02	12/20/02
18	Contractors Submit Management Plans	1 day	12/20/02	12/20/02
19	User Rates Management Plans	1 day	12/23/02	12/23/02
20	All data put into modified DIM	1 day	12/23/02	12/23/02
21	Contractors are Prioritized	1 day	12/23/02	12/23/02
22	PO Selects Best Value	1 day	12/24/02	12/24/02
23	Pre Award Period	3 days	12/25/02	12/27/02
24	Pre Award Meeting	1 day	12/30/02	12/30/02
25	Final Paperwork	1 day	12/31/02	12/31/02
26	Award	1 day	01/01/03	01/01/03

TOTAL   44 Days

Attachment 7.1b: Design-Bid-Build Schedule (Large or Complex Projects)

NO	TASK	DURATION	START	FINISH
1	SETUP PHASE	11 days	11/01/02	11/15/02
2	Advertisement	10 days	11/01/02	11/14/02
3	Registry Meeting	1 day	11/15/02	11/15/02
4	Pre Bid Meeting Notice	1 day	11/15/02	11/15/02
5	PAST PERFORMANCE INFORMATION PHASE	17 days	11/18/02	12/10/02
6	Companies prepare reference list	5 days	11/18/02	11/22/02
7	Companies submit lists to the User	1 day	11/25/02	11/25/02
8	Data Collection	10 days	11/26/02	12/09/02
9	Past Performance Line Generated	1 day	12/10/02	12/10/02
10	BIDDING PHASE	21 days	12/11/02	01/08/03
11	Pre Bid Meeting	1 day	12/11/02	12/11/02
12	Contractors Prepare Bids	10 days	12/12/02	12/25/02
13	Contractors Prepare Management Plans	15 days	12/12/02	01/01/03
14	Contractors Submit Bids	1 day	12/26/02	12/26/02
15	Contractors Submit Management Plans	1 day	01/02/03	01/02/03
16	User Rates Management Plans	1 day	01/03/03	01/03/03
17	Key Personnel Interview	2 days	01/06/03	01/07/03
18	User Rates Interviews	1 day	01/08/03	01/08/03
19	SELECTION PHASE	10 days	01/09/03	01/22/03
20	All data put into DIM	1 day	01/09/03	01/09/03
21	Contractors are Prioritized	1 day	01/09/03	01/09/03
22	PO Selects Best Value	1 day	01/09/03	01/09/03
23	Pre Award Period	5 days	01/10/03	01/16/03
24	Pre Award Meeting	1 day	01/17/03	01/17/03
25	Final Paperwork	2 days	01/20/03	01/21/03
26	Award	1 day	01/22/03	01/22/03

TOTAL 59 Days

Attachment 7.1c: Design-Bid-Build Schedule (Small or Simple Projects*)

NO	TASK	DURATION	START	FINISH
1	SETUP PHASE	11 days	11/01/02	11/15/02
2	Advertisement	10 days	11/01/02	11/14/02
3	Registry Meeting	1 day	11/15/02	11/15/02
4	Pre Bid Meeting Notice	1 day	11/15/02	11/15/02
5	PAST PERFORMANCE INFORMATION PHASE	17 days	11/18/02	12/10/02
6	Companies prepare reference list	5 days	11/18/02	11/22/02
7	Companies submit lists to the User	1 day	11/25/02	11/25/02
8	Data Collection	10 days	11/26/02	12/09/02
9	Past Performance Line Generated	1 day	12/10/02	12/10/02
10	BIDDING PHASE	13 days	12/11/02	12/27/02
11	Pre Bid Meeting	1 day	12/11/02	12/11/02
12	Contractors Prepare Bids	10 days	12/12/02	12/25/02
13	Contractors Prepare Management Plans	10 days	12/12/02	12/25/02
14	Contractors Submit Bids	1 day	12/26/02	12/26/02
15	Contractors Submit Management Plans	1 day	12/26/02	12/26/02
16	User Rates Management Plans	1 day	12/27/02	12/27/02
17	SELECTION PHASE	10 days	11/01/02	11/14/02
18	All data put into DIM	1 day	11/01/02	11/01/02
19	Contractors are Prioritized	1 day	11/01/02	11/01/02
20	PO Selects Best Value	1 day	11/01/02	11/01/02
21	Pre Award Period	5 days	11/04/02	11/08/02
22	Pre Award Meeting	1 day	11/11/02	11/11/02
23	Final Paperwork	2 days	11/12/02	11/13/02
24	Award	1 day	11/14/02	11/14/02

TOTAL 51 Days

*For small or less complex projects, the key personnel interviews are not necessary.

Attachment 7.1d: Fast-Track Schedule*

NO	TASK	DURATION	START	FINISH
1	SETUP PHASE	6 days	11/01/02	11/08/02
2	Advertisement	5 days	11/01/02	11/07/02
3	Registry Meeting	1 day	11/08/02	11/08/02
4	Pre Bid Meeting Notice	1 day	11/08/02	11/08/02
5	PAST PERFORMANCE INFORMATION PHASE	0 days	11/08/02	11/08/02
6	Companies prepare reference list	0 days	11/08/02	11/08/02
7	Companies submit lists to the User	0 days	11/08/02	11/08/02
8	Data Collection	0 days	11/08/02	11/08/02
9	Past Performance Line Generated	0 days	11/08/02	11/08/02
10	BIDDING PHASE	8 days	11/11/02	11/20/02
11	Pre Bid Meeting	1 day	11/11/02	11/11/02
12	Contractors Prepare Bids	5 days	11/12/02	11/18/02
13	Contractors Prepare Management Plans	5 days	11/12/02	11/18/02
14	Contractors Submit Bids	1 day	11/19/02	11/19/02
15	Contractors Submit Management Plans	1 day	11/19/02	11/19/02
16	User Rates Management Plans	1 day	11/20/02	11/20/02
17	SELECTION PHASE	6 days	11/01/02	11/08/02
18	All data put into DIM	1 day	11/01/02	11/01/02
19	Contractors are Prioritized	1 day	11/01/02	11/01/02
20	PO Selects Best Value	1 day	11/01/02	11/01/02
21	Pre Award Period	2 days	11/04/02	11/05/02
22	Pre Award Meeting	1 day	11/06/02	11/06/02
23	Final Paperwork	1 day	11/07/02	11/07/02
24	Award	1 day	11/08/02	11/08/02

TOTAL   20 Days

*Assumes that the initial performance lines have been collected.

Attachment 7.2: Advertisement / Announcement Example

NOTICE TO PROPOSERS

The <Owner's Name> is soliciting qualified contractors for <Job Name>. Written notice of intention to propose is due by <Due Date, Time>. Intention to propose via FAX <Fax Number> is acceptable.

The project will be awarded using a best-value procurement process. Under this process, the bidder will propose a roofing system it will install, and guarantee the performance of the system for a stated period during which it will make all necessary repairs and touch-ups. The process considers price, past performance history, and risk management in the selection of a successful proposal.

An educational meeting will be held on <Date of educational meeting> to discuss the award process and project requirements. Vendors (contractors and manufacturers) are highly encouraged to attend this meeting. The meeting will be held at: <Time of Meeting, Date of meeting> at the <Location of Meeting and Address>.

Only proposals submitted by vendors with the necessary contractor licenses and who fulfill all of the requirements will be considered. The <Owner's Name> reserves the right to reject any or all bids, proposals, statements, and to waive technicalities.

Attachment 7.3: Risk Assessment Plan Rating Sheet

Instructions:

The risk assessment plan should <u>not</u> contain any names or products that may be used to identify who the contractor is. If the plan does contain any proprietary information, the plan should be disqualified.

Plans that contain any technical terms, any means and methods (unless it affects the performance in a significant manner), or any material technical descriptions should receive low ratings.

Criteria are rated on a scale of 1-10, with 10 being the best and 1 being the worst. All plans should start from an average (or 5 rating) and go up and down depending on the relative value. If a plan stands out it should get a 10. If none of them seem any different, they should all get an average score of 5. If a plan is so bad that the rater feels like they should not get the project, they should be rated a 1.

Rating:

NO	CRITERIA	ALTERNATIVES				
		1	2	3	4	5
1	Structure of the Plan (Organized, concise, brief, and added value)					
2	Identification of Risk Areas (In terms of cost, schedule, and quality)					
3	Plan to Minimize Risk					
4	Increase of Value (Cost reduction or added quality)					

Total Points _____

Average Score _____

By signing your name below, you state that you have based your scores on the contents of each management plan and that you have had no prior knowledge of any and whom they belong too. You further agree that there is no collusion or conflict of interest between yourself and any other party involved.

Name: _____   Date: _____

Attachment 7.4: Interview Rating Sheet

Interview Rating Sheet

Instructions:

Personnel should be rated based on the manner in which they respond to questions. They should be quick, concise, and give the impression that they have already built the facility.

The interview criteria are rated on a scale of 1-10, with 10 being the best and 1 being the worst. If an interview stands out, they should get a score of 10. If they don't seem to stand out they should get an average score of 5. If the interview is so bad that the rater feels like they should not get the project, they should be rated a 1.

Rating:

NO	CRITERIA	ALTERNATIVES				
		1	2	3	4	5
1	Ability to understand the risk assessment plan					
2	Identification and minimization of risk (In terms of schedule, cost, and quality)					
3	Identifying the critical components of the job					
4	Identifying how the entire team was selected (Why subs, and key personnel were chosen)					
5	Identifying what activities will be done differently					
6	Comfort level of getting the job done					
7	Ability to use a construction interface (Only passing critical information just in time)					

Total Points _____

Average Score _____

By signing your name below, you state that you have based your scores on the contents of interview. You further agree that there is no collusion or conflict of interest between yourself and any other party involved.

Name: _____   Date: _____

Attachment 7.5: Contract Cover Sheet

Contract Cover Sheet

The contractor agrees to perform all work as specified in the following documents:

1. The Request For Proposal (along with any addendum).
2. The Contractors Bid Proposal.
3. The Contractors Risk Assessment Plan.
4. The Pre-Bid Meeting Minutes.
5. The Pre-Award Meeting Minutes.
6. (Any other user issued document/requirement)

The contractor agrees to perform all the work mentioned (in the above mentioned documents) at the price and the duration submitted in their bid proposal.

The total lump sum cost submitted in their bid
proposal is: $ _____

The total construction duration submitted in their bid
proposal is: _____ Days (Calendar)

Contractor Team

     General Contractor   _____

     Site Superintendant   _____

     Project Manager   _____

     Electrical Sub   _____

     Mechanical Sub   _____

     Roofing Sub   _____

     Waterproofing Sub   _____

This bid package includes:

     ☐ Risk Assesment Plan
     ☐ Cost Breakouts
     ☐ Bid Bonds/Insurance

The Contractor accepts full responsibility for delivering this project as intended by the owner (delivering on-time, within budget, and meeting the quality requirements). The owner will not accept any change orders except for changes in scope or unforeseen events (as determined by the owner).

_____   ___/___/_____

Contractor Name: Date:

_____   _____

Name of President / Owner: Signature of President / Owner:

Attachment 7.6: Performance Criteria

NO	CRITERIA	UNIT
1	Ability to manage the project cost (minimize change orders)	(1-10)
2	Ability to maintain project schedule (complete on-time or early)	(1-10)
3	Quality of workmanship	(1-10)
4	Professionalism and ability to manage (includes responses and prompt payment to suppliers and subcontractors)	(1-10)
5	Close out process (no punch list upon turnover, warranties, as-builts, operating manuals, tax clearance, etc. submitted promptly)	(1-10)
6	Communication, explanation of risk, and documentation (construction interface completed on time)	(1-10)
7	Ability to follow the users rules, regulations, and requirements (housekeeping, safety, etc...)	(1-10)
8	Overall customer satisfaction and hiring again based on performance (comfort level in hiring contractor again)	(1-10)
9	Total number of different jobs	(#)
10	Total number of different customers	(#)

Attachment 7.7: Data Collection

"How To Prepare For A Performance Survey"

Overview

The objective of this process is to identify the past performance of a vendor. This is accomplished by sending customer evaluation survey forms to past users (a maximum of 50 different projects will be evaluated). The users will return the forms, and the ratings will be averaged together to obtain a company's past performance information rating.

This is a deliberate process. The better organized you are the smoother the inspection will go. Continuous and clear communication is the key. If you have any questions please send an email to the point of contact below. *No phone calls, please.*

ORGANIZATION: <Name of Organization>
CONTACT: <Contact Name>
EMAIL: <Contact Email Address>

Guidelines

1. The data <u>must</u> be submitted on an Excel spreadsheet. (No word-processing documents or databases!) The data must be complete and accurate.
2. The points of contact, telephone numbers, and fax numbers need to be verified prior to submission. Please call all of your references ahead of time to let them know that they will be receiving a survey evaluation. You should make all of your references aware of the importance of the survey and the importance of receiving a high rating.
3. When you are done compiling your data, you will be required to <u>email</u> the file to purchasing@calhigh.org.
4. *The vendor is responsible for obtaining confirmation from Contract Services stating that the file was received.*
5. *The vendor is responsible for sending a survey form to all of their references and making sure that the references return the survey to the owner.*

Vendor Profile

We must have all the information in order to be qualified.

1. Are you a Contractor or Manufacturer   _____
2. Company Name: _____
3. Office Address, City, State, Zip: _____
4. Point of Contact: _____
5. Phone Number: _____
6. Fax Number: _____
7. Email: _____

Reference / Project Information

The following fields should be entered in a spreadsheet file. We must have all the information in order to be considered for qualification. <u>All fields are required!</u> If you do not submit all the information required, there will be no credit given for the reference!

Reference Information:

POINT OF CONTACT	Person who will answer customer satisfaction questions about your company and about the roof that was installed.
COMPANY	Name of the company where the point of contact is employed.
PHONE NUMBER	Point of contacts current phone number (including area code).
FAX NUMBER	Point of contacts current fax number (including area code).

Project Information:

USER NAME	Name of the company or institution that purchased the system (i.e. Cactus School District, Rock Industries, City of Austin).
BUILDING NAME	Name given to the building (Bird High School A-Wing, Warehouse B, etc.).
STREET ADDRESS	Street address of the building. (135 East Campbell)
CITY	What city is the building located in? (Phoenix)
STATE	What state is the building in?
ZIP	What is the zip code?
DATE INSTALLED	Date when the roof was completed. It must be a four-digit year. *Please enter DD/MM/YYYY.*
SIZE	What was the cost of the project? (55000)

Example

	A	B	C	D	E	F	G	H	I	J	K	L	M
1	NO	CONTACT	COMPANY	PHONE	FAX	USER	BUILDING	STREET	CITY	STATE	ZIP	DATE	SIZE
2	1	Joe Smith	ASU	5555689887	5559865454	ASU	Enginnering	123 Orange St.	Temp	AZ	85018	11/15/2001	68000
3	2	Sue Robets	ABC Inc	6549873216	6853216541	Delta	Warehouse	38 N Maple	Phoenix	AZ	85285	12/18/1997	32000
4													
5													

Attachment 7.8: Roof Survey Form Example

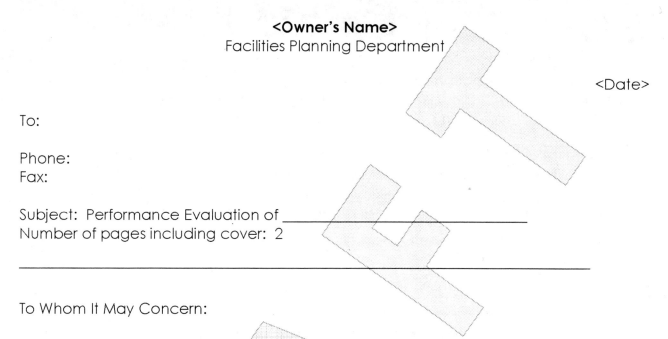

\<Owner's Name\>
Facilities Planning Department

\<Date\>

To:

Phone:
Fax:

Subject: Performance Evaluation of _____
Number of pages including cover: 2

To Whom It May Concern:

\<Owner's Name\> has implemented a process that collects past performance information on various roofing contractors and manufacturers. The information will be used to assist \<Owner's Name\> in the procurement of various roofing projects.

The company listed above has chosen to participate in this program. They have listed you as a past client that they have done work for.   Both the company and \<Owner's Name\> would greatly appreciate you taking a few minutes out of your busy day to complete the accompanying questionnaire.

Please review all items in the following attachment and answer the questions to the best of your knowledge. If you cannot answer a particular question, please leave it blank. Please return this questionnaire to us by \<Date Deadline for Surveys\>.

Thank you for your time and effort.

\<Contact for the Owner\>
\<Owner's Name\>

Contractor Name: _____

Point of
Contact: _____

Please evaluate the performance of the contractor (10 means you are very satisfied and have no questions about hiring them again, 5 is if you don't know and 1 is if you would never hire them again because of very poor performance).

NO	CRITERIA	UNIT	
1	Ability to manage the project cost (minimize change orders)	(1-10)	
2	Ability to maintain project schedule (complete on-time or early)	(1-10)	
3	Quality of workmanship	(1-10)	
4	Professionalism and ability to manage (includes responses and prompt payment to suppliers and subcontractors)	(1-10)	
5	Close out process (no punch list upon turnover, warranties, as-builts, operating manuals, tax clearance, etc. submitted promptly)	(1-10)	
6	Communication, explanation of risk, and documentation (construction interface completed on time)	(1-10)	
7	Ability to follow the users rules, regulations, and requirements (housekeeping, safety, etc...)	(1-10)	
8	Overall customer satisfaction and hiring again based on performance (comfort level in hiring contractor again)	(1-10)	

Please evaluate the performance of each roof identified below (if the owner will be evaluating more than one roof, please make a copy the section below for each roof to evaluate):

User Name: _____   Date
                                        Installed: _____

Building Name: _____ Roof Area: _____

NO	CRITERIA	UNIT	
1	Has the roof ever leaked since the contractor installed it?	Circle	Y / N
2	If the roof leaked, was it repaired?	Circle	Y / N
3	Does someone walk on the roof more than 12 times per year?	Circle	Y / N

Thank you for your time and effort. Please fax this form to 999-999-9999

Attachment 7.9: Example Request for Proposal (RFP)

The Performance Information Procurement System (PIPS)

The Performance Information Procurement System (PIPS) is a best-value process that considers additional factors besides price. The major components of this process will be addressed in the sections below.

Section 1: Important Dates
A project schedule will be provided. All times and dates are subject to change. The following are important tasks:

No	Task	Date (Example)
1	Educational Meeting	(1/15/04)
2	Vendor Reference List Submittal	(1/28/04)
3	Pre-Bid Meeting & Site Walk	(2/13/04)
4	Risk-Assessment Plan & Supplemental Form Submittal	(2/27/04)
5	Bid Proposal Submittal	(3/5/04)
6	Pre-Award Meeting (best-valued contractor only)	(3/16/04)

Section 2: Educational Meeting
An educational meeting will be held to discuss the selection process and project requirements.

Section 3: Past Performance Information
Past performance information will be collected on all vendors (contractors and manufacturers). Vendors are required to identify and submit their best projects. Vendors will be required to send out customer evaluations to each of their clients. Vendors are also responsible for making sure their clients return the surveys back to the owner. The State reserves the right to verify and confirm any information submitted in this process. Such verification may include, but is not limited to, speaking with current and former clients, review of relevant client documentation, site-visitation, and other independent confirmation of data.

Section 4: Risk-Assessment Plan (RAP) & Supplemental Form
All bidders must submit a Risk-Assessment Plan and a Supplemental Form for each project in which they expect to participate. The Risk-Assessment Plan (RAP) must NOT contain any information identifying the Contractor or Manufacturer (if it does the proposal will be disqualified and the bidder will be considered non-responsive). This is required to minimize any evaluator bias. All proprietary information should be contained in the Supplemental Form. The Supplemental Form and the Risk Assessment Plan will be treated as complementary documents.

The Risk Assessment Plan must not be longer than 2 pages front side of page only. The RAP should address the following items in a clear and generic language:

1. What risks the project has. (Areas that may cause the contractor not to finish on time, not finish within budget, cause any change orders, or be a source of dissatisfaction with the owner).
2. Explanation of how the risks will be avoided / minimized.
3. Provide a project schedule documenting general milestones.

4. Propose any options that could increase the value of their construction.
5. Explain the benefits of the Risk Assessment Plan. Address the quality and performance differences in terms of risk minimization that the owner can understand and what benefit the option will provide to the user. No brochures or marketing pieces. (No product names!)

The Supplemental Form shall include the following:
1. Contractor and manufacturer's names.
2. Type of roof system (BUR, MOD, SPF, etc).
3. A copy of the warranty.
4. Contractor's signature.

Section 5: Proposal Submittal

Each Contractor shall submit a Proposal Form for each project (which includes cost, project duration, and other general information). The Contractor must also submit a Proposal Form for every system they are proposing (if they are proposing more than one system for the same roof).

Section 6: Warranty Review

Warranty Exclusions / Value of the Warranty: The owner shall identify the value of the manufacturers warranty period for the purpose of risk minimization. The Proven Performance Period is either the adjusted service period (calculated from the manufacturers past projects) or the actual warranty period (the owner shall use the smaller of two in order to identify the true capability of the system). One year will be subtracted from the Proven Performance Period for each of the following exclusions (unless the warranty is amended by the manufacturer's document):

1. Traffic on the roof.
2. Ponding, standing water, or require positive drainage.
3. Materials not made by manufacturer.
4. Metal flashing.
5. Animals.
6. Mechanical damage.
7. Failure of owner to use reasonable care or maintenance (roof inspections).
8. Acts of parties other than the Manufacturer or Contractor.
9. Solid or liquid deposits (solvents, grease, oils, fats, and any other chemicals).
10. Changes in building use.
11. Limits on the maximum dollar limit (maximum liability shall be no greater than the original installation, etc).

Removal of Existing Membrane: The manufacturer is required to cover all materials down to the structural deck if the existing membrane is not removed. The following shall be required in writing at the time of bid submittal from the roofing manufacturer: "The manufacturer accepts liability for the nonperformance of any material down to the structural deck for the duration of the warranty. If any of the materials of the existing or installed roofing system become defective, absorb water, lose their original shape, blister or delaminate, or cause leaking, the manufacturer will immediately restore the existing and overlaid roofing system at the manufacturer's cost."

Elastomeric coating system: If the system being selected uses an elastomeric coating system, a technical review of the warranty may be performed. The owner may perform the Factory Mutual Severe Hail (FM-SH) test on as many roofs they feel are necessary to evaluate the performance of the system (all roofs must pass the test). The following items will be required for all elastomeric coating systems:

1. The Manufacturer must have at least 3 roofs that are at least half the age of the warranty period submitted. (Example: If the manufacturer offers a 20 year warranty, then the manufacturers reference list must have at lease 3 roofs that are at least 10 years old or older).
2. All roofs contained on the vendors reference list must not have had any recoating (since the original installation).
3. The average coating thickness of the roofs will be the minimum coating that shall be accepted for the systems to be installed. (The owner may require additional mils to be installed based on the age of the roofs).
4. All elastomeric coating system Warranties must contain the following statement; "the system can perform with ponding water and can pass the FM-SH test during any time of the warranty period. If it does not pass the test (as identified by the owners personnel,) the manufacturer, at their own expense, will recoat the roof to meet the FM-SH test." If this is not in writing from the manufacturer, the bidder will be disqualified due to the risk of heavy traffic and hailstorms.

The owner will make the final judgment on whether the warranty minimizes risk.

Section 6: Method of Award

A modified Displaced Ideal Model, as explained at the Educational Meeting, will be used for each project to determine the best-valued contractor. The model will analyze: past performance information of the contractor and manufacturer, the Risk-Assessment Plan ratings, cost proposal, warranty reviews, and other project requirements. The method of award will be as follows:

1. Each project will be awarded independently. There is a prioritized list of roofs.
2. The owner shall choose either the highest ranked proposal or the highest ranked proposal within the budget and recommended for award. The owner may negotiate with the highest ranked proposal even if it is over the budget estimate.
3. The owner may decide not to allow a single system (modified bitumen, SPF, etc...) to be awarded more than 60% of the total number of jobs (based on square feet) to minimize risk of nonperformance.
4. The owner may decide not to allow a single contractor to be awarded more than 33% of the total number of jobs (based on square feet) to minimize the risk of nonperformance.
5. Contractors will be allowed to withdraw without penalty.

Section 7: Pre-Award Meeting / Award / Post Construction Rating

Upon notice of being selected as the best-valued contractor, the contractor will review the entire project in detail. The contractor shall answer any technical and/or performance issues from the owner. The contractor shall then have an engineer or architect stamp the specifications, roof plan, and detail drawings. The contractor agrees that they will complete the job on time, within budget, and with no contractor-initiated cost change orders.

When the project is completed, the owner will rate the contractor/manufacturer on their performance on the job. The rating will be incorporated into their past performance rating.

Attachment 7.10: Interview Question Sheet

Questions for Interview of the Site Superintendent and Project Manager

Risk Assessment Plan

1. Prioritize and tell us how you will minimize the largest risks to this project in terms of cost, time, and customer expectation?
2. What would you do differently on this project due to performance based approach?

Value of Key Personnel

1. Why were you selected for this project?
   a. How many project managers/site superintendents are in your company?
   b. Where do you place yourself in terms of ability to minimize risk?
   c. How do you come to that conclusion?
   d. What is the difference between you and the other project managers?
2. What are your personal goals on this project?
3. What are your strengths/weaknesses?
4. How do you measure your performance on this project?

Performance Based Construction

1. Are you comfortable with documenting all risk during project in terms of cost, time, and client expectation and quality, reporting it weekly, and having your record being used as the project record?
2. Who is your counterpart on this project? Why were they selected? Who will be the point of contact on this project?
3. How were your subcontractors selected?
4. When did you select them?
5. How are you ensuring that you will get the best craftspeople?
6. Do you feel comfortable with all components will be barcoded with the same performance?

Differences (comment and record)

8

Six-Sigma Applications in Construction

Introduction

There are three major participants in the delivery of construction: the client, the client's professional representative (designer, engineer, construction manager, inspector), and the contractors. The client defines the construction requirement, the client's representative transforms the requirement into a construction requirement that can be understood by the contractor, and the contractor performs the construction. The construction industry has had the following characteristics over the past thirty years:

1. The industry has become price based.
2. The industry uses minimum standards and requirements as the basis of tendering .
3. Construction management or project management has become the most critical component of construction.
4. The industry has had poor performance when compared to other manufacturing industries in terms of on time, customer satisfaction and minimized cost changes.
5. The industry is solving some of the same problems it solved 30 years ago.
6. The research community has investigated many of the concepts of optimization including partnering, continuous improvement, business process re-engineering, lean construction, and supply chain management studies, but has yet to significantly impact the construction performance.
7. The industry is now trying to solve the nonperformance problem by identifying the value of all the components.

Construction Industry Structure

The construction industry can be defined by competition and performance (Chapter 4). The price pressure has moved the majority of construction work into the price based Quadrant I. This means that the construction industry is simply responding to the client's request for low price, minimal quality, and high risk construction. This is a simple example of demand and supply.

As the number of outsourcing owners who pass the risk to performing contractors increase, the number of highly trained construction professionals and craftspeople will increase. As the number of priced-based owners increase, the demand for less experienced construction professionals and craftspeople will increase. The clients are actually "controlling" the percentage of highly trained craftspeople that a contractor can hire. If clients gravitate to the price based approach, the industry will encourage less trained personnel. This also creates the need for more construction managers to minimize construction nonperformance.

Management is a sign of inefficiency. Management is not required for contractors who are intelligent, acting in the best interest of the client, and minimizing the risk of nonperformance with expertise. Management is only required in Quadrant I, when the adversarial price-based environment forces the contractors to use the less experienced construction workers.

Quadrant II is the best value environment. Contractors have to compete based on performance and price. Performance includes past performance and the ability to identify, prioritize, and minimize risk on a future project. By definition, high quality contractors send their best personnel (get credit for high performing team components) and select the highest performing subcontractors within the budget. High performing contractors do their own quality control. If quality control is being done, external management and control is not required. If external management and control is being exercised, quality control will not be performed (Deming 1982).

The difficulty with the best value Quadrant II environment is that clients (and their representatives) do not know how to effectively compare both performance and price. Clients cannot predict what they are going to get. Clients have no method to competitively compare price and performance to their satisfaction, and gravitate toward their comfort level, which is price based.

Six-Sigma & DMAIC

Deming is the father of continuous improvement. His statistical control process and 14 points of continuous improvement are the forerunners of Six-Sigma. Six-Sigma is a rigorous and disciplined methodology that uses data and statistical analysis to measure and improve a company's operational performance by identifying and eliminating "defects" in manufacturing and service-related processes (iSixSigma LLC, 2004a). The goal of Six-Sigma is to increase profits by eliminating variability, defects, and waste that undermine customer loyalty (iSixSigma LLC, 2004b).

DMAIC, an integral part of the Six-Sigma Quality Initiative, refers to a data-driven quality strategy for improving processes. DMAIC is an acronym for five interconnected phases: Define, Measure, Analyze, Improve, and Control (iSixSigma LLC, 2004c). DMAIC is a cyclical process as shown in Figure 8.1.

The DMAIC process steps are as follows (GE.com 2004):

D – Define. This phase defines the Customer, including:
1. Defining who the customers are, what their requirements are for products and services, and what their expectations are.
2. Defining the project boundaries and the timeline.
3. Defining the process to be improved by mapping the process flow.

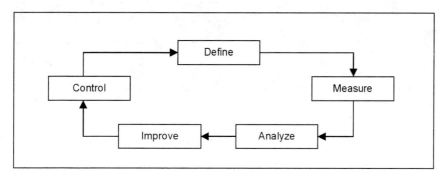

Figure 8.1: DMAIC Cycle (GE.com 2004)

M – Measure. This phase measures the performance of the Core Business Processes, including:
1. Developing a data collection plan for the process.
2. Collecting data from many sources to identify expectations.
3. Analyzing customer survey results to identify potential shortcomings.

A – Analyze. This phase analyzes the data collected and the process map to determine the root causes of defects and opportunities for improvement. This is done by:
1. Identifying gaps between current performance and goal performance.
2. Prioritizing opportunities to improve.
3. Identifying sources of variation.

I – Improve. This phase improves the target process by designing creative solutions to fix and prevent problems. This is done by:
1. Creating innovative solutions using technology and discipline.
2. Developing and deploying implementation plan.

C – Control. This phase controls the improvements to keep the process on the new course. This is done by:
1. Preventing reverting back to the "old way."
2. Requiring the development, documentation and implementation of an ongoing monitoring plan.
3. Institutionalizing the improvements through the modification of systems and structures (staffing, training, incentives).

Literature review (Young, 2001, Pullman, 2004, iSixSigma LLC, 2004a-d, Godfrey, 2002) showed the application of Six-Sigma in various domains. Some of these domains included finance, healthcare, automobile, and aerospace. However, a literature search did not identify any Six-Sigma implementations in the construction industry. If PIPS and the performance based environment continues to increase in popularity, a documented process such as Six-Sigma is required to assist contractors continuously improve.

Six-Sigma Application

Six-Sigma can be used by contractors to broaden the performance of the construction industry. The following is a proposal to implement Six-Sigma in conjunction with the PIPS environment.

D – Define. The customer in construction is the client. Construction performance should be defined as on time, no contractor generated cost change orders, and meeting the expectation of the clients or facility owners. Performance should be non-technical. All performance information must be related to the following:

1. Finishing early.
2. No contractor generated cost change orders.
3. Exceeding the expectations of the owner.

M – Measure. This phase measures the performance of the contractor's processes. Figure 8.2 briefly depicts a typical high-level process of a performance based construction environment.

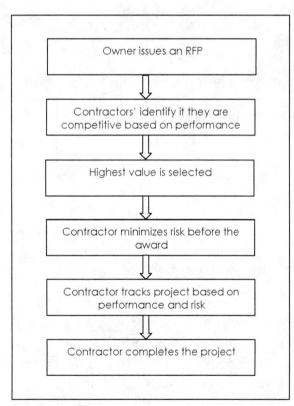

Figure 8.2: Typical high level process map in the performance environment

Measurement occurs in:
1. Past performance information.
2. The ability to identify, prioritize and minimize risk.
3. The measurement of relative value when considering general ability to perform and the ability to perform on the current unique project.
4. Measuring the contractor's ability to manage the risk of their project by proper documentation.
5. Measuring the contractor's performance after the project is completed.
6. Modification of the contractor's past performance rating.

An important measurement of the contractor's performance during the project is the measurement of the number of times they submit the risk assessment report in a timely fashion, and the percentage of times the report is accurate. These measurements affect the end of project performance rating.

In the performance environment, the outcome depends on the performance of the contractor. Once an owner selects and awards a project to the contractor, there's very little that an owner can do to change the eventual outcome. This concept has been validated by the PIPS tests. The contractor should know their capability to perform before the bid, should be measuring their performance and minimizing risk during the project (without the aid of the client's representatives), and communicate to the client in terms of the performance information. Contractors should be measuring:

1. Performance of competing contractors.
2. Performance of all key personnel within the company.
3. Performance of critical subcontractors.
4. Performance of projects for different owners.
5. Profit margins of projects for different owners, personnel, and subcontractors or general contractors.

A – Analyze. Contractors should be constantly evaluating their performance. A performance-based environment minimizes the subjective decision making of the owner. Tools are available in the statistical world, which can help in performing a root cause analysis. Some of these include:

1. FMEA – Failure Mode Effect Analysis
2. Ishikawa Diagram or Fishbone diagram
3. The 5 Why's

The details of the above tools can be found in reference (Hoerl & Snee, 2002). This analysis will lead to the conclusion that the root cause of failure of construction projects lies in either the construction delivery process or the process by which a contractor performs the construction. This is analogous to the common cause variation in the statistics world. In other words, the lack of performance is not *project specific* but *process specific*. This difference is depicted in Figures 8.3 and 8.4.

Normally, project specific actions are taken to achieve the desired results due to nonperforming processes. These actions are reactive, non-efficient, and not performance based. The process-based solution is to treat construction as a process that can be continually improved. This justifies implementing continuous improvement. Continuous improvement can only be accomplished with measurement and analysis of performance information. The process approach will ignore the project specific data and identify the root causes of nonperformance.

The process will be analyzed based on the results to minimize risk of nonperformance. The modified Displaced Ideal Model (Chapter 10) analyzes the risk before the project. Based on price and performance, the model identifies differential in the ability to perform to the customer's expectations. Analysis of the price component can also identify if the owner picks up additional risk if they override the prioritization of the model and select the lowest bidder. Contractors can improve their competitiveness if they study the results of the relative distancing model (State of Hawaii Audit Report).

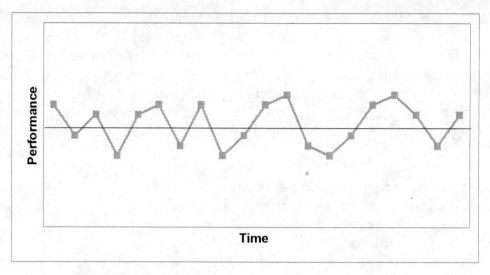

Figure 8.3: Common Cause variation (Process Specific)

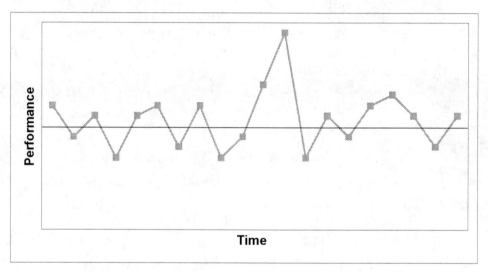

Figure 8.4: Special Cause variation (Project specific)

I – Improve. The performance based environment of PIPS forces the contractors to continuously improve to stay competitive. Contractors who do not have a continuous improvement or DMAIC process, will not be successful in the performance-based environment. In both the State of Hawaii, and State of Utah environments, contractors who depended on project specific solutions, were not successful (Kashiwagi & Byfield, 2002). In both cases, it ended up being detrimental to the owner's efforts to maintain a performance based environment. In the State of Utah, contractors who perceived they were performers objected to the performance-based environment, and convinced the government to return to a more project specific environment. This meant less performance information, more subjective decision making by the client's experts, and no requirement for a contractor to have a continuous improvement program. In the State of Hawaii program, a contractor who could not win projects based on performance protested the process. The contractor was not fully educated and did not have a DMAIC process in place. The contractor ended up performing very poorly.

The State of Hawaii PIPS roofing program test had the following characteristics (Kashiwagi & Savicky 2003):

1. Time period of over four years.
2. Procurement of 100 roofs.
3. The performance of six contractors was tracked over the four years.
4. Contractors with DMAIC processes in place were more successful.
5. Contractors without DMAIC processes did not participate.
6. The performance based contractors did work twice as fast, had a no leaking record, and provided enforceable warranties for 10 -15 years, an increase of over 10 years from the low-bid environment.

Lessons learned from the two experiences show that it is critical for contractors to implement Six-Sigma practices to make a performance-based environment sustainable. If this is not done, the following detrimental results will occur:

1. Motivate nonperforming contractors to protest the process with the claim that it is noncompetitive and exclusionary.
2. Frustrate nonperforming contractors who do not understand performance.
3. Give support to non-value added management type personnel who would much rather revert to the status quo, inefficient processes that favor commodity contractors and bureaucratic managers.
4. Create an environment of confusion where performance and value are not understood.

In both Hawaii and Utah PIPS programs, an implementation of a DMAIC program with the contractors would have improved the sustainability of the program.

C – Control.   It is vital that contractors understand that they must control their own performance and performance information. The performance-based environment will provide a motivation to continuously improve. By definition of the performance-based environment, the client does not control the contractor. Therefore, the way for the client to control the environment is to ensure that the contractors are keeping their owner performance information and controlling their performance. The client then controls by forcing the contractors to control themselves, using the performance-based environment to minimize the risk of a nonperforming contractor getting a project.   The risk to the process is then defined by nonperforming contractors destabilizing the environment with political pressure. The most important function of the client's representatives becomes to ensure that the performance information is being kept, managed, and used by the contractors. The environment will then regulate itself by forcing contractors to practice the most value added processes.

The best value process is defined as having contractors who will (See Figure 8.5):

1. Self measure their performance and compete based on performance (past performance and the ability to minimize risk on the unique project).
2. Minimize the project construction risk by analysis of performance and risk information before the award.
3. Improve their performance by setting performance goals while managing their project by measuring risk.
4. Be measured after construction, using the performance ratings to affect their future past performance rating of the entire construction team.

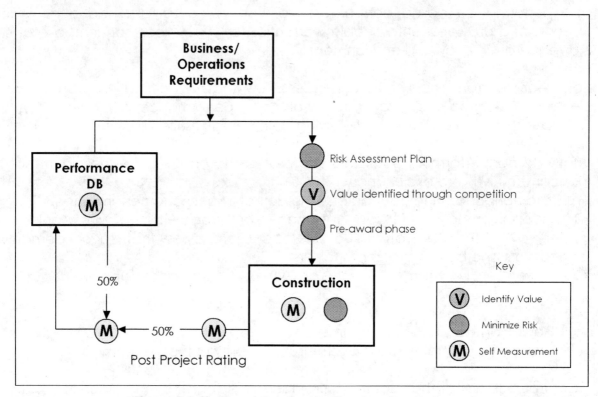

Figure 8.5: Six-Sigma Solution to Construction Delivery

The process results in the following:

1. Contractors are motivated to submit their best personnel because the process uses a best value award (performance and price).
2. By having the entire construction team receive the same rating, high performance personnel do not want low performing personnel that bring risk of nonperformance.
3. The process requires the winning contractor to do a high-level risk business plan (cost, time, and expectation) and a detailed business plan (minimize all identified risk, detailed schedule, coordination of all drawings and specifications, and identification and clarification of all potential problems).
4. The individual ratings create an environment of pride in the construction personnel.

Process Solution Results

The process solution has been tested over the past ten years on 380 projects ($240M). It has resulted in 98% customer satisfaction, minimized up to 80% of the construction management requirements (Serikawa 2002, Kundsen 2000, Kashiwagi 2004). Where data was available to compare prices, the cost of best-value construction did not cost more (in terms of transaction costs). At the State of Utah, University of Hawaii, State of Hawaii, and the Dallas Independent School District (DISD), the construction first cost was less. In the procurement of a $45M environmental wet laboratory at the Georgia Tech campus, the performance-based solution was cheaper than the low bid solution, and would have finished over 33% earlier. Although the data is limited, preliminary analysis of projects result in the hypothesis that a highly managed project in the price based environment may be inefficient and more costly, inferring that the solution to construction nonperformance may be due to the client's delivery system and not the inability of the construction industry to perform. This may explain the following:

1. Why ten years of construction research focused on the technical solution (more efficient management, more construction expertise, more construction management, and more efficient construction methodologies) has not significantly improved construction performance.
2. Why partnering, lean construction and continuous improvement efforts have not motivated contractors to increase their performance in the price-based environment.
3. Why the construction industry has had a bad reputation and has not attracted enough quality personnel (Tompkins 2001, Krizan and Winston 1998, ENR 2001).
4. Why construction output has decreased over time (Russell 1991).

Using Performance-Based Concepts in the Low-Bid Environment

The performance-based environment differs from the price-based environment in that performance information is collected and used to minimize risk. Performance information is used to minimize the opportunity of nonperforming contractors to get work. The research has identified the following concepts:

1. Price and performance have no correlation. Clients can pay too much for nonperforming work, and too little for high performing work.
2. Nonperforming contractors gain a competitive advantage when the construction specifications are very detailed in means, methods, and materials. Nonperforming contractors would not know how to do or bid the work if the detailed methods and means were not given. Performers do not need all the details because they know construction.
3. Nonperforming contractors cannot minimize risk. When forced to compete based on the ability to perform and minimize risk (to actually minimize the risk before construction), nonperforming contractors do not have a competitive advantage.

4. A performance-based environment minimizes the motivation of contractors to bid low and "buy" the project.

The performance environment can be used for both Quadrants I and II. However, the usage of the information will differ in the two environments. In the low bid environment, the PIPS process will change (Figure 8.6: Price Based PIPS). Performance information will be collected on all the participants. However, the performance information will not be used to select or disqualify any contractor. Instead, the performance concept will be used in the following ways:

1. All the contractors' critical elements will be performance lined.
2. The contractors will compete based on the low bid, and the award will be made to the low bidder.
3. The low bidder will enter a preconstruction phase where they will be forced to review the plans and specifications with all their key components. They will be required to identify and seek clarification for anything that is not constructible. They will be required to propose any modifications, identifying both the cost and time requirements.
4. If the review results in a significant cost increase, the contractor will be awarded a predetermined stipend or allowance, and the project will be redesigned and rebid. If the contractor is allowed to proceed into construction they will retain the risk of the project.
5. The contractor will then be required to manage their project based on the documentation of risk. They will be required to submit the weekly report 95% of the time, and with 95% accuracy.
6. The contractor's performance will be rated at the end of the project, and the rating will be used in any future project in the performance-based environment.

The hypothesis is that the modified PIPS or performance-based process will improve the performance of the price-based contractor, and that the process-based solution can also be used in the price-based environment.

This leads to the conclusion that performance information cannot be used the same way in the performance based sector and the low-bid sector (Chapter 25). Performance information in the low bid sector can only be used to:

1. Change policies to exclude nonperformers.
2. Explain nonperformance.
3. Disqualify contractors because they cannot manage their own projects.
4. Make it more expensive for low bid contractors to get a project.

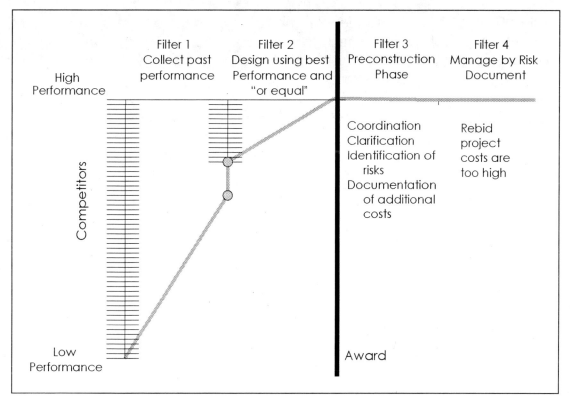

Figure 8.6: Price Based PIPS Process

Impact on FAA and USAMC Organizations

The Six-Sigma application of PIPS and performance information forces:

1. Documentation of the performance of best value and other contractors.
2. Minimization of technical management and direction of the client's representative.
3. Minimization of technical decisions made by the client.
4. Minimization of construction directives made by the designer.

An obstacle for using Six-Sigma is the bureaucracies of the client. By the time the overall boss of the organization gets any information on a project, it has been filtered several times. The information environment comes with a negative feature: it is uncontrollable. Like time and space, you cannot put a border around an information environment. It will end up measuring everyone.

Using the construction risk minimization report or the construction interface (Chapter 8 and 25), the research hypothesis for the Federal Aviation Administration (FAA) projects and the US Army Medical Command (USAMC) projects was to form the information environment within the client's representatives. The hypothesis is that the use of the risk information to prioritize multiple projects has the capability to optimize the client's organization - delivering construction. Figure 8.7 shows an organizational chart with four levels of managers. The top level is the facility management manager (FM). The second level is the project manager/procurement person. The third level is the "in the field" project manager. The fourth level are the contractors who are actually accomplishing the construction work.

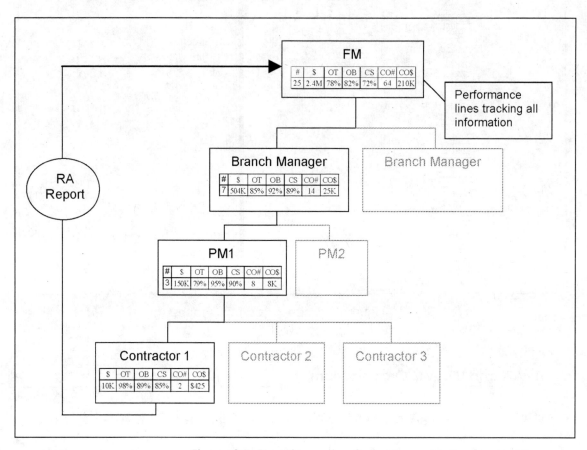

Figure 8.7: FM Information System

If the managers are making decisions, they are accepting risk. When they make the wrong decision, the managers will screen any information that goes to the FM. By sending the contractor's risk information directly to the FM, it allows the FM to analyze the following information:

1. Number of projects.
2. Cost of projects.
3. Percentage of projects that are on time, on budget, and meeting quality expectations.
4. Number of projects of each of the third level project managers.
5. Percentage of projects at risk.
6. Percentage of projects where the contractor is not performing.
7. Projects that are at most risk.
8. Who is responsible for the projects that are at risk.
9. Performance of every level of management.

A process is proposed for taking the Risk Assessment (RA) reports from the contractors and asking them to email the report directly to the FM. A simple program will be written which will strip the RA attachment from the email, and put it into an analysis database. The analysis database will output the FM's performance numbers, will identify where the FM's risk is, and which participants are causing risk. Once this information environment is established, the project managers will:

1. Not want to make decisions.
2. Hire the best available contractors (effective and efficient).
3. Minimize the risk, according to Pareto's law (20% of problems cause 80% of the risk).

Project managers will minimize their decision making, hire the best contractors, facilitate performance, and minimize their risk by identifying which contractors are low performers. The project managers will take on the appearance of leaders who influence instead of managing and directing (Maxwell 1998). The entire FM organization can now be measured. Each component will maintain the detailed information, responsibility, and be measured by the resulting client's performance information.

The overall information system will require only the party at risk for nonperformance to document the risk. The timely information, which does not require any of the FM's personnel to do any effort to deliver the information to the FM, will now be motivated to ensure that the risk is minimized. It forces partnering, sharing of information, efficiency (minimization of risk with the least effort), and personal responsibility to increase the performance of the construction.

Conclusion

Construction research results, construction performance results, and successful business practices results, support the hypothesis that construction nonperformance is caused by the client's price-based delivery process and the non-value adding functions of construction management and inspection. It also confirms that the solution may be process-based.

Documented results of construction research have shown that the only success in the industry has been with processes that give the contractor more control over their construction. PIPS or performance-based results are significantly different from price-based results. The process' critical components include performance information, the identification and minimization of risk before award, the ability to minimize risk using construction expertise, and using the project rating to influence future competitive ratings. The application of Six-Sigma has defined, measured, analyzed using different levels of performance, influenced improvement, and controlled, the construction performance deviation by using the process control of PIPS.

Chapter 8 Review

1. An information environment has what two unique characteristics which are often misunderstood?
2. If it takes a detailed explanation to explain a contractor's performance, is that an information environment? Why or why not?
3. What is the impact of the boss getting performance and risk information?
4. What is DMAIC?
5. How does PIPS assist in analyzing and controlling nonperformance.
6. How is performance information used in the low bid arena?
7. What should be measured in the delivery of construction or services?
8. What is the impact on the project managers on the lowest levels caused by the delivering of risk information that is documented by the contractor at risk and giving it to the head of the organization?
9. A true information environment forces project managers to do what two actions?
10. If DMAIC is implemented, the client will identify if the situation requires a _____ or a _____ solution.

References

CIB (2000, May). *The State of the Construction Industry Report*. Construction Industry Board. (11), Retrieved from http://www.dti.gov.uk/construction/stats/soi/soi11.htm.

Darshit, Parmar. (2004). Low Bid and PIPS Procurement Hypothesis Testing. Internal Report at PBSRG submitted on April 1, 2004.

Deming, E. W. (1982). *Out of the Crisis*. Cambridge, MA: Massachusetts Institute of Technology.

Egan, J. (1998). Rethinking Construction: The Report of the Construction Task Force. *Department of Trade and Industry*, 1-37.

ENR Staff Writer. (2001). It takes only one job to create proven technology. *Engineering News Record*, 247[6], 56.

GE Capital Vendor Financial Services (2004). *DMAIC Process.* Retrieved from http://www.ge.com/capital/vendor/dmaic.htm

Godfrey, A.B. (2002, February) *The Honeywell Edge*. Retrieved from http://www.asq.org/pub/sixsigma/past/vol1_issue2/honeywell.html Also in Six-Sigma Forum Magazine, 1(2), no page given.

Herbsman, Z. and Ellis, R. (1992). Multiparameter Bidding System—Innovation in Contract Administration. *Journal of Construction Engineering and Management*, 18[1], 142-150.

Hoerl, R.W. and Snee, R.D. (2002). *Statistical thinking: improving business performance.* California: Wadworth Group – DUXBURY.

iSixSigma LLC (2004a). *What is Six-Sigma?* Retrieved from http://www.isixsigma.com/library/content/six-sigma-newbie.asp

iSixSigma LLC (2004b). *Six-Sigma*. Retrieved from http://www.isixsigma.com/dictionary/Six_Sigma-85.htm

iSixSigma LLC (2004c) *DIMAIC Problem Solving Methodology*. Retrieved from http://www.isixsigma.com/dictionary/DMAIC-57.htm

iSixSigma LLC (2004d) *Ford Embraces Six-Sigma*. Retrieved from http://healthcare.isixsigma.com/library/content/c010614a.asp

Kashiwagi, D. (2004). *Best Value Procurement: Theory & Practice Manual.* Tempe, AZ: PBSRG, Arizona State University.

Kashiwagi, D. & Savicky, J. (2003) The Cost of 'best value' Construction. *Journal of Facilities Management,* 2(3), 285-295.

Kashiwagi D. & Byfield R. (2002) Testing of Minimization of Subjectivity in 'Best Value' in Procurement by Using Artificial Intelligence Systems in State of Utah Procurement. *ASCE: Journal of Construction Engineering and Management,* 128 (6), 496-502.

Krizan, W.G. and Winston, S. (1998). Scarcity of Skilled Workers Will Put Brakes On Growth. *Engineering News Record*, 240[4], 95, 98, 101.

Kundsen, L. (2000). Analysis of PIPS at the State of Utah. *State of Utah, Division of Facilities Construction and Management,* Sent to John Savicky on August 31, 2000.

Maxwell, JC. (1998). *21 Irrefutable Laws of Leadership*. Nashville, Tennesse: Thomas Nelson, Inc. Post, N. (1998, May 11). Building Teams Get High Marks. *Engineering News Record (ENR)*, 240 (19), 32-39.

Murray, M. (1993). A Construction Contract for the Year 2000. *Concrete International*, June, 60-61.

NEL Staff Writer. (2003). What is a knowledge worker? *National Electronic Library for Health*, Feb5.

OFPP Staff Writer (1998). A Guide to Best Practices for Performance Based Service Contracting. Office of Federal Procurement Policy, Retrieved on October 1, 1998, from http://www.arnet.gov/Library/OFPP/BestPractices/PPBSC/BestPPBSC.html

Pullman Memorial Hospital (2004). *Raising the Bar – A Quality Model for Hospitals (news release)* Retrieved from http://www.pullmanhospital.org/current_news_releases/raising_the_bar.htm

Rice, H. (1995). A Collective Wake-Up Call: The Point is Profit. *Painting & Wallcovering Contractor*,57[3], 32,34.

Rosenbaum, D.B., Rubin, D.K., and Powers, M.B. (2002). The Nation's C-Schools : Undergraduate construction programs raise skills and expectations, but face own challenges. Engineering News Record, Retrieved from http://www.enr.construction.com/features/education/archives/011029a.asp

Russell, J. (1991). Contractor Failure: Analysis. *Journal of Performance of Constructed Facilities*, 5[3], 163-180.

Serikawa, C. (2002, June 28). Letter written to PBSRG. *University of Hawaii at Manoa, Facilities Planning and Management Office, Manoa, HI, USA.*

Snider, K. and Walkner, M. (2001). Best Practices and Protests: Toward Effective Use of Journal of Performance of Constructed Facilities Past Performance as a Criterion in Source Selections. *Journal of Public Procurement*, 1[1], 96-122.

Tompkins, S. (2001). Construction Industry Faces Potential Labor Crisis. *Cost Engineering*, 43[11], 36.

Waddick, P. (2004). *Six-Sigma DIMAIC Quick Reference – Analyze Phase*. Retrieved from http://www.isixsigma.com/library/content/six_sigma_dmaic_quickrefanalyze.asp

Young, J. (2001, November) *Driving Performance Results At American Express*. Retrieved from http://www.asq.org/pub/sixsigma/past/vol1_issue1/driving.html Also in Six-Sigma Forum Magazine, 1(1).

Zeleny, M. (1982). *Multiple Criteria Decision Making*. New York: McGraw Hill.

9
Getting Started

Introduction

Facility owners (FO), facility managers (FM), construction managers (CM), and designers and engineers (A/E) should become more involved with the PIPS and Best Value Procurement to:

1. Minimize the risk of nonperformance.
2. Procure performing construction (on-time, on-budget, and meeting quality expectations).
3. Improve the existing process.
4. Reduce management, overhead cost, and time.
5. Do more with less.
6. Obtain the best value.
7. Create a "win-win" relationship.

If you are a FO, FM, CM, or A/E, and do not have these motivations, the implementation of PIPS may revert individuals back to a price-based mentality with all its inherent problems.

Cost of Implementation

The cost of implementation depends on the following factors:

1. The core team's level of understanding of the IMT/PIPS concepts.
2. The complexity and number of projects.
3. The amount of political risk (see Chapters 14 and 21).
4. The availability of IMT/PIPS training personnel at Arizona State University.

The following are costs at different levels of implementation:

1. Test cases: $10K - $50K
2. License from ASU: one time charge of $25K (includes annual on-site education and updates to process)
3. Implementation with assistance from ASU: $75K - $150 per year (depending on scope of work)

How to Implement PIPS

There are some basic principles that users must understand before implementing PIPS. The majority of organizations (whether public or private) are "Type C" organizations. The majority of their employees are "Type C" individuals (they control, manage, make decisions etc). This does not mean that these organizations cannot implement PIPS. However, these companies should be very careful in the manner in which PIPS is implemented. The following principles are key factors to the long-term success of PIPS:

1. A small "Core Group" should be identified (Chapter 14). They should be "Type A" individuals with common personal goals.
2. Do not educate individuals that are not involved with projects using the PIPS process since their first reaction will be fear of change. Type C individuals will feel threatened by the process.
3. Change is a slow and hard process. Therefore, the implementation of PIPS should be gradual. Do not try to change the entire organization overnight; this will not work.
4. The process must create a "win-win" relationship.
5. The process should not be cost-reduction oriented but rather to increase efficiency.

Through past implementations, the author has found that not abiding by these principles has been the major stumbling block when implementing PIPS. The process should not be implemented to replace any other system, including the low-bid process. The PIPS process should be implemented slowly, and should be considered another "tool" that the owner can use when procuring construction.

Core Group

Identify a core group of personnel. A core group must include:

1. Procurement personnel (one who contracts the project).
2. Project manager (one who is responsible for the entire project).
3. High-level manager who can make decisions on policy and support the decision when challenged.
4. Legal representative (to make sure the rules and laws permit the concept of awarding on performance and price).
5. Designers (who will identify the requirement, complete the request for a proposal, and make decisions if required).

The success of the implementation will depend on having these key players. These key players should have a Type A approach to problems.

Selecting the Test Project

Test projects should be selected to minimize political risk, but still justify the cost of implementation. The projects should have the following characteristics:

1. Small or repetitive projects (under $5M).
2. Less complex projects (roofing, painting, system projects such as HVAC replacement, fire alarm replacement, etc.).

The projects should be small and simple enough that the core team can finish the project within a year. Under no circumstances should a non-core team individual be allowed to participate in the design, management, or inspection of the first few projects.

The implementation of the process should not be accelerated. Even if the results are good, the user should be patient. Change is slow. The core team should be careful to document the results of the test project. The client should also document the performance of the status quo process. The author has noted that most owners do not know their own performance. One of the major problems with implementing PIPS is that the owner's representatives do not document their performance. The documentation is the most important feature of this process.

The core team should not be overworked. Past experience shows that when the owner realizes how successful PIPS can be, the core team is inundated with projects. Also, the fees for the A/E and consultants should not be minimized. Allow them to participate and learn by doing the process. Over time the designers will be able to do more projects for a larger profit (an increase of 200 to 500%).

Introduce PIPS to all interested parties as an alternative procurement process. As stated earlier, the process should not be used to replace the low-bid process or any other process. The change in the scope of the implementations should be continuous and as slow as possible.

Identify The Goals For The PIPS Implementation

Identify goals when implementing PIPS or a best value approach. These goals should be monitored and documented on each test. Goals may include:

1. Performance (on-time, on-budget, meeting quality expectations).
2. Reduction of change orders.
3. Customer satisfaction, the owners should document the quality of the contractor.
4. Contractors adding value to the project (identified by the performing contractor).
5. Getting more quality contractors to participate and bid with their best performing personnel (increased competition).

6. Minimization of management time, design corrections, and construction. Time on every project should be documented. Training time and management time should be documented separately.
7. Minimization of protests and litigation.

Training Requirements

The PIPS is a system of the information age. The requirements of the information age or "information worker" are different then those from the construction industry of the last twenty years. PIPS core teams cannot receive enough training. The PIPS requirements (releasing control, allowing performing contractors to do their best to minimize the owner's risk, discontinue making decisions, and stop managing the construction) are not natural actions for most design and construction managers.

Construction managers are taught to make decisions, control construction, and make things happen. This is the current status quo of perceived "value" of project managers in the industry. PIPS requires a Type A leader and not a Type C manager (see Chapter 3). Training and education for the PIPS core team and contractors is one of the most important components of the process. Recommended training includes:

1. A minimum of three days of intensive training during the implementation.
2. Attendance at any PBSRG presentation of PIPS.
3. Annual two day training at Arizona State University.
4. Monthly contact with PBSRG personnel.

The temptation of the PIPS core team has been to get busy and not refine and improve their information worker characteristics. Attention to the IMT basics guarantees the success of PIPS.

Schedule

The best way to understand PIPS is to use the schedule of activities as an explanation. In Chapter 7, Attachments 7.1a, 7.1b, 7.1c, and 7.1d, show a schedule of implementing PIPS on a design-build project, a large and small design-bid-build project, and a competitive emergency award. The major events are:

1. Registry or education meeting.
2. Past Performance Information data collection.
3. Pre-bid meeting.
4. Bids, risk assessment plans and interviews.
5. Prioritization using a modified DIM.
6. Pre-award meeting.

Major Responsibilities of the Project Manager and Designer

The major responsibilities of the user's representatives (user's project manager and designer) are to:

1. Advertise projects to contractors and invite them to attend the registry, education, or pre-bid meeting.
2. Hold the education meeting (and give a presentation on PIPS). Give contractors the reference submittal forms to send out to their references.
3. Receive performance data from the references.
4. Create past performance lines or barcodes.
5. Select the review team members.
6. Receive and rate the risk assessment plans.
7. Input data (past performance, perceived value, and price) in the model and prioritize the bidders.
8. Make the selection. The user can override the model due to information not in the system. See Chapter 7 for impact of override.
9. Do a technical review of "best value" by allowing the contractor to coordinate the design documents with the critical personnel and subcontractors, clarify any misunderstandings, and ensure that the contractor is comfortable with minimizing the risk identified by all the competing contractors.
10. Award contract.
11. Assist contractor in being successful by using the construction interface.
12. Do a write-up project at the end of construction.
13. Update contractor's performance numbers with 25% rating.

Managing PIPS

A project manager (PM) should be assigned responsibility for tracking the schedule and events, documenting how the process is working, and providing the required documents. The PM should remember the following:

1. The PIPS rules should be followed with no exceptions.
2. Do not let subjective opinions of contractors (based on their past experiences) alter PIPS rules.
3. All questions and answers must be documented in writing (email or fax).
4. Do not do a technical review until the pre-award period. The contractor should conduct the technical review and present it to the client's representative in a non-technical form.
5. Allow the awarded contractor to minimize risk.
6. Complete the closeout ratings.

Construction and Information Interface

During construction, the owner's construction project management should be minimized. The contractor should be in control of the project, unless the project needs to be shut down due to contractor nonperformance. A construction interface (see Chapter 25) should be used to pass the owner critical performance information.

Conclusion

The PIPS is an evolving process and modifications are continually being made to it. Reasons for modifications should be done to minimize risk (both political and construction nonperformance). Modifications are also being made to fit policy and regulation requirements of users. Not all the modifications made will minimize risk, however, the overall process (including any modifications) will still reduce the relative risk of non-performance over the low-bid system (see Attachment 9.1).

The objective of the PBSRG is to continually improve the process. Users should keep in touch with PBSRG through annual training and on the Internet at www.pbsrg.com. It is important to realize that the objective of PIPS is to minimize risk within the user's constraints. Risk is defined as the inability to predict the future outcome. PIPS can always be modified to fit the constraints of the user. As users continue to make modifications (that do not follow IMT), they increase the chance of construction nonperformance. All modifications should be checked with IMT concepts to ensure that risk is minimized.

Chapter 9 Review

1. What are the best projects to first implement PIPS on?
2. What is the most important part of the test?
3. How should the test be done?

Attachments

Attachment 9.1: PIPS Checklist

Attachment 9.1

PIPS CHECKLIST

ONE-TIME SETUP & USER EDUCATION

1	Have all of the users key personnel been educated on PIPS (procurement officer, contracting officer, facility manager, information worker)?	☐ Yes	☐ No
2	Has your legal department reviewed and approved the process?	☐ Yes	☐ No
3	Are there any modifications that need to be made to the PIPS process?	☐ Yes	☒ No
4	Has a core group been established?	☐ Yes	☐ No
5	Has a PIPS Administrator been selected?	☐ Yes	☐ No
6	Has an information worker been selected?	☐ Yes	☐ No
7	Were these individuals at all of the meetings / presentations?	☐ Yes	☐ No

PILOT PROJECT INFORMATION

1	Has a test / pilot project been selected?	☐ Yes	☐ No
2	Estimated budget?	☐ Yes	☐ No
3	Estimated award date?	☐ Yes	☐ No
4	Estimated completion date?	☐ Yes	☐ No
5	Type of project?		

     ☐ General Construction
     ☒ A/E Selection
     ☐ Maintenance and Service
     ☐ Renovation & Repair (roofing, painting, flooring)

Documentation

1	Has the advertisement been prepared?	☐ Yes	☐ No
2	Has the RFP been prepared?	☐ Yes	☐ No
3	Does the RFP contain the following information:		
	Educational Meeting (date, time, location, mandatory)	☐ Yes	☐ No
	Past Performance Information (critical areas, survey form)	☐ Yes	☐ No
	How to prepare for a survey (setting up the reference list)	☐ Yes	☐ No
	Risk Assessment Plan contents (no names, only risk)	☐ Yes	☐ No
	Bid Proposal (attachment to the RA Plan)	☐ Yes	☐ No
	Overall weighting scheme	☐ Yes	☐ No
	Short-list date / Interviews	☐ Yes	☐ No
	Pre-Award Meeting outline	☐ Yes	☐ No
	General schedule of critical dates	☐ Yes	☐ No
4	Has the Risk Assessment Plan rating sheets been approved?	☐ Yes	☐ No
5	Has the interview rating sheets been approved?	☐ Yes	☐ No
6	Has PBSRG seen all other documentation that will be issued for this project?	☐ Yes	☐ No

Education / Criteria / Weights

1	Do vendors have to attend the Educational Meeting to bid on the project?	☐ Yes	☐ No
2	Has the criteria been established?	☐ Yes	☐ No
3	Have you established the overall weighting scheme?	☐ Yes	☐ No
4	Have you established the individual weights?	☐ Yes	☐ No
5	Are any other factors necessary in the selection (i.e. minority/women factor)?	☐ Yes	☐ No

Past Performance Information

1	Can you use past performance information?	☐ Yes	☐ No
2	Can you use numerical ratings (1-10 scores)?	☑ Yes	☐ No
3	What is the maximum number of projects each vendor can submit?		
4	What are the critical areas that need to be surveyed?		

Risk Assessment Plan

1	Have you selected the evaluation committee?	☐ Yes	☐ No
2	How many pages do you want the risk assessment to be?	☐ Less than 2	☐ Less than 5
3	If a plan contains names/marketing information will it be disqualified for failing to follow directions (non-responsive)?	☐ Yes	☐ No
4	Have all of the evaluation committee members been educated on PIPS?	☐ Yes	☐ No
5	Do the members understand that the plan should be non-technical and identify/minimize risk (value added)?	☐ Yes	☐ No
6	Do the members understand that the ratings should be done individually (they must not be group ratings)?	☐ Yes	☐ No
7	Are there at least 3 individuals rating the RA Plans?	☐ Yes	☐ No
8	Has the Bid Proposal Form been reviewed?	☐ Yes	☐ No

Interview

1	Are you going to interview any key personnel?	☐ Yes	☐ No
2	Are you going to short-list to reduce the number of firms to interview?	☐ Yes	☐ No
3	If yes, how many firms will be short-listed?	☐ Yes	☐ No
4	Have you selected the interview rating members?	☐ Yes	☐ No
5	Have all of the members been educated on PIPS?	☐ Yes	☐ No

Pre-Award/ Award

1	Will you give the highest-ranked firm a list of all of the risks (without any solutions)	☐ Yes	☐ No
2	Does the PIPS Administrator understand that this meeting is to go over any outstanding items, and for the firm to do a complete technical review to make sure that there are no issues?	☐ Yes	☐ No
3	Does the PIPS Administrator understand that you can override the system and make a subjective decision on the award (to minimize any political risk)?	☐ Yes	☐ No

10

Modified Displaced Ideal Model (MDIM)

Introduction

The most difficult task in best-value procurement is identifying the value of construction services. Owner representatives are forced to make decisions because they have a lack of information. In the absence of information, they have considered all alternatives as equals. They have not found a consistent method of identifying the relative performance and value of their procured construction services. They have been in an environment for the past 20 years where "value" was a marketing term, which had no supporting documented performance. As discussed in Chapter 4, the void of performance information and the lack of a way to compare performance information and price (value) has resulted in focusing on price and making decisions based on relationships. Owner representatives bring risk because they:

1. Make decisions based on a lack of information.
2. Procure services without knowing what is true performance and value.
3. Tend to trust those they know (relationships).

The author proposes to minimize risk caused by owner decision-making by providing a computer processor with no bias. The goal of the computer processor is to:

1. Calculate value (performance and price) using performance information.
2. Provide documentation for the justification of purchasing value.
3. Consistently produce high quality results.
4. Allow the user to define performance in the user's terms based on the user's risks and objectives.

It is important to note, that the processor does not have to do the entire job of risk minimization. Chapter 7 discussed the filters that work in combination with the processor to ensure the identification and procurement of the best value. The purpose of the model is to identify best value. It will prioritize based on numbers. The contractors have control over the numbers. All the numbers are non-technical. Contractors are motivated to compete their best personnel. The model will not make a subjective decision and it will not disqualify any contractor.

PIPS is a process that forces a contractor to knock itself out of the competition. Therefore, if a contractor is weak in a certain criteria, the weakness may cause the contractor to be knocked out of competition. Contractors' weaknesses are always measured in relative terms. In critical areas of major differential between contractors, contractors with high relative performance should be given more credit than if there is very little differential. Other requirements of the processor should be:

1. It is capable of functioning with many criteria and many alternatives.
2. It is reproducible.
3. It allows numbers to be used without translation. The translation of numbers is the introduction of personal bias.
4. It meets the perceptions of different owners for different requirements.
5. It is fast and quick.
6. It is easy to operate.
7. It makes the contractors concentrate on value.
8. It is simple to analyze and easy to understand.

Selection of an Artificial Intelligence Decision-Making Model for PIPS

There are many different forms of decision-making models, including:

1. Arithmetic averaging matrix
2. The Analytical Hierarchical Process (AHP)
3. Linear programming
4. Neural Networks
5. Cluster Analysis
6. Analytical Network Process (ANP)
7. Data Envelopment Analysis (DEA)
8. Factor Analysis
9. Expert Systems

The author does not recommend using these models for one or more of the following reasons:

1. The model is very complex (requires an "expert" to run the model).
2. The model requires someone to translate numbers. For example the model cannot consider past performance numbers and the number of references submitted (the model can't compare apples to oranges).
3. The model cannot compare objective and subjective data.
4. The model allows user bias and subjectivity, thus allowing the project managers to easily pick their favorite contractors.
5. The model uses pair-wise comparison between alternatives and attributes, which makes it very difficult to use on projects with large number of contractors and criteria.
6. The model cannot prioritize a list of contractors (the model can only group similarities or differences).
7. The model cannot select the best value efficiently (in a fast and cost effective manner).
8. The model requires extensive programming and "learning".

After analysis of the different decision-making techniques, the Displaced Ideal Model (DIM) (Zeleny 1982) was selected, modified, and tested successfully for the PIPS process. The DIM was selected for the following reasons:

1. The model functioned with large numbers of criteria and alternatives.
2. The model works the same way every time. It does not change or learn.
3. It does not require numbers to be translated.
4. It can incorporate the perceptions of different owners for different requirements.
5. It is fast and simple to use.
6. It motivates the contractors to be competent in all critical areas.
7. It motivates the contractors to concentrate on value and continually improve without management.
8. It is easily checkable, correctable, and easy to debug.
9. It is easy to understand..

The DIM is one of the few models that will work with many criteria and relatively fewer alternatives. It also meets all of the other requirements of the PIPS model. A common understanding of artificial intelligent multi-criteria decision making models is that the models think on their own and learn as they process. The objective of the artificial intelligent model is to copy a human being's processing or brain. It is also desired for the artificial intelligent model to mimic an intelligent person. The author however, does not agree with this perception. The author in Chapter 2 and 3, identifies that human decision-making is constrained. It can only learn when it perceives the information. And because it learns, it is assumed to lack the perception of information. The only reason it would make decisions, is because it lacks sufficient information that will predict the constraints of the initial conditions and the future outcome. It then goes back into its previous information base of events (which does not cover the current event) and tries to find an event that is close to the current event. It then assumes that the event is about the same, and the decision is made to act in a similar way. Explaining it another way, when someone does not have sufficient information, they go back to their previous experiences and make a subjective (lacking all information) decision.

By definition, everyone who learns is constrained and lacks information. Instead of copying a subjective or biased modeling process, the author selected the DIM because of its following characteristics:

1. Has no bias or subjectivity.
2. Uses all possible information.
3. Makes the decision as if it had all information.
4. Does not learn.
5. Minimizes subjectivity and bias in the decision making process.

Another way to minimize bias is for the processing model to be able to use numbers that represent measurements, subjective ratings of past performance and current capability, and percentages without any translation. *When the numbers are translated, bias enters into the numbers, and the true value and meaning of the numbers can be diluted.* For example, instead of the user saying that a 9 or 10 rating means satisfied, the model uses the straight data (ratings). This prevents the user from having to decide if a contractor with 6 past projects should get the same rating as a contractor with 5 past projects.

Some models cannot consider the amount of references. It therefore does not motivate the contractor to have more experience, and dilutes the value of a contractor who may have received all 10s. If the best value contractor on the current project has a past performance of 9.5, it then motivates the contractor to get a rating on the project of at least 9.5 if the project weighting is 50% of the future performance rating. The DIM takes into account:

1. The number of references.
2. The exact performance numbers.
3. The current capability to identify and minimize risk as well as past performance.

Many modeling techniques use past cases to identify an optimal way of thinking. Instead of accepting how an owner thinks, the models can identify a better way to describe the requirement. This can be done by advising the owner that he or she would be better off having an expert identify their true wants or needs.

The DIM allows *an owner to represent his perception and expectations.* The objective with PIPS is to deliver performance to the owner. Many design professionals and design consultants attempt to identify what performance is to the owner. The author has designed PIPS to eliminate all time attempting to explain to the owner what performance is. An owner's expectations are unique. They know what makes them happy in terms of performance (budget, time, and quality expectation). It is the contractor's responsibility to meet the owner's expectations as well as they can.

The purpose of the modeling is to identify which contractor is the closest match to the owner's expectations. The bias of the owner enters the DIM as the owner's requirements (in terms of all factors that represent performance). The requirement is biased. PIPS wastes no time in trying to change this bias. The bias represents the owner. Its simplicity and ability to accept a "biased" requirement, regardless of the "level of consistency" in the relationship of the weighting between criteria, make it unique. The owner can use the modeling over and over for different projects by changing the weighting.

The DIM can be automated on a spreadsheet. PBSRG has made the model to be self-generating by entering the number of alternatives and the number of criteria. The data is copied into the spreadsheet with the criteria, the weights are entered, and the model runs itself. The model runs instantly. The operation of the model takes less than five minutes to set up once the data is compiled in spreadsheet format.

The DIM finds the relative distance of each alternative's value from the best value in each critical criterion. If an alternative has a very poor number, that alternative becomes noncompetitive. This prevents a contractor who is very weak in one criterion from trying to make it up in another criteria. A best value-performing contractor must be competent in all areas.

What separates the DIM from all other modeling techniques is that it has an information factor. The information factor identifies which factors have the largest differential. The easiest way to understand the concept is to consider making a selection between four alternatives, which are represented by three criteria. If all alternatives have the same value for one of the criteria, the user will make their decision based on the other criteria. If all the numbers are the same in that criterion, there is no information in that criterion, and the criterion becomes meaningless. The selection will be made where there is differential. No differential means no information. Differential means information. Those contractors who have the highest performance where there is differential, will have the competitive advantage. Those contractors who have the highest value where there is relatively no differential, will not have much of an advantage. The information factor has the following impact on contractors:

1. It motivates contractors to find the criteria with the most differences and improve in those areas.
2. Because of the large number of criteria, and different combinations of site superintendents, project managers, and critical subcontractors, it is very difficult for contractors to compete with other contractors. It forces contractors to compete against themselves, offering the very best value within the budget.
3. It forces the contractors to concentrate on value, instead of low price. The only reason to compete against another contractor is to increase value by either increasing performance or dropping price. The only reason to look at the competition is to drop price. This process makes it unprofitable to drop prices.
4. It minimizes the importance of a contractor's competitive advantage if it is in an area of very little differentiation.

The DIM is a very robust model. The model can identify for each contractor what their weaknesses are and where they can improve. Once the model is set up, students can play "what if" scenarios. The DIM also forces the project manager to have the right information, to document the entire process, and to be able to respond quickly to inquiries to errors and potential problems. Due to the relative prioritization of factors, the model also assists the project manager (PM) to do sensitivity analysis to debug any potential errors.

Modification of PIPS

The modeling has gone through very little change over years of development and testing (1994 - present). The changes that have been made include:

1. Separating price and performance. Both owners and contractors were not comfortable with including the price factor in determining performance. In many states, the state procurement laws specified that the performance and price should be calculated separately. The DIM was modified to account for these two factors.

The two factors are combined using a linear relationship between price and performance numbers in terms of percentage of the best number. The percentages are then multiplied by the weights, and the contractor with the most points is awarded the project. The construction industry participants were much more comfortable with this structure.

2. <u>Increasing spread.</u> Past performance criteria that were rated on a 1-10 scale, did not always have a large enough impact in the model due to the small variation in their spread. A modification was made to subtract the lowest number in all the "1-10" rated criteria from all the "1-10" criteria numbers.

DIM Model Explanation

The DIM is easy to understand. It competes and prioritizes the alternatives based on the distance away from the best values of the alternatives. It uses the weights placed on the different criteria by the owner and an information factor that identifies which criteria have no information. It uses the concept of entropy, or confusion caused by the lack of differential. DIM operates the same way every time, prioritizing the alternatives based on the three major factors (# of references, exact performance numbers, current capability to identify and minimize risk as well as past performance), the distance from the best value multiplied by the weighting factor, and the information factor. The model has been run 350 times and has a very high rate of identifying performance (98%).

Kosko discusses the theory of relativity and fuzzy logic (Kosko 1993). Zadeh discusses the theoretical foundation of the DIM (Zadeh 1993). Zadeh's book has an example of the DIM, which can be copied unto a spreadsheet. This book also includes a simple spreadsheet model of the DIM at the end of the book.

The following keywords are commonly referred to in the DIM:

Attribute: This refers to a single performance criterion, such as "ability to maintain schedule" or "quality of workmanship".

Alternative: This refers to each company or contractor.

Entropy: This can be defined as the amount of confusion. Entropy is defined as a number times the natural log of the number. It describes dispersion or the movement toward confusion. The opposite of entropy is information, or a very clear differential. Another explanation is that with information, the outcome is clear, with entropy, the outcome is very unclear.

Normalization: This is defined by relating a set of values to one another, accomplished by adding all of the values and then dividing each value by the total sum. Normalization always results in every number being between 0 and 1. Therefore, every number is relative to every other number in a decision making sense.

DIM Model Mathematical Explanation

A detailed explanation of the mathematical equations can be found in the book, "Multiple Criteria Decision Making" by Milan Zeleny (1982). An explanation using mathematical equations and symbols is presented below. The process can be divided into two modules:

1. Identifying fuzzy membership functions.
2. Recognizing the importance of attributes that describe the alternatives. This is further divided into the user's perception of importance and the intrinsic amount of information generated by the competing alternatives.

For the following set of pairs: $\{x^k_i, d^k_i\}$ $i = 1,\ldots\ldots,m$, $k = 1,\ldots\ldots,n$, where d^k_i is a membership function mapping the scores of the ith attribute into the interval [0,1]. Hence the degree of closeness (distance) to x^*_i for individual alternatives could be computed as:

a. If x^*_i is a max. Then $d^k_i = x^k_i / x^*_i$
b. If x^*_i is a min. Then $d^k_i = x^*_i / x^k_i$
c. If x^*_i is a feasible goal value or Coomb's ideal value, for example, x^*_i is preferred to all x^k_i smaller and larger than x^k_i, then $d^k_i = [\frac{1}{2} \{ (x^k_i / x^*_i) + (x^*_i / x^k_i) \}]^{-1}$
d. If, for example, the most feasible score is labeled by zero regardless of its actual closeness to x^*_i, we can define: $x_{i*} = \text{Min } x^k_i$ and $d^k_i = [(x^k_i - x_{i*})/(x^*_i - x_{i*})]$
e. The above four functions d^k_i indicate that x^j is preferred to x^k when $d^k_i < d^j_i$

To measure the attribute importance, a relative weight is given to every attribute. This reflects the decision maker's expectation based on their cultural, psychological, and environmental background.

The more distinct and differentiated the scores, or in other words, the larger the contrast intensity of the ith attribute values, the greater the amount of decision information contained in and transmitted by the attribute. The less differentiation, the less information the attribute has, and the less likely the owner is to make the decision based on that attribute. An attribute importance λ_i, is assigned to the ith attribute as a measure of its relative importance in a given decision.

For the vector $d_i = (d^1_i \ldots d^m_i)$ characterizes the set D in terms of the ith attribute and let $D_i = \sum^m_{k=1} d^k_i$ $i = 1 \ldots n$. Then the entropy measure of the ith attribute contrast intensity is $e(d_i) = -K \sum^m_{k=1} (d^k_i / D_i) \ln(d^k_i / D_i)$.

If all d^k_i became identical for a given i, then $d^k_i/d_i = 1/m$, and $e(d_i)$ assumes its maximum value, that is, $e_{max} = \ln m$. Thus by setting $K = 1/e_{max}$, we achieve $0 \leq e(d_i) \leq 1$ for all d_i's. Such normalization is necessary for comparative purposes.

We shall also define total entropy as: $E=\sum^n_{i=1}e(d_i)$ or $m(Lnm)$. Because weights $\lambda\tilde{}_i$ are inversely related to $e(d_i)$, we shall use $1-e(d_i)$ rather than $e(d_i)$ and normalize to assure that $0\leq\lambda\tilde{}_i\leq 1$ and $\sum^n_{i=1}\lambda\tilde{}_i=1$: $\lambda\tilde{}_i=[1/(n-E)][1-e(d_i)]$ n= number of criteria.

Both wi and $\lambda\tilde{}_i$ are determinants of importance in parallel fashion. The most important attribute is always the one that has both w_i (owner's perception) and $\lambda\tilde{}_i$ (differential)t their highest possible levels. The overall importance weight (information and weight) λ_i can be formulated as follows: $\lambda_i=\lambda\tilde{}_i.w_i$. Or after normalization: $\lambda_i=[\lambda\tilde{}_i.w_i]/\sum^n_{i=1}[\lambda\tilde{}_i.w_i]$ i=1,......,n. Calculation of relative distance R_i of each variable would then be: $R_i=\lambda_i[1-d^k_i]$ i=1,......,n.

DIM General Steps

The steps will now be explained in simpler terms. The DIM has the following general steps:

1. The owner identifies the requirement in terms of relative weights. The model then identifies the normalized weight (WFn) for each attribute.
2. The performance data is collected and input into the model.
3. DIM identifies the optimal value of each attribute from all of the alternatives.
4. DIM divides each value of every attribute by the optimal attribute value for a maximum best value, and inversely for a minimum best value. This makes the data for each attribute relational to all others, and each value of every attribute a percentage from the best value.
5. DIM normalizes the data to make all values relative and related for all of the attributes. This provides a relationship between values within and between different attributes.
6. DIM applies the entropy equation, which is a natural logarithmic function, to identify the entropy of each value for every attribute (factor of confusion). For numbers that are similar, the criteria has a high entropy or confusion value. The entropy is then summed for each attribute.
7. DIM divides each attribute's sum by the maximum possible entropy for every attribute, which is the natural log of the number of alternatives. This gives a percent of entropy for each attribute in relation to each other.
8. DIM calculates the percent of information for each attribute as the opposite of each attribute's entropy (each value subtracted from 1) and normalizes the values to determine the normalized information factor (IFn) for each attribute.
9. DIM subtracts each value calculated in Step 3 from one to determine each attribute's distance from the best attribute (which has a value of 1,) resulting in the distance from the best (DFB) for every alternative's attributes.
10. DIM multiplies the normalized weighting factor (WFn) by the normalized information factor (IFn). These values are then normalized and multiplied by each alternatives distance from the best (DFB) value.
11. DIM adds the values together for each alternative to determine the alternative's total relative distance (RD) from the best. The lower the total relative distance, the closer the alternative is to being the best value.

Running of the Automated DIM Model

Arizona State University licenses the PIPS process and an automated DIM spreadsheet processor. The model is hosted on Microsoft Excel. It requires the project manager to input the number of criteria and the number of alternatives. A model is generated and the project manager then copies the performance information, criteria, and weights into the model. The model then shows the following pages:

1. Weights and criteria (Attachment 10.1)
2. Performance data (Attachment 10.2)
3. Prioritized performance numbers (Attachment 10.3)
4. Criteria that made a difference, and the strengths and weaknesses of the contractor's performance (Attachment 10.4)
5. Final prioritization based on performance and price (Attachment 10.5)

Test Results

The following groups have run the DIM:

1. State of Hawaii, Chris Kinimaka (over 100 times).
2. State of Hawaii DOT, Jamie Ho (three times.)
3. Dallas Independent School District, Mike Cekowski (11 times).
4. Denver Hospital, Mark Bollig (3 times).
5. University of Hawaii, Charlie Serikawa (35 times).

The following groups are testing the process in the next year (2003-2004):
1. US Coast Guard.
2. Federal Aviation Administration.
3. Harvard University.
4. US Army Medical Command.

The process has been run 380 times and has resulted in 98% performance. The times when PIPS did not produce results was with the following:

1. A DOT project where a low bid specification was used, and where the client's representative did not allow the contractor to manage their own project. The environment was one of management and control. The process did pick the best team with the best personnel. The contractor identified very early in the project that their site superintendent was not the best suited for a performance based project. They ended up releasing the site superintendent and putting a performance based replacement with less experience on the project. There were other extenuating circumstances with the project, however the client's political environment prevented the project from being successful. The plusses on the project was that the paving smoothness far exceeded the normal paving smoothness (the major objective of the project,) the smoothness was predicted

from the interview of the paving superintendent, the users around the project were satisfied, the contractor received high ratings from the client's project managers.

2. The State of Georgia ran two PIPS projects. In one case they went low bid due to perceived high prices and found out that they paid more than the performance based bid (Chapter 23.) In the second case, the DIM picked the second low bidder, and the contractor had great performance. However, the contractor was given a low bid contract, and the owner did not appreciate the inflexibility of the price based contract.

3. United Airlines hired a design-build contractor who had never done a design-build project. The UA management maximized the risk by advancing the contractor a large portion of the $600K budget, before the contractor produced. The contractor ended up not paying some of the subcontractors, delaying the project completion. Amazingly, the high performance site superintendent and some of the critical subcontractors finished the work.

4. The State of Utah ran a project and selected the price based contractor on the project. The Project was poorly designed and the State of Utah did not run the pre-award phase. The project resulted in change orders.

5. The State of Hawaii ran a project (Maili mechanical renovation) where the committee overrode the model results, and picked the price based contractor. The contractor ended up losing key personnel and not performing.

6. A roofing project in Hawaii did not finish on time. the contractor received bad material on the project, and stopped the project. After receiving the correct material, they finished the project to the satisfaction of the client and users.

7. Another Hawaii roofing project was done poorly and reported a leak. Both the material supplier and the contractor did not have the best performance numbers. As predicted, the roof did not meet the satisfaction of the client or building user. The contractor was the low bidder on the project. The risk was predicted before the construction.

The DIM, through various modifications and tests had the following results:

1. 98% of the time selected the best value, high performance contractor.
2. Identified risk before the award.
3. Made it difficult for non-performers to compete.
4. Made it impossible to compete based on price.
5. Forced the contractors to offer the best value.
6. Was easily corrected when errors were identified in the data.
7. Was explained successfully in the administrative hearing by the State of Hawaii personnel under cross-examination.
8. Was validated as an acceptable process through a State of Hawaii administrative hearing (Chapter 21.)
9. Was run by five different individuals who understood the DIM, understood and explained the results, and led to successful construction.

Conclusion

The DIM has the following characteristics:

1. Forces contractors to bid their best value, and then compete with other contractors for the best valued best value.
2. Gives credit to the best performance, does not penalize contractors in the mainstream, but penalizes a contractor who has a nonperforming number in a critical category.
3. Mathematical functions reflect the IMT philosophy.
4. Minimizes subjectivity.
5. Identifies risk in terms of distance.
6. Successfully picked the best value that performed 98% of the time.
7. Makes it very difficult for a contractor with a nonperforming team member to win the bid.

The DIM is a critical component of PIPS. The State of Utah, the University of Hawaii, and the State of Hawaii have all tried to run a process without the DIM. They are all back to low bid procurement with the poor performance of the priced based sector which looks solely at price.

Chapter 10 Review

1. What does the DIM stand for?
2. What is the DIM?
3. How is the DIM related to PIPS?
4. What are the three main factors used in the DIM?
5. Give an example of how the Information Factor (IF) works?
6. How is the DIM different from other selection models?

References

Blake, John. (2000). *An Introduction to Data Envelopment Analysis.* IENG 4564, Design and Optimization of Service Sys. Retrieved from http://www.emp.pdx.edu/dea/homedea.html

Gupta, P.K., & Mohan, M. (1994). Problems in Operations Research (Methods and Solutions). Sultan Chand & Sons.

Hartigan, J.A. (1975). *Clustering Algorithms.* New York: John Wiley.

Hastie, Tibshirani, and Friedman (2001). *The Elements of Statistical Learning Data Mining.* Springer-Verlag.

Hillier, F.S., & G.J., Liebermann. (1967). Introduction to Operations Research, Fourth Edition. Oakland, CA: Holden-Day, Inc.

Kosko, Bart. (1993). *Fuzzy Thinking, The New Science of Fuzzy Logic.* New York: Hyperion.

Morrison, D.F. (1976). *Multivariate Statistical Methods* (2nd edition). New York : McGraw-Hill.

Nydick, R.L., & Hill, R.P. (1992). Using the analytic hierarchy process to structure the supplier selection procedure. *International Journal of Purchasing and Materials Management*, 28 [2], pgs. 31-36.

Rama, Nathan. (2000). Retrieved from DataEnvelopmentAnalysis/HUT/September-December.

Richard A. Johnson and Dean W. Wichern Everitt. (1993). *Applied Multivariate Statistical Analysis fifth edition.*, B.S. Cluster Analysis (3rd edition). London : Edward Arnold.

T.L. Saaty. (1980). Analytic Hierarchy Process, McGraw-Hill.

Winston, Patrick Henry. (1993). *Artificial Intelligence (Third Edition)*. Reading, Massachusetts, Addison-Wesley.

Zadeh, Lofti. (1993). *Fuzzy Logic for the Management of Uncertainty;* J.B. Wiley & Sonsal Acquisition Regulation (27 Dec 1999), FAC 97-15, 15.101

Zeleny, Milan. (1982). Multiple Criteria Decision Making. New York: McGraw Hill.

Attachments

Attachment 10.1: Example of Weighting Sheet
Attachment 10.2: Sample Performance Data Sheet
Attachment 10.3: Prioritized Numbers (Relative Distance)
Attachment 10.4: Criteria that Made a Difference
Attachment 10.5: Final results

Attachment 10.1: Example of Weighting Sheet

Weights

NO	CRITERIA	WEIGHTS
GC1	Ability to manage the project cost	0.00666
GC2	Ability to maintain project schedule	0.00666
GC3	Quality of workmanship	0.00666
GC4	Professionalism and ability to mange	0.00666
GC5	Close out process	0.00666
GC6	Communication, explanation of risk, and documentation	0.00666
GC7	Ability to follow the users rules, regulations, and requirements	0.00666
GC8	Overall customer satisfaction and hiring again based on performance	0.00666
GC9	Number of different people surveyed	0.00666
GC10	Number of different projects surveyed	0.00666
PM1	Ability to manage the project cost	0.008325
PM2	Ability to maintain project schedule	0.008325
PM3	Quality of workmanship	0.008325
PM4	Professionalism and ability to mange	0.008325
PM5	Close out process	0.008325
PM6	Communication, explanation of risk, and documentation	0.008325
PM7	Ability to follow the users rules, regulations, and requirements	0.008325
PM8	Overall customer satisfaction and hiring again based on performance	0.008325
PM9	Number of different people surveyed	0.008325
PM10	Number of different projects survyed	0.008325

Attachment 10.2: Sample Performance Data Sheet

NO	CRITERIA	(1-10) (#) (-)	Option 4	Option 3	Option 2	Option 1
1	Risk Assessment Plan Rating	(1-10)	6.00	6.50	6.92	1.75
2	Interviews	(1-10)	6.81	6.82	7.65	3.48
3	Schedule (Days)	(#)	84	60	140	60
GC1	Ability to manage the project cost	(#)	8.98	9.40	9.64	9.38
GC2	Ability to maintain project schedule	(1-10)	9.45	9.29	9.60	9.31
GC3	Quality of workmanship	(1-10)	9.58	9.43	9.64	9.69
GC4	Professionalism and ability to mange	(1-10)	9.55	8.71	9.74	9.85
GC5	Close out process	(1-10)	9.19	9.00	9.46	9.23
GC6	Communication, explanation of risk, and documentation	(1-10)	9.45	9.00	9.58	9.38
GC7	Ability to follow the users rules, regulations, and requirements	(1-10)	9.62	9.50	9.72	9.69
GC8	Overall customer satisfaction and hiring again based on performance	(1-10)	9.63	9.29	9.76	9.85
GC9	Number of different people surveyed	(#)	20.00	7.00	20.00	13.00
GC10	Number of different projects surveyed	(#)	20.00	7.00	20.00	12.00
PM1	Ability to manage the project cost	(1-10)	8.83	9.67	9.69	9.00
PM2	Ability to maintain project schedule	(1-10)	9.53	9.67	9.63	9.33
PM3	Quality of workmanship	(1-10)	9.78	9.67	9.69	9.67
PM4	Professionalism and ability to manage	(1-10)	9.64	9.33	9.79	9.83
PM5	Close out process	(1-10)	9.08	8.50	9.53	9.17
PM6	Communication, explanation of risk, and documentation	(1-10)	9.47	9.33	9.60	9.33
PM7	Ability to follow the users rules, regulations, and requirements	(1-10)	9.81	9.33	9.81	9.50
PM8	Overall customer satisfaction and hiring again based on performance	(1-10)	9.75	9.67	9.75	9.83
PM9	Number of different people surveyed	(#)	14.00	3.00	10.00	6.00
PM10	Number of different projects surveyed	(#)	12.00	3.00	10.00	6.00

Attachment 10.3: Prioritized Numbers (Relative Distances)

NO	CRITERIA	0.341 Option 4	0.351 Option 3	0.157 Option 2	0.645 Option 1
1	Risk Assessment Plan Rating	0.139	0.114	0.094	0.347
2	Interviews	0.030	0.030	0.009	0.113
3	Schedule (Days)	0.019	0.000	0.037	0.000
GC1	Ability to manage the project cost	0.000	0.000	0.000	0.000
GC2	Ability to maintain project schedule	0.000	0.000	0.000	0.000
GC3	Quality of workmanship	0.000	0.000	0.000	0.000
GC4	Professionalism and ability to manage	0.000	0.000	0.000	0.000
GC5	Close out process	0.000	0.000	0.000	0.000
GC6	Communication, explanation of risk, and documentation	0.000	0.000	0.000	0.000
GC7	Ability to follow the users rules, regulations, and requirements	0.000	0.000	0.000	0.000
GC8	Overall customer satisfaction and hiring again based on performance	0.000	0.000	0.000	0.000
GC9	Number of different people surveyed	0.000	0.006	0.000	0.003
GC10	Number of different projects surveyed	0.000	0.006	0.000	0.004
PM1	Ability to manage the project cost	0.000	0.000	0.000	0.000
PM2	Ability to maintain project schedule	0.000	0.000	0.000	0.000
PM3	Quality of workmanship	0.000	0.000	0.000	0.000
PM4	Professionalism and ability to manage	0.000	0.000	0.000	0.000
PM5	Close out process	0.000	0.000	0.000	0.000
PM6	Communication, explanation of risk, and documentation	0.000	0.000	0.000	0.000
PM7	Ability to follow the users rules, regulations, and requirements	0.000	0.000	0.000	0.000
PM8	Overall customer satisfaction and hiring again based on performance	0.000	0.000	0.000	0.000
PM9	Number of different people surveyed	0.000	0.017	0.006	0.013
PM10	Number of different projects surveyed	0.000	0.014	0.003	0.009

Attachment 10.4: Criteria That Made A Difference

NO	CRITERIA	Distance Sums	0.3412 Option 4	0.3512 Option 3	0.1573 Option 2	0.6448 Option 1
1	Risk Assessment Plan Rating	0.6943	0.1389	0.1144	0.0940	0.3470
2	Interviews	0.1813	0.0298	0.0296	0.0088	0.1130
3	Schedule (Days)	0.0839	0.0185	0.0001	0.0370	0.0001
GC1	Ability to manage the project cost	0.0005	0.0001	0.0001	0.0001	0.0001
GC10	Number of different projects surveyed	0.0159	0.0001	0.0063	0.0001	0.0039
GC2	Ability to maintain project schedule	0.0005	0.0001	0.0001	0.0001	0.0001
GC3	Quality of workmanship	0.0005	0.0001	0.0001	0.0001	0.0001
GC4	Professionalism and ability to manage	0.0005	0.0001	0.0001	0.0001	0.0001
GC5	Close out process	0.0005	0.0001	0.0001	0.0001	0.0001
GC6	Communication, explanation of risk, and documentation	0.0005	0.0001	0.0001	0.0001	0.0001
GC7	Ability to follow the users rules, regulations, and requirements	0.0005	0.0001	0.0001	0.0001	0.0001
GC8	Overall customer satisfaction and hiring again based on performance	0.0005	0.0001	0.0001	0.0001	0.0001
GC9	Number of different people surveyed	0.0133	0.0001	0.0056	0.0001	0.0031
PM1	Ability to manage the project cost	0.0005	0.0001	0.0001	0.0001	0.0001
PM10	Number of different projects surveyed	0.0383	0.0001	0.0137	0.0031	0.0092
PM2	Ability to maintain project schedule	0.0005	0.0001	0.0001	0.0001	0.0001
PM3	Quality of workmanship	0.0005	0.0001	0.0001	0.0001	0.0001
PM4	Professionalism and ability to manage	0.0005	0.0001	0.0001	0.0001	0.0001
PM5	Close out process	0.0005	0.0001	0.0001	0.0001	0.0001
PM6	Communication, explanation of risk, and documentation	0.0005	0.0001	0.0001	0.0001	0.0001
PM7	Ability to follow the users rules, regulations, and requirements	0.0005	0.0001	0.0001	0.0001	0.0001
PM8	Overall customer satisfaction and hiring again based on performance	0.0005	0.0001	0.0001	0.0001	0.0001
PM9	Number of different people surveyed	0.0520	0.0001	0.0173	0.0063	0.0126

Attachment 10.5: Final Results

Overall Best Value

Rank	Contractor	Total Points	Relative Distance	Distance Points	Price	Price Points
1st	Option 2	98.14	0.157	60.00	$ 411,009.00	38.14
2nd	Option 4	67.00	0.341	27.66	$ 398,500.00	39.34
3rd	Option 3	60.33	0.351	26.87	$ 468,637.00	33.45
4th	Option 1	54.64	0.645	14.64	$ 391,926.00	40.00

Performance Factor	60
Price Factor	40

11

How to Select A General Contractor

Introduction

This chapter will discuss the selection of a general contractor (Chapter 15 covers the selection of a specialty contractor). Selecting a general contractor's team is different from selecting a specialty contractor because:

1. The project is more complex. There are more entities and coordination between entities.
2. The projects are longer in duration and usually have higher costs.
3. It is more difficult for the general contractor to control the project.

PIPS uses the following concepts:

1. Leadership: Assigns responsibilities to performing persons and groups and allows them to do their work.
2. Minimization of management and control: Minimizes the amount of client's management over the general contractor.
3. Information: Minimizes the information passed to different parties to performance and risk information.

The differences between using PIPS to select a specialty contractor and a general contractor are:

1. Due to the complexity and number of entities, the role of the site superintendent and project manager are critical.
2. The general contractor's past performance is important, but is not more important than the critical subcontractors: electrical, mechanical, waterproofing, and any major systems being installed.
3. The risk assessment plan that identifies, prioritizes, and minimizes risk, is more important than past performance. This takes into account that the model penalizes contractors who have low performance far from the mean of the other contractors.
4. The bidding process will impact the value of the risk assessment plans. On general contracting projects, contractors have a difficult time transitioning from the low price mentality to the performance-based mentality. Therefore, subcontractors wait until the last minute to submit their bids. This puts pressure on the general contractors to quickly submit their plan and appropriate team members.

5. Due to the complexity of having many factors, general contractors are forced to compete against themselves, submitting the best possible value they can offer within the budget.
6. The pre-award period is much more important due to the increased complexity of the construction requirement. During the pre-award period, the contractor must ensure that they know how to minimize risk, coordinate all design requirements between the key individuals, and clarify any un-constructible items.
7. The general contractor, project manager, site superintendent and critical subcontractors are not only at risk, but are risks to each other. At the end of the project, the entire team receives the same rating. Subcontractor prices may fluctuate based on the contractor and key personnel on the project.
8. The contractor interface (Chapter 25) is used during construction to force the contractor to manage the project by identifying, documenting, and minimizing risk.
9. Contractor closeout becomes more important.

The same PIPS recommendations apply when selecting general contractors:

1. Do not limit the pool of potential contractors.
2. Do not limit the major systems to a specified design, but entertain alternatives with equal performance.
3. Use performance information as much as possible.
4. Do not make decisions.

PIPS Process

The process is the same as in a specialty contractor selection:

1. Design and request for proposal.
2. Education meeting (required for general contractors and their specialty contractors).
3. Collection of the past performance information of all critical team members.
4. Pre-bid walkthrough.
5. Submittal of the risk assessment plan and the contract documents (bid price, bonds, licenses, and team composition).
6. Rating of the risk assessment plans.
7. Short-listing if required.
8. Interview of the key personnel on the team.
9. Prioritizing the options based on past performance, risk assessment plan, and interviews.
10. Pre-award period.
11. Award and construction.
12. Rating of construction work.

A tentative schedule is shown in Attachment 7.1a. It is important to note that the education meeting and collection of the performance information does not have to be done repeatedly.

Policy Decisions

The following questions should be answered before the invitation to the Education Meeting is sent out:

1. Can the budget of the project be listed?
2. Should contractors over the budget be disqualified?
3. Is the client pre-qualifying the participating contractors?
4. Which subcontractors are critical (and should be performance lined)?
5. What is the maximum number of references a contractor can submit?
6. Who will references include (will the contractors or the users decide)?
7. Are there any prequalification for references?
8. Which contractors should attend the education meeting?
9. Should the education meeting be combined with the pre-bid meeting/site walk?
10. Are any systems being performance rated?
11. What is the maximum number of pages of the risk assessment plan?
12. What is to be included in the risk assessment plan?
13. Should the risk assessment plan be submitted at the same time as the bid packages?
14. Should the contractors be short-listed before the interviews?
15. Who should be interviewed? The site superintendent? The project manager? Should they be interviewed together or separately? Should anyone else be allowed in the interview?
16. Who is on the rating committees?
17. Who is handling the reference and contract documents?

Should the budget of the project be listed?

The author proposes that the budget should be listed. Any contractor who uses the entire budget without any contingency is not a performing contractor. When selection is based on performance and price, the true performers will always do a better job if they have all information available. There are three factors to minimize risk: expectations (design), time, and cost (budget). Without any of the three factors, the high performers will be forced to minimize risk by subjectively creating the client's expectation level.

The performer is rarely going to be the low bidder. Therefore, the low bidder will gain their advantage by proposing a lower cost. The low performer will not increase their cost if they knew the budget, because they would be giving away their advantage (low price). Expectation, time, and budget are interrelated. Without all three, the contractor cannot maximize the impact of risk minimization. If the budget is not given, the performing contractor will be forced to guess if the expectation is within the budget.

PIPS projects have been done both ways. Releasing the budget does not influence the spread of prices because of high competition. The PIPS projects have never had a budget problem because there are no contractor generated cost change orders.

Should contractors above the budget be disqualified?

Contractors within the budget should be prioritized first. Contractors over the budget should not be disqualified, but prioritized last. High performing contractors that know they are over budget should identify why there is a differential in price. If a lower costing contractor is awarded the project, the lower costing contractor will be forced to minimize the risk identified by the high priced contractor. In this way, a contractor over the budget is regulating the quality and value delivered by the other contractors. The quality that they would have delivered at the higher price will have to be delivered by the lower priced option. This forces the high quality contractors to identify and differentiate their quality.

Is the client pre-qualifying the participating contractors?

The client should not prequalify unless there are political constraints. If prequalification is done, the risk is increased. The problems with prequalification and using a set number of contractors include:

1. The contractors are not truly competing with competitors who have highly skilled personnel. Long-term relationships do not lead to high performance. High performance results from intense competition and continuous performance (Quadrant II characteristics). Performers continually measure their performance and attempt to continually improve.
2. Prequalification always puts the emphasis on price. Even though the client may say they consider performance and value, price is still in the back their mind. If it is not, the contractor would truly act in the best interest of the owner, and minimize the risk of the owner.
3. Long-term relationships allow the client's representatives to get heavily involved with projects. When this happens, the risk is shared and the motivation of the contractor is not to unilaterally minimize risk. If there are political forces in the environment, it becomes much more comfortable for the contractor to partner and share the risk with the client's representative. This type of relationship requires the client's representative to have tremendous expertise. This relationship can result in performing construction, however it is not as consistent and sustainable.

Which subcontractors are critical and should be performance lined?

Any specialty subcontractor whom does over 25% of the work should be performance lined. Any system that is over $50K or 25% of the project budget should be performance lined. Any subcontractor that deals with an area where the client has had problems in the past should be performance lined.

What is the maximum number of references a contractor can submit?

The author recommends 40 references.

Who will references include?

Good candidates for references are facility owners, maintenance and operations personnel, general contractors, and designers.

Are there any prequalification for references?

Clients can request references to come from commercial facilities, renovation projects, and projects that are in-operation buildings.

Which contractors should attend the education meeting?

All critical contractors and subcontractors should attend the meeting. The author highly recommends owners to direct all contractors not to send advertising or marketing personnel to the meeting. The author also recommends to owners not to allow general contractors to explain PIPS requirements to all critical subcontractors. General contractors have been trained to control specialty subcontractors. PIPS proposes that in a true information and performance based environment, the general contractor becomes a coordinator instead of a controller. General contractors may not be capable of explaining this new environment to the specialty contractors.

Should the education meeting be combined with the pre-bid meeting/site walk?

The education meeting will function as a prequalification meeting. After the education meeting, some contractors may withdraw due to the performance requirements. The author proposes to have an education meeting the first time PIPS is tested. In later runs, it may be combined with the pre-bid meeting.

Are any systems being performance rated?

Any system that is over $50K, 25% of the project budget, or has been a severe nuisance to the client, should be performance lined.

What is the maximum number of pages of the risk assessment plan?

If the project is under $500K, the risk assessment plan should be a maximum of two pages. Over $500K, the maximum number of pages should be 10.

What is to be included in the risk assessment plan?

Chapter 7 discusses the details of the risk assessment plan. The risk assessment plan should analyze risk in terms of cost, expectation, and time. It should then identify how the risk will be minimized. It should quickly cover the who, why, when, where, and how. It should identify what is going to be done to perform at a higher level, what value the contractor will bring that is different, what will be done that minimizes the need for owner participation, and how the contractor will monitor and measure their own performance.

The client must not direct the contractors with specific forms, items, or format. This will only train the contractors to give the client what they ask for and no more. Allow the contractors to be creative and identify what they truly know. After all, they are meant to be identifying how they are going to construct the job. If none of the contractors delivers a valuable risk assessment plan, they all get the same RA plan score. The selection will then depend on the past performance and the interview score. This will still deliver a high performance contractor.

Should the risk assessment plan be submitted at the same time as the bid packages?

If the project is complicated, and the input of the critical specialty contractors can be used in the risk assessment plans, the RA plan should be turned in a couple days after the submittal of the bids. However, the plans can be submitted simultaneously for more simplistic projects.

Should the contractors be short listed before the interviews?

If there are more than five contractors, the contractors can be shortlisted.

Who should be interviewed? The site superintendent? The project manager? Should they be interviewed together or separately? Should anyone else be allowed in the interview?

For general construction projects over $250k, the site superintendent and the project manager should be interviewed. For projects under $250K, only the site superintendent should be interviewed.

Who is on the rating committees?

The rating committee should consist of individuals from the facility, the design team, and the owner's project manager.

Who handles the reference and contract documents?

An individual who is not on the review/selection team should handle all the reference information and the contract submittals. The analysis of performance data can be outsourced. The bid person should ensure that they have copies of everything before the data is sent to PBSRG or other 'data crunching' organizations. The data organization team will input data, identify data that puts the client at risk, and formulate performance lines that the client can use.

Contractor Actions

The contractors are given an RFP that explains the entire process. It is important that the contractors be given a checklist of critical activities that they must do including:

1. Attend the educational meeting.
2. Know the critical dates.
3. Submit reference lists for general contractors, site superintendents, project managers, and critical subcontractors to the owner.
4. Submit a risk assessment plan.
5. Send out surveys to all references and have the references send them back to the owner.
6. If short-listed, make sure the site superintendent and project manager are prepared for the interview.
7. If prioritized and selected as best value by the project manager, the general contractor must participate in a pre-award phase to confirm the risk assessment plan, coordinate design with key personnel, and clarify any discrepancies.

Contractors are responsible for identifying the client's risks, and how the risks will be avoided. The contractors must understand that the performance of all the key elements is being measured. The contractor is responsible for measuring themselves, and identifying their own strengths and weaknesses. The contractors are competing against themselves and are responsible for their own actions.

Measurements During the Process

The owner is asking the contractors to measure themselves before the bidding, as a team during the bidding, and when construction is over. The measurements will put people in a continuous improvement cycle. The author recommends that the performance measurements be given back to the contractors so that they can compare themselves against their competitors. If a contractor wants to argue with their references about their rating, they have no one to blame but themselves.

Conclusion

PIPS is the same process whether run to select a specialty subcontractor or a general contractor's team. PIPS forces contractors to define who they are, measure their own relative performance, and allows the user to analyze their proposal in a very nonbiased fashion. The contractor is then motivated to continuously improve by tracking their own quality and performance, and thereby controlling their own destiny. Contractors who are high performers and who minimize the risk of the clients will feel very confident in this process.

Chapter 11 Review

1. Why do the majority of GCs not want to have the critical subcontractors rated?
2. Should the critical subcontractors be educated?
3. Why do subcontractors not want to give value engineering ideas to the general contractor?
4. Should the risk assessment plan and the contractor's bid on a complex project be turned in at the same time? Why or why not?
5. What are the key criteria on a GC project?
6. Should the budget be released to the contractors? Why or why not?
7. Does PIPS work better on a large, risky project or a smaller single trade project? Why?

12

Designers: Problems, Selection, and Design

Introduction

For the past 30 years, the designer's role has been the controlling function in the delivery of construction. As the client started demanding a better value, the designer has attempted to deliver construction as a commodity. The resulting performance has not met the expectations of the user. Reacting to the poor construction performance (not being, on time, on budget, or meeting quality expectations), building owners are moving to alternative delivery processes that consider "best value." Best value construction is not a commodity and should not have to be managed and inspected. Best value construction does not require means, methods, and minimum specifications.

The poor performance in the design-bid-build process has forced designers and consultants to move more into construction management and inspection. The need for expertise in planning, programming, and design is being diminished. The designer's ability to minimize the owner's risk has been reduced. Fees, functions, and hours have also been reduced. Designers have responded by minimizing their liability through insurance, and minimizing their risk by forcing the owner to make more design decisions. Ironically, it is the designers planning, programming, and design skills that bring the client the most value.

Design Industry Status Quo

Designers have defined their function by delivering construction as a commodity. They have used materials, means, methods specifications, and minimum standards to define the commodity. The commodity was then bid by contractors and awarded to the lowest bidder. The owners attempted to minimize the risk caused by using marginal services and systems through construction management and inspection by professionals (designers and engineers). However, the resulting construction performance has been inconsistent and has not met the expectations of the owners in most cases.

Owners have reacted by moving to alternative delivery processes that deliver construction as a non-commodity (consider the price and performance of the contractor and systems) to increase the performance of construction. If construction is not a commodity, designers find themselves in a precarious position. Since they propose to deliver construction as a commodity, they acquired the following problems:

1. They were forced to define the construction requirement using minimum standards. Minimum standards encourage contractors and manufacturers to deliver the cheapest possible performance.
2. They were forced to completely identify and describe every construction requirement. The design is no longer an intent, but a regulatory document which describes the minimum requirement. Anything that is not described becomes a potential change order.

Designers Become a Source of Risk in the Low Bid Arena

Instead of assisting the owner in communicating the intent and identification of the construction requirement, the design professional has now become a source of potential risk for nonperformance. Their efforts may result in lower quality, lower performance, and less value (Butler 2002). Even when the designer does a great design in terms of detailed means, methods, material specifications, and drawings, the designer actually becomes a bigger source of risk. This is easily understood by looking at the PIPS process (Figure 12.1). The question that explains this is, "If the designer does a more complete design in terms of details, which contractor will benefit more, the high performer, or the low performer?"

The answer to this question is the low performer. The high performer already knows how to do the construction. It is the low performer who will not be able to effectively bid on the project if they are not given exact instructions on how to do the construction. In some cases, they will not be able to bid because of their lack of construction expertise. This reasoning is also emphasized by the fact that when PIPS is run, the poor performing contractor must also find a way to identify, prioritize, and minimize risk to the owner. By definition, poor performing contractors cannot do this. Therefore, designers should do their expertise: identifying, prioritizing, and minimizing risk in transforming an owner's requirement into a non-technical construction requirement. Any issue should not be solved technically, but by using performance numbers. Technical specifications can be used if it is easier, but any "or equals" should be approved by using performance numbers.

Designers Have Become Commodities

The designers have minimized their liability and risk by acquiring insurance. However, the insurance companies minimize their own risk by constraining the functions of the designers. Ironically, designers are being directed on what they can and cannot do by their insurance companies. In minimizing their risk, the insurance companies minimize the designers' decision making (decisions result in risk). Designers, therefore, ask the owners to define what is required in terms of programming and planning; they then respond to the owners' directions. This illustrates how designers are losing their ability to identify and lower the risk to the owners (in terms of cost, time, and quality expectations). The author proposes that many designers cannot identify risk to the owners, prioritize the risks, and minimize the risks. As designers lose their ability to identify and minimize the owners' risk, the differential between the designers disappears. Designers then become a commodity and will be selected based on price.

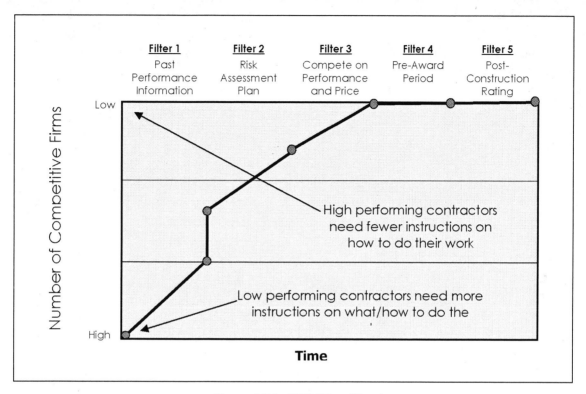

Figure 12.1: PIPS Filter Chart

Many designers are in denial. They claim that they are qualification-based and not price-based. However, with no differential in true performance (identifying, prioritizing, and minimizing risk), they become price based. In the truest sense, qualification based processes are price-based. Qualification looks for minimum standards to see if a designer is qualified. If they are, they are compared with the other designers who are also qualified. Once an owner identifies that designers are qualified, it will become a price-based issue. Designers will react in the following ways to clients in the price-based environment:

1. Use their relationship with the user to attempt to influence selection.
2. Not follow instructions that minimize bias or help the owner identify performance.
3. Perceive the requirement to prove their past performance and identify, prioritize, and minimize risk as too much work.
4. Ask the user to identify exactly what is required so that they can price out their bid.

A service is either price based (commodity) or it is performance based. It cannot be both. If the above four characteristics exist, the environment is price based, because the conditions would not exist if it were a performance based environment.

Standards Are Another Source of Risk

The delivery of construction as a commodity is one of the major reasons for construction nonperformance. Standards are set based on minimums. Recall the example of the ASTM standard (explained in Chapter 4) that shows the following:

1. Each manufacturer (A, B, C...) tests their material using the ASTM test to identify the physical characteristic measurement.
2. The chart (Chapter 4, Figure 4.2) shows all the measurements.
3. The lowest value for each characteristic becomes the ASTM standard.
4. The last column is the ASTM standard. It usually does not represent a product, but a combination of the lowest values.

The ASTM standard has no correlation with performance. Once the ASTM standard is identified, each manufacturer is now motivated to minimize the performance of their product until it meets the minimum standards. The objective is to lower the cost of the material as long as the physical characteristics are above the ASTM standard. The way the standards are set, motivates manufacturers, to continually lower the value of their products. Standards are a source of lowering value and increasing the risk of failure.

Standards are never set to increase performance. Standards are required in the low bid sector. If the service or product is being specified, it is being sold as a commodity. Commodities are always price based. However, because the best value is the lowest price when using minimum standards, the designer's specification, which includes minimum standards, now becomes a source of construction risk. The designers are directing the contractors to deliver construction:

1. As cheap as possible.
2. Forcing contractors to assume that all things will go right.
3. Assuming that the specifications and drawings are flawless.

These actions increase the risk of the project. By defining construction as a commodity, designers and their design documents, become a source of risk. They force everyone to think in terms of low price, low quality, and to deny responsibility when something goes wrong.

Current State of Designers

Many designers have lost their capability to identify, prioritize, and minimize, the risk in terms of cost, time, performance, and quality expectations. When asked to compete based on performance, many designers will not be able to. Instead they will try to use the same low bid tactics that they have always used (personal relationships, marketing and sales brochures, and social events such as dinners, golfing, or sports events). When a designer exhibits these characteristics, the client should be wary.

To escape from being a source of risk, designers must learn how to use performance information to quantify and improve on their performance. They must learn how to identify, prioritize, and minimize risk in terms of cost, time, and expectation. They must learn not to use minimum standards and stop directing, controlling, and managing the contractor. Designers can be motivated to change if clients select designers using PIPS. However, in the beginning, designers who operate as a performance-based entity may have a distinct advantage.

PIPS Process For the Selection of Designers

The PIPS selection process for designers is the same as for contractors. The following are the major steps:

1. Invitation sent to the designers.
2. Educational meeting.
3. Collection of past performance. Designers and subcontractors (mechanical and electrical engineers) are asked to submit 20 references. The lead designer is also asked to submit references.
4. Risk assessment plan. Identify, prioritize, and minimize risk of the owner in the project.
5. Shortlist based on past performance and risk assessment plan score.
6. Interview the lead designer.
7. Selection based on past performance, risk assessment plan, interview, and price.

Invitation to the Designers

The invitation should help the designers decide if they want to attend the educational meeting. If the first project is not in the designer's expertise, it is better that the designer knows ahead of time. It is important for the client to minimize the effort and cost of the designers. It is also important to advise the design firms not to send their marketing people to the educational meeting. They may have no technical background, and they may not understand the importance of following the PIPS instructions.

The designers must be told the following:

1. The owner will award to a designer based on performance and price.
2. Brief description of the project.
3. The designers will be asked to minimize the risk of the client.
4. The PIPS process is different from the traditional qualification based process.
5. The educational meeting is mandatory.
6. The design firm president or a project manager should attend.
7. Designers should be instructed to bring a business card with an email address.
8. Designers should be told to be in place 30 minutes ahead of the meeting's start time. Any person arriving after the meeting has started, will not be allowed into the room and will be disqualified from project.

Educational Meeting

The first time PIPS is being used to select designers, the educational meeting must be done correctly. The client must ensure the following:

1. The project is defined in terms of the client's requirements.
2. The schedule is set in terms of when the design needs to be completed.
3. The owner must decide how the designer will be selected.
4. The client gives complete control of the design to the designer.
5. The designers understand the PIPS process and understand exactly what is required.

The client must give all information they have on the project to the designers. If information is withheld, the performers who minimize risk will be at a disadvantage. Even though the requirements for past performance information and risk minimization is written in a request for proposal, it should be repeated in detail during the education meeting.

Past Performance Information

Design firms are asked to submit:

1. A list of 20 references on their firm.
2. A list of 10 references each, on the lead designer, mechanical, and electrical engineers.

The design firm is then requested to send a survey form to their references, and request that the references send the forms back to the client. The design firm is requested to submit only good references, and discuss the importance of the survey with their reference before sending the reference to the client.

A design firm needs to go through this experience only once. The past performance becomes a permanent record. There is only two ways to improve the past performance record:

1. Do more projects well.
2. Get the reference to upgrade the rating.

Case Study of the Denver Health and Hospital Authority

In 2002, the Denver Health and Hospital Authority (DHHA) implemented the (PIPS) process for the selection of a designer, for a medical research building. The DHHA's objectives for running the PIPS process were to:

1. Identify if PIPS can differentiate between the performances of different designers.
2. Identify if PIPS can successfully select the best potential designer.
3. Validate the perception of the current state of the design community.

The project selected was a new medical research laboratory. The scope of the project was $5M-$12M, with a potential estimated design fee of $1.2M. The risk of the project included: the method of funding the location of the research laboratory, the need to maximize the performance of the hospital, and the assurance that the project would be completed satisfactorily.

The next step in the process was the submission of the references. Fourteen design firms and six engineering firms submitted references. The firms were then instructed to submit their team proposals. Three firms were disqualified for either failing to list a lead designer or listing a lead designer with no past performance information. One design firm did not have the capability to compete on this project.

The submitting of the risk assessment plans was next. The purpose of the plan was to identify which design firms could identify, prioritize, and minimize the risk to the owner. The plans were to be brief and simple (no more than 6 pages), and they would have to be in non-technical terms. To prevent bias, the plans could not contain any names that could identify the firms involved. Out of ten risk assessment plans, one firm was eliminated since their plan contained the firm's name (contrary to repeated instruction not to do so). This reduced the competition to nine design firms. The plans were given to the review committee for rating. The DHHA review committee comprised of two facility representatives and two medical personnel representatives. Every member independently rated each plan. As it turned out, they all selected the same alternatives.

The following observations were made:

1. Some design firms wanted the owner to identify the scope in clearer terms. They stated that it was difficult to cost.
2. No design firm prioritized the identified risks.
3. No design firm performed a quick analysis of cost, quality, and design time.
4. All plans contained marketing information (did not differentiate based on performance) that did not have to be included.
5. Only three plans addressed the site's unique characteristics and clearly identified the risks.
6. No plan addressed why the designer was chosen for the project.
7. No plan identified how the designer would rate performance and how the designer would improve their design performance on the project.

Short-listing of firms

The past performance information and the risk assessment plan ratings were inputted into the DIM processor, which prioritized the design firms (Table 12-1). Out of the nine design firms, the selection committee selected the top four prioritized firms (A3, A6, A13, and A14) to move on to the second phase of interviews and bid proposals.

Table 12-1: DIM Prioritization

Rank	Design Firm	Score
1	A3	10.00
2	A13	5.21
3	A6	4.84
4	A14	4.42
5	A10	4.39
6	A5	3.75
7	A9	2.66
8	A4	2.43
9	A11	2.25

The largest differentiator, in the performance areas, was the risk assessment plans.

Final Selection

After the firms were short-listed, the lead designers were interviewed. The purpose of the interview was to verify that the risk assessment plan and the lead designer's perception were identical. Both are critical, however, it is most critical to know that the lead designer understands the risk and how to minimize the risk, and does not need to be managed by the firm or the user. Any case to the contrary requires management and direction, leading to inefficiency and risk. Table 12-2 displays the results of the interview scores.

Table 12-2: Cost Proposals and Interview Scores

Firm	Cost	Interview Score
A14	$ 1,049,230	9.52
A6	$ 895,000	8.41
A3	$ 1,171,000	7.61
A13	$ 961,200	7.33

As shown in Table 12-2, all of the bid proposals were within the acceptable budget ($1.2M). The largest differentiators in the final selection of the performance areas, were the interviews' and management plans' scores. Table 12-3 shows the results of the final model based on performance and price.

Table 12-3: Final Prioritization Order

Rank	Firm	Total Score	Performance Points	Price Points
1st	A14	9.63	7.50	2.13
2nd	A6	9.38	6.88	2.50
3rd	A3	6.79	4.88	1.91
4th	A13	6.66	4.33	2.33

The DHHA identified the following reactions from design firms:

1. At the out briefing meeting, several designers vocalized that the process required them to do too much work, was not worth their time, and that most designers were uncomfortable with the process.
2. Not all the designers showed up for the out briefing.
3. Some designers attempted to use their personal relationships with the owner to change the process.
4. One design firm identified that the process gave them a new method to differentiate themselves from other design firms.

The owner and users were very comfortable with their selection. The best value designer won approval from the DHHA governing board.

Conclusion

The results of the DHHA case study support the following hypothesis:

1. Design firms are focusing more on marketing and personal relationships to win projects, rather than on minimization of the user's risk.
2. Design firms have lost their capability to identify, prioritize, and minimize risk, in terms of cost, time, and quality.
3. Design firms do not want to change, and consider the owner forcing them to differentiate themselves, as too much work.

Performance construction is delivered with better planning, programming, design (design work), and construction (contractor work). If designers continue to attempt to use tools that use minimum requirements, deliver construction as a commodity, and attempt to manage and control construction work, their value and professionalism will be minimized. Designers need to return to their core competencies of planning, programming, and designing. They need to be able to identify, prioritize, and minimize the owner's risk through high performance design work. Using performance-based processes to select designers will motivate designers in this direction (Post 2000).

Chapter 12 Review

1. What should a designer do, if he/she needs to do a lot of work in responding to the risk assessment plan?
2. What factors will PIPS consider in selecting the best value?
3. Which factor is the most important in the design selection? Which is second most important?
4. Why is the risk assessment plan minimized to five pages?
5. What should be included in the risk assessment plan?

References

Butler, J. (2002). Construction Quality Stinks, *Engineering News Record (ENR)*, 248 [10], p. 99.

Kashiwagi, D. & Johnson, K. (2002). The Impact on the Changing Construction Industry on Architectural and Engineering Design Services. *The 1st International Conference CIB-W107 – Creating a Sustainable Construction Industry in Developing Countries,* South Africa, pp. 455-464.

Post, N. (2000). No Stamp of Approval On Building Plans: Contractors sound off over difficulties with bid documents. *Engineering News Record (ENR),* 244 [17], pp. 34-37, 39, 42, 45-46.

Attachments

Attachment 12.1: A/E Survey Questions
Attachment 12.2: A/E Interview Questions
Attachment 12.3: Risk Assessment Plan Rating Sheet
Attachment 12.4: Interview Rating Sheet

Attachment 12.1: A/E Survey Questionnaire

To: _____
Phone: _____
Fax: _____

Subject: Past Performance Survey of _____
(Name of design firm and/or individual/(s) being surveyed)

The XXXXX is implementing a process that collects past performance information on design firms and key personnel.   The information will be used to assist the XXXXX in the selection of design firms to perform various agency projects.   The firm/individual listed above has chosen to participate in this process.   They have listed your firm as a client for which they have previously performed design services.   We would very much appreciate your taking the time to complete this survey.

Rate each of the criteria on a scale of 1 to 10, with 10 representing that you were very satisfied (and would hire the firm/individual again) and 1 representing that you were very unsatisfied (and would never hire the firm/individual again).   Please rate each of the criteria to the best of your knowledge.   If you do not have sufficient knowledge of past performance in a particular area, leave it blank.

Client Name: _____
Project Name: _____

NO	CRITERIA	UNIT	RATING
1	Ability to meet the customers expectations	(1-10)	
2	Ability to manage costs (minimal design & construction change orders)	(1-10)	
3	Ability to maintain project schedule (completed on time or early)	(1-10)	
4	Comfort level in hiring the firm/individual again based on performance	(1-10)	
5	Ability to increase value (quality of design)	(1-10)	
6	Ability to identify and minimize the users risk	(1-10)	
7	Ability to close out (proper documents, assisting contractor to perform)	(1-10)	
8	Leadership ability (minimized the need of owner direction)	(1-10)	

Please fax the completed survey, no later than February 20, 2004, to my attention at either (555) 555-5073 or (555) 555-9219. Thank you for your time and effort in assisting the XXXXX in this important endeavor.

John Smith
Contracting Officer - XXXXX

Attachment 12.2: A/E Interview Questions

A/E INTERVIEW QUESTIONS

1.   Why were you picked for this project?

2.   What personal qualities/traits will assist you to perform on this project?

3.   What is your major objective on this project?

4.   Do you feel comfortable with minimizing the risk instead of depending on the client to minimize the risk?

5.   What are you going to do differently on this project than on previous projects you have worked with?

6.   What makes you think that you can do this project in the shortened time frame?

7.   Walk through the project in major steps and identify where the risks are and what will be done to minimize the risk.

8.   Identify the risks on this project in terms of time, resources or funding, and expectation.

9.   What risk does the owner bring to the project?

10. How will you pass information during the project?

11. Why were the other individuals/firms chosen for this project?

Attachment 12.3: Risk Assessment Plan Rating Sheet

Instructions:

The risk assessment plan should <u>not</u> contain any names or products that may be used to identify who the contractor is. Plans that contain any technical terms, any means and methods (unless it affects the performance in a significant manner), or any material technical descriptions should receive low ratings.

Criteria are rated on a scale of 1-10, with 10 being the best and 1 being the worst. All plans should start from an average (or 5 rating) and go up and down depending on the relative value. If a plan stands out it should get a 10. If none of them seem any different, they should all get an average score of 5. If a plan is so bad that the rater feels like they should not get the project, they should be rated a 1.

No	Criteria	1	2	3	4	5
1	Structure of the Plan (Organized, concise, brief, non technical)					
2	Identification of Risk Areas (In terms of cost, schedule, and quality)					
3	Plan to Minimize Risk					
4	Increase of Value (Cost reduction or added quality)					

Total _____

By signing your name below, you state that you have based your scores on the contents of each plan and that you have had no prior knowledge of any plan and whom they belong too. You further agree that there is no collusion or conflict of interest between yourself and any other party involved.

Name: _____   Date: _____

Attachment 12.4: Interview Rating Sheet

Instructions:

Personnel should be rated based on the manner in which they respond to questions. They should be quick, concise, and give the impression that they have already built the facility.

The interview criteria are rated on a scale of 1-10, with 10 being the best and 1 being the worst. If an interview stands out, they should get a score of 10. If they don't seem to stand out they should get an average score of 5. If the interview is so bad that the rater feels like they should not get the project, they should be rated a 1.

		ALTERNATIVES				
NO	**CRITERIA**	**1**	**2**	**3**	**4**	**5**
1	Ability to understand the risk assessment plan					
2	Identification and minimization of risk (In terms of schedule, cost, and quality)					
3	Identifying the critical components of the job					
4	Identifying how the entire team was selected (Why subs, and key personnel were chosen)					
5	Identifying what activities will be done differently					
6	Comfort level of getting the job done					
7	Comfort level in working with a high performing contractor					

By signing your name below, you state that you have based your scores on the contents of interview. You further agree that there is no collusion or conflict of interest between yourself and any other party involved.

Name: _____   Date: _____

13

Movement to "Best Value" Using the FAR

Introduction

The U.S. Federal Government has been attempting to move from the low-bid award system to a "best-value" (or performance contracting) delivery system (Office of Federal Procurement Policy 1992, Federal Acquisition Streamlining Act 1994, Winston 1999). The Federal government has identified that their current procurement system has the following characteristics (General Government Division 1990, Office of Federal Procurement Policy 2000, Charles 2002):

1. Poor performance and value.
2. By using means and methods specifications, the federal government is retaining all the risk and liability.
3. Inefficiency.

However, the federal government has not been successful in using performance contracting (Burman 1997, Trimble 2003, Department of Defense 2001). The following supports this:

1. There is little documentation identifying where any federal government agency has tracked the continuous value and performance of their contractors and their contracting group in terms of being on time, on budget (with no contractor generated cost change orders), and meeting the user's expectations of quality.
2. There is no documentation on the impact of the performance of designers, contractors, and users on the performance of contracting groups.
3. There has been no documentation of a method to identify if best value or performance contracting efforts have resulted in performance or an increase in performance over a period of time.

Procurement and contracting agents have many reasons for not changing, including:

1. Complexity of the FAR.
2. Inability to release control.
3. Fear of change.
4. Fear of losing their job.
5. A lack of understanding of the construction industry.
6. A lack of a structural process that minimizes their risk in best value procurement or performance contracting.

Most federal agency procurement or contracting officers will only do something new if:

1. Someone else does it first.
2. Someone directs them to do it.
3. Someone tells them exactly how to do it, releasing them from any liability.

This objective of this chapter is to introduce procurement and contracting officers to the RFP option in the FAR and to show that PIPS can be modified to meet the FAR. This chapter will:

1. Identify that the FAR allows the use of best value (or performance contracting).
2. Review the difficulties for federal agencies to implement a performance based procurement process.
3. Identify how to modify PIPS to meet the requirements of the FAR.
4. Differentiate between policy and the FAR.

Federal Acquisition Regulation (FAR)

The majority of procurement done by the Federal Government is governed by the Federal Acquisition Regulation (FAR). Federal agencies are directed to Section 36 for FAR directives on procuring construction services (FAR 36):

> "When a requirement in this part is inconsistent with a requirement in another part of this regulation, this Part 36 shall take precedence if the acquisition of construction or architect-engineer services is involved." (FAR 36.101b)

Many federal government groups and procurement agents still maintain that the best value in construction is the lowest bid. The FAR clearly states that to award using the sealed bid, the following requirement must be met:

> "Contracting officers shall acquire construction using sealed bid procedures *if the conditions in 6.401(a) apply....*" (FAR 36.103b).

Section 6 has the following (FAR 6.401):

> (a) Sealed bids. Contracting officers shall solicit sealed bids if-
>
> (1) Time permits the solicitation, submission, and evaluation of sealed bids;
>
> (2) *The award will be made on the basis of price and other price-related factors;*
>
> (3) It is not necessary to conduct discussions with the responding offers about their bids; and
>
> (4) There is a reasonable expectation of receiving more than one sealed bid.

It has been proven that construction cannot be delivered successfully as a commodity (Chapter 4). Movement to alternate delivery systems, which consider the relative performance or expertise of the contractors, shows that it is necessary to discuss the delivered construction with the offers. The testing of PIPS has shown that discussions with the offers solve the non-performance issues of construction (Chapter 7). It is shown in the transaction cost analysis of the State of Hawaii (Chapter 21) and the University of Hawaii (Chapter 22) that the result of delivering construction with discussions with offers minimizes the user's first cost of delivering construction. The theoretical foundation of IMT, KSMs, and successful business practices shows that delivery of construction performance is related to the experience level of the contractor. *The successful delivery of construction requires the award will be made based on factors other than price or price-related factors. The low bid award, sealed bid process is designed to procure commodities* (all the same), and the delivery of construction does not meet the requirements of FAR 6.104(a). The delivery of construction cannot be considered a commodity.

Because construction is not a commodity, further information and discussion is needed to understand a contractor's bid. A contractor's bid should identify their level of performance that is associated with the bid, and be responsible to meet that level of performance. FAR 6.04(b)(1) states that the contracting officer can request for competitive proposals or use the request for proposal (RFP) process. The wording of 6.04(b)(1) is listed below:

> (b)　　Competitive proposals (see Part 15 for procedures).
>
> 　　(1)　　Contracting officers may request competitive proposals if sealed bids are not appropriate under paragraph (a) of this section.

The FAR then directs the contracting officer to look in Part 15 for details on how to do the RFP. FAR 15 allows contracting officers to use any process or any combination of processes in the FAR (best-value, one-step or two step, or performance contracting) to procure contracting services (FAR 15.101):

> "*An agency can obtain best value in negotiated acquisitions by using any one or a combination of source selection approaches. In different types of acquisitions, the relative importance of cost or price may vary. For example, in acquisitions where the requirement is clearly definable and the risk of unsuccessful contract performance is minimal, cost or price may play a dominant role in source selection. The less definitive the requirement, the more development work required, or the greater the performance risk, the more technical or past performance considerations may play a dominant role in source selection.*"

The FAR offers exceeding latitude to the contracting officers, spelling out that the awards do not have to go to the lowest priced option (FAR 15.101-1):

> "A tradeoff process is appropriate when it may be in the best interest of the Government to consider award to other than the lowest priced offeror...When

using a tradeoff process, all evaluation factors shall be clearly stated in the solicitation...This process allows the Government to accept other than the lowest priced proposal. Their perceived benefits of the higher priced proposal shall merit the additional cost."

The FAR even allows the contracting officer to make a decision, explain the rationale, and document the occurrence, but does not require the contracting officer to quantify the decision in any way (FAR 15.308):

"The source selection authority's (SSA) decision shall be based on a comparative assessment of proposals against all source selection criteria in the solicitation. While the SSA may use reports and analyses prepared by others, *the source selection decision shall represent the SSA's independent judgment.* The source selection decision shall be documented, and the documentation shall include the rationale for any business judgments and tradeoffs made or relied on by the SSA, including benefits associated with additional costs. *Although the rationale for the selection decision must be documented, that documentation need not quantify the tradeoffs that led to the decision.*"

Therefore, the FAR allows federal agency procurement offices to use any variation of performance contracting or best-value procurement. The FAR also states that the procurement agent must document the decision, but no quantification of the tradeoffs needs to be documented. The only requirement is that the contracting officer document their decision making process.

Obstacles in Using Best Value

The Office of Federal Procurement Policy (OFPP) defines "Past Performance Information" as relevant information regarding a contractor's actions under previously awarded contracts, specifically the contractor's (OFFP Letter 92-5):

1. History of conforming to specifications and to standards of good workmanship.
2. Record of containing and forecasting costs on any previously performed cost reimbursable contracts.
3. Adherence to contract schedules, including the administrative aspects of performance.
4. Proclivity for reasonable and cooperative behavior and commitment to customer satisfaction.
5. Business-like concern for the interest of the customer.

It is the federal government's policy that executive agencies shall use past performance information (OFFP Letter 92-5):

1. Prepare evaluations of contractors' performance on all new contracts over $100,000. Evaluations shall be made during contract performance at the time the work under the contract is completed.

2. Use past performance information in making responsibility determinations in both sealed bid and competitively negotiated procurements.
3. Specify past performance as an evaluation factor in solicitations for offers for all competitively negotiated contracts expected to exceed $100,000 except where the contracting office determines that such action is not appropriate. Such determinations shall be in writing and included in the contract file. As an evaluation factor, past performance should be used to assess the relative capabilities of competing offers and to help assure greatest value source selections.
4. Allow newly established firms to compete for contracts even though they lack a history of past performance.

The last point in the above document confuses the issue of the use of past performance. Newly established firms do not have past performance. The directive seems contradictory. It is statements such as these, and the misunderstanding of what past performance is used for, which prevents many contracting agents from understanding how to do best value or performance based contracting.

The FAR states that to be determined a responsible contractor, the contractor must have a satisfactory performance record. A contractor shall not be determined responsible or non-responsible solely on the basis of lack of performance history, *except as provided in 9.104-2 (9.104-1)*. Section 9.104-2 states that when it is necessary, special standards may be used that are desirable when experience has demonstrated that unusual expertise are needed for adequate contract performance. However, the goal of PIPS is not to create work or risk.

When best value or performance contracting is to be utilized to deliver construction (Quadrant II), both performance factors and price are to be used. Because the award will go to the best value that meets the budgetary constraints of the agency, there is no need for the use of additional minimal requirements beyond the existing bonding and license requirements currently in place. *Therefore, the use of performance information as a minimal qualification is not required.* This invalidates the use of performance information to pre-qualify or eliminate contractors. This also minimizes the need for government agencies to use negative performance information to eliminate a contractor from competition.

An information based performance procurement system should not discriminate against a particular contractor for a lack of past performance history. Discrimination is the act of unfairly, subjectively, and selectively discriminating against a contractor for a specific characteristic that the contractor may possess. An information based performance procurement system will minimize the subjective decision making of the contracts and other decision-making personnel of the agency. Every contractor should have the opportunity to show and have considered his or her best construction potential.

The federal government has several past performance databases and performance models. Databases include:

1. The U.S. Air Force (USAF) Contractor Performance Assessment Reporting System (CPARS).
2. The Defense Logistic Agency (DLA) Automated Best Value Model (ABVM).
3. The Army Corps of Engineers (USACE) A&E Contract Administration Support System (ACASS) and Construction Contract Appraisal Support System (CCASS).
4. The National Institute of Health (NIH) Contractor Performance System (CPS).
5. The Federal Aviation Administration's (FAA) Qualified Vendor List (QVL).

The shortcomings with the above-mentioned databases include:

1. No method of applying the past performance numbers from projects that were unique with different conditions to the current project without subjective translation. The subjective translation is usually into values that demonstrate that the contractor meets a perceived minimum standard. This makes the potential best performance a moot issue and encourages an award to the lowest bidder.
2. The inability to break out the performance of the key components including the site superintendent, lead craftsperson, and critical subcontractors who performed on the projects.
3. The majority of the projects were not awarded to the contractors with the understanding that their performance on the project would dictate their future competitiveness.
4. No method of maintaining a useable "performance number" on a contractor once work is completed.
5. No method of using the past performance number to recognize the potential for high performance in the award of a construction project.

The federal government is using performance information for qualification purposes. This usage of performance information identifies whether or not the contractors meet the minimum standards of an agency and encourage the use of a low-price award once the agency has pre-qualified the contractors. This is the objective of two-stage procurement, pre-qualification, and award to the lowest-priced qualified contractor. This process is no different from a well-enforced, low-bid award, which does not consider past performance and the contractor's ability to minimize risk on a unique project. The process still requires regulatory means and methods specifications, inspection, and construction management. This is the Quadrant I environment that has led to poor construction performance, and higher construction delivery costs. These concepts are incongruent with performance contracting where the user provides the contractor with a requirement and allows the contractor to determine means and methods, to accept liability for the project, and to finish on schedule while meeting budget and quality expectations.

The current structure for all existing best value contracting systems uses a high degree of subjectivity and minimizes the value of performance information. The current use of past performance information does not:

1. Motivate contractors to continuously improve.
2. Motivate the contractor to minimize the risk of nonperformance.

3. Factor in the capability to identify and minimize risk on a new project in terms of price, time, and quality.
4. Transfer the risk of nonperformance to the contractor.
5. Directly factor current project performance into the contractor's future past performance line.

Federal government agencies end up maintaining huge databases of "difficult to use information." The value of the information is minimized because a government decision maker will interpret the information before it is used. The key to the current use of performance information is the decision making of the contracting officer. The author proposes that whenever there is subjective decision making, the direction of the awards is always to the low bidder. This is easily seen by the following IMT and KSM analysis (Figure 13.1):

1. A lack of information leads to decision-making.
2. Decision-making is only done when information is lacking. If there is a preponderance of information, everyone will agree, and decision-making is not needed.
3. When information is lacking, risk is high.
4. Decision-making brings risk.
5. A lack of information will make alternatives look alike.
6. When alternatives look alike, the best value is the lowest price.
7. The lowest price brings the highest risk.

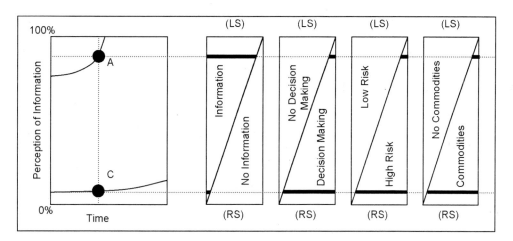

Figure 13.1: KSM (Information, decision-making, risk, and commodities)

Instead of supporting the procurement of value, the procurement groups have become procurement of commodities. To be successful they must:

1. Minimize decision-making.
2. Release control and direction of the contractors and vendors. There is no precedence where control led to high performance.
3. Help measure performance using relative numbers.

Case Study with the U.S. Coast Guard

The Coast Guard Civil Engineering Group, headquartered in Washington D.C., was introduced to PIPS in October 2001. A presentation made to all installation commanders in December 2001, met with an enthusiastic response. With the intended objective of implementing the process throughout the entire U.S. Coast Guard, twenty U.S. Coast Guard procurement and facility personnel attended a two-day education and training session at Arizona State University in February 2002. The procurement and contracts personnel presented the following ideas:

1. The process does not meet the FAR's procurement requirements.
2. U.S. Coast Guard contracts officers cannot run the process.
3. The process is not needed, as current processes are already delivering performing construction.
4. The Coast Guard already documents past performance with the National Institute of Health (NIH) system and does not need another performance database.
5. The Coast Guard procurement policies mandate that the contracts officer negotiate with the best offer.

The procurement and contracts personnel then briefed the legal office on their understanding of PIPS and requested a legal review of the system. The following is a list of concerns and the responses (Eder 2002).

1. A major concern was that the Coast Guard contracting officer would lose control of the contracting function. The legal review stated, *"There is the danger that purchasing or using an outside PIPS consultant to independently evaluate actual proposals might be a prohibited activity."*

   This confirmed that the procurement group did not understand that PIPS is a process that is run by the procurement and contracts group. The underlying fear of losing the procurement function made it seem as though PIPS made it unnecessary for procurement and contracts personnel. In the early stages of PIPS development, the information based PIPS seemed so efficient, procurement agents felt threatened by the process. PBSRG is a research office, which educates and continually modifies PIPS in order to make it more efficient and capable of meeting the policies of each unique user.

2. The Coast Guard does not use the term pre-qualification. *"If PIPS were to be utilized by the Coast Guard, this federal procurement term (pre-qualification) should be renamed or dropped to avoid confusion."*

   The purest form of PIPS does not use prequalification. PIPS allows all contractors to compete to the final selection. Although it can be used with a two-step process, it is not recommended unless it is the only way to meet the policies of the user.

3. The Coast Guard was concerned that the cost of data collection would eliminate some of the contractors. *"Any associated costs were reasonable so as not to materially discourage contractors from competing for the contract."*

   This cost is minimal and is usually borne by the user and not the contractors.

4. Another concern was that a *"... contractor with no past performance may be ineligible to compete for awards under the performance driven PIPS program."*

   This is a policy issue and not a PIPS issue. PIPS is a process to procure a non-commodity item. If a service is a commodity, and past performance is not required, PIPS should not be run. However, if the service is not a commodity, and the user wanted to allow contractors without past performance to bid, the user should weight past performance "0" or very low, and the selection will be based on capability to identify and minimize risk and price.

5. The Coast Guard had issue with the reliance on numerical ratings in the selection of the best value and was concerned that the *"...FAR requires documentation of the relative strengths, weaknesses, and risks of the proposals.... The PIPS program does not appear to provide a way to 'un-crunch' the computer generated numbers into narrative, or easily explain the meaning and value of the numbers."*

   The PIPS program uses a modified Displaced Ideal Model to prioritize alternatives (Chapter 7 and 10). It identifies the relative strengths and weaknesses of each alternative according to the owner's perception of performance, the values of the competitors, and the distance away from the best values. This numerical description is information that the contracting officer can use in the award justification. The PIPS model puts the information in a very user-friendly format. Instead of data, it is transformed into information, making it simpler for the contracting officer to make and justify their decision.

6. The legal review raised another award justification issue. It stated, *"...At the very heart of federal-negotiated-best value-procurement process is the requirement that source selection authorities perform tradeoff analysis showing why a higher priced offer is worth the price premium, or why a lower priced offer is not worth the savings".*

   The author agreed with the Coast Guard thought process. The DIM identifies relative performance and allows the contracting officer to do a trade off analysis between price and performance. The DIM, does the trade-off analysis and prioritization with no bias. However, if the contracting officer, who has to justify the award, desires to use their individual bias to override the model results, the contracting officer has the option.

7. The procurement and legal personnel concerned about the "Lack of Competitive Range & Discussion Components" in PIPS stated, *"It does not incorporate some certain basic negotiated contract FAR Part 15 procedures. One is the lack of*

competitive range for discussions.... It is unclear if the PIPS program allows for 'clarifications' of proposals before an award".

To clear up this misunderstanding, PIPS allows for clarifications to the proposal during the interview stage. After one vendor is interviewed, the other vendors can be interviewed and clarifications sought. At this stage, specifications can be made available or technical questions can be asked. There is no set limit on the amount of clarification that can be sought. Once the clarifications of bids are made, the interview is rated and the model is run.

8. The legal personnel were concerned about the ability to direct contractors on improving their bids when using PIPS. They quoted FAR 15.306(d)(3) *"...requires that significant weaknesses, deficiencies, or other aspects of a proposal being considered for award be discussed that could materially enhance the proposal's chance for award. In turn, these discussions must be held with all offers within the competitive range, a range that must be determined if any discussions are in fact held. It seems inconceivable that no aspect of any exchange at a typical PIPS pre-award meeting would qualify as a FAR discussion".*

When using PIPS the contracting officer does not want to direct the contractor on what to do. When the owner directs the contractor, the owner accepts the risk. The way the contracting officer can assist the contractor to improve their proposal is by alerting the contractor to any additional risk that they are not aware of. This allows a contractor to reassess their proposal, ensuring that they will perform. A competitive range of prices can be preset from 75% of the budget to the budget. This does not preclude an owner from conducting best and final discussions with the contractors or from going back to all contractors with new information.

PIPS does not set a limit on the extent of discussion with the offerors. That is set by policy of the owner. PIPS does not override policy (PIPS can be modified to meet policy). The pre-award meeting is an opportunity for the best value contractor to confirm to the owner that the project can be accomplished. It is also an opportunity to clarify project requirements. Clarifications are allowed by the FAR before the award of a project.

9. The next issue involves the "Use of Price & Disclosure of the Ceiling Price Issue". The Coast Guard stated, *"PIPS appears to require that the owner provide some sort of cost ceiling at the outset of the competition".*

The setting of a ceiling price is policy and does not impact PIPS. A budget figure or a range of prices can be given to the contractors. It is noted that if the owner does not release budget figures to the contractors, the contractors are faced with additional risk. The contractors who will minimize the risk are the higher performing contractors. The withholding of information will make the risk minimization contractors less competitive. The lower performing contractors who use lower price as their competitive advantage are not affected by the identification of the budget figure.

Most contracting personnel use the withholding of the budget figure to ensure that the contractors don't take the entire budget. However, if the award is by low bid, the low bidder will get the project. The low bidder does not price based on the budget. The practice of withholding the budget is based on a lack of trust, inefficiency, and an illogical thought process. If the contracting officer would like to give a range instead of a budget, the range should be as small as possible.

10. The Coast Guard did not previously consider only good references but perceived that *"[The] PIPS program requires contractors to solicit past performance scores only from owners who would give them high performance marks.... PIPS expressly does not want to factor negative performance"*.

The current government policy is based on prequalification and low bid. However this is a policy incorporated by the owner. The owner can implement other policies which are inefficient, hard to manage, bring the opportunity of litigation, and minimize the purpose of using past performance. Past performance can include: best as defined by the contractor, best plus what the user has experience with, or the last ten jobs that the contractor completed. This is a policy statement and not a PIPS rule.

The procurement personnel thought performance information must be released before the award. However, PIPS owners have not released any information, or model results, before the award. The type of information released after the award is determined by the user's policy.

11. The procurement personnel asserted, *"...Any rigid PIPS requirement for no cost increase to the contract price would have to be modified"*.

There is no rigid PIPS requirement for no contractor generated cost increase change orders. There is a performance-rating factor at the end of the project, and a contractor can be penalized for originating cost increase change orders in order to make a profit on the project. However, it does not stop a contractor from generating a cost increase change order. The PIPS structure is simply designed to minimize cost increasing change orders.

12. The legal review closed with the following remark: *"It would be legally difficult if not impossible to exclusively rely upon the PIPS system as a stand-alone source selection tool"*.

This statement was made during the their initial analysis of PIPS without an understanding of the process. It is very important to understand the following:
   a. PIPS is a theoretical concept that increases the value of construction projects. It must be implemented according to the user's policy, in this case, the Coast Guard and the FAR. Therefore, it is not a stand-alone process and is not intended to be contrary to the FAR, nor should it be used in such a manner.

    b. It is not a process that should be used exclusively.

    c. It should be tested and confirmed to work in the FAR environment.

    d. It does require the facility and contract personnel to be educated.

Modifications to PIPS to meet the "Letter of the Law" perception of the FAR have been done. Some of the modifications are now recommended whether or not the FAR requirements need to be met. The modifications include:

1. After the management plans are submitted and rated, the identified risks should be sent back to all the contractors. The contractors should be given an opportunity to change their price and their management plan. The management plan rating remains unchanged.

2. After the DIM is run to prioritize the options, the model results should be given to the contracting officer. The contracting officer has the option of awarding to the top prioritized contractor or awarding to another party, based on the value of the other contractors.

Case Study of the Corps of Engineers

The Corp of Engineers (COE) has it's own interpretation of the FAR:

FAR 15.305 Proposal evaluation.

(a) Proposal evaluation is an assessment of the proposal and the offeror's ability to perform the prospective contract successfully. An agency shall evaluate competitive proposals and then assess their relative qualities solely on the factors and subfactors specified in the solicitation. Evaluations may be conducted using any rating method or combination of methods, including color or adjectival ratings, numerical weights, and ordinal rankings. The relative strengths, deficiencies, significant weaknesses, and risks supporting proposal evaluation shall be documented in the contract file.

The major obstacle with the COE procurement is their interpretation of the above section. The US Army Source Selection Guide, which is the interpretation of the FAR, states:

"When using the tradeoff process, you evaluate the non-cost portions of the proposal and associated performance and proposal risks using rating scales. These scales must be included in the SSP and may consist of words, colors, or other indicators, with the exception of numbers. (Numerical rating systems appear to give more precise distinctions of merit, but they may obscure the strengths, weaknesses, and risks that support the numbers.)" (US Army Source Selection Guide, Chapter 5 "Rating Scales" page 15.)

This is the biggest "mumbo jumbo", bureaucratic, direction that sets apart the FAR. If numbers cannot be used, then colors or descriptions must take their place. It results in the following:

1. Impossible to prioritize alternatives with multiple factors.
2. Forces the contracting officer to make a subjective decision.

3. Makes past performance information a "moot" issue.
4. Forces contracting officers to transform colors to numbers, do the calculation in their head, and transform it back into colors once the final number is calculated.

The only result of this direction is non-direction. The only possible reason for such a practice, is to give the contracting officer a position where they cannot be questioned. This is a case where the FAR is OK, but the interpretation of the FAR does not make sense. "Numerical rating systems...may obscure the strengths, weaknesses, and risks that support numbers." Customer satisfaction ratings, performance periods, percentage of successes....are numbers. These numbers should not be interpreted. This direction takes the Army back into the dark ages.

How can a procurement agent consider multiple criteria, many of them objective and very hard to misunderstand, when every number has to be transformed to a color.

At one point in time, numerical criteria are in a numerical format. The procurement officer should use the DIM as an information generator. Colors can be transformed to numbers and input into the model. The DIM is run, and the alternatives are listed in terms of distances from the best number. This information becomes an input to the procurement agent, who must then look at all the primary numbers which are changed into colors and make a decision.

This is the biggest change in PIPS, allowing the procurement agent to take the output of the DIM, and use it as an input to their final decision. However, the numerical output of the DIM cannot be used directly as the justification of value. the procurement agent must transform all numbers to colors.

This change in PIPS is shown in Figure 13.2. The following changes are reviewed:

1. All risks that are identified are given back to all the contractors, allowing them to change their price. However, their risk assessment plan rating is not changed. Remember, because numbers cannot be used, color ratings must be given to the RA plan rating, and the color is transformed back into numbers to run the model.

2. Interviews can be conducted as a part of the information feed (FAR 15.)

3. Clarification is done with the best value contractor. This is the pre-award phase.

4. The contracting officer writes up a recommendation that is based on colors. This shields the contracting officer, because the subjective color is not attackable.

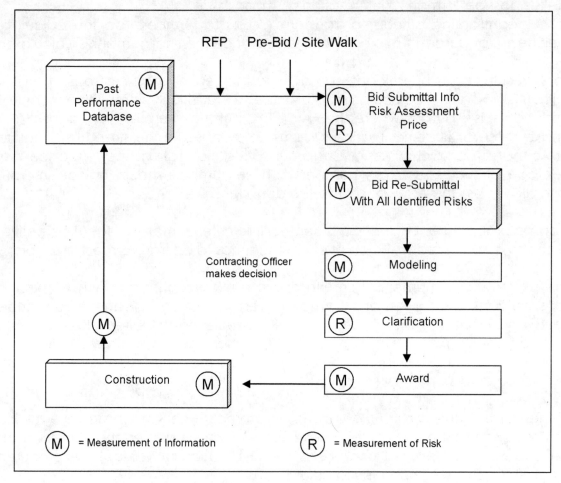

Figure 13.2: PIPS with the FAR

Conclusion

The FAR allows for performance contracting and best value procurement in the federal government. If construction is identified as a non-commodity item, the request-for-proposal process meets the conditions of the FAR. PIPS can be used to meet all of the conditions of the FAR. Federal contracting officers should use PIPS as a tool within the policies and requirements of the FAR. PIPS is the only process with documented results of value and performance. If any federal agency would like to test out PIPS, they should contact the author at the website www.pbsrg.com.

Chapter 13 Review

1. If there is a conflict between PIPS and the user's policy, can PIPS still be legally implemented?
2. Can PIPS be modified to meet all the rules and regulations of the user?
3. Does PIPS meet the requirements of the FAR?

References

Burman, A. (1997, October 1). Putting Past Performance First. *GovExec*. Retrieved from http://govexec.com/procure/articles/1097mark.htm

Charles, M. (2002 February). Proposal Allows States to Use Design/Build On Federally Funded Projects. *Civil Engineering* 72 [2], p. 34.

Department of Defense. (2001, May 1). A Guide to Collection and Use of Past Performance Information (Version 2). Deputy Under Secretary of Defense.

Eder, E. A. (2002, February 26). Subject: Performance Based Procurement System (PIPS), United States Coast Guard HQ Legal Office, Chief Office of Procurement Law Addressed letter to Chief Office of Procurement Management, February 26.

Federal Acquisition Regulation. (2001 September). Issued by the: General Services Administration Department of Defense National aeronautics and Space Administration. Federal Acquisition Circulars through 97-27. Volume I – Parts 1 to 51.

Federal Acquisition Streamlining Act. (1994). Federal Acquisition Streamlining Act of 1994. S.1587, SEC. 1091. Policy Regarding Consideration of Contractor Past Performance.

General Government Division. (1990, January 18). Federal Construction: Use of Construction Management Services. *United States General Accounting Office*. Report to Congressional Requesters.

Office of Federal Procurement Policy. (1992, December 30). Policy letter no. 92-5. Past Performance Information. Section 6(a) OFPP Act, 41, U.S.C. 405.

Office of Federal Procurement Policy. (2000, May). Best Practices for Collection and using current and past performance information. Office of Management and Budget: Executive Office of the President.

Trimble, S. (2003, July 1). IG Finds DOD Has Mishandled Most Performance-Based Contracts. *Aerospace Daily*. Retrieved July 7, 2003, from http://www.aviationnow.com/avnow/search/autosuggest.jsp?docid=122350&url=http%3A%2F%2Fwww.aviationnow.com%2Favnow%2Fnews%2Fchannel_aerospacedaily_story.jsp%3Fview%3Dstory%26id%3Dnews%2Fmis07013.xml.

Winston, S. (1999, October 4). Pentagon Pumps Up Performance. *Engineering News Record*, 243 [14], p. 10.

14

PIPS Core Group:
Information Workers and Industry Advisory Group

Introduction

The PIPS is an information-based procurement system. It is used when an owner is outsourcing a function that is not a part of their core competency. Outsourcing by the author's definition requires no management or control. It requires minimum expertise or knowledge by the owner's representative. The only "knowledge work" that is required is in the identification and selection of the best value, and the use of information to minimize risk (which is done by the PIPS process and the DIM processor). The key to successfully implementing PIPS is in understanding that it requires "information workers."

The PIPS uses an information environment and a nonbiased processor to generate the knowledge or information. The DIM processor then uses the information to identify the best value. The only knowledge work (value added skill) of the PIPS team is the use of performance information to minimize risk. This requires the owners' representatives to be information workers, or users of information. Their knowledge work is how to capture and use information, which requires no technical expertise.

The person who manages the information that is used in the various phases of PIPS, and who compiles and stores the performance information, is the most critical individual in the PIPS core team. If the proper information is maintained, it allows the PIPS program manager, project managers, and administrators to be information workers with minimal political risk.

Based on case studies, if the information manager is not doing their function, the core team will be making decisions and will have political risk. The degree to which the owner's representatives fail to get involved with the knowledge of the construction function that they are procuring, will dictate the success of their PIPS program. Failure to understand this concept has led to the end of two implementation efforts (the States of Hawaii and Utah).

Information Environment

The information environment of the future has two types of knowledge workers: knowledge workers who do technical functions that minimize risk (designers, contractors' personnel, vendors) and information workers who use information to outsource to performers who minimize risk (project managers). The next generation construction environment will not have a position of an independent construction manager (construction manager who does not work directly for the contractor). This is a redundant function that brings risk due to the reliance on a decision maker who has no risk. In the future information environment, there will be very few managers representing the owner who minimize risk due to their technical expertise.

Managers are those who "direct, control, or manage" other people. The management function is inefficient and does not add value. Managers should never manage someone who is not in their own company. The less a manager manages the personnel in their own company, the more efficient their company will become. Therefore, construction design professionals must either be a true designer/engineer, or work for the contractor using their design skills to minimize risk. Even though the construction manager who represents the client may currently be in high demand, their function is one of redundancy, based on inefficiency, and a source of confusion.

There are two phases for the implementation of PIPS: initial implementation, and widespread usage. Both phases are constrained by the capability of the user's personnel to change and be information workers. PIPS must first be tailored to fit the user's environment. A PIPS expert must accomplish this. The core team will continually modify the system. However, to have a successful implementation, the PIPS process must be modified to fit the perception, the legal requirements, and the capability of the core team.

The initial test requires a core team composed of personnel who understand IMT. Once the process has been run, the structure of PIPS will run itself. In other words, the structure is self-enforcing. The structure will run itself if it is allowed to run "undisturbed." Therefore, the core team is required to implement, but once it is implemented, the structure will force the process to be run. The core team requires more understanding of what not to do than what to do. Once the process is in place, the process will be very difficult to disturb due to the rules that will be put in place. Naturally, the process or information environment will minimize subjectivity, political influence, and risk. All these elements are functions of a non-information environment, which are only there due to a lack of information and a lack of trust.

The information environment is a "leadership environment." It minimizes decision making of managers. It allows every entity to identify itself. It then forces all entities to compete and continuously improve. If an entity is not competitive, it must get competitive or it cannot survive. A manager, who by definition makes decisions, is the only real threat to the process. If no one manages, the environment stays pristine.

Phase I requires a PIPS expert and a core team. The core team should be educated, watch initial tests of PIPS, and then run the process themselves under the guidance of PIPS experts. Performance databases should be setup in the initial tests. The core team will be the future experts and trainers in phase II. They must be highly receptive to IMT/PIPS. Once the process is set up, participants in the next phase do not have to have a full understanding of IMT.

PIPS Core Team

The main participants in a PIPS core team include:

1. An executive (who understands efficiency, performance and directs the use of PIPS)
2. Executive oversight group (formed by an executive as a support group to assist in determining the speed of implementation)
3. An administrator (solves disputes in PIPS)
4. A PIPS manager (manages the program)
5. A performance information manager (keeps the information current)
6. Project managers (processes the projects)
7. An industry advisory committee that ensures the information worker and core team are doing their responsibilities

Executive

There are two elements that are required for the executive in a PIPS implementation: position and leadership. The executive is someone at a very high level, either inside or outside of the PIPS group. The executive directs the use of PIPS because the user has risk and needs efficiency and performance. The executive wants information in terms of time, money, and quality expectations.

The executive is a visionary person who has a personal objective to become efficient, minimize waste, and deliver performance. The executive must be able to:

1. Have total confidence in the PBSRG PIPS expertise.
2. Put the best personnel on the core team.
3. Control the pace of implementation.
4. Allow the core team to do their job.
5. Ensure that the core team is providing the performance information.
6. Provide political shelter. The executive must be high enough to cut off opposition from within the organization.

The executive must be a leader and not a manager. The more of a manager the executive is, the more expert the core team needs to be. A leader will be able to influence political people, maximize the use of information to cut off political agendas, and ensure that the core team is successfully discharging their tasks as information workers. The executive, who is a leader, understands that education is the most critical element of the implementation.

A true leader will use information, and will not set the performance numbers (expectations). The leader will allow everyone to identify their own capabilities (by performance barcode and then let them improve by measuring differential between the performance numbers). A leader understands:

1. That the core group is constrained by who they are.
2. The contractors and designers are constrained.
3. That the constraint includes a rate of change.
4. That any type of expectation makes the entity inefficient.

The executive may organize an executive oversight committee, which assists the executive in a bureaucratic organization to gain acceptance of replacing bureaucracy with an information environment. The executive oversight committee ensures political protection and is a staff group to the executive.

Components

The other four components must understand that they are information workers. Their knowledge work or expertise is their ability to identify, collect, and use performance information to minimize political risk. In the test cases, there has been minimal construction risk, because what is procured will always be better than what was procured before PIPS.

Ironically, in PIPS, the knowledge worker is an information worker (Attachment 14.1). All participants in the core team must be able to understand IMT, and know what performance information is needed to minimize political risk. The PIPS identifies performers who minimize construction risk. The ultimate protection of the PIPS program will be the performing construction contractors (industry advisory group). Core team members who think that they are the guardians of the PIPS program do not understand IMT, and sooner or later will try to control the PIPS program.

Administrator

The administrator is a person who makes decisions on the PIPS program when the core team is faced with a decision. This protects them from their own subjectivity do to undue influence of contractors and clients who do not understand the process. It also gives the contractors the knowledge that PIPS is an open and transparent process, and not a subjective process.

Program Manager

A program manager manages the PIPS program. The program manager's responsibilities are not a full time position unless the client is running a large number of PIPS projects. Their responsibilities include selecting the projects, and giving the presentations to executives, clients, and political decision makers.

Project Manager

The project manager is the person who runs the PIPS process. This is a key person in the core team. They are the most knowledgeable core team members of IMT/PIPS. They are the major interface between the contractor and client. The project manager is the first level supervisor of the information manager.

Information Manager

The information manager (IM) is the foundation of the PIPS team. If the IM does not have the right information at the right time, the rest of the PIPS team is forced to make decisions and use technical expertise to minimize political risk. The IM is the most critical component.

If the facility owner's group is small, or has a relatively small construction and maintenance program, one person can do the functions of the administrator, manager, and project manager. The information manager (IM) should be a different individual.

If the facilities group is of sufficient size, the administrator, manager, and project manager should be different people. Every person's responsibilities will be minimized if they are information workers. The project manager's and the information manager's (IM) position are the only full time positions. The other positions are part time PIPS workers who use information to minimize political risk. If the other jobs become full time, it is only because the administrator and program manager do not understand their function and IMT/PIPS. If the PIPS program is developed properly, the other functions will not have enough work to keep them busy full time. The PIPS program's success is predicated on the minimization of effort of the owner's facility and project management and their transition to information workers.

Industry Advisory Group

The industry advisory group is a group of industry participants (other clients, owners, designers and engineers, contractors, and manufacturers) who understand that PIPS is the only way to stabilize the construction industry and create a "win-win" relationship. The members must be voluntary, have positive feelings about PIPS, and must be willing to educate others and defend the program.

The industry advisory group, made up of high performers, will become the true protectors of the program. The purpose of the industry advisory group is not to ensure that PIPS meets the needs of the industry. The purpose is to support the PIPS core group to form an information environment that transfers the risk of nonperformance to the contractors, designers, and vendors.

The industry advisory group cannot gain a competitive advantage through their efforts because they do not see any proprietary performance information. Due to the blindness of the risk assessment plan reviews, interviews, and past performance ratings, the industry core group cannot put any undue pressure on the process. They must convince the industry that the program is for the good of the industry.

The performers in the industry realize that if there is no performance environment, they are truly at risk. In the end, everyone is at risk if the process is inefficient. However, the performing industry participants realize that if their performance is not recognized, they cannot gain a competitive advantage. The industry advisory group should be informal, voluntary, and should ensure that the core team is doing its job. The core group should approve the industry advisory group members. Any industry member, who does not act in the best interest of PIPS, should be removed from the advisory group. The core group must approve industry advisory members.

The industry advisory group should not be confused with a regulatory group. The industry advisory group gives "informal" advice and support to the core team. They also allow the core team to see how performers think and validate the principles of IMT. The advisory group can also ensure that the core team is doing its quality control.

If any formal group is formed to give the views of the industry, this will be a different group, and may include personnel from the industry advisory group. The industry advisory group should be committed enough to give political support to the core group.

Functions of the industry support group include:

1. Meet or hold telecom at least once a month.
2. Review the performance line of the core group at least once a month.
3. Identify performers in the program, and have a recall roster of all performers who support PIPS to answer questions from an industry point of view. (I thought that the Industry group would not have access to the P-lines as mentioned above.)
4. Give suggestions to the core group on how to be more efficient.

The industry advisory committee or support group is a critical element of the PIPS environment. In both the states of Hawaii and Utah, the project managers did not set up and correctly use the industry core group.

Requirements for PIPS Core Team Members

Core team members are information workers. The core team members need the following characteristics:

1. Understand IMT. This is the most critical requirement. This is the telltale sign of whether someone will become efficient and adept at PIPS.
2. Comfortable with Dr. Dean. One quickly will see that there is very little differentiation between Dr. Dean and IMT/PIPS.
3. Quickly understand the differential between PIPS and what they have done in the past.
4. Become a proponent of IMT.
5. Use IMT in their own life.
6. Explain things in their personal and professional life in terms of IMT.
7. Explain things in terms of performance information.
8. Rate their performance in terms of things that are measurable.
9. Become leaders instead of managers.
10. Educators (the ability to speak, explain, understand people).
11. Understand constraints, but do not feel controlled by the environment.

12. Interested in the group and not self-focused.
13. Self-confident.
14. Understand that the most important knowledge is what they do not know.
15. Able to downplay their own technical expertise.
16. Understand their individual constraints and weaknesses.
17. Do not attempt to control anyone else.
18. Delegate to others.
19. Work hard, but always minimize the amount of work everyone does.
20. Understand win-win.
21. Operate as a businessperson.

When selecting and organizing the core team, experience in management should not be the major consideration. The above requirements should take precedence. It will be easier to teach the individual what they need to know about the technical and management side, than it will be to teach the IMT/PIPS side. By definition, the status quo is what is causing the problem. The PIPS is different.

One of the problems with learning PIPS is that IMT/PIPS is conceptual and theoretical. However, it is also a tool to pre-qualify people to work on the core team. Past participants in PIPS have identified that there is very little differential between people's level of comfort with Dr. Dean and IMT/PIPS. Therefore, when selecting individuals to participate in the core team, exposure to Dr. Dean and IMT is one of the easiest and effective tests to select core team members.

It is also important to realize that the objective of PIPS is outsourcing and the minimization of management. Therefore team members should not be managers (control, direct, and make decisions), but users of information who enjoy educating and allowing others to solve the problem. Experience has shown that the best core-team members are not technically oriented, think about the big picture, and are not bureaucratic.

Purpose of the Performance Information

The purpose of information is to reduce risk. The risks to a PIPS program include: political risk, performance risk, and construction risk.

History of PIPS tests shows that the biggest risk to the PIPS program is the political risk. The risk of non-performing construction in PIPS is less than 4%. If the PIPS program manager has poor construction results, tests have shown that the program manager is usually controlling the process and making decisions. The political risk includes the following incorrect perceptions:

1. Performance based projects cost too much.
2. PIPS projects unfairly minimize competition and it selects the same contractors over and over.
3. PIPS gives an unfair advantage to certain contractors.

4. PIPS is too difficult to maintain.
5. PIPS does not minimize effort.
6. The status quo process has the same results as PIPS.

Political risk exists because people oppose change, and oppose the identification and assignment of responsibility. The PIPS minimizes political influences, forces participants to accept responsibility, and identifies performance and nonperformance. Political influence is any influence that has another objective rather than the optimization of construction performance. Political pressures are brought to bear because people fear that the performance based concept and environment will threaten their future "inefficient" functions, services, influence, or the amount of work they receive.

The core team must always have a strategic plan to minimize political risk. They should:

1. Identify and prioritize the political risk (internal and external of the organization).
2. Have the performance information that proves PIPS minimizes cost, risk, and overhead from the previous methodology.
3. Move slowly with the transition, always leaving a place for the bureaucratic personnel to survive and an alternative for the non-performing contractors to get work.
4. PIPS should never replace the low-bid system. The low-bid system is the only methodology for the core team to show that PIPS brings value in terms of cost, time, and quality.

The method of those attacking the PIPS program is very predictable. They will use the following strategy:

1. They will claim that there currently is no problem in the way the owner does procurement.
2. They will claim that the owner is getting the same performance as the rest of the industry.
3. They will claim that they already have a very similar program to PIPS.
4. They will question the theoretical correctness of the process and the DIM processor.
5. They will question the added value of the process.
6. They will attack the credibility of the PIPS core team, claiming that they do not have the expertise and capability to manage the PIPS program.
7. They will bring political pressure on those who they have supported politically.
8. They will try to identify those who are threatened by the process and build a team, which defends the status quo.
9. They will attack the PIPS program information, and management of the information.
10. They will protest jobs if it is possible.
11. They will try to show that the PIPS team is not responding to them.
12. They will try to cause confusion.
13. They will resort to questioning the integrity and management capability of the PIPS core team members.

The irony of the efforts of the opponents of PIPS is that they will never use performance information. They will use confusion and innuendo. In every test case, this has proven to be true. Therefore, the way to minimize political risk is to:

1. Have current performance information in a simple, readily available format. Information cannot be technical information.
2. Have performance information of the status quo project procurements including case studies of projects that have gone very wrong.
3. Make the contractors, designers, and key personnel responsible for verifying the performance information.
4. Initiate an education program that continually educates designers, contractors, users, and facility representatives.
5. Make a list of industry participants who form an advisory board for the owner.
6. Hold regular meetings of the industry support group to quality control and optimize the process.
7. Make a list of all other PIPS users and their case studies.
8. Have a knowledge of all other performance based procurement efforts.
9. Retain a relationship with the Performance Based Studies Research Group (PBSRG) to get assistance whenever it is required.

Updated Performance Information

The rule is simple: He, who has the gold, makes the rules. He, who has more information than anyone else, will always be perceived as more credible. The information worker must be responsible for having the performance information updated in a timely fashion. The information must be easily accessible by the information manager and all other core team members.

The information manager must have the following information:

1. Total number of projects completed, in process, and planned.
2. Type of projects.
3. Performance ratings on the completed projects both PIPS and non-PIPS projects.
4. Cost and change order information on the projects.
5. Punch list information on the projects.
6. Project completion (early, on-time, or late).
7. Number of contractors who bid and won PIPS projects.
8. Award analysis of each project based on budget, low bid, unit price, and the average bid.
9. Number of projects that do not have performance ratings.
10. Contact information on the raters (names and telephone numbers).
11. List of contractors who have performance ratings.
12. List of supporters of PIPS including users, contractors, manufacturers, industry personnel, and user personnel (name, description, telephone number, email number).
13. Award selection (DIMs) for all projects.

14. Analysis of all past projects identifying areas of differentials.
15. List of projects with high risk.
16. List of contractors who have performance issues.
17. List of risk items for the PIPS program.
18. Location of all PIPS documents.
19. Status of all PIPS projects.
20. Schedules of all PIPS projects.
21. Case study of every PIPS project which includes risks, bid and award information, performance information, points of contacts or raters, and lessons learned.
22. Documentation of information work during the week including audits, meetings, identification, prioritization, and action of minimization of risk items.
23. Audit reports by industry support members of the required information.

Self Analysis of the PIPS Information Worker

The work of the information manager is the heart and soul of the PIPS program. This is a full time function. The training of the information manager should start at the beginning of the PIPS program. The information will slowly build up, but the information worker must maintain, analyze, and pass information from the very beginning. As described above, the information worker should be responsible for performance information of the status quo projects. This should also include the documentation of failed projects. The information worker should be fully educated in the IMT/PIPS theory.

The information work should be audited monthly by a member of the industry support group and weekly by the PIPS program manager. If the information worker does not have the information updated 90% of the time, or errors are found over 10% of the time after the first couple months, the information manager should be replaced.

If the information worker does not perform, it is very difficult to convince others that PIPS is successful. Contractors, who are at risk in a performance-based program, expect the PIPS core group to perform by having the correct information. The PIPS process involves change. Most people do not like change. Therefore, they will criticize PIPS and demand information. The information worker can "make or break" the PIPS team.

The information must then be made available to the rest of the PIPS team in hard copy, and electronic copy every Monday morning. This information may not change from week to week, but still must be presented. The better the information worker's work, the less work every else in the core group is required to do.

The PIPS program will not fail due to non-performing construction. It will fail because the information worker is not doing their job (nonperformance). The opponents of PIPS will not attack the results of the PIPS program. They will attack the ability of the core group to correctly run the PIPS program.

Importance of Understanding the Information Structure and the DIM

The expertise or knowledge work of running PIPS is to understand the information environment and what information is. The DIM creates information and describes the event. Therefore, the information worker is merely the mechanic of the information environment. They have no opinion, no perception, and no technical expertise of what is performance. The expertise is IMT and how the DIM captures the event. They explain the results of the DIM, which represent the results of the event.

The information worker runs the models. Although every person should understand the models, the information worker should know the model better than anyone else. The information worker should know the following:

1. Performance of the existing low bid system.
2. How projects were awarded.
3. Percentage of projects that went low-bid.
4. Percentage of projects with change orders.
5. Percentage of projects that did not finish on time, on budget, and meet quality expectations.
6. The weaknesses of the system.
7. Problem projects, contractors, and systems.
8. Areas of potential improvement.
9. The reduction of costs and time brought about by the program.

Continuing Education

Due to the current status of the majority of construction industry participants, the PIPS effort will receive opposition from both industry participants and the client's own personnel who do not want to see change, efficiency, and assignment of responsibility. At the State of Hawaii and University of Hawaii, some government personnel opposed the PIPS efforts due to the attention it drew to their own performance and due to the loss of their perceived control in the process. These personnel were identified by the following characteristics:

1. Focused on the identification of problems and had no concrete solution or documentation of the problem and solution.
2. Stated that the problem was complex.
3. Did not want to implement new concepts.
4. Were very active but did not document their actions in terms of performance.

The PIPS core group needs to have support not only from the Advisory Group, but also from:

1. Facility personnel around the country who have either run PIPS or support PIPS.
2. Industry personnel (designers, contractors, or vendors) who support a value added process and environment.

3. PBSRG personnel.

Owners or users of PIPS should attend the annual education seminar at Arizona State University (usually held in the first week of February). This is a time when they can coordinate with other users of PIPS, be reeducated about PIPS, and review case studies (lessons learned) from other users that have made modifications to the process.

The most important part of PIPS is the education and regulation of the construction performance by the industry. It is important to allow participants from the industry who have an affinity for PIPS and performance to assist the PIPS user.

Conclusion

The implementation of PIPS has two phases: initial testing/implementation, and proliferation of the process. The first phase requires a core team. The core team is required to understand IMT. When the PIPS structure is set, the second phase requires PIPS project managers to understand PIPS, but not IMT. The second phase requires PIPS rules to be set, and the project managers will follow the rules. It is always advantageous for project managers to understand IMT. However, the understanding of IMT is difficult, conceptual, and abstract. Test results have shown that project managers in construction are able to run PIPS without understanding IMT if the PIPS structure has already been setup.

A PIPS expert is usually required to train the core team. However, project and procurement managers who understand the theory of leadership, outsourcing, and efficiency, should be able to run PIPS.

PIPS is an information environment and requires the information worker to have the correct information and understand the process. The only risk to PIPS is political risk. Political risk will come in the form of misperceptions. The foundation of PIPS is the correct information. The successful implementation of PIPS will be based on the core team's ability to have the correct information at the right time.

Chapter 14 Review

1. List the members of the core group.
2. Who is the most important member of the group? Why?
3. What information should the Information Worker keep?
4. What is the greatest risk to PIPS?
5. What is the purpose of the Industry Advisory Group?

Attachments

Attachment 14.1: Information Worker Checklist

Attachment 14.1: Information Worker Checklist

Information Worker Checklist

The information worker must have the following documentation updated and accurate every week:

1. Performance of the existing low bid system.
2. Areas of differentiation.
3. How projects were awarded.
4. Percentage of projects that went low-bid.
5. Percentage of projects with change orders.
6. Percentage of projects that did not finish on time, on budget, and meet quality expectations.
7. The prioritized risks of running PIPS.
8. Problem projects, contractors, and systems.
9. Areas of potential improvement.
10. The reduction of costs and time brought about by the program.
11. Performance line of PIPS and standard projects.

15

Maintenance and Repair Example: Roofing

Introduction

PIPS was initially run on the procurement of roofing systems. It is one of the most straightforward, simplistic systems to run PIPS. This chapter will explain the roofing industry and walk through the PIPS process when procuring roofing. The chapter addresses the procurement of built-up roofing "or equal" warranties, past performance information, the perceived value of a roofing system before procurement, and how to leverage performance from a roofing manufacturer and contractor. For results on roofing procurement, see Chapter 21 Case Study: State of Hawaii.

Roofing Steps

The following steps should be taken when procuring roofing projects:

1. Education on the roofing industry environment.
2. Legal review of PIPS.
3. Identification of the legal requirements of PIPS.
4. Policies on roofing systems.
5. Setting up the PIPS process for a one step design-build process.
6. Identify the roofing requirements.
7. Request for Proposal (RFP).
8. Educational meeting.
9. Collecting past performance information.
10. Pre-bid meeting, site walk.
11. Submittal of bids and Risk Assessment Plan.
12. Review of the Risk Assessment Plans and proposals.
13. Identifying the value of the proposed roofing system.
14. Prioritization of the bidders.
15. Pre-award discussions.
16. Award.
17. Construction.
18. Final documentation.

A schedule is attached in Attachment 15.1.

Legal Review

The user must determine if they can legally implement PIPS. The user must have a request for a proposal process that considers both performance and price. This may include a design-build process or a two-step process. The two-step process was run by the Dallas Independent School District (DISD), which is discussed in Chapter 24. A presentation should be made to the legal and procurement office for approval.

The process must be modified to meet the requirements of the legal and procurement offices. Modifications are best made in conjunction with PBSRG to ensure the integrity of the PIPS process.

If the user cannot do an RFP or design-build project, the user must use a specification specifying a proven roofing system. The author proposes a 20-year, five-ply built up roof system to be the proven roofing system. The specification must include an "or equal" clause. The user will determine if systems are "equal" and if their performance information meets or exceeds the performance information of the specified roofing system (average performance period, percentage of roofs not currently leaking, percentage of roofs that never leaked, customer satisfaction, meeting FM-SH test requirements for the length of the warranty, and light mechanical and traffic damage).

Understanding the Roofing Industry Environment

It is important for the user to understand that the roofing industry environment is one of: indemnification, finger pointing, providing the cheapest possible roofing systems, installing roofing systems that have not been fully tested over an adequate period of time, and marketing (fancy brochures, the use of corporate names, and warranties that offer minimized protection for the user). There is no requirement for roof system performance information (service period, leak records, customer satisfaction, and contractor/manufacturer's quality) in the roofing industry.

Many roofing manufacturers and contractors claim that they have performance information, but cannot produce it when requested. PBSRG has done research with a couple of roofing manufacturers to identify the problems by documenting performance information (Alpha manufacturers, Alpha contractors, and Custom Seal, Chapters 16 and 18).

Roofing problems account for a major part of construction and litigation problems. The lack of stability within the roofing industry is caused by failure to continually improve performance and maintain the ability to perform.

The roofing industry has responded to poor performance by requiring roofing experts. The experts specify, procure, and inspect roofs for the owners. Although there are some very knowledgeable roofing experts, the average roofing expert can often have the following characteristics:

1. Previously an unsuccessful roofing contractor.
2. Partnered with a major manufacturer and receives payment from both the owner and the roofing manufacturer.
3. Receives the roofing specification directly from the manufacturer.
4. Does not have any performance information on the roofing systems or contractors.
5. Does not understand the ASTM or FM standards, their origination, and meaning (Chapter 4).
6. Does not have a professional degree or license.

Many times a professional designer or engineer will employ the services of a roofing consultant (or expert) with the hope that the roofing expert understands roofing products. The author has come to the following deductive conclusions about the roofing industry:

1. Roofing manufacturers and contractors do not keep the performance information on their roofs; therefore, are not interested in the performance of their installed roofing systems (as documented in the DISD case study).
2. There is a lack of performance information in the roofing industry.
3. When asked to provide references, roofing contractors and manufacturers have had to go through a lot of work to produce minimal information.
4. Roofing warranties are a marketing gimmick. Warranties are not a true picture of roofing system value. Many times a 20 year roofing warranty will be assigned to a brand new product, from a roofing manufacturer who has been in the business for less than five years (see NRCA Warranty Bulletin Attachment).
5. Roofing manufacturers and contractors should not be trusted to perform to owner's expectations. They should prove it.
6. Roofing performance information (50 references) showing, system performance periods, customer satisfaction, leaking rates, and percentage of roofs still leaking, should be requested from every contractor and manufacturer.
7. Buying roofing systems based only on low price is a method practiced only by uninformed owners. It is this practice that is responsible for poor roofing performance.

The roofing manufacturers and contractors have used the environment of no performance information to confuse owners, avoid liability, and create a new function for roof experts. The owners' emphasis on price has caused non-performing manufacturers to produce cheaper roofing systems that barely meet minimum requirements and bring increased risk to building owners (Chapter 4). Ironically, the resulting poor performance and risk, strengthens the justification for more experts, standards, management, and inspection. All these functions are non-value added. There is no greater example of a Quadrant I low bid environment that confuses responsibility, has non-value added functions, and where non-performers may make a greater profit than performers.

Implementing PIPS will identify performing roofing manufacturers and contractors, and bring the owner the best value. In every case, PIPS tests have identified performing roofing contractors and manufacturers, who the owner did not know existed. In many cases, the owner procured successful roofing systems that experts previously told them would not work. In the case of the Dallas Independent School District (DISD), the owner procured roofs that were previously banned due to the nonperformance of manufacturers and contractors (who were claiming that they could duplicate the quality of the performing contractors and manufacturers).

An advantage of PIPS is that it forces competition of the best performing manufacturers and contractors in each roofing system. It will force contractors and manufacturers to:

1. Prove they can perform and track their performance.
2. Minimize the risk of the owner.
3. Take over the responsibility of the roof.
4. Minimize the owner's need to maintain the roof.
5. Compete with other systems that perform.
6. Minimize the owner's need to give directions on what to do, what materials to use, and how to do it.
7. Increase the value of the roofing system by working as a team to minimize the risk of future nonperformance.
8. Give the owner "true performance protection" beyond the warranty protection usually given by manufacturers.

Policies on Roofing Procurement

The first rule of PIPS is to always be logical. Past users of PIPS have implemented certain policies, which have minimized risk. Policies may be impacted by the following factors:

1. The types of roofing systems have been previously installed at the site.
2. Type of roofing systems that can be maintained by the in-house staff.
3. Systems that have catastrophic failure modes may not be used.
4. Roofing systems that cause environmental hazards, which may be excluded due to smell, carcinogenic materials, or cannot be done within the required time frame.
5. Roofing manufacturers who want the user to accept risk by not accepting responsibility for materials that they do not manufacture.
6. Roofing systems that cannot take traffic, mechanical abuse, or hail damage.
7. Roofing systems that require consistent maintenance.
8. Roofing systems that cannot be repaired by the owner.
9. Roofing manufacturers who have systems that have been previously installed on the owner's roofs, which still have problems.

The author recommends the following policies:

1. Require a "built-up-roof or equal".
2. Roofing contractors must waterproof the roof and surrounding surfaces.
3. Document the contractor and manufacturer's performance on the project, and use this information to potentially disqualify nonperformance of a contractor or manufacturer from future work.

4. Minimize risk with a joint and several warranty.
5. The manufacturer or contractor must have proven performance of the roofing system within 150 miles of the site. The contractor's performance should be defined as the major category of system: single ply, modified bitumen, built up roof, and sprayed polyurethane foam. The manufacturer's system must be the same system that they are proposing. The client's technical representative will make a decision required on differing systems.
6. When procuring a large number of roofs, the client will minimize its risk by using multiple contractors and short installation durations.

High Performance "Built Up Roof or Equal"

Minimizing the risk should be the client's only interest. The requirement needed to minimize risk is a high performance built-up roof or a roof of "equal" quality. Built-up roofs are more durable and easier to maintain than other systems. The roof system should be able to maintain its durability over time. The roof system should also minimize deterioration of the roof due to mechanical damage, maintenance, animals, foot traffic, and hail.

The client should avoid systems that _could_ work or systems where several contractors cannot consistently make the system work. Every contractor thinks their roof system is the best. Clients need to avoid manufacturers' products and systems that need constant maintenance or recoating. The end cost of procuring a roof that has to be recoated, costs the client more than doing the procurement just once.

All roof systems, especially those with protective coatings (including Spray Polyurethane Foam (SPF) Roofing systems) will pass the Factory Mutual Severe Hail (FM-SH) test for the entire duration of the roofing warranty. The client can perform the test at any time during the warranty period. If the system fails the test (as determined by the client), the contractor and manufacturer will replace the system (materials and labor) or add material to bring it back to the original conditions.

The contractor and manufacturer can be asked to prove that the roof system can pass the hail test during the performance period. This is done by conducting hail tests on existing systems, which is at least half the warranty period, or during the installation before acceptance. The ability to pass the FM-SH test shall be expressly written and signed by the manufacturer and included along with the manufacturers warranty. This statement is important when considering SPF systems, since there are such a vast range of available SPF systems and coatings. There have been many documented cases in which poor quality SPF systems have failed and not performed. However, there are also many cases of high quality SPF systems that last 20 years without leaking (See Chapter 16 Alpha Roof System). The FM-SH test is a great test of durability of the roof system. The test will identify if the roof system is not durable (coating is deteriorating, coating is too thin, coating is made of bad materials, or the SPF does not have sufficient structural strength). If a roof system does not pass for any reason, corrections have to be made until it can pass the test.

Responsible for Waterproofing the Roof and Surrounding Surfaces

The contractor is not being directed to remove the existing system. They are being directed to waterproof the existing building roof. However, the manufacturer should accept liability for the nonperformance (as determined by the owner) of any material, down to the structural deck, for the duration of the warranty. If any of the materials of the existing or installed roofing system: becomes defective, absorbs water, loses its original shape, blisters, delaminates, or causes leaking; the manufacturer will immediately stop the leaking and restore all materials to a dry and stable condition. This includes any materials that may have been left on the structural deck and was overlaid by the new roofing system. This should be in writing as a part of the warranty if the contractor is proposing to overlay the existing waterproofing membrane. This minimizes the owner's risk and puts the contractor and manufacturer at risk.

Documented Performance of Contractor and Manufacturer

The performance of the contractor and manufacturer will be documented. After the roof system is installed, the contractor and manufacturer will be legally bound by the warranty. If the roof leaks, and the cause is not covered by the warranty, the contractor and manufacturer do not need to respond (based on the warranty clauses). However, the poor performance will have a negative impact on the contractor and manufacturer's future performance rating, which will be used on future projects. The technical engineers also may not use that roof system in future work. Therefore, poor performance can impact the contractor and manufacturer in two ways:

1. Technical disqualification - Disqualify the roofing system type in future procurements because it does not perform as advertised.
2. Noncompetitive based on past performance - Make the system manufacturer and contractor noncompetitive in future work if they are allowed to participate.

Joint and Several Warranty

PIPS is a risk minimization process. The goal is to minimizes the risk of the owner. It attempts to find performing contractors and manufacturers that have the expertise and systems to minimize risk. It seeks to make those that minimize risk more competitive than vendors, who are trying to shed risk back to the client. PIPS identifies and differentiates any alternatives that minimize the client's risk.

One of the risk minimization options in warranties is the "joint and several" warranty. It means that the contractor and manufacturer are jointly and severally responsible for the roof. When both entities are in business, there is a contract between them that covers all aspects of nonperformance. This is a legal document that identifies what both parties will do to solve any nonperforming roof issue. If one of the entities goes out of business, the entity still in business is legally responsible to fix any nonperformance issues. The author recommends giving 25% extra value to any contractor/manufacturer who propose a joint and several warranty, that is supported by a legal contract, signed between the contractor and manufacturer.

Proven performance in the Local Area

The author proposes to constrain the contractor and manufacturers' references, to be within the area of the users building ("...all references must be within a 150 mile radius of our facility..."). This will achieve two things:

1. It will ensure that the contractor is local and can service the roof for the duration of the warranty period.
2. It ensures that the roofing system works in the local environment.

Minimization of Risk (Time and Quality)

Any roofing contractor is constrained by their trained craftspeople. If a contractor is given too much work, their performance may suffer. If they are given too much time, a phenomena is that their performance begins to vary. If a client has a number of roofs, the client should hire multiple contractors and give narrow windows for installation. The client may minimize their risk by setting limits on the percentage of roofs that a single system or contractor can receive. This will ensure competition, and minimize the risk of one contractor receiving all the projects and not being able to complete in a timely and performing fashion.

If the client implements these steps, they will greatly minimize risk before PIPS is even implemented. They will be procuring:

1. Roofing systems that equal the performance of built up roof systems.
2. Leak free roofs.
3. Durable roof systems (pass FM-SH test for the length of the warranty).
4. Contractors and manufacturers who are liable.
5. Joint and several warranties.
6. Contractors who will service the roofs.
7. Highly competitive and quick installation.

If the client does not implement these principles, they are increasing their risk of procuring performing roof systems over time. The above policies are not requirements of the PIPS process. These are user policies that are implemented above and beyond PIPS to minimize the risk of nonperformance.

Setting Up the PIPS Process

Once the legal and procurement issues have been settled, and the policies have been identified, the user can begin to work with the PIPS process. The process is covered in detail in Chapter 7. The following items should be covered during this phase:

1. The user should identify the procurement officer (PO) that will be the main point of contact for this project. The PO should create a committee/team that will be used to evaluate the risk assessment plans (and interviews if required). The author does not recommend doing an interview for roofing procurement.
2. A project schedule should be created (Attachment 1).
3. An advertisement should be published informing the contractors and manufacturers about the education meeting (Chapter 7, Attachment 7.2). The advertisement should include any qualifications, a description of the method of award, and any unacceptable systems. The educational meeting can either be mandatory or non-mandatory. The author recommends that the educational meeting be made mandatory.
4. A request for proposal (RFP) should be generated in time for the pre-bid meeting. It is advantageous to have the RFP done as soon as possible. In some cases the education meeting and the pre-bid meeting can be the same meeting if the RFP is already completed.

Educational Meeting

The user performs the following at the education meeting:

1. Identify the contractors and manufacturers that are interested in participating. The Client's representative will have a sign-in roster that asks for name, company, telephone number, and email address of the contractor or manufacturer's representative. Each manufacturer's representative must represent only one manufacturer. It is advantageous to have a computer and have the attendee's type in their information. It is also recommended to collect business cards.
2. Educate all parties that a "built-up roof" or equal is being procured. There will be no discussion on entertaining other options. The FM-SH test will be a requirement on all roofing systems for the duration of the warranty.
3. Contractors and manufacturers are required to have references. The collection of the performance information shall be covered. The client's representative shall review the format of the reference list (Chapter 7, Attachment 7.7) and the survey methodology.
4. Surveys are sent to the references by the contractors and manufacturers (Chapter 7, Attachment 7.8); this can be done on a diskette or by email.
5. Contractors and manufacturers are given the construction window and point of contact for questions (email address).
6. Contractors and manufacturers must understand that this is a partnership, and that if the contractor does not perform; the manufacturer will also be affected. If the manufacturer has no references, any contractor who is planning to use their material will be at a distinct disadvantage. Contractors and manufacturers must also realize that the other can impact their future performance rating.
7. Take questions by the attendees. Answer all questions in writing after the meeting.

Collecting Past Performance Information

One of the requirements for PIPS is submitting a maximum of 50 references to show past performance (50 is the maximum, 1 is the minimum). Contractors and manufacturers who turn in more references will have the competitive advantage, because it minimizes the risk of nonperformance. PIPS is a risk minimization process. The contractor and manufacturer with the oldest performing roofs, the most satisfied customers, the least number of leaking roofs, the greatest number of roofs that have never leaked, and the highest customer satisfaction, will have the competitive advantage.

The contractor and roofing manufacturer (of the system that the contractor is using) shall submit a spreadsheet of references to the procurement officer. The format is given at the educational meeting. The information for each of their references includes (Chapter 7, Attachment 7.7:):

1. Point of contact representing the reference with telephone number, fax number, and email address.
2. Company name.
3. Address of location of the roof.
4. Date the roof was installed.

This reference list is sent to the procurement officer by the deadline given at the education meeting. The contractor and manufacturer then contact their references, explain the importance of the reference referral, ask them to fill it out, and send it to the client's procurement officer (See Chapter 7, Figure 7.6). The procurement officer has no responsibility to ensure that the references respond. If the references do not respond, the contractor and manufacturer will be less competitive.

It is very important that the contractor understands that they must partner with a manufacturer's system. If the manufacturer they select does not have any references returned, the contractor will have a very poor opportunity of winning the bid. This is a partnering approach. The contractor has to check with the manufacturer and ensure that they are sending in references. A contractor cannot win on their references alone.

PIPS ensures that:

1. The contractor can install the proposed system.
2. The manufacturer's proposed system has proven performance.
3. The contractor and manufacturer's system has to be the same system (i.e.: BUR, modified bitumen, SPF, single ply – PTO, reinforced PVC, EPDM rubber). If the contractor's system does not match the manufacturer's system, the bid is non-responsive.

The owner has the option to inspect any of the referenced roofs. The owner should only inspect the roofs that put them at risk (roofs that differentiate the contractor/manufacturer's performance). The contractor and manufacturer will be responsible to show any of the referenced roofs. If anything is found to make the user doubt the validity of the references, the owner can inspect every roof on the reference list.

The contractor and manufacturer are encouraged to submit different references (i.e. vendors should submit 50 different projects done for 50 different owners, instead of 50 roofs done for one owner). However, if one reference has more than one roof, that is acceptable.

On the deadline date, the procurement officer will compile each contractor and manufacturer's performance line (totals and averages of all the references' information). This is the past performance information (PPI) for the vendor.

Request For Proposal (RFP)

The user should issue the RFP before or at the pre-bid meeting. The RFP contains the following:

1. Contract and legal requirements of the owner (bonding, insurance, licenses, etc...)
2. A description of the condition of the existing roof system.
3. The performance criteria and relative weights.
4. Any special requirements of the owner due to the site conditions, owner operations, preferences, or working conditions.
5. Requirement of the risk assessment plan, legal and contract requirements, and bid price sheet.

The description of the roofing requirement (given by the owner) can include the following:

1. A roof plan and moisture survey.
2. A cross section view of the roof including the existing deck, insulation, waterproofing membranes.
3. A core sample giving information on any asbestos or other hazardous material that requires abatement.

The RFP should also include all policies that will be used in the procurement for the prioritization and award. This includes:

1. This procurement is for a roof that has the characteristics of a 20 year "built up roof."
2. The client has the right to have the manufacturer and contractor verify that the roof system being proposed passes the durability requirements of the FM-SH test, on an aged roof that is at least half the service period of the proposed warranty period.
3. All roof systems will have the requirement to pass the FM-SH test for the duration of the warranty provided. If the system cannot pass the test, either at installation or anytime during the warranty, the manufacturer and the contractor shall, at no cost to the owner, bring the roof to a level that passes the FM-SH test. This shall be in writing from the manufacturer and be a part of the manufacturer's warranty.

4. If a contractor or manufacturer has no references or very few references, the bid will not be competitive unless everyone else has no references.

5. How the winning contractor performs will influence the future competitiveness of the contractor and manufacturer. Nonperformance of either party will minimize the competitiveness of the partner. If the roof leaks, and remains unchecked and not repaired, the performance line of both contractor and manufacturer will be penalized, even though the warranty may not cover the leaking or damaged roofing. The contractor and manufacturer are both at risk. Both should ensure that the other party in the partnership performs.

6. The risk assessment plan will be rated on a relative basis.

7. The potential value of the roofing system will be based on the minimum proven performance and the modified warranty period.

8. The performance of the installed system will count at least 25% of the future performance of both the contractor and manufacturer. The performance can be modified anytime during the warranty period based on the performance of the roofing system.

9. The contractor may withdraw from the bid at any time before the pre-award meeting, based on the inability to minimize the owner's risk. This can be done with no penalty, even though there is a bid or performance bond.

10. Time to construct is a very important issue. The clock is turned on as soon as the award is made. If it is a design-build contract, the contractor must generate any drawings required to get the building permit. The drawings must include a roof plan, current and new configuration, and any required details. This should not be a difficult task. In most cases: the moisture survey roof plan, the core sample results and the manufacturer's specification and details; comprises a roof design. The contractor needs to get the package stamped by an engineer.

11. The contractors and manufacturers should be given an easy to understand explanation of how the award will be made (Figure 15.1).

12. The base bid must be within the overall budget of the roofs being bid.

13. Roofs will be awarded according to a prioritized list, if there is more than one roof.

14. The prioritization of the contractors by the model will then be given to the contracts person. The contracts person has the right to keep the prioritization or modify it in the best interest of the owner.

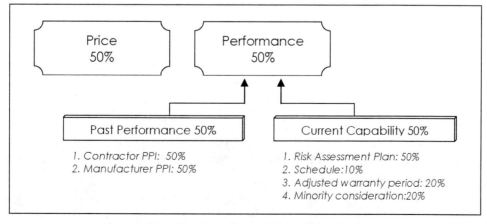

Figure 15.1: Explanation of Selection Factors

The RFP directs the contractor to submit a bid package that can quickly be divided into two packages: a bid package meeting all of the client's legal contractual requirements, and a management plan package. The bid package includes:

1. The signed contract documents.
2. A price breakout, which includes, activities, unit prices, and total cost; time to construct in number of days; unit price costs of replacing the roofing deck, if required; and any value added activities, which are not a part of the basic bid package.
3. An unsigned draft of the manufacturer's warranty for the roofing system.
4. The manufacturer's name and roof system.

The other package is the risk management plan. It should be no longer than two pages. It should include:

1. Advantages of the roofing system in terms of cost, performance, and time.
2. The risk of leaking or nonperformance due to the environment, traffic, or roof configuration.
3. How the contractor and roofing system will minimize the risk.
4. Added value of the contractor's option including items in the base bid or above and beyond the base bid along with cost, time, and quality explanations.

The plan will be rated "blind." The plan should not include any names of manufacturers, contractors, or individuals. If the plan includes any names, the submittal will be identified as non-responsive.

Pre-bid Meeting

The pre-bid meeting includes a quick review of the project and a site walk. The users should schedule a day or two to visit the site. The pre-bid meeting will discuss the contents of the RFP. After the pre-bid meeting is performed, the user should quickly issue meeting minutes to all companies that attended.

Review of the Risk Assessment Plan and Proposals

The contractors will submit their bids and risk assessment plans. If any plan contains a proprietary name it should be eliminated. The proposals should also be reviewed to make sure that everything has been submitted properly. The committee members then review the plans, and the scores are combined to get an overall average for each company.

The committee should be educated on how to rate the plans before hand. The plans should clearly identify risk, how it will be minimized, and identify how value will be added.

The plan should not be more than two pages. One page should be a cost breakout and the other page should be a description of the risk or problems, minimization of risk, and added value. What is within the base bid and what is added value should be clearly defined. Any unknown item should be bid in terms of unit price. Differential should be explained in terms of performance, cost, and time. The following are examples of differential:

1. Number of days to construct.
2. Noise and dust creating activities performed after-hours or during weekends.
3. Installing an elastomeric coating in four coats instead of two coats, because it lengthens service period by 33%.
4. Raising all mechanical equipment 12 inches above the roof deck.
5. Repainting all flashings.
6. Providing new roof flashings.
7. Covering all exposed roofing the same day.
8. Checking roofing properties on a daily basis.
9. Stopping installation if the roofing materials do not meet specifications.
10. Installing three plies instead of two.
11. Sloping roof with tapered insulation.
12. Adding drains.
13. Innovative flashing detailing.

If the cost of any value added feature increases the price above the budget, the contractor is at risk. The contractor should decide which items will be included in the base and which are not. The risk assessment plan becomes a part of the contractor's contract.

Perceived Value of the Warranty

> "Too often, the only thing about a warranty that a building owner considers is length. This is probably the least important part. When considering whether to obtain a warranty, building owners must understand that warranties are written by the attorneys of the issuer for the benefit of the issuer." – (Warseck 2003)

In simple terms, the warranty does not protect the owner; it protects the manufacturer and contractor. Roofing warranties are being used to sell roofs. If the roof has problems, the manufacturers will make a financial decision if they will support the warranty. If the problem is too severe, they will walk away from the warranty. This results in litigation in the roofing industry. Once a roof owner has a bad roof, the damage has been done. Owners should not make a decision based on a roof warranty length.

Warranties protect the manufacturer. This is done through the warranty exclusions, or the fine print of the document. Warranty exclusions are rules that protect the manufacturer if any problems arise. The following is a list of common exclusions that can be found on many warranties:

1. All roofing systems require periodic maintenance to keep your warranty in effect.
2. Ponding water is not allowed on the roof.
3. Roofs must have slopes.
4. Roof drains must be kept clean.
5. The system should not be exposed to acids, solvents, greases, oil, fats, or chemicals.
6. This warranty is void if there is a change in building use or purpose.
7. All flashing, drains, skylights, equipment, and any other rooftop accessories must be properly maintained at all times.
8. The warranty does not include damage caused by winds in excess of 55 MPH.
9. This warranty does not cover damage caused by installation.
10. This warranty does not cover leaks resulting from materials supplied by others.
11. This warranty does not cover damage resulting from other than occasional traffic.
12. This warranty does not cover damage caused by animals or insects.
13. This warranty does not cover damage caused by failure of the owner to use reasonable care in maintaining the system.

The list of exclusions may be different for each manufacturer and each product. However, the objective of the warranty exclusions is to protect the manufacturer and tell the owner when the manufacturer has no responsibility. If we examine the previous mentioned exclusions, we will see that many of them are highly subjective. For example, item 13 states: "This warranty does not cover damage caused by failure of the owner to use reasonable care in maintaining the system." Who decides if the owner used reasonable care in maintaining the system? What is "reasonable" care? Obviously one owner may say that they did maintain the roof properly, and the manufacturer may say that they did not. In the end, the lawyers will be brought in and their objective will be to outlast the building owner.

If a problem does occur with the roofing system, and the owner has not met the conditions specified in the exclusions, the manufacturer may either honor the warranty or only cover the cost of replacing their material. They will not cover the cost of labor, which is the larger cost in many cases.

Performance information is more reliable to predict future performance than warranties. The warranty is only as good as the manufacturer and contractor. Users should use the following to identify the perceived value of the warranty:

"...Identify the minimum of the proven service period or the warranty period, then subtract one year for each of the following exclusions (unless the warranty is amended by the manufacturer's document):

1. Traffic on the roof.
2. Ponding, standing water, or require positive drainage.
3. Materials not made by manufacturer.
4. Metal flashing.
5. Animals.
6. Mechanical damage.
7. Failure of owner to use reasonable care or maintenance (roof inspections).

8. Acts of parties other than the Manufacturer or Contractor.
9. Solid or liquid deposits (solvents, grease, oils, fats, and any other chemicals).
10. Changes in building use.

The following should not be considered a deductible exclusion:

1. Settlement of the building or acts of God.

Performing this task does not change any legal obligations of the manufacturers, but it does give credit to those manufacturers that are reducing the risk of the owners more than the others are.

Selection of a Contractor

All of the data that has been collected thus far will be inputted into a modified Displaced Ideal Model (see Chapter 10). Once the contractors are prioritized, the Procurement Officer (PO) will review the result. The PO still has the option to override the system and award to a different alternative if they feel it is in the owner's best interest.

Award and Construction

Once the PO has selected the best-valued contractor, the contractor then prepares for the pre-award meeting. The contractor should prepare for the pre-award meeting by, seeking any clarifications, doing destructive testing, completing their drawings if it is a design-build, and answering any owner questions.

The contractor then gives a presentation at the pre-award meeting. It is important to note that until the pre-award meeting, the contractor can withdraw from the project with no penalty. When the project is awarded, the contractor agrees to perform the project as specified in the, RFP, the pre-bid meeting minutes, risk assessment plan, bid proposal, and pre-award meeting minutes.

During construction the user should help facilitate the contractor with any problems that they might encounter. The PO should also identify the members that will evaluate the contractor. When the project is complete, the PO should get the ratings from the evaluation members which may count up to 50% on the contractor's new rating.

Final Documentation

The user should minimize documentation. It should include: the selection models, the winning risk assessment plan, and the closeout ratings. Opportunities should be taken to optimize the process (minimize effort in management and control).

Chapter 15 Review

1. What is a joint and several warranty?
2. What are the important components of a joint and several warranty?
3. Why do most contractors and manufacturers not offer a joint and several warranty?
4. If a roof leaks, is a manufacturer and contractor legally required to fix the leak in the PIPS system? Why or why not?
5. Why is the FM-SH test required for SPF roofs in non-hail areas?
6. Who usually creates the specification data sheet and specifications for roofing projects?
7. What is the perceived value of the roofing warranty?
8. What is the difference between perceived and actual value of the roofing warranty?
9. How does a client compare the value of a roofing system when it goes over the existing and a roofing system which requires the existing system to be removed before the installation of the new roof system?
10. How is the perceived value of the roofing warranty derived?
11. What are added criteria that show the performance of the roofing system?
12. How are the manufacturer and contractor forced to be partners in PIPS?
13. What is the client's action if the roof leaks?

References

Dodson, M. (1995, May/June). Selling Quality. *Western Roofing*, p. 4.

Garrison, T. (2003 October). "Do roof auctions provide better value to building owners?" *Professional Roofing*, pp. 21-24.

Graham, M. (2002, September). NRCA's performance standards initiative. *Professional Roofing*, 32 [9], p. 80.

Holf, J. (2003, March). Exploring Industry Expectations: a survey reveals consensus, as well as conflict, regarding how key industry groups view quality. *Professional Roofing*, 33 [3], pp. 18-23.

NRCA. (1993, April). Consumer Advisory Bulletin: Roofing Warranties. *National Roofing Contractors Association*, [1].

NRCA. (1993, April). Consumer Advisory Bulletin: Selecting a Professional Roofing Contractor. *National Roofing Contractors Association*, [2].

Patterson, M. (1996, February). Starting at the top. *Buildings Magazine*, pp. 54-56.

Sharp, S.A. (2002, June). What are the Standards? *Professional Roofing*, 36 [6], pp. 39-40.

Warseck, K. (2002, October). Reroofing: What Do You Get for You Money? *Building Operation Management*, 49 [10], pp. 76,78.

Warseck, K. (2003, February). Finding the Value of Roofing Warranties. *Building Operating Management*, 50 [2], pp. 53, 54, 56, 58-59, 60, 62, 64.

Attachments

Attachment 15.1: Roofing Schedule
Attachment 15.2: Sample Moisture Survey
Attachment 15.3: Industry Roof Statements
Attachment 15.4: NRCA Advisory Bulletin

Attachment 15.1: Roofing Schedule Example

No	TASK	DURATION	START	END
1	**EDUCATIONAL MEETING**	**11 days**	**1/1**	**1/15**
2	Announcement Posted	10 days	1/1	1/14
3	Education/Registry Meeting	1 day	1/15	1/15
4	**DATA COLLECTION**	**20 days**	**1/16**	**2/12**
5	Companies prepare reference lists	8 days	1/16	1/27
6	Companies submit lists to the user	1 day	1/28	1/28
7	Companies send out surveys	10 days	1/28	2/10
8	Past Performance Information (PPI) generated	2 days	2/11	2/12
9	**BID INFORMATION**	**16 days**	**2/13**	**3/5**
10	Pre-Bid / Site Walk Meeting	1 day	2/13	2/13
11	Contractors prepare / submit risk assessment plans	10 days	2/16	2/27
12	Contractors prepare / submit cost proposals	5 days	3/1	3/5
13	Risk assessment plans evaluated	3 days	3/1	3/3
14	**SELECTION PROCESS**	**20 days**	**3/4**	**3/31**
15	All data transferred into DIM	2 days	3/4	3/5
16	Contractors are prioritized	1 day	3/8	3/8
17	PO selects best value	1 day	3/8	3/8
18	Pre-Award Period	5 days	3/9	3/15
19	Pre-Award meeting	1 day	3/16	3/16
20	Award paperwork	10 days	3/17	3/30
21	Award	1 day	3/31	3/31

Attachment 15.2: Moisture Survey

ROOF INVESTIGATION
ELEMENTARY SCHOOL BUILDING "A" & "D"

The nuclear moisture survey roof investigation and report was conducted on Roof "A" (CLASSROOM) & "D" (ADMINISTRATION), at XXXX ELEMENTARY SCHOOL on August 13, 2000. This report includes identifying problem areas on roofs, giving assessment of roofs' condition, and core sample results.

A.   OVERALL CONDITION:

The roofs to be inspected shall be given a condition rating of good, fair, or bad.

A roof having a good condition rating means:

1.   There are no problems that require immediate corrective work.
2.   There are no noticeable visual damages that may cause leaks.
3.   There are no noticeable moisture problems on the moisture surveyed roof plan.

A roof having a fair condition rating means:

1.   There are minor problems that may result in leaks.
2.   There are noticeable visual damages that may result in leaks.
3.   There are noticeable moisture problems on the moisture surveyed roof plan.

A roof having a bad condition rating means:

1.   There are major roofing problems to the roof that are causing leaks.
2.   There are major moisture problems on the moisture surveyed roof plan.

B.   IDENTIFYING CONDITIONS OF ROOFING ITEMS BELOW:

Building "A "Roof- Classroom:

Roof "A" is a built-up capsheet roofing. The roofs are gable roofs in shape. The overall condition of roof "A" being investigated appears to be in fair condition.

1.   The nuclear moisture survey of this roof shows little moisture migration throughout the roof area.
2.   The roof appears to have been spot mopped. This causes moisture to migrate in various directions.
3.   The capsheet is pulling away from the ends of the building.
4.   The caulking is drying out on the Diamond Head side of the building.
5.   The capsheet granules are coming off, exposing the asphalt membrane below to the weather.
6.   There is a lot of rubbish on the roof beneath the trees.
7.   The ridge membrane is starting to deteriorate.
8.   Cracks are occurring at the base of the vent pipes.
9.   The edge flashing appears to be all right.

Building "D "Roof- Administration:

Roof "D" is a built-up capsheet roofing. The roofs are gable roofs in shape. The overall condition of roof "D" being investigated appears to be in fair condition.

1. The nuclear moisture survey of this roof shows moisture migration throughout the roof area.
2. The roof appears to have been spot mopped. This causes moisture to migrate in various directions.
3. The capsheet is pulling away from the ends of the building.
4. The capsheet granules are coming off, exposing the asphalt membrane below to the weather.
5. Cracks are occurring at the base of the vent pipes.
6. The gooseneck vents appear to be all right.
7. The edge flashing is pulling away in some places and caulking is worn in other places.

AREAS PROBED FOR MOISTURE:

Probe #1:Deck = 0%
Probe #2:Deck = 0%
Probe #3:Deck = 0%
Probe #4:Deck = 0%

Brief description of roofing make up starting from top:

· Capsheet
· 2 ply membrane
· Base sheet
· Rosin sheet

ASBESTOS TEST RESULTS ON PROBE #---, CORING ONLY

RESULTS:

No	Layer	Laboratory Sample Description	Type*	Percentage
1	Whole sample basis	Black roofing core with silver paint	Chrysotile	Trace
2	Black material	Black roofing core with silver paint	AND	<1%
3	Silver paint	Black roofing core with silver paint	Chrysotile	5%
4	Whole sample basis	Black roofing core	AND	<1%
5	Whole sample basis	Black roofing core	AND	<1%
6	Whole sample basis	Black roofing core	AND	<1%
7	Whole sample basis	Black roofing core	AND	<1%
8	Whole sample basis	Black roofing core with brown fibrous layer	Chrysotile	Trace
9	Black material	Black roofing core with brown fibrous layer	Chrysotile	Trace
10	Brown fibrous later	Black roofing core with brown fibrous layer	AND	<1%
11	Whole sample basis	Black roofing ore with brown fibrous layer	AND	<1%
12	Whole sample basis	Block roofing core with brown rocky surface & traces of silver paint	Chrysotile	Trace
13	Black material	Black roofing core with brown rocky surface & traces of silver paint	AND	<1%
14	Silver paint	traces of silver paint	Chrysotile	Trace

*AND=Asbestos not detected

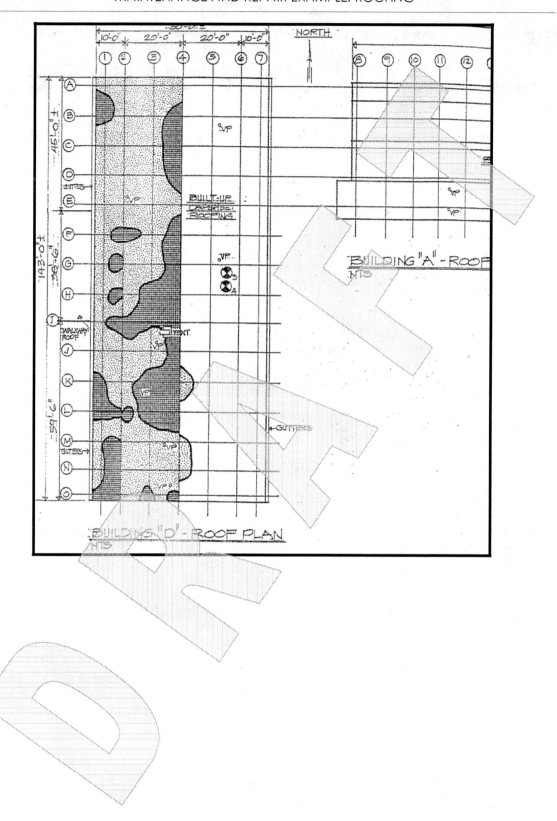

Attachment 15.3: Industry Roof Statements

1. Graham, Mark. (2002, September). NRCA's performance standards initiative. Professional Roofing, 32 [9], pg. 80.

NRCA is undertaking an initiative to develop and maintain meaningful performance standards for roof systems. However, through NRCA's involvement, it has realized the values established in many of these standards are not necessarily based on what is required to achieve satisfactory field performance.

2. Sharp, Stephen A. (2002, June). What are the Standards? Professional Roofing, 36 [6], 39-40.

An ASTM International standard for TPO's is on its way to racking a consensus. ASTM standards often are viewed as reflecting the lowest common denominator for many products. The standard that finally is issued may reflect the consensus of manufacturers' minimum requirements for a laboratory-tested roof. It is most unlikely the standard can ensure a product's performance in the field.

An ASTM standard probably won't hurt much. But it's unlikely to change the way products perform. As usual, the changes that are needed in any product likely will come about based on performance, or lack thereof, at the expense of all involved. As a result, the industry could face a continuing challenge to define a "standard" TPO membrane.

3. Warseck, Karen. (2003, February). Finding the Value of Roofing Warranties. Building Operating Management. 50 [2], pg. 53, 54, 56, 58-59, 60, 62, 64.

Too often the only thing about a warranty that a building owner considers is length. This is probably the least important part. Building owners must understand that warranties are written by the attorneys for the issuer for the benefit of the issuer. Warranties have become a marketing tool.

As an example, when PVC roofing first went on the market, a manufacturer whose product line included shower curtains decided to expand into roofing. Its material, although quite good for shower curtains, was unsuited for use as a roofing membrane. Many failures occurred.

Another area to pay attention to is maintenance requirements. Most manufacturers require that the owner conduct twice-yearly inspections of the roof and document the findings. Failure to carry out these inspections and to repair small defects promptly can be taken to mean that the owner is not maintaining the roof and that the warranty is null and void.

4. Warseck, Karen (2002, October). Reroofing: What Do You Get for You Money? Building Operation Management, 49 [10], pg. 76,78.

"Pay me now or pay me later."

The old saying that you only get what you pay for is true in roofing. Quality takes time and costs a little bit more, but the small increment in upfront price is usually worth paying. The savings occur in the long term when the roof does not have to be replaced as quickly, when tenants are happier with a dry building and when the facility executive can go home at night without worrying about that 3 a.m. call "The roof is leaking-again"

Roofers know that the facility executive is not really looking for the best solution, but rather the cheapest price. When price is the overriding criterion, cheap is better and more likely to win the job for the contractor. But cheap usually means thinner, less durable materials.

Another potential problem is that the architect or engineer may not have a good understanding of what a reproofing project involves. That can be true even if they have designed hundreds of roofs on new construction. The result can be inferior work.

Good contractors do have costs that other contractors will not, including training, insurance and workers compensation, salaries to keep superior mechanics in an employee-driven job market, and equipment. All these things add up, but without them, the contractor cannot provide superior work. In addition, it takes time to do the details that make the difference between long roof life and a short-term disaster.

5. Dodson, Marc (1995, May/June). Selling Quality. Western Roofing. Pg. 4.

How can you sell on quality when the bidding system in the construction industry is based solely on who can bid the job at the lowest possible price?

The Midwest Roofing Contractors Association commissioned a study to find out what building owners and roofing contractors considered important. Roofing contractors thought that owners considered prices as the most important item in bidding a job, while owners rated the quality of the job as their number one concern and price a distant third.

Why would an owner take the lowest bid for a roof and then turn around and add to that cost by hiring a roofing consultant to ensure the quality of the job? Roofing consultants have added an entire new category to this industry merely by ensuring the quality of the roofing application and the owners are willing to pay handsomely for it."

6. Holf, James. (2003, March). Exploring Industry Expectations: a survey reveals consensus, as well as conflict, regarding how key industry groups view quality. Professional Roofing, 33 [3], pgs. 18-23.

Although significant strides have been made to improve roof system performance during the past decades, the roofing industry continues to cling to a limited definition of quality. At a time when many industries are viewing quality in broad terms of customer satisfaction, the roofing industry (as well as the entire construction industry) continues to cling to a more narrow definition of quality as "conformance to requirements".

Conformance to requirements defines quality as satisfying a set of specifications rather than satisfying a customer. It ignores the potential mismatch between what is specified and what the customer needs or wants.

7. Garrison, Ted. (2003 October). "Do roof auctions provide better value to building owners?" Professional Roofing, pgs. 21-24.

Roof auctions have become attractive because building owners and developers are under constant pressure to lower construction and maintenance costs while attempting to maintain quality materials and workmanship. However, roof auctions do not accomplish this objective. In fact, roof auctions can result in higher overall costs, lower quality and increased litigation.

Building owners who have used roof auctions have been disappointed by the results because of higher project costs and poor workmanship. Roof auction bidding doesn't guarantee the lowest price. There are many hidden costs, including change orders that tend to increase a project's financial price.

Roofing work is not a commodity and should not be purchased according to price alone. Building owners should understand a bid evaluation must include a quality aspect. When there is strong competition, competitors tend to improve their skills to stand out from their competition.

8. Patterson, Maureen. (1996, February). *Starting at the top.* Buildings Magazine, Pgs. 54-56.

Today's building owners and facilities managers place a high priority on the performance of their roofing systems.

I'd really encourage you to do some homework on those [contractors] people, check references, do things along that line to make sure that you're comfortable with the people you're dealing with, because roofing turns out to be a very large investment for building owners. After all, the three major reasons for roof failures are poor workmanship, inadequate design specifications, and bad materials.

Though I wouldn't necessarily exclude them or not take the warranty – because if there's a product failure there're nice to have – it should never be used as a basis for selection of a roof system.

In a June survey conducted by Buildings Magazine respondents were asked to rate how important certain characteristics were in deciding which brand of roofing to purchase.

No	Criteria	Very Important	Important	Not So Important
1	Maintenance cost	73%	26%	0.30%
2	Installed Cost	60%	37%	3%
3	Product Reputation	49%	41%	5%
4	Life Cycle Cost	63%	30%	5%
5	Factory Trained Support	27%	49%	19%
6	Manufacturer Reputation	30%	52%	5%
7	Warranty Term	54%	35%	9%
8	Contractor Recommendation	17%	37%	40%

When asked if they are outsourcing the management of their roofing installations 51% said no and 38% said yes. For those that said yes, 57% said they were outsourcing with a consultant, 40% with a contractor, and 19% with a manufacturer.

Attachment 15.4: NRCA Advisory Bulletin

Roofing Warranties

"The relatively recent introduction of numerous systems utilizing rubbers, plastics, modified asphalts and other synthetic materials caused manufacturers to focus attention upon the warranties they offered and to employ long-term warranties as a marketing tool. The National Roofing Contractors Association (NRCA), in the interest of the roofing consumer, acknowledges the following concerns relative to manufacturers' roofing warranties."

"The length of a roofing warranty should not be the primary criterion in the selection of a roofing product or system because the warranty does not necessarily provide assurance of satisfactory roofing performance."

" A long-term warranty may be of little value to a consumer if the roof does not perform satisfactorily and the owner is plagued by leaks."

" It is suspected that in some cases the length of the warranty was established without appropriate technical research or documentation of in-place field performance."

" Increased liability risk associated with long-term warranties has contributed to the recent demise of some manufacturers resulting in unanticipated and costly expenses for extensive roof repairs by roofing consumers."

"Roof warranties typically do not warrant that the roof system will not leak or is suitable for the project where it is installed. Even the most comprehensive manufacturer warranties that cover material and workmanship generally provide only that the manufacturer will repair leaks that result from specific causes enumerated in the warranty."

" Warranty documents often contain restrictive provisions which significantly limit the warrantor's liability and the consumer's remedies in the event that problems develop."

" Long-term warranties are largely reactive...."

"Manufacturers who focus their sales efforts primarily on the relevant and proven merits of those products and systems best designed to serve the specific needs of the roofing consumer."

" Manufacturers who base warranties for membranes or systems solely upon an honest and realistic appraisal of their proven service life..."

" NRCA believes that the roofing consumer, with the assistance of a roofing professional, should focus his purchase decision primarily on an objective and comparative analysis of proven roofing system options that best serve his specific roofing requirements and not on warranty time frames."

Selecting A Professional Roofing Contractor

" It pays to remember that all roofing contractors are not alike. NRCA recommends that you pre-qualify your roofing contractor to get the job done right the first time."

" There is no foolproof method for selecting a professional, but there are a number of things you can do to help you make the decision possible when evaluating contractors."

" Check for a permanent place of business..."

" Don't hesitate to ask the roofing contractor for proof of the insurance he carries. In fact, insist on seeing copies of both his liability coverage and his workers' compensation certificates."

" Check to see if the roofing contractor is properly licensed or bonded."

" Make sure the contractor is financially stable."

" Look for a company with a proven track record that readily offers client references and a list of completed projects."

" Have your contractor list the roofing manufacturers with which his firm has licensed or approved applicator agreements."

" Have the contractor explain his project supervision and quality control procedures."

" Carefully read and understand any roof warranty offered and watch for provisions that would void it."

" Choose a company committed to the safety and education of its workers."

" Keep a healthy skepticism about the lowest bid. If it sounds too good to be true, it probably is."

16

Manufacturer's Use of PIPS: Alpha Program

Introduction

Neogard is a manufacturing company which produces urethane coating with the highest documented performance over the past twenty years. They have used quality raw materials to produce a urethane coating for sprayed polyurethane foam roof systems that has documented performance of over 25 years. Neogard is the only manufacturer who has issued a joint and several warranty with its high performing roofing systems.

Neogard began to see the roofing marketplace exhibit, the Quadrant I low price, commodity environment (Chapter 4) in the 1990s. It became harder for them to compete as their competitors were issuing warranties with twice the service period with less coating material. Neogard realized that to stay profitable and maintain its high performance, they would have to find a new way to sell their products. They could not sustain themselves in the SPF roofing industry without moving from a Quadrant I low price environment to a Quadrant II high performance environment.

In 1995, Mike Steele, the CEO of Neogard, realized that the same technology that building owners used to minimize the risk of nonperformance could be used to help Neogard minimize the risk of price based owners and nonperforming contractors. He approached PBSRG with the objective of designing a delivery system that could deliver high value to intelligent building owners with risk (Quadrant II). Steele also realized that by maintaining high quality, Neogard could become more efficient, minimize their risk, result in very satisfied owners, and maximize their profit. He realized just like building owners, he could not minimize risk by using minimum standards and regulation. It was too risky and too costly. He requested PBSRG to use IMT concepts and an understanding of PIPS to transform Neogard into a company that could leverage the high performance of the Neogard roofing systems instead of low price.

Background of the Sprayed Polyurethane Foam Industry

The construction industry has attempted to use specifications and minimal standards to regulate performance of construction services and systems (Quadrant 1). Without any motivation to increase value, construction materials and systems are made as economical as possible. The materials are installed with the most economical workforce. The Quadrant I environment (Chapter 4) has shifted the risk from the manufacturer to the owner without the owner's perception. This is well documented by the many marketing schemes involving warranties (Chapter 13).

The impact of this environment on the spray polyurethane foam (SPF) roofing industry has been to make the SPF roof system an inexpensive system with inconsistent performance results. This has resulted in roof failures and the minimization of market share (3-5% over the past ten years). Documented performance information has shown that when high quality contractors install the SPF roof system with performing materials, the SPF roof system performs as well as a traditional BUR or modified bitumen system.

Coated sprayed polyurethane foam (SPF) roofing has been commercially installed since the 1960s. Performance studies of the SPF roofing systems in 1983-1997 identified the following performance results (Kashiwagi and Moor 1992, Kashiwagi 1996):

1. When installed by "quality oriented" contractors, the SPF roofing systems have proven performance periods of 15 to 20 years. Recoating the SPF roof systems could extend the service period.
2. The SPF systems can be installed successfully in all regions of the country. However, in areas with frequent rain showers, the SPF system is not the most economical system due to the dry conditions required for installation.
3. The SPF system is a more complex roofing system (equipment and installation), which requires the contractor's craftsmen to have a higher level of training and to make more technical decisions. The lack of trained craftspeople affects the quality and performance of the SPF roofing systems.

Historically, the SPF system was sold as a "cheaper" roofing system than the conventional "built-up" roofing systems. SPF can be installed cheaper than the traditional systems due to the capability to be installed over an existing waterproofing membrane. The SPF roof system is also monolithic, seamless, lightweight, and has the largest insulating capability of any roofing material. The rationale used by the industry, was that more facility owners and designers would select the SPF roof system to save money. This strategy was not successful over the last 20 years due to the following factors:

1. Premature failures.
2. SPF material system problems.
3. Changing formulations.
4. The lack of proven performance and research into system performance.
5. Perceptions of SPF systems not being durable.
6. A lack of trained, business oriented contractors who minimized risk and maximized their profit

These results have stayed relatively constant over the last 20 years. In an attempt to gain a larger share of the roofing market, SPF and coating manufacturers have:

1. Altered the material content to make the coating system more "economical".
2. Reduced the amount of required coating material to warranty a system to make the system cheaper.
3. Sold coatings that could not resist weathering, ponding, or traffic.
4. Allowed contractors with inadequate training to install systems.
5. Used past performance of other manufacturers' high performance to convince a new owner that their installations would have the same performance.
6. Altered the formulation of the coating and SPF and sold the systems without proper field-testing.

These practices led to the following results:

1. Extremely low prices. In some areas of the country, coated SPF systems are installed with a first price of $1.00 per square foot.
2. Premature failure of some SPF systems due to a change in raw materials or SPF composition.
3. Premature chalking of coating systems due to a lower percentage of elastomeric material.
4. Reversion and cracking of some high solids, aliphatic urethane coating systems.
5. Aesthetically unpleasing SPF roof system installations.
6. The inability for manufacturers and contractors to respond to problems due to inadequate profit margins.
7. A very low market share (approximately 3-5%).

Performance studies in 1980s and 1990s (Kashiwagi) identified requirements to stabilize the marketplace and identify the true value of the SPF roofing systems installed by quality oriented contractors and manufacturers. The requirements were:

1. SPF manufacturers should quality control production and distribution.
2. SPF and coating manufacturers and contractors should collect performance information on their systems.
3. A joint and several warranty should be issued by the SPF, coating manufacturer, and contractor.
4. A difference must be identified between systems with "high proven performance" and systems with "no documented performance."

In a meeting at Arizona State University in the mid 1990s, the major manufacturers rejected these concepts. In the past ten years, these major manufacturers have not been able to increase their marketshare.

Business Problem

The problems faced by the SPF manufacturers and contractors are not unique in the roofing or construction industry. It is well documented that roofing product specifications using minimum standards have no direct correlation with performance of the installed system (Cash 1991, Kashiwagi 2000). This is due to the following factors:

1. Variation in installation site conditions.
2. Variation in contractor skill in installing the roof system.
3. Variation of installation environmental conditions.
4. Variation in the system materials.
5. Variation in the maintenance of the installed system.

With conventional technical and engineering analysis techniques, it is difficult to identify the potential factors that influence performance. It is also difficult to select a representative random sample that can be used to identify causes of nonperformance. The roofing industry has not been successful in quantifying performance criteria that will predict nonperformance of roofing systems (Cash 1991, Kashiwagi 2000). This has resulted in problematic analysis of roof failures, "after the fact."

Manufacturers and contractors in the construction industry are being forced into a "commodity" role (low price, leverage volume). Manufacturers in the "commodity" mentality, push volume instead of quality and value.

Facility owners and their representatives (designers, consultants, and inspectors) are faced with the following dilemmas:

1. Are forced to select a system from those that they have personal knowledge of, and estimate the value of the system.
2. Do not use systems that they do not have a personal knowledge of.
3. Do not use systems that have failures (regardless of the cause of failure including nonperforming materials and contractors).
4. Do not use high performing contractors and products if they do not have a personal knowledge of their performance due to their higher price.
5. Are forced to be an expert of manufacturer and contractor warranties, which many times offer no real owner protection.
6. Are forced to be an expert and direct the contractor on how to install the system through the use of specifications.
7. Attempt to demand a level of excellence from the contractor that is not well understood and difficult to quantify.

The Alpha Research Program

SPF and coating manufacturers were approached in 1994 to participate in a performance based program, which would:

1. Rate the performance of each manufacturer's product and contractor installation.
2. Identify the performance constraints of each system.
3. Develop an Alpha specification and warranty which is based on proven performance and which minimizes exclusions.
4. Produce quality control processes for the use of SPF on "performance oriented" projects.

5. Differentiate performance based project results from price based "commodity" project results.
6. Develop an information-based approach to marketing, warranties, contractor qualifications, and staff operations that can be successful in an "information environment."
7. Invest funding into the research program to develop the above objectives.

Only one coating manufacturer agreed to participate in the research project. The coating manufacturer (Neogard) then persuaded a SPF manufacturer to join the program (BASF). The following reasons were given by other manufacturers for nonparticipation:

1. Owners are not interested in a "high performance" SPF roofing system.
2. Owners are only interested in economical roof systems, which have the lowest first cost.
3. There are not enough contractors who can meet high performance requirements. The lack of contractors will limit the manufacturer's sales.
4. Not all manufacturers have performance information on their systems. Some of the past performance may not be conducive to marketing, based on performance.
5. Manufacturers are not used to fund research to identify performance. Funding is usually put into advertising, marketing, and getting sales. (The author quickly realized that manufacturers do not know how to sell based on "performance information.")
6. Some manufacturers felt that the "information approach" would not work.

The SPF industry was not the only sector of the roofing marketplace that was invited to participate in the Alpha program. In the mid 1990s, a concentrated effort was made to involve BUR, modified bitumen, and single ply manufacturers to participate in the Alpha program. Several manufacturers showed interest, however the current "commodity" and "marketing" (flashy brochures, prepared specifications, and sales pitches) approach of most manufacturers made it very difficult to even consider an "information oriented" system. In the status quo marketplace, the most successful contractors were the ones with the largest sales. Moving to a system of performance instead of volume is a difficult step. Test results in the states of Hawaii, Maryland, and Texas verified that the majority of roofing manufacturers are not interested in identifying and improving the performance of roofing systems.

Design of the Alpha Program

The Alpha program was created with the following objectives:

1. Develop a manufacturer and contractor roofing delivery system and environment that is based on performance information.
2. Identify the proven performance of SPF roofing systems installed by quality contractors and manufacturers.
3. Post the performance information on the Internet. (www.pbsrg.com)

4. Develop a process to quality control the SPF roofing product (material composition and installation) to maximize the performance period.
5. Develop a process that will increase the customer's value by using the past performance of the contractor as a criterion for extended warranties.
6. Develop an information system whereby contractors can continuously monitor their performance and compare the performance against other performing contractors.

The participating manufacturers and contractors realized that the nonparticipating (less performing manufacturers and contractors) would also use the performance information to represent the capability of their products and installations. They would claim that their performance was the "same" as the Alpha vendors. However, the Alpha participants realized that in order to reduce their own risk of nonperformance, to continuously improve, and to service their customers in a manner that would lead to repeat business, a structure of performance information was necessary.

The Alpha Program was designed using the theoretical foundation of Information Measurement Theory (IMT). The Alpha program requirements include:

1. Contractor performance criteria and requirements.
2. Manufacturer performance criteria and requirements.
3. Contractor and manufacturer performance numbers that can be used by procurement systems that require documented performance information.
4. An information system maintained by third party university research group, that gives the contractor, manufacturer, and facility owner the same information.
5. Constant improvement of performance.
6. Disqualification from the Alpha program on failure to meet the requirements set by the performing contractors.
7. The ability to identify performing facility owners who require "best value" and risk minimization.

Contractor Performance Criteria and Requirements

Ten of the highest performing contractors with documented performance were selected by Arizona State University to identify the contractor performance criteria and requirements for an Alpha contractor. It was not a requirement to install the coating manufacturer's product. The contractors selected the performance criteria (See Table 16-1).

The contractor requirements were selected based on the following IMT principles:

1. Performers have high past performance.
2. Performers use performance information to track their performance. Those who are uncomfortable or who cannot understand the importance of performance information are often not performers.
3. Performers will perform when something goes wrong.
4. Performers can be educated on the importance of an information environment.

5. Performers will train their personnel.
6. Performers will take responsibility for the success of the industry.

Over the past five years, contractors who are financially stable, performance oriented, use performing products, and track their performance, have remained in the Alpha program. The program has become uncomfortable and costly for those contractors who are not natural performers.

Table 16-1: Contractor and Manufacturer Performance Requirements

CONTRACTOR:	
Minimum years of experience	5
Random Survey of Roofs	Every other year
EMR Rating	Publish
Minimum insurance requirements.	$500,000
Maintenance inspection programs.	Annual
ASU check on all roof applications	Annually
Subcontract requirements:	None allowed
All roofs documented at ASU	5,000 SF or larger
% of roofs do not currently leak	98%
% Customer Satisfaction	98%
24 hour response to leaks	Yes
Warranty covering labor	Yes
Educational presentations w/ASU	Minimum (1/year)
ASU Conference Participation	Yes
FOAM MANUFACTURER	
Sampling requirements:	ASU Design
Database of product performance	ASU documented
Warranty Covering SPF defects	Manufacturer's
SPI Accredited	
COATING MANUFACTURER	
Warranty Length	15 years
Type of Warranty	Manufacturer's
Bird Pecking, FM-SH, 90 MPH Wind	Yes
Full maintenance	Yes
Independent Third Party Testing	Yes
Proprietary Details	Yes
SPI Accredited	

Manufacturer Requirements

The coating manufacturer then increased the "real value" of the high performance system with the following changes:

1. Provided an Alpha program and specification.
2. Increased the joint and several warranty from ten years to fifteen years for roofing systems.

3. Included a "full service" warranty with exclusions limited to "Acts of God" and similar catastrophic acts. All other exclusions were eliminated based on the decrease of risk.
4. Included hail damage in the warranty, which is comparable to the Factory Mutual Severe Hail test (1-3/4 inch steel ball dropped by 17 feet nine inches). This resulted from extensive testing of aged SPF roof systems.
5. Used independent third party testing to document "in-field" quality control.
6. Persuaded an SPF manufacturer to join the Alpha team and offer the first ever "joint and several" SPF warranty.
7. Increased the coating and SPF material requirements to further reduce risk of nonperformance.

The coating and SPF manufacturer identified the Alpha program as a separate roofing program from all other SPF roofing systems. The contractors were required to meet all contractor qualifications. Contractors were also required to do the following to be qualified to install the Alpha system:

1. Pass an exam on Information Measurement Theory or the measurement of differential, performance, and industry structure.
2. Agree to a joint and several warranty that makes the contractor liable with the manufacturers for the length of the warranty; not only for leaking, but also defects to the roof systems.

A "joint and several" warranty differs from a regular warranty in the following way: It makes all parties, contractors and manufacturers, individually liable for nonperformance of the installed system. The joint and several warranty of the Alpha system minimizes the risk of nonperformance in the following manner:

1. Provides maximum legal coverage for the owner. The SPF and coating manufacturer have "joint and several" warranties along with the contractor's joint and several warranty.
2. Shows past performance of warranty providers. The contractor is required to show high performance (98% roofs not leaking and customer satisfaction).
3. Performs quality control of materials and installation of warranted roofs. The manufacturers are required to meet a QC plan for the delivery of material that is based on past performance and designed by the Performance Based Studies Research Group.

BASF is the first SPF manufacturer in the history of the SPF industry to offer an Alpha material delivery process and a joint and several warranty for the SPF. This is a shocking departure from the traditional SPF roofing practices.

Contractor Proven Past Performance

Contractor past performance is collected in two ways:

1. Annual checks with owners of all SPF roofs installed by the contractor.

2. Every other year random surveys of 50 roofs installed by the contractor.

The results of both of these information gatherings are compiled and posted on the Internet at pbsrg.com under the research projects. Alpha contractor requirements include:

1. Maintain a 98% customer satisfaction.
2. Maintain a 98% of roofs not leaking.
3. Document facility owner rating in the categories of professionalism, performance, honesty, and hiring again based on performance.

Many roofing contractors do not practice these "common sense" business practices. From past experience with contractors, the author has not identified a contractor who was keeping the information in a useable format before being approached by PBSRG or a facility owner using PIPS. These practices minimize the possibility of nonperformance or failure. These are business issues and not technical issues.

Surveying Alpha contractors assumes that "best or successful practices" have been used to install the SPF systems. The performance data has been collected in the States of California, Wyoming, Ohio, Kentucky, New York, Virginia, Texas, Indiana, Kansas, and Michigan. The performance numbers do not seem to be affected by the different environmental conditions. The common factor between the sites is the performance of the contractor. The 2003 Alpha contractor performance numbers are listed in Table 16-2, and the individual contractor numbers and the Alpha system performance numbers are listed in the Attachments.

The most important performance results are:

1. SPF systems installed correctly have a proven performance period of 29 years.
2. The 661 SPF systems have an average proven performance period of 14 years.
3. The SPF roofs have a leaking rate of less than 1 percent.

Table 16-2: Performance of SPF Roof Systems Installed by Alpha Contractors

Application Profile	Units	Value
Total Square Feet Installed	#	22,693,301
Percent of Roofs with Traffic Greater than 12 Times per Year	%	22
Maximum Service Period (years)	#	29
Adjusted Service Period (years)	#	14
Average Service Period (years)	#	.9
Number of Roofs that Never Leaked	#	232
Number of Roofs that Still Leak	#	-
Percent of Roofs that Never Leaked	%	60
Percent of Roofs that Still Leak	%	-
Percent of Roofs not Requiring Maintenance	%	11
Percent of Satisfied Customers	%	99
Percent of Jobs Completed on Time	%	97
Number of Roofs Inspected	#	661
Number of Customer Responses	#	393

Based on 393 responses from the 661 owners (64% response), the Alpha contractors were rated by their long time customers (10 being best) in Table 16-3.

Table 16-3: Customer Satisfaction Ratings

CRITERIA	AVERAGE
Contractor's ability to communicate	8.93
Contractor's management ability	8.95
Professionalism	9.11
Level of honesty	9.34
Overall performance	9.09
Comfort level on hiring again based on performance	9.22

These performance numbers show that if SPF systems are installed by experienced, trained craftspeople, and backed by performing contractors and manufacturers, the risk of nonperformance is minimized. Customers are satisfied with the performance of both the contractor and the system.

PBSRG research has found a commonality between the following contractor traits:

1. High performance.
2. Measurement and analysis of performance information leading to continuous improvement.
3. Sound business practices which lead to longevity and minimization of risk.
4. Repeat business based on performance.

Alpha Information System

The Alpha information system is designed to give performance information to the owner, the contractor, and the manufacturers. All Alpha contractor performance lines are posted on the Internet at www.pbsrg.com under the "Alpha" program. Any facility owner who uses an Alpha contractor can use the Internet to report any problems and upgrade or downgrade their performance rating.

The impact of the performance information includes the following:

1. Roofing contractors pay more attention to what they are doing.
2. Owners have quick responses to problems. If the problem is not solved within two weeks from the time the owner notified ASU through the Internet, the contractor could lose their Alpha status.
3. Nonperformance information assists the manufacturers to respond to minimize risk.

The information system is the only performance information rating system in the roofing industry. For facility owners who are seeking value and minimized risk, the performance information, along with contractor's profile information, allows the facility owner to get best value and roofing service without the usual risk.

The performance information also allows the contractors to continuously improve their performance. The performing contractors meet annually to review their performance numbers, and get training on the latest performance techniques to monitor performance.

The Alpha Program has evolved as the top quality control program in the roofing industry. No other manufacturer or contractor group has a program which includes quality control checks every year, random inspections every other year, and an entire process and materials set up for a third party review. Performance information makes contractors and manufacturers liable for performance, makes it more difficult to hide behind marketing and warranties, and quickly identifies performance or nonperformance.

Modifying the Alpha Requirements

In analyzing the objective of the Alpha program, the manufacturers have identified that in order to make the Alpha Program stronger, they need to have more high performing contractors. The original requirements of the Alpha program were that contractors could only participate if they have been in business for over five years. This requirement was modified. Research performed by PBSRG has proven that the Alpha system is very durable (see Chapter 15). Preliminary results show that a 10 mil minimum system lasts 20 years. The system passed the FM-SH test for 12 out of the 15 samples after 19 years of infield service. Entry into the Alpha program can be achieved in two ways:

1. They must have a minimum of five years experience and can document 50 high performing elastomeric-coated SPF roof systems.
2. They do not have to have a minimum of fiver years experience, but they must be able to document that they have installed 10 "Alpha-like" roofs with total area being over 150,000

An Alpha contractor would still have to meet all of the other requirements. This includes: submitting their entire roof list, submitting to random inspections every other year, submitting a list of all roofs installed every year, and maintaining 98% customer satisfaction and 98% of roofs not leaking.

Conclusion

The Alpha program is a prototype information-based program in the roofing industry that incorporates documented contractor and system performance. The Alpha system does not minimize the owner's risk through a warranty but by quality control, high system performance, and a performance based contractor.

Manufacturer and contractor relationship in the program is based on performance. The performance information forces continuous improvement. The objective of the

Alpha program is to change the structure of the SPF industry to a high performance product sector and a commodity sector. The high performance sector will run based on performance information and the commodity sector will run based on low price.

The performance data has shown that the Alpha SPF contractor installed system is comparable to any of the high performance roofing systems (29 year performance, 98% of roofs not leaking, and 98% of customers satisfied). The Alpha program information system minimizes the causes of risk currently in the roofing industry (lack of training, improper installation, premature failure, lack of performance information, lack of liability in case of problems). It protects the manufacturer, contractor, and facility owner against any poor quality. The Alpha program increases the value of the SPF system by ensuring that it is installed correctly with high performance materials. The Alpha SPF system will increase the market share of SPF roof systems.

The Alpha program is in its seventh year of development. The coating and SPF manufacturers are both pleased with the potential of the program. The program has had the following results:

1. Minimized the risk of the coating manufacturer who was previously forced to pay for nonperformance of the SPF used under its coating.
2. Identified high performance contractors, which has allowed the manufacturer to raise their warranty period 50% without accruing additional risk.
3. Provided an information system for the manufacturers, which structures their warranty system. The warranty system protects the owner and the contractor and manufacturers.
4. Attracted facility owners who are seeking "best value."
5. Given facility owners the capability to gain best value considering price and performance.
6. Differentiated their products and installed system from an industry that has been hampered by a lack of performance information, failures, quality control, product modifications, and a lack of quality contractors.

The Alpha program allows the performers to identify their performance and reduce risk by knowing where performance could be increased. The Alpha program then forces the contractors and manufacturers to minimize everyone's risk by using "joint and several" warranties to make the constructors liable for performance.

The Alpha program is not limited to SPF roof systems. The authors encourage all manufacturers to minimize risk of nonperformance by using performance information. Performance information has the potential to change the environment of the roofing industry.

Chapter 16 Review

1. What is the Alpha program?
2. What are the past performance requirements of the Alpha contractors?

3. How are the manufacturers using performance information to market themselves?
4. Can the Alpha research program be developed for other types of roofing systems?
5. Can the Alpha research program be developed for other types of systems (not roofing related)?
6. What are the most important factors in buying a roof?
7. How do contractors bring risk to the owner?
8. What type of systems will a contractor install?
9. A high performance manufacturer will maximize profit by _____.
10. When a high performance manufacturer meets a price-based owner, they will deliver _____.
11. Who does the warranty protect?
12. A joint and several warranty is different from an ordinary warranty in what two ways?
13. What brings the greatest risk to a contractor?
14. The current construction industry forces manufacturers and contractors to leverage _____ and _____.
15. A high performance manufacturer must do what to leverage their performance?
16. What does a high performance manufacturer do with the performance information?
17. What is the relationship between a high performance contractor/manufacturer and PIPS?
18. What is the advantage of a high performance contractor in PIPS?
19. Is the Alpha roof the best roof?
20. When manufacturers make cheaper systems, who absorbs the risk?
21. A manufacturer who does not keep performance information is banking on the owner not asking them to _____.
22. What is the difference between the Alpha program and PIPS?
23. Why would the Alpha manufacturers be interested in PIPS?
24. Who has the advantage in PIPS?

References

Cash, C.G. (1991) The Effect of Heat Aging on Load-strain Properties of Glass Felt Reinforced Asphalt Built-Up and Polyvinyl Chloride Roofing Membranes, and the Effect of Ultraviolet Accelerated Exposure on Polyvinyl Choloride Membranes. 1991 Third International Symposium on Roofing Technology, NRCA, 1991, p. 1-6.

Kashiwagi, D.T., Moor, W.C., Nuno, J.P., and Badger, W.B. (1992) The Effect of Artificial Intelligence on the Determination of Roof Performance and Test Standards. *VIII Congreso Internacional: Association Internacional De La Impermeabilizacion,* Madrid, Spain, 96-111 (1992).

Kashiwagi, D. (1996). Performance Issues of Sprayed Polyurethane Foam Roof Systems. Professional Roofing, Vol 19, Jan 1996, pp. 49 – 58.

Kashiwagi, D. (2000). Artificial Intelligent Performance-Based Procurement System. *Construction Congress VI,* Orlando, FL, 49-58.

Attachments

Attachment 16.1: Alpha Contractor Performance Lines
      Attachment 16.1a: Dallas Urethane, Inc.
      Attachment 16.1b: Insulated Roofing Contractors, Inc.
      Attachment 16.1c: JVC Company.
      Attachment 16.1d: Phoenix Coatings, Inc.
      Attachment 16.1e: Phoenix 1 – Restoration & Construction Ltd.
      Attachment 16.1f: PROCO Inc.
      Attachment 16.1g: S&J Contractor Inc.
      Attachment 16.1h: Washington Roofing & Insulation, Inc.
      Attachment 16.1i: Wattle & Daub Contractors, Inc.

Attachment 16.1a: Dallas Urethane, Inc.

Dallas Urethane, Inc.

Alpha Roofing Performance Line

System Information

Information
Valid Thru:
January
2004

No	Criteria	Average
1	Average square feet installed	24,359
2	Average square foot of roof per penetration	1624
3	Percent of roofs with slope less than 1/4"	73%
4	Percent of roofs with traffic greater than 12 times/year	35%
5	**Maximum service period**	**16 years**
6	Adjusted service period	13 years
7	Average service period	8 years
8	Percent of roofs that never leaked	65%
9	Percent of roofs that leaked and were fixed	35%
10	**Percent of roofs that still leak**	**0%**
11	Age sum of all roofs that never leaked	234 years
12	Age sum of all roofs that do not leak	383 years
13	Percent of roofs not requiring maintenance	39%
14	Percent of roofs with more than 5% ponded water	47%
15	Percent of roofs with less than 1% deterioration	98%
16	**Percent of satisfied customers**	**100%**
17	**Percent of jobs completed on time**	**98%**
18	**Number of roofs inspected**	**58**
19	**Number of roof evaluations**	**46**

Contractor Performance Information

No	Criteria	Average
1	Contractor's ability to respond to emergencies in days	1.38
2	Contractor's ability to communicate	9.42
3	Contractor's management abilities	9.53
4	Professionalism of contractor	9.52
5	Contractor's level of honesty	9.67
6	Overall performance of contractor	9.45
7	Comfort level in hiring contractor again	9.57
8	**Number of different customer responses**	**30**

Attachment 16.1b: Insulated Roofing Contractors, Inc.

Insulated Roofing Contractors, Inc.

Alpha Roofing Performance Line

System Information

Information
Valid Thru:
January
2005

No	Criteria	Average
1	Average square feet installed	72,380
2	Average square foot of roof per penetration	2,135
3	Percent of roofs with slope less than 1/4"	60%
4	Percent of roofs with traffic greater than 12 times/year	16%
5	**Maximum service period**	**27 years**
6	Adjusted service period	20 years
7	Average service period	12 years
8	Percent of roofs that never leaked	65%
9	Percent of roofs that leaked and were fixed	35%
10	**Percent of roofs that still leak**	**0%**
11	Age sum of all roofs that never leaked	161 years
12	Age sum of all roofs that do not leak	279 years
13	Percent of roofs not requiring maintenance	0%
14	Percent of roofs with more than 5% ponded water	0%
15	Percent of roofs with less than 1% deterioration	100%
16	**Percent of satisfied customers**	**100%**
17	**Percent of jobs completed on time**	**100%**
18	**Number of roofs inspected**	**50**
19	**Number of roof evaluations**	**26**

Contractor Performance Information

No	Criteria	Average
1	Contractor's ability to respond to emergencies in days	1.25
2	Contractor's ability to communicate	9.75
3	Contractor's management abilities	9.88
4	Professionalism of contractor	10.00
5	Contractor's level of honesty	10.00
6	Overall performance of contractor	9.62
7	Comfort level in hiring contractor again	10.00
8	**Number of different customer responses**	**8**

Attachment 16.1c: JVC Company

JVC Company

Alpha Roofing Performance Line

System Information

Information Valid Thru: August 2005

No	Criteria	Average
1	Average square feet installed	29,329
2	Average square foot of roof per penetration	2428
3	Percent of roofs with slope less than 1/4"	100%
4	Percent of roofs with traffic greater than 12 times/year	0%
5	**Maximum service period**	**30 years**
6	Adjusted service period	30 years
7	Average service period	14 years
8	Percent of roofs that never leaked	52%
9	Percent of roofs that leaked and were fixed	48%
10	**Percent of roofs that still leak**	**0%**
11	Age sum of all roofs that never leaked	229 years
12	Age sum of all roofs that do not leak	503 years
13	Percent of roofs not requiring maintenance	14%
14	Percent of roofs with more than 5% ponded water	0%
15	Percent of roofs with less than 1% deterioration	100%
16	**Percent of satisfied customers**	**100%**
17	**Percent of jobs completed on time**	**100%**
18	**Number of roofs inspected**	**52**
19	**Number of roof evaluations**	**31**

Contractor Performance Information

No	Criteria	Average
1	Contractor's ability to respond to emergencies	9.75
2	Contractor's ability to communicate	9.32
3	Contractor's management abilities	9.46
4	Professionalism of contractor	9.46
5	Contractor's level of honesty	9.50
6	Overall performance of contractor	9.50
7	Comfort level in hiring contractor again	9.64
8	**Number of different customer responses**	**14**

Attachment 16.1d: Phoenix Coatings, Inc.

Phoenix Coatings, Inc.

Alpha Roofing Performance Line

System Information

Information Valid Thru: January 2005

No	Criteria	Average
1	Average square feet installed	23,404
2	Average square foot of roof per penetration	609
3	Percent of roofs with slope less than 1/4"	15%
4	Percent of roofs with traffic greater than 12 times/year	8%
5	**Maximum service period**	**12 years**
6	Adjusted service period	10 years
7	Average service period	7 years
8	Percent of roofs that never leaked	55%
9	Percent of roofs that leaked and were fixed	45%
10	**Percent of roofs that still leak**	**0%**
11	Age sum of all roofs that never leaked	159 years
12	Age sum of all roofs that do not leak	283 years
13	Percent of roofs not requiring maintenance	11%
14	Percent of roofs with more than 5% ponded water	13%
15	Percent of roofs with less than 1% deterioration	100%
16	**Percent of satisfied customers**	**98%**
17	**Percent of jobs completed on time**	**98%**
18	**Number of roofs inspected**	**54**
19	**Number of roof evaluations**	**40**

Contractor Performance Information

No	Criteria	Average
1	Contractor's ability to respond to emergencies	10.00
2	Contractor's ability to communicate	9.44
3	Contractor's management abilities	9.47
4	Professionalism of contractor	9.56
5	Contractor's level of honesty	9.78
6	Overall performance of contractor	9.53
7	Comfort level in hiring contractor again	9.62
8	**Number of different customer responses**	**32**

Phoenix 1 – Restoration & Construction Ltd.

Alpha Roofing Performance Line

System Information

No	Criteria	Average
1	Average square feet installed	42,739
2	Average square foot of roof per penetration	922
3	Percent of roofs with slope less than 1/4"	100%
4	Percent of roofs with traffic greater than 12 times/year	5%
5	**Maximum service period**	**28 years**
6	Adjusted service period	20 years
7	Average service period	13 years
8	Percent of roofs that never leaked	30%
9	Percent of roofs that leaked and were fixed	68%
10	**Percent of roofs that still leak**	**2%**
11	Age sum of all roofs that never leaked	149 years
12	Age sum of all roofs that do not leak	529 years
13	Percent of roofs not requiring maintenance	0%
14	Percent of roofs with more than 5% ponded water	0%
15	Percent of roofs with less than 1% deterioration	98%
16	**Percent of satisfied customers**	**100%**
17	**Percent of jobs completed on time**	**100%**
18	**Number of roofs inspected**	**48**
19	**Number of roof evaluations**	**40**

Information Valid Thru: July 2005

Contractor Performance Information

No	Criteria	Average
1	Contractor's ability to respond to emergencies	10.00
2	Contractor's ability to communicate	9.67
3	Contractor's management abilities	9.67
4	Professionalism of contractor	10.00
5	Contractor's level of honesty	10.00
6	Overall performance of contractor	9.92
7	Comfort level in hiring contractor again	10.00
8	**Number of different customer responses**	**6**

Proco, Inc.

Alpha Roofing Performance Line

System Information

Information Valid Thru: November 2004

No	Criteria	Average
1	Average square feet installed	15,536
2	Average square foot of roof per penetration	840
3	Percent of roofs with slope less than 1/4"	54%
4	Percent of roofs with traffic greater than 12 times/year	12%
5	**Maximum service period**	**17 years**
6	Adjusted service period	10 years
7	Average service period	7 years
8	Percent of roofs that never leaked	94%
9	Percent of roofs that leaked and were fixed	6%
10	**Percent of roofs that still leak**	**0%**
11	Age sum of all roofs that never leaked	114 years
12	Age sum of all roofs that do not leak	124 years
13	Percent of roofs not requiring maintenance	53%
14	Percent of roofs with more than 5% ponded water	18%
15	Percent of roofs with less than 1% deterioration	97%
16	**Percent of satisfied customers**	**100%**
17	**Percent of jobs completed on time**	**100%**
18	**Number of roofs inspected**	**39**
19	**Number of roof evaluations**	**17**

Contractor Performance Information

No	Criteria	Average
1	Contractor's ability to respond to emergencies	10.00
2	Contractor's ability to communicate	9.86
3	Contractor's management abilities	9.86
4	Professionalism of contractor	9.86
5	Contractor's level of honesty	9.86
6	Overall performance of contractor	9.86
7	Comfort level in hiring contractor again	9.86
8	**Number of different customer responses**	**7**

Attachment 16.1g: S&J Contractor Inc.

S&J Contractors, Inc.

Alpha Roofing Performance Line

System Information

Information Valid Thru: March 2005

No	Criteria	Average
1	Average square feet installed	17,492
2	Average square foot of roof per penetration	1581
3	Percent of roofs with slope less than 1/4"	94%
4	Percent of roofs with traffic greater than 12 times/year	20%
5	**Maximum service period**	**18 years**
6	Adjusted service period	10 years
7	Average service period	5 years
8	Percent of roofs that never leaked	63%
9	Percent of roofs that leaked and were fixed	30%
10	**Percent of roofs that still leak**	**7%**
11	Age sum of all roofs that never leaked	56 years
12	Age sum of all roofs that do not leak	111 years
13	Percent of roofs not requiring maintenance	30%
14	Percent of roofs with more than 5% ponded water	8%
15	Percent of roofs with less than 1% deterioration	98%
16	**Percent of satisfied customers**	**100%**
17	**Percent of jobs completed on time**	**100%**
18	**Number of roofs inspected**	**53**
19	**Number of roof evaluations**	**27**

Contractor Performance Information

No	Criteria	Average
1	Contractor's ability to respond to emergencies	9.84
2	Contractor's ability to communicate	9.91
3	Contractor's management abilities	9.81
4	Professionalism of contractor	9.86
5	Contractor's level of honesty	9.95
6	Overall performance of contractor	9.91
7	Comfort level in hiring contractor again	9.95
8	**Number of different customer responses**	**22**

Washington Roofing & Insulation, Inc.

Alpha Roofing Performance Line

System Information

No	Criteria	Average
1	Average square feet installed	19,305
2	Average square foot of roof per penetration	3526
3	Percent of roofs with slope less than 1/4"	42%
4	Percent of roofs with traffic greater than 12 times/year	0%
5	**Maximum service period**	**19 years**
6	Adjusted service period	18 years
7	Average service period	9 years
8	Percent of roofs that never leaked	91%
9	Percent of roofs that leaked and were fixed	9%
10	**Percent of roofs that still leak**	**0%**
11	Age sum of all roofs that never leaked	189 years
12	Age sum of all roofs that do not leak	194 years
13	Percent of roofs not requiring maintenance	35%
14	Percent of roofs with more than 5% ponded water	50%
15	Percent of roofs with less than 1% deterioration	65%
16	**Percent of satisfied customers**	**100%**
17	**Percent of jobs completed on time**	**100%**
18	**Number of roofs inspected**	**26**
19	**Number of roof evaluations**	**23**

Information
Valid Thru:
May 2005

Contractor Performance Information

No	Criteria	Average
1	Contractor's ability to respond to emergencies	10.00
2	Contractor's ability to communicate	10.00
3	Contractor's management abilities	10.00
4	Professionalism of contractor	10.00
5	Contractor's level of honesty	10.00
6	Overall performance of contractor	9.83
7	Comfort level in hiring contractor again	10.00
8	**Number of different customer responses**	**6**

Wattle & Daub Contractors, Inc

Alpha Roofing Performance Line

System Information

Information
Valid Thru:
May 2005

No	Criteria	Average
1	Average square feet installed	15,077
2	Average square foot of roof per penetration	1044
3	Percent of roofs with slope less than 1/4"	26%
4	Percent of roofs with traffic greater than 12 times/year	0%
5	**Maximum service period**	**24 years**
6	Adjusted service period	20 years
7	Average service period	14 years
8	Percent of roofs that never leaked	86%
9	Percent of roofs that leaked and were fixed	14%
10	**Percent of roofs that still leak**	**0%**
11	Age sum of all roofs that never leaked	487 years
12	Age sum of all roofs that do not leak	571 years
13	Percent of roofs not requiring maintenance	15%
14	Percent of roofs with more than 5% ponded water	11%
15	Percent of roofs with less than 1% deterioration	100%
16	**Percent of satisfied customers**	**100%**
17	**Percent of jobs completed on time**	**100%**
18	**Number of roofs inspected**	**53**
19	**Number of roof evaluations**	**44**

Contractor Performance Information

No	Criteria	Average
1	Contractor's ability to respond to emergencies	10.00
2	Contractor's ability to communicate	10.00
3	Contractor's management abilities	9.71
4	Professionalism of contractor	10.00
5	Contractor's level of honesty	10.00
6	Overall performance of contractor	10.00
7	Comfort level in hiring contractor again	10.00
8	**Number of different customer responses**	**7**

17

Hail Resistance of the Alpha Sprayed Polyurethane Foam Roof System

Introduction

The case of the Alpha Sprayed Polyurethane Foam (SPF) roof system development is a performance based program that not only assists clients to get high performance SPF roofing systems, but also motivates the manufacturer and contractor to maintain the highest performance. The Alpha system was developed to be used in hailstorm areas. The proven performance of the system showed that it could resist up to 3.5 inch diameter hailstones in severe hailstorm areas if installed correctly. The manufacturers (BASF/Neogard) recognized by in-field test results that the Permathane system when installed correctly with a high quality SPF had high durability for over twenty years. The manufacturers created the Alpha program (Chapter 16) and the Alpha roof system, and issued a 15 year joint and several contract covering all forms of defects. The manufacturers also realized that no other elastomeric coated SPF system had the durability to resist the hailstorm damage. This led to the issuance of the first FM-SH hailstone warranty for roofing systems. The Alpha roof system development is covered in this chapter. It is important to note that the Alpha roof system is differentiated by documented in-field performance information, and the warranty is determined by running the FM-SH test on the roof. Any or equal would have to pass the same performance requirements with documented test results.

History of Hail Resistance of the SPF Roof Systems

Sprayed Polyurethane Foam (SPF) roof systems have been installed since the 1960s. The success of the SPF roof system has been documented by a U.S. Air Force thesis and a performance report published by the National Roofing Contractor's Association (Kashiwagi 1984; Kashiwagi et al 1999). However, in the last 15 years, the use of SPF roof systems has declined to less than three percent of the roofing market (Hinojosa et al 2002). Although the SPF roofing system has outstanding performance, the durability of the system in hailstorm areas has been called into question.

In the 1990s, the occurrence of hailstorms and resulting hailstorm damage, encouraged owners to identify roofing systems that could minimize damage and the ensuing cost of insurance. Two major roofing manufacturers, Neogard and BASF, used a combination of performance information, in-field testing methods, and contractor performance requirements to minimize the risk of hailstone damage. The research program became known as the "Alpha" program.

A hail resistant roof system brings value to a building owner in a hail area (such as Texas, Oklahoma, and Kansas) in two ways:

1. They receive lower insurance rates (a deductible of 1% of the building cost) from insurance companies if the roof is a hail resistant system that protects against large hailstone damage.
2. A hail resistant roof system protects the school against hailstone damage, delivering a direct savings to the school.

Hail Resistance of Elastomeric Coated SPF Roof Systems

In 1996, the Performance Based Studies Research Group (PBSRG) at Arizona State University (ASU) conducted a hail resistance test of SPF roofing systems. The tests used the Factory Mutual #4470 Class I test, also known as the Factory Mutual Severe Hail test or FM-SH test. The FM-SH test is designed to test the hail resistance of roof coating systems against simulated severe hail (1.75 inches in diameter). The test consists of dropping a 1.75" steel ball (0.79 lbs) from a height of 17ft-9.5 inches onto a roofing sample. The ball must be dropped ten times and the system cannot fail on any of the drops (failure is considered to be any signs of cracking, splitting, separation, or rupturing). The authors selected this test procedure due to its simplicity. The 1996 tests resulted in the following conclusions (Kashiwagi et al 1996a, Kashiwagi et al 1996b):

1. Using laboratory samples and the FM-SH test, the Permathane polyurethane coating was the most resistant SPF coating system.
2. There was a very large differential between the hail resistance of silicone, acrylic, and polyurethane coating systems.
3. The Permathane system was the only elastomeric coating that passed the laboratory test with a 30-mil DFT (dry film thickness) average (15-mils DFT min) coating thickness using 40-PSI (compressive strength) SPF. Silicone coatings did not pass the test, even with a 45-mil DFT average coating thickness. Newly applied acrylic coatings passed with thicker coatings; however, after aging, they quickly lost their elongation and failed the test procedure.
4. Simulated aging tests specified by ASTM and FM had no correlation to the in-field test results of actual aged systems, which have also been confirmed by other authors (Cash et al 1993, Stenman et al 1994, Lounis et al 1998).
5. The Permathane coated roofs (when tested in the field) were the only systems that passed the FM-SH test. The roof systems were installed with a coating system of 3 gallons per 100 SF (approximately 30-mils DFT average and 10-mils DFT minimum thickness), which passed the FM-SH test during their twelfth year of service.
6. There was also a large differential between the durability and longevity of the performance of different manufacturers' products, especially within the generic urethane coatings. Some urethane coatings (Permathane is an exception) have suffered "reversion" (returning to a liquid or semi-liquid state), aging, and cracking. The Permathane coating was the only urethane coating with a documented

service period. The Permathane coating is also the only urethane coating that has been documented to pass the FM-SH test after 10 and 12 years of service.

Permathane coated SPF systems are the only SPF system with documented performance in hailstorm areas. The 15–20 year existing Permathane coated SPF roofs were installed with a 30-mil DFT average, 10-mil DFT minimum specification. This system was warranted for five years and performed for 20 years.

Case Study at Torrington (Wyoming)

Two Permathane roofs installed in 1983 at Torrington, Wyoming, were examined to identify the performance of the system. The first roof was a 46,000 square-foot flat school roof with the following history:

1. The roof was installed in 1983 as a 5-year system (30-mil DFT average, 10-mil DFT minimum).
2. The roof was exposed to a severe hailstorm in 1985 (observed hail of 1.75 inches in diameter). The hail caused indentations in the system, but no failures were identified.
3. The FM-SH test was performed on the roof in 1996 after 13 years of service. The system passed since there were no identifiable failures in the protective coating.
4. The roof was exposed to another severe hailstorm in 1999 (observed hail of 1.75 inches in diameter). The hail caused indentations in the system, but once again, there were no identified failures.
5. The roof had never been maintained during its service period.

In 2002, after 19 years of service, the FM-SH test was once again performed on the roof. The system passed 8 out of 10 drops. At the 19-year point of time, with an average minimum coating thickness of 28 mils, the roof failed the test due to breakage in two of the drops (to pass the FM-SH test, the roof must pass all ten drops). The thickness of the coating at the break was 10-mils DFT.

The roof was recoated in 2003 using a 10-year specification (38 mils average and 20 mils minimum). The roof was re-tested using a 2-inch diameter steel ball (2 drops), a 3-inch diameter steel ball (1 drop), and a 4-inch diameter steel ball (4 drops). These drops simulated the effects of oversized hail (baseball and softball sized hail). The test resulted in no breakage of the protective urethane coating. Table 17-1 analyzes the slit samples taken in the latest tests. The samples show the original 5-year system with an overall minimum thickness of 9 mils and an average thickness of 28 mils. The newly recoated system has an average thickness of over 50 mils.

A second roof in Torrington (the Vo-Tech building) was also tested in 2003 with the FM-SH test. The roof is approximately 16,000 square-feet and was also installed in 1983. Ten drops of the 1.75 inch steel ball were performed and the system passed 8 of the 10 drops. Measurement of the slit samples showed that the two drops that broke had an average coating thickness of about 10 mils.

Table 17-1: Slit Sample Analysis of the Torrington Middle School

No	Criteria	Original Spec	2002 Test	2003 Test	Alpha Spec
1	Overall minimum thickness DFT of coating	10	9	50	20
2	Overall maximum thickness DFT of coating	n/a	50	50+	n/a
3	Average minimum thickness DFT of coating	n/a	17	50+	n/a
4	Average maximum thickness DFT of coating	n/a	37	50+	n/a
5	Average thickness DFT of coating	20	28	50+	45
6	Number of slit samples	n/a	18	7	n/a

In 2001, the buildings' user was asked to rate the performance of these roofs after approximately 18 years of service. Table 17-2 shows that the owner was completely satisfied and the systems did not have any leaks since they were installed. The owner also stated that the Middle School roof had <u>never</u> had any maintenance performed since the roof was installed.

Table 17-2: User Evaluation of the Torrington Roofs (Childs 2001)

No	Criteria	Scale	Middle School	Vo-Tech
1	Contractor's ability to communicate	(1-10)	10	10
2	Contractor's management abilities	(1-10)	10	10
3	Professionalism of the contractor	(1-10)	10	10
4	Contractor's level of honesty	(1-10)	10	10
5	Overall performance of the contractor	(1-10)	10	10
6	Comfort level in hiring the contractor again	(1-10)	10	10
7	Was the job completed on time?	(Y/N)	Yes	Yes
8	Are you satisfied with the contractor?	(Y/N)	Yes	Yes
9	Has your roof ever leaked since it was installed?	(Y/N)	No	No

The results of the FM-SH tests and customer satisfaction evaluations validated that the 5-year Permathane coated SPF system maintained its durability and longevity for up to 20 years. It also validated that the 5-year Permathane system could resist FM-SH size hailstone damage for over 20 years (if the minimum coating thickness was over 10 mils). The recoated roofs at Torrington currently have over 50 mils of coating. Based on the performance of the 20 mils system (5-year system), the performance of the newly installed Permathane system should exceed <u>20 years</u>.

The Alpha Roof System

The two manufacturers involved in the Alpha program developed a long-term, strategic plan to minimize risk. The philosophy is to minimize risk rather than leveraging the volume of sales. Therefore, based on actual performance results, the manufacturers have created an Alpha roofing system that has the following requirements:

1. A quality controlled SPF, which has a density of 3 lbs/cubic-ft and an in-place compressive strength of 50-PSI.

2. A three-coat Permathane polyurethane base coating. The system has a minimum thickness of 20-mils (dry film thickness) and an average of 45-mils DFT (double the thickness of the existing Permathane roofs).
3. Granules are installed over a Permathane top-coat of 9 mils.

Since the manufacturers realized that this system would reduce their risk, they modified their 10-year warranty to provide a 15-year non-prorated maintenance agreement. The warranty does the following:

1. Limits exclusions to acts of God and building movement.
2. Accepts liability for all materials, including existing BUR down to the roof deck.
3. Offers a joint and several warranty for the coating system, based on a written contract between the coating manufacturer and contractor to cover all damage (except acts of God and building movement). If either party goes out of business, the remaining party agrees to accept full responsibility for the warranty.
4. Offers the only joint and several warranty on the SPF.
5. Provides a warranty on the roof against Factory Mutual Severe Hail damage for the entire duration of the warranty.

The Alpha system was designed to minimize risk by proving that the roofs could withstand the FM-SH hailstone damage without requiring recoating. Unlike most roofing system warranties, which shift risk to insurance companies or building owners, the Alpha system minimizes the risk with its durability and strength.

Case Study at Carrollton (Texas)

The first documented performance of the Alpha system in an actual hailstorm was conducted at Carrolton (TX). Two recently installed urethane roofs, 70 feet apart at the same site, were exposed to severe and oversized hailstones (up to 2.9 inches in diameter).

The two roofs had the following characteristics (Table 17-3):

1. The first roof (Administration building) was a 15-year Alpha system (45-mil DFT average, 20-mil DFT minimum Permathane coating) with a SPF compressive strength of 50 psi. The roof was 25,000 square-feet.
2. The second roof (Annex building) was a 10-year Permathane coated SPF system (38-mil DFT average, 20-mil DFT minimum Permathane coating) with a SPF compressive strength of 40 psi. The roof was 11,000 square-feet.

Due to the close proximity of the two roofs (70ft apart), it is assumed that the hailstones hit both systems. However, the non-Alpha roof sustained much greater damage. The authors analyzed the two roofs and identified that the high compressive strength of the SPF system (49-PSI vs. 41-PSI) was the largest difference between the two systems (however, it is important to note that the coating thickness and coating properties also play a critical role in the durability of the system, which will be explained later in this report).

Table 17-3: System Information of the Carrollton Roofs

No	Criteria	Unit	ADMINISTRATION BLDG	ANNEX BLDG
1	Thickness of foam	Inch	1.5	1.0
2	Compressive strength of foam	PSI	49.3	41.1
3	Required average coating thickness*	Mils	45	38
4	Required minimum coating thickness*	Mils	20	20
5	Manufacturers warranty period	Years	15	10

* As required by the manufacturer

The size and distribution of the hailstones were documented on the non-Alpha roof (Annex building). Table 17-4 illustrates the number and size of hail indentions in 100 SF of a randomly selected roof area on the Annex building (which was representative of the more heavily damaged area).

Table 17-4: Random Hail Impact Observation*

No	Criteria	Results
1	Number of hail impacts less than 1 inch diameter indentation	100
2	Number of hail impacts between 1.0 – 1.5 inches diameter indentation	40
3	Number of hail impacts greater than 1.5 inches diameter indentation	2

*Observation was made on a 10' by 10' area, chosen at random.

FM-SH Hail Test

The FM-SH hail test was performed on both roofs (10 drops on each roof). Both systems passed the test on all of the drops, which show that the 38-mil and 45-mil DFT systems can withstand the damage of 1.75-inch hailstones. To confirm the validity of the FM-SH test, the indentation diameters and depths were measured and compared against the actual hail damage on the two roofs (Table 17-5).

Table 17-5: Hailstone Indentation vs. FM-SH Test Indentation

No	Criteria	Hailstone (Actual)	Steel Ball (FM Test)
1	Average Diameter (Alpha)	1.2	1.2
2	Average Depth (Alpha)	0.33	0.25
3	Average Diameter (Non-Alpha)	1.5	1.5
4	Average Depth (Non-Alpha)	0.50	0.45

On the non-Alpha roof (Annex building), the FM-SH test resulted in an indentation diameter of 1.5 inches and a depth of 0.45 inches (average of 10 drops). Out of 20 randomly observed hail indentations, the average indentation diameter was 1.5 inches and the depth was 0.50 inches.

On the Alpha roof (Administration building), the FM-SH test resulted in an indentation diameter of 1.2 inches and a depth of 0.25 inches (average of 10 drops). Out of 18 observed hail indentations, the average indentation diameter was 1.2 inches and the depth was 0.33 inches.

Visual observations indicated that both roofs were exposed to severe and oversized hail. There was even evidence of hailstones over 2.75 inches in diameter (maximum observed indentation diameter). Based on the indentation diameter of the FM-SH test, Table 17-6 illustrates the maximum observed hailstone that impacted the roofs.

Table 17-6: Maximum Size of Hailstones

No	Criteria	1.75 Hail Indentation Diameter	Maximum Observed Hail Indentation	Actual Maximum Hailstone Size
1	Non Alpha Roof (Annex Building)	1.5	2.5	2.9
2	Alpha Roof (Administration Building)	1.2	2.0	2.9

The maximum size hailstone indentation was 2.5 inches in diameter on the Permathane roof, and 2.0 inches in diameter on the Alpha roof. These observations showed that both roofs were exposed and resisted oversized hail of up to 2.9 inches in diameter (Figure 17.1).

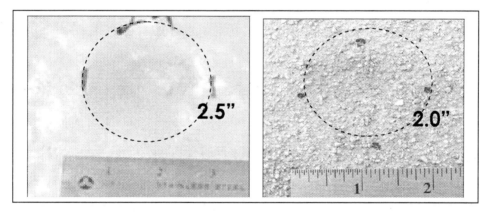

Figure 17.1: Maximum observed hail impact (2.5 inch impact on Annex building and 2.0 inch impact on Administration building). Both represent actual hailstones of 2.9 inches in diameter

Coating Analysis

Fourteen slit samples were taken on the Alpha roof. Four of the slit samples were taken at four spots where hailstones damaged the Alpha coating. The Alpha System requires an average thickness of 45-mils DFT and a minimum thickness of 20-mils DFT. After analyzing the damaged samples in Table 17-7, the average minimum thickness was observed to be 11 mils (9 mils below the specification). The average diameter of the indentations on the four breaks was 1.1 inches, which indicates that the damage was caused by severe hail of up to 1.75 inches. The average thickness of the damaged samples was only 16 mils, compared to the 45 mils specified by the manufacturer.

Table 17-7: Coating Thickness Analysis of the Alpha Roof

No	Criteria	Damaged	Non - Damaged
1	Average Minimum Coating Thickness	11	35
2	Minimum Coating Thickness	9	15
3	Average Coating Thickness	16	39
4	Maximum Coating Thickness	24	45
5	Number of Samples	4	10

The ten non-damaged Alpha samples were approximately 23 mils thicker than the damaged samples. The damage from the hail occurred in locations where the contractor had installed too little coating. The contractor quickly repaired the spots to meet the manufacturers specification and to reduce the risk of future hailstorm damage.

Fourteen slit samples were also taken on the non-Alpha roof. Six of the samples were from hailstone-damaged areas (the average impact diameter was 1.3 inches). The 10-year system specifies that the average thickness must be 38 mils and the coating must not be thinner than 20 mils. After analyzing the damaged samples (Table 17-8), the minimum thickness observed was 15 mils and the average thickness was 21 mils, which are below the manufacturers specifications. The non-damaged samples met the minimum and average requirements.

Table 17-8: Coating Thickness Analysis of the Non-Alpha Roof

No	Criteria	Damaged	Non - Damaged
1	Average Minimum Coating Thickness	15	32
2	Actual Minimum Coating Thickness	10	20
3	Average Coating Thickness	21	38
4	Maximum Coating Thickness	28	43
5	Number of Samples	6	8

Based on the limited sampling, the Alpha roof did not meet the manufacturer's specifications for average coating dry-film-thickness (33 mils instead of 45 mils). However, the minimum thickness requirement was almost 50% over (28 mils instead of 20 mils) the specification. The average thickness requirement is heavily dependent on the SPF roughness, and the method of application of the coating. Clearly, the systems failed in areas that lacked coating. The samples that did not exhibit failure had approximately 20 mils more of coating.

Figure 17.2 illustrates how a roof may have areas of low and high coating thickness. A key component in the installation of a coated SPF roofing system is dependent on the skill level of the craftsman. Figure 17.2A shows a non-uniform SPF surface. The uneven surface causes the coating to fill up the low spots (valleys) and leave the high spots (peaks) with very little coating. If a high spot is struck by hail, it is more likely that the system will suffer damage in that area (due to less coating). However, very skilled craftsmen may be able to install smoother SPF (Figure 17.2B), which allows a more uniform coating thickness across the roof (with very few low and high spots).

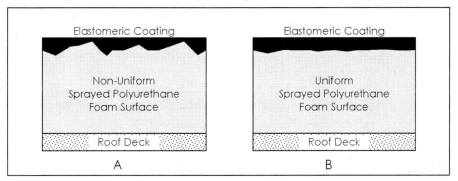

Figures 17.2: Sprayed Polyurethane Foam (SPF) Roof System Showing
Uniformly and Non-Uniformly Applied SPF Surface

A method to meet the minimum and average coating requirements can be accomplished by rolling the coating in <u>multiple</u> passes, as required in the Alpha specification.

SPF Analysis

Based on the analysis of the slit samples of the damaged and undamaged samples, damage (penetration of coating) occurs where an insufficient amount of Permathane coating is applied. However, this did not explain why the Alpha roof did not show as many visible signs of hail impact as the non-Alpha roof system, located at its side. After further analysis, the author determined that the compressive strength of the Alpha SPF played a major difference between the two systems (49-PSI vs. 41-PSI). This is the first time that the importance of the SPF quality has been so graphically identified.

Neogard's Permathane urethane coating is the only documented system to resist FM-SH damage for extended periods of times, greatly exceeding the duration of the warranty. A combination of both insufficient coating and low compressive strengths may increase the potential of failure in both the coating damage and hailstone indentations. The author highly recommends that facility owners require a high quality SPF (with proven documentation of the delivery of 50-PSI compressive strength SPF, and a quality control process) that will minimize the possibility of low compressive strength SPF being installed. The difference in cost of a high quality Alpha SPF over a low-bid, is pennies per square foot. Owners are not taking advantage of value when they procure SPF at the lowest price.

Conclusions

The analysis of the Alpha and non-Alpha roofs indicates:

1. The Permathane urethane coating system does not deteriorate as some other urethane coating systems do. Analysis has shown that the coating deterioration has been minimal over 20 years of in-field service.
2. The Alpha system minimizes the risk from FM-SH level of damage and allows the manufacturers to offer a 15-year joint and several maintenance agreement, which covers damage from hailstones up to the FM-SH level (1.75 inch).
3. The Alpha roof system can also minimize damage over the level of the FM-SH damage (up to 2.9 inches) if installed properly.
4. The skill level of the contractor's craftsperson will increase the value that the owner receives. A skilled contractor will be able to install a more uniform coating (lowering the probability of having spots where the coating is thin).
5. Hailstone indentations can be attributed to low SPF compressive strength. Hailstone damage (breakage) can be attributed to the type of coating system and the thickness of the system.
6. The 10-year Permathane roof system can resist hail damage, but is not warranted against a FM-SH level of damage.
7. The Alpha system requires the use of higher quality SPF (with a 50-PSI compressive strength instead of 40-PSI compressive strength), thicker Permathane coating, and high quality applicators. The quality of the applicators is achieved by requiring that the Alpha contractors participate in a continuous improvement program based at Arizona State University. The Alpha contractors must maintain a high level of performance (98% of roofs not currently leaking, and 98% customer satisfaction).
8. The Permathane urethane system has proven longevity and durability equal to built-up/modified bitumen roofing systems.
9. The Permathane roof system is renewable, and when recoated at the 20-year point in time, it can take almost twice the level of damage (the Torrington roof was tested against larger sized hailstones than the FM-SH test requires).

These test results validate other test results and observations on other roofs in Dallas (TX) and Big Springs (TX), and show that the Alpha coating system can resist up to 3-inch hail (Kashiwagi et al 1996a, Kashiwagi et al 1996b). One of the major problems with elastomeric-coated SPF roof systems is the deterioration of the coating's physical properties, which may jeopardize the systems capability to resist hail over a period of time. The authors conclude that using proven documentation of the systems' ability to resist hail over a specific time period severely minimizes the risk of failure. The skill level of the contractors craftsmen are also a key issue in regards to the smoothness of the SFP surface.

Recommendations

Many owners have stopped using elastomeric-coated SPF roof systems due to the nonperformance of coating systems and contractors. The documented performance of the Permathane/Alpha roof system shows that it is equal to a high performance 20 year modified bitumen or built up roof. The author recommends that users requiring hail resistant roof systems specify the Alpha system with the following requirements:

1. Require documentation <u>proving</u> the performance of the product in the field rather than accepting "industry" recommendations or laboratory testing results. (Many SPF elastomeric-coated roof systems have FM-SH test ratings. However, these results could not be duplicated by either laboratory tests or in-field tests conducted by the author).
2. Systems should be tested with the FM-SH test to prove that the system can resist the FM-SH level of damage.
3. The proven performance should be at least 50% of the required warranty period.
4. Require the system to have a warranty that covers all material down to the roof deck.
5. Require the system to have a warranty that states that the system must pass the FM-SH test during the <u>entire</u> duration of the warranty.
6. Require a joint and several warranty, which includes a legal contract between the manufacturers and the contractor stating that they will correct any problems including hail damage.

Acknowledgments

The author would like to thank the following participants for their assistance in this research study:

1. John Savicky, lead researcher and data collector, PBSRG.
2. Johnny Hibbs, (Carrollton Farmers Branch Independent School District) for permitting PBSRG to inspect and test the Administration and Annex buildings.
3. Bob Childs, (Goshen County School District - Torrington) for permitting PBSRG to inspect and test the Middle School and Vo-Tech buildings.
4. Thom Tisthammer, Wattle & Daub.
5. Ted Sellers, Phoenix I Restoration.
6. Neogard and BASF for their support and technical assistance.

Chapter 17 Review

1. How can a building owner use performance information to minimize risk?
2. What is the difference between marketing information and performance information?
3. How is a warranty on the Alpha system enforced?
4. What is a joint and several warranty? How is it different from a regular roof warranty?
5. How many elastomeric coated SPF roof systems can pass the FM-SH test? How many systems have documented performance on in-field weathered systems?
6. How does the Alpha system ensure durability to other types of traffic?

7. Why did the Factory Mutual tests give FM-SH ratings to other systems if the test results cannot be duplicated and if field tests do not support their results?

References

Cash, C. & Kan, F. (1999). On the Study of Crack-Initiation Fracture Toughness of Fiber Glass Asphalt Shingles. *Roofing Research and Standards Development 4th Volume*, ASTM STP1349, pp. 132-151.

Childs, B. (2001). Owner Response to Roof Evaluation. Performance Based Studies Research Group (PBSRG), Tempe, AZ.

Childs, B. (2002). Owner Response to Roof Evaluation, Performance Based Studies Research Group (PBSRG), Tempe, AZ.

Hinojosa, O. & Kane, K. (2002). A Measure of the Industry. *Professional Roofing*, 32[4], pp. 24-28.

Kashiwagi, Dean T. (1984). *The Economic Feasibility of the Polyurethane Foam Roof System*. Master's Thesis, Arizona State University, Tempe, AZ.

Kashiwagi, D. & Pandey, M. (1996a). Oversize Hail Resistance and Performance Analysis of Elastomeric Coated SPF Roof Systems. *Performance Based Studies Research Group*, Tempe, AZ, ISBN: 1-889857-11-4.

Kashiwagi, D. & Pandey, M. (1996b). Hail Resistance of SPF Roof Systems. *Performance Based Studies Research Group*, Tempe, AZ, ISBN: 1-889857-00-9.

Kashiwagi, D. (1999). Standards for 'Oversized' and 'Severe' Hail Resistance of Elastomeric Coated Sprayed Polyurethane Foam Roofing Systems. *American Society for Testing and Materials*, West Conshohocken, PA.

Kashiwagi, D. & Tisthammer, T. (2002). Information Based Delivery System for Sprayed Polyurethane Foam on Roofing. *Journal of Thermal Envelope & Building Science*, 26[1], pp. 33-52.

Lounis, Z., Lacasse, M., Vanier, D. & Kyle, B. (1999). Towards Standardization of Service Life Prediction of Roofing Membranes. *Roofing Research and Standards Development 4th Volume*, ASTM STP1349, pp. 3-18.

Stenman, H., Mech, M., Paroli, R., & Lei, W. (1994). Maximum Tensile Load and Elongation Properties of Heated Built-Up Roofing Membranes at Selected Cold Temperatures. *Roofing Research and Standard Development*, 3rd Volume, ASTM STP 1224, pp. 78-86.

Sellers, T. (2003). Contractor Participation in Roofing Survey. Performance Based Studies Research Group (PBSRG), Tempe, AZ.

Tisthammer, T. (2002). Contractor Participation in Roofing Survey. Performance Based Studies Research Group (PBSRG), Tempe, AZ.

18

Manufacturer's Simplified Use of Performance Information

Background

Mayle Construction, a roofing contractor, was introduced to IMT concepts in 1990. The owners of the company (Steve and Bob Mayle) were dissatisfied with their current suppliers who were not using performance information to improve roofing products. In 1996, Steve Mayle created a manufacturing group named Custom Seal Inc, which manufactures a high quality single-ply thermal plastic roofing membrane.

Steve Mayle has been the pioneer in the documentation of single ply roofing systems. Taking his knowledge, experience, and expectations of being a high performance contractor, he formed Custom Seal as a single ply roofing manufacturer who would continually improve the performance of the single ply system, continually track the performance of their products and systems, and use performing contractors.

In 1998, Custom Seal partnered with the PBSRG to implement IMT concepts within the organization. Custom Seal wanted to establish a rigorous performance monitoring system to evaluate their contractors and the overall performance of their roofing system. The goal of Custom Seal was to:

1. Maintain 100% customer satisfaction and no leaking roof within their system.
2. Identify high quality contractors that could install Custom Seal's products properly.
3. Differentiate their products from other roofing manufacturers.
4. Increase the quality of work for the end users (owners).

This would differentiate Custom Seal as the only single ply manufacturing company who had a third party University tracking the performance of every industrial roof system sold.

The Continuous Improvement Program

A continuous improvement program was developed by the PBSRG in order to accomplish Custom Seal's goals. The following requirements were set:

1. Any contractor that installs a Custom Seal product is required to submit project/roof information to Custom Seal.

2. The information is then sent to PBSRG. The PBSRG generates surveys that are sent out to the end users. Once the end users evaluate the contractors, the PBSRG inputs the information into a database to generate past performance lines.
3. The contractor is required to correct any problems that have been identified by the owner. If the contractor does not repair a leaking roof, they will be taken off of the approved applicator list.

Custom Seal separated their applicator list into three different levels based on performance information. Table 18-1 illustrates the performance requirements of each level. Contractors that perform at higher levels will minimize risk (on time, no change orders, and meet the quality expectation of the client). This reduces the risk to the end user as well as to Custom Seal.

Table 18-1: Custom Seal Levels of Performance

Criteria	Level 1 High Performing Contractor	Level 2 Performing Contractor	Level 3 Certified Contractor
Minimum roof area	250,000	100,000	50,000
Average performance ratings	9.5 – 10.0	8.5 – 9.4	8.0 – 8.4
Minimum response time	2 days	2 days	2 days
Percent of roofs that do not leak	100%	100%	100%

Performance Information

Data collection began in 1999 on 15 contractors that installed 183 industrial roofs. Customer survey results showed that 99% of the customers were satisfied, 94% of the roofs were completed on time, 72% of the roofs never leaked, and all the roofs that did leak were repaired. In 2003, Custom Seal had 42 contractors on over 900 roofs. Table 18-2 illustrates the performance information of the Custom Seal contractors over the past five years.

The results of the five-year study has shown the following:

1. 95% of the customers were satisfied.
2. 94% of the jobs were completed on time.
3. 68% of the roofs never leaked.
4. Less than 1% of the roofs are currently leaking.

Table 18-2: Custom Seal Performance Lines (1999-2003)

ROOF INFORMATION	1999	2000	2001	2002	2003
Total Number of Contractors Surveyed	15	17	21	30	42
Total Number of Roofs	183	332	506	760	909
Total Roof Area (Million sq ft)	1.3	2.5	3.8	7.3	8.5
Maximum Age of Roofs (in years)	3	4	6	7	8
Average Roof Age (in years)	2	2	2	3	3
Average Roof Area (sq ft)	9,066	7,076	11,796	9,663	9,383
Number of Roofs over 15,000 sq ft	26	39	54	102	118
Total Area of Roofs over 15,000 (Million sq ft)	0.9	1.3	1.9	4.6	5.2
ROOF PROFILE & PERFORMANCE					
Number of Different Job Responses	121	210	180	309	389
Number of Roofs that Never Leaked	87	182	103	197	262
Number of Roofs that Still Leak	0	0	0	2	0
Percent of Roofs that Never Leaked	72	78	55	65	69
Percent of Roofs that Still Leak	0	0	0	1	0
Percent of Roofs that Leaked & Repaired	28	22	45	34	31
Percent of Roofs not Requiring Maintenance	55	57	59	44	44
Percent of Satisfied Customers	99	92	94	97	95
Percent of Jobs Completed on Time	94	94	88	97	97
Percent of Roofs with Traffic	33	12	16	8	10
CUSTOMER EVALUATIONS					
Contractor's Ability to Communicate*	8.5	8.6	8.6	9.0	9.1
Contractor's Management Abilities*	8.7	8.4	8.2	9.0	9.1
Contractor's Level of Honesty*	9.7	8.6	8.6	9.3	9.2
Professionalism of Contractor	9.0	9.2	9.2	9.1	9.4
Overall Performance of the Contractor*	8.7	8.8	8.9	9.1	9.2
Comfort Level in Re-hiring Contractor*	9.2	8.7	8.8	9.2	9.2
Number of Days to Response	2.2	2.3	2.0	1.5	2
Number of Customer Responses	183	209	163	263	340

*The maximum rating score is "10"

Figure 18.1 illustrates the average performance of the contractors over the past five years. The figure shows that the contractors perform at a fairly consistent level of performance.

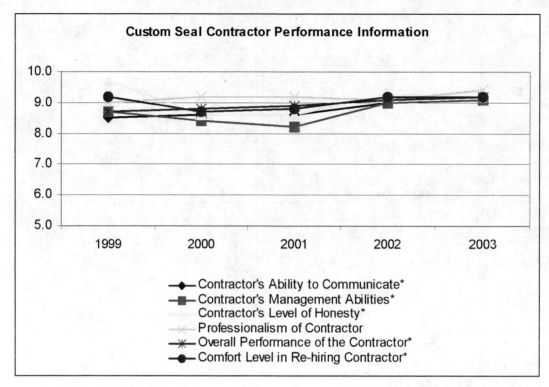

Figure 18.1: Past Performance Information on Custom Seal Contractors

Conclusions

Custom Seal is the only single ply manufacturer who is doing the following:

1. Attempts to call every industrial roof owner annually to monitor their customer satisfaction.
2. Responds to every leaking roof.
3. Has a third party University doing the verification of performance.
4. Posts the numbers on their website.
5. Gathers performance information about their contractors and allow performance to dictate relationships instead of sales.
6. Gives all owners a third party, University point of contact to call if there are any problems with the roofing system.

Custom Seal is a performance-based manufacturer. Steve Mayle, the president of the company, personally reviews the performance numbers every year. He has implemented an information environment that minimizes the risk of the clients, contractors, and Custom Seal.

19

United Airlines Case Study

Introduction

The United Airlines (UAL) San Francisco Maintenance Center is responsible for performing many high-risk functions 365 days a year. The facility department is faced with the difficulty of maintaining approximately 5 million square feet of office space, 135 acres of land, seven hangars, and various other buildings. Traditionally, projects were awarded using the low-bid process, resulting in costly change orders and low quality work.

Ron Campbell (Project Manager of UAL) became aware of PIPS and the Performance Based Studies Research Group in 1996. After hearing about the process and results from the FAA storm damage repair and roofing results from the Phoenix metropolitan area, he decided to test the system at his facility. He became the visionary at UAL, procuring the highest quality construction work that was seen on the site. Campbell realized that a properly maintained facility, rather than repeatedly replacing poorly installed work, could save UAL thousands of dollars. The process was run on 32 projects with outstanding results.

Construction Results

The Dock-7 renovation project convinced Ron Campbell (and other personnel at UAL) that the PIPS process was far superior to the traditional low-bid process that they were accustomed to using. Traditionally, UAL used specifications, consultants, and inspectors in attempt to obtain high performing products and services.

The Dock-7 building consisted of the following:

1. The current roof was riddled with leaks.
2. The exterior metal was decaying due to the poorly painted surfaces.
3. The floor was unfinished.

The dock was constantly being used to maintain aircrafts and the building could only be shutdown for very short periods of time (30 days). The building needed three different types of work done (roofing, painting, and flooring), which would all have to be accomplished during the same timeframe.

Ron Campbell used the PIPS process to procure three high-quality contractors. The immediate obstacle was the absence of a general contractor coordinating work between the three trades (UAL partnered with three independent subcontractors). The challenges that the project manager and the contractors faced were that:

1. The building could only be shut down one time. All the work had to be accomplished during the shut down. None of the contractors knew the work would be simultaneous work.
2. The roofing work caused debris to fall onto the floors.
3. The power-wash performed by the painter caused the floors to get wet.
4. The floorer could not work on the floor with debris falling down from the roof or water on the floor.
5. The new roofing material was placed near the hanger doors, which prevented access to an entire wall for the painter.

The contractors were not initially aware that other work would be done at the same time. They quickly realized that they had a problem. Without any intervention from the project manager, the contractors proposed the following:

1. The flooring contractor proposed to work during the evening.
2. The roofing contractor agreed to work during the day (during normal hours).
3. The painting contractor adjusted their schedule to work during the weekends.

The project manager was surprised to see that the contractors quickly identified the problems and also provided solutions to the owner without forcing the owner to make a decision for them. This was unlike anything that the project manager had experienced. All three contractors worked together to minimize the destruction of each other's work. The shift changes that were proposed by the contractors occurred without any intervention from the owner. All three trades were able to complete their work on time (actually 1 day ahead of schedule), with very high quality, and most impressively, <u>without any change orders</u>.

This project illustrates how performing contractors work together to minimize the risk for themselves, as well as for the owner. The owner was surprised at the high quality of work. He was also impressed when the contractors did not ask for any change orders in order to accomplish the work during non-business hours. The contractors understood that doing the job once (and properly) would result in greater profit than trying to delay their work and issue change orders.

High Quality Painting

The most important aspect of any painting project is preparing the surface, or "prep work." In low-bid work, it is fairly difficult to specify how to do high quality "prep work." Ron Campbell was no stranger to this concept. He stated that previous painters simply sprayed over the original paint with very little "prep work" done. The painters sprayed over rust and unclean surfaces, which caused the paint to peel off soon after it was installed.

The project manager stated that they were forced to paint and repair previous paint work every other year. He decided to use PIPS to hire a high quality contractor to paint approximately 115,000 square feet of the hangers. The project manager awarded to the highest prioritized contractor that was within their budget.

The awarded contractor proposed to do the work in a longer time period than it took most of the other bidders, but this was due to the intensive amount of "prep work" on the surfaces. The contractor power-washed all the surfaces. They then prepped all of the walls. In certain areas on the parapet walls, large cracks had formed, which caused water to infiltrate the building. The painter stated that painting over the crack would not prevent water infiltration. The painter cleaned the cracks and then injected the cracks with high-strength epoxy to seal them from water infiltration. The painter then painted over the epoxy to form a smooth surface with the existing wall. It was the amount of "prep work" that made the difference between what UAL had previously seen, and what they received under PIPS. The contractor completed the work on time, with no change orders, and with very high quality.

In 2004, the site was re-inspected by PBSRG. Although the hanger walls were dirty (since they had not been washed), there were no signs of deterioration after 5 years of infield service. This was impressive since the site sits a couple hundred yards from the San Francisco Bay, which creates very salty and damp conditions. Current employees at the facility stated that this was the best work that the facility had ever procured. Ironically, Ron Campbell stated that it took the PIPS painter less time and less money to do the high quality work than what UAL would have received awarding to the low-bid contractor.

High Quality Roofing & Flooring

Campbell re-roofed almost every roof on the UAL Maintenance site. He procured built-up roofs, modified bitumen roofs, and sprayed polyurethane roofs. None of the roofs currently leak. He also coated five hangar floors. Four years later, an inspection shows the floors having very little deterioration. Between the roofs, floors, painted hangar doors, and waterproofing of all the tanks, Ron Campbell has left the mark of performance on the SFO UAL site.

Conclusion

The United Airlines maintenance facility implemented PIPS for over 2 years. The project manager (Ron Campbell) was the key success in making the system work. During this time period, the project manager ran PIPS on every type of project that he was involved on, including:

1. General construction
2. Roofing
3. Painting
4. Flooring
5. High-speed roll-up doors
6. Elevator installation
7. Underground storage tanks
8. Submersible pumps
9. Environmental projects

The results of the projects were far superior than anything that had been procured at the facility. The results of the PIPS projects can be seen in the following table (19.1). Lessons learned included:

1. Quality construction was procured with less management and inspection.
2. The quality construction lasted twice as long as the low-bid awarded construction.
3. Performers gravitated to UAL.
4. The performing construction minimized maintenance and repair.
5. By using performance information at the right time, UAL minimized the amount of technical specifications it used.

Table 19-1: Results of PIPS projects at United Airlines

Criteria	Results
Total number of projects	32
Total award amount	$13 Million
Users comparison - Low Bid vs. Performance-Based	3:09
Overall satisfaction of PIPS	100%
Overall quality of construction procured using PIPS (10 max)	9
Percent of PIPS contractors that would be hired again	95%
Percent of project finished on time	98%
Percent of projects finished within budget	100%
Percent of projects with no change orders	100%
Number of companies that were evaluated (PPI)	75

The research done at UAL shows that by minimizing management, inspection, and control by the user, quality actually increases. The Dock 7 case study also identifies that high quality contractors are focused on creating "win-win" relationships and minimizing the risk for themselves as well as the owner. The research illustrates the importance of contractors working with a Type A project manager. Most managers fear that PIPS will eliminate their control and functions. Without the visionary beliefs of Ron Campbell, the system would have never been tested at the site.

20

State of Utah Case Study

Overview

Until 1999, PIPS had not been run on any large projects. Late in 1998, another visionary facility/construction manager, Richard Byfield, the Director of the Division of Facilities Construction and Management (DFCM) for the State of Utah, attended the fall PIPS conference at ASU. They had previously heard of the PIPS process (called the Performance Based Procurement System (PBPS) at that time) through presentations at the National Association of State Facility Managers (NASFA). Richard Byfield saw PIPS as the only possible methodology to increase performance.

Byfield implemented the process on five multi-million dollar construction projects (totaling approximately $86 Million in construction). The projects were unique since:

1. They were the largest projects ever tested using PIPS.
2. This was the first test on a large general contractor job.
3. The projects were complex, and required the need for many performing subcontractors.

This chapter will review the state of the industry in Utah, concentrate on the University of Utah Housing project case study, and include the details and results of all the Utah tests, and lessons learned.

State of Utah Construction Environment

The State of Utah construction environment exhibited the characteristics of the "low-bid" environment (Kashiwagi 2002):

1. Change orders other than scope and unforeseen site conditions were at 5.7% (1.2% over the contingency construction budget measured over a ten year period).
2. Construction was not being completed on time.
3. There were construction problems that have led to litigation or the State of Utah paying the contractor for delays and change orders.
4. Use of DFCM's construction managers' time was ineffective due to problems caused by "low-bidding" contractors.
5. Low-bid contractors were extremely successful at getting contracts.

6. Subcontractors were selected using only price. Some general contractors claimed that price was not the only selection criteria, but the selected subcontractors almost always had the lowest price.
7. There was a lack of liability of designers due to confusion over construction problems. Therefore, all costs flowed to the owner.

University of Utah Housing Project (2000 Winter Olympic Village Housing)

The (DFCM) was facing one of its most critical projects in the fall of 1998; the construction of the University of Utah Housing Phase II which would provide the housing and beds for the 2002 Winter Olympics. The $131M project was divided into two phases, Phase I (which included a portion of the housing and utility installations for Phase II) and Phase II (the balance of the housing).

The University had selected the master planner and designer for the project, despite DFCM's suggestion of hiring a different designer. When problems occurred due to the designer, the University of Utah staff blamed DFCM. It was one of the most political situations the author had seen.

From Phase I, it was evident that the master planner was having difficulty with the overall design and coordination of the multiple contractors on site. The following were documented:

1. Phase I was behind schedule (3 months). The only contractor on schedule was a design-build contractor who had more control over the design and was not selected using "low-bid."
2. Design services for Phase II were behind schedule (3 months) and would not be completed in time for the contractors to bid.
3. It would be very difficult to meet the deadline for Phase II construction completion of May 2000 using the "low-bid" procurement delivery system.

The process was implemented in an environment of political unrest between the University of Utah staff and DFCM, between the DFCM and some of the contractors in Phase I, and between the master planner and designer, and DFCM and the contractors.

PIPS Implementation

There were a number of obstacles to overcome in the Phase II project. The following problems were occurring in Phase I:

1. The architect was having difficulty meeting the design dates, and the construction in Phase I was not being completed as initially scheduled.
2. The architect/construction coordinator could not stop the slipping schedule and delays.

3. The architect/construction manager, general contractors, subcontractors, and the State of Utah and University of Utah construction managers required a new "way of doing business."
4. The construction environment was in a "low-bid," litigious, and "non-trusting" environment.
5. The project would have to be awarded in three months, with the specifications and drawings not yet completed.
6. The design and coordination had already used almost the entire contingency funding, resulting in very little room for error in Phase II.
7. The project was due to be completed before June 2000, making the installation of the landscaping very difficult.

There were unique pressures on the PIPS test. The University of Utah housing project was a substantial project ($53M). Due to the lack of a similar "performance based" system, the largeness of the project, and the radical change that PIPS brought to the State of Utah construction procurement philosophy, the following occurred:

1. Highly successful contractors who did not usually bid government work were attracted into participating.
2. "Successful" contractors were attempting to define "performance" for the State of Utah. This resulted in these contractors having a difficult time understanding the simple PIPS and IMT concepts taught in the educational seminars. Some of the contractors took a "personal" approach, that if they did not win, the system was flawed.
3. The openness of the PIPS allowed the participating contractors to set the performance criteria and show their performance capability. The opportunity seemed to stun the contractors. Contractors were used to "marketing" themselves, and not differentiating based on performance. A few of the contractors made "obvious" errors in their proposals, which support the above idea of "not being ready for a performance based approach."

Performance Data Collection

Past performance information was collected on the general contractor, critical subcontractors, and the project manager and site superintendent. Performance lines were collected on 86 contractors.

The contractors were instructed to give only their best references, and were told to contact their references to inform them on the importance of the survey. Despite these instructions, some contractor references resulted in poor performance numbers. This illustrated that some contractors do not understand whether they perform or not. The following data describes the unusual level of success of the data collection process:

1. Number of surveys: 1,931
2. Total number of contractors surveyed: 86
3. Percentage of surveys returned: 69%
4. Average number of criteria per survey: 42

Table 20-1: Criteria Weights

No	Criteria	Weights
1	Price	20
2	Management Plan	10
3	Contractor Interview	10
4	Site Superintendent Performance	5
5	Site Superintendent Interview	5
6	General	20
7	Electrical	5
8	Mechanical	6
9	Framing	4
10	Plumbing	4
11	Masonry	3
12	Drywall	3
13	Roads	3
14	Landscaping	2

The weights for the performance criteria were set by the user and are shown in Table 20-1. The price and performance of the general contractor were weighted the heaviest. The management plan and interview were also weighted heavily.

Performance Information Procurement System Results

A major "successful" contractor did not bid the project due to political considerations connected to the 2000 Olympics. Five general contractors bid on the project. Table 20-2 shows the performance information and price for each firm.

Table 20-2: Contractor Raw Scores

		Firm 1	Firm 2	Firm 3	Firm 4	Firm 5
1	Price	$55.6M	$50.3M	$48.8M	$52.6M	$49.9M
2	Management Plan	8.43	6.21	4.24	5.31	5.73
3	Contractor Interview	8.94	9.06	9.13	7.25	6.52
4	Site Superintendent PPI	9.71	9.46	9.09	9.24	9.36
5	SS Interview	8.97	8.75	9.10	5.57	6.75
6	General PPI	9.09	9.19	8.40	8.96	8.52
7	Electrical PPI	8.93	8.41	8.41	9.02	8.41
8	Mechanical PPI	8.44	8.45	8.45	9.10	8.45
9	Framing PPI	7.80	8.41	8.52	8.30	8.33
10	Plumbing PPI	9.30	8.65	8.65	8.66	8.65
11	Masonry PPI	8.15	8.41	8.50	9.01	9.01
12	Drywall PPI	8.72	8.36	8.00	8.00	8.72
13	Roads PPI	9.23	8.23	8.23	8.80	8.80
14	Landscaping PPI	8.20	8.20	8.20	9.41	8.20

The contractors were told that there were two major requirements that had to be met:

1. The project must be complete by May 1, 2000, including the landscaping.
2. The project budget was $53M. Any bid over $53M would be non-responsive.

The highest performing contractor's bid was $55M. This contractor was a joint venture between the design build contractor who had worked on Phase I of the Housing Project, and another general contractor. The contractor gave the following reasons for their high priced bid submittal:

1. There were flaws in the design, which would raise the project cost over the budget of $53M. The major flaw was the omitting of the FHA requirements of the housing units, which eventually ended up costing the State of Utah approximately $3M for Phase I. The contractor claimed that their price included the FHA requirements.
2. The contractor knew the expectations of the owner because of their personal experience in the Phase I work.
3. At the time of the bid, the design for the village center (cafeteria facility for the new housing units) was not completed and bid as an allowance (later ended up costing $11M instead of $7M).

The contractor requested to change the bid a day after the bid submittal.
They did not "fully realize" that the over budget proposal would eliminate their bid. The contractor should have done the following, which is allowable under the PIPS rules:

1. Identified the design flaws or unstated requirements and priced them as additives.
2. Identify the risk of working with the State of Utah and set rules and requirements, which would reduce the cost.

However, because their bid was above the stated budget requirement, they were eliminated as non-responsive.

Contractor #2 was the second highest performer with a bid of $49M. However, their projected completion date of their landscaping was two months beyond the May 1, 2000 deadline set by the University of Utah. Contractor #2 gave the following arguments:

1. Substantial completion of the project would be May 1, 2000.
2. It was impossible to finish the landscaping in the spring by May 1, 2000. The spring season was not long enough to do the landscaping effectively.

The contract documents called for substantial completion, including landscaping, by May 1, 2000. The University wanted no landscaping to occur once students occupied the facility. Additionally, they wanted no landscape material tracked into the units. Contractor 2 was eliminated as being non-responsive. They protested the bid award and the bid protest was denied due to the following facts:

1. Contractor #2 specifically asked in the pre-proposal meeting if the deadline for landscaping could be beyond May 1, 2000. The addenda listed their question with the answer "no."
2. The pre-proposal meeting presentation, which was also part of the addenda, covered the requirements that would eliminate a bid as non-responsive. The requirements were to be within budget, and finishing all landscaping by May 1, 2000.
3. The University requested that the landscaping be done by May 1, 2000 due to the projected immediate use of the housing units.
4. The successful bidding contractor (Contractor #3) had proposed a way to minimize risk and finish on time. They proposed to install much of the landscaping the previous year (1999), and repair any "dead" or damaged items at the end of the construction period (2000). Their submitted landscaping budget included the cost of repairs.

Contractor #3 was awarded the contract. It should be noted that the landscaping and finish of several buildings actually were completed beyond May 1, however the contractor was delayed through no fault of its own, resulting in the landscaping being finished in July 2000. Contractor #2 did not understand that the legal requirement was "to have a construction plan finish by May 1, 2000, if the contractor is allowed to perform on their proposal."

Contractor #1 and #2 were both disqualified due to a lack of understanding of the difference between PIPS and the policy requirements of the State of Utah. Requirements cannot be altered by the PIPS. PIPS has to work within the constraints of the user's requirements. The objective of PIPS is to measure differences to prioritize alternatives to meet a unique requirement.

Contractor #3 had the following differentiating characteristics:

1. They had not bid on State work in the past.
2. They assigned the "best" personnel to the project. Both the project manager and the site superintendent were extremely knowledgeable about the project. They were quick thinking, logical, and passed information very quickly.
3. They had a workable plan that finished within the contract period.
4. They were creative in handling the critical areas of framing, sheetrock, and landscaping.
5. Additionally, they were the "low-bid" on the project.

Construction of the University of Utah Housing

The following occurred during the construction period:

1. The Phase I contractors (particularly the infrastructure contractor) were not finished on time, delaying the start of the PIPS contractor.
2. The design was not complete. Specifically related to utilities and site engineering requirements. Critical design components such as finished grade were not available until four months into Phase II. One of the issues was the fact that the

designer thought that the project was a design-build project once the contractor was awarded the contract. A major point in PIPS is that where there is a full design, the designer remains responsible for design. However, the performing contractor is responsible for asking for clarifications for any issue causing confusion or designs that are not constructible.

3. The performing contractor changed his "proposed construction plan" twice to attempt to get construction under way immediately. In both cases, the designer had information that was not passed on to the contractor. A pre-award meeting would have solved this issue before the contract was awarded. However, the issues dragged on for three months, preventing the contractor from starting.

4. One of the critical construction requirements, the $7M Village Center design was completed five months late. The contractor was asked to submit a $7M allowance in their bid. However, the Village Center final cost was $11M.

5. The designer had difficulty staffing the construction management/engineering support functions.

6. DFCM and the University released the lead design firm, which was responsible for overall construction management. The University of Utah personnel took over the daily construction coordination and management. It is interesting to note that the designer was not selected under the PIPS process.

The Village Center project was substantially complete on May 11, 2000. The contractor was paid $350K acceleration fee to make up the lost time (3-4 months). The contractor identified to the author that the entire fee went to the specialty contractors. All but one of the remaining 10 buildings, the landscaping, and punch list items were completed by the end of August. The State of Utah made the determination that the contractor was delayed due to incomplete project drawings and a failure to respond to the contractor in a timely manner throughout the project.

A major lesson learned on this project is a procedural step in the PIPS. The PIPS has a "pre-award and partnering" meeting before the award. Before the meeting the following is accomplished:

1. The contractor reviews the drawings in detail with their critical subs.
2. Identifies all items which cannot be constructed or have incomplete information.
3. Submits a list of requests for information to the designer.
4. Discusses the responses at the pre-award meeting.
5. A construction information interface should be agreed to and implemented.
6. The pre-award meeting minutes and agreements become a part of the contract.

The pre-award meeting has the following advantages:

1. The contractor can carefully coordinate with their critical subcontractors.
2. Errors or issues in the design are identified before construction.
3. The designer is forced to respond to the contractor's RFIs in a timely manner.
4. The information at the pre-award meeting identifies responsibilities, ensures that information will be passed in a timely fashion, and creates a partnering environment.

This meeting was not held before the award for the University of Utah Housing project. The partnering meeting was held after the award. The contractor did not get needed information from the designer. It is significant to note that the designer did not alert the contractor during the partnering meeting that their construction plan could not be accomplished based on the late finish of Phase I contractors, and other information that was not passed to the contractor. As previously stated, the project took three to four months to get into construction. The lack of an information system led to confusion, difficulty in solving the problems, and finally the transfer of the construction coordination from the lead designer to the University of Utah.

Analysis of the PIPS Implementation

The project was awarded within the scheduled 2-1/2 month procurement time. This included the two free education sessions, data collection, management plan and interviews reviews, and the prioritization based on all the information. It also included the review of two protests on issues, which did not address the PIPS.

The process selected an innovative contractor with a clear plan of success. The successful contractor was well within budget, had excellent personnel, and had a plan to meet the user's needs by creative contracting. The contractor addressed the landscaping and framing by using innovative scheduling and prefabrication.

The construction finished on time and on budget. All change orders were owner directed scope changes and time acceleration. The contractor did all that could be done to finish on time, within the bid price. The contractor, with the aid of one of the subcontractors, finished the village center ($11M) in 11 months and opened the center on schedule.

An analysis was performed to compare the results of the PIPS contractor with the Phase I low-bid and design-build contractors (Tables 20-3 and 20-4).

Table 20-3: Delivery System Performance Results

	Low Bid	Design Build	Performance Based
Days added to schedule	234	332	105
Actual days added until substantial completion	279	184	105
Percent change in scope	12.9%	19.4%	8.9%
Percent change in unknown events	1.3%	0.8%	0.9%
Percent change in error	2.4%	4.8%	1.3%
Percent change in omissions	1.5%	0.8%	1.6%

Table 20-4: Contractor Comparison

	Low Bid	Design Build	Performance Based
Change in scope	12.9%	19.4%	8.9%
Change in unknown events	1.3%	0.8%	0.9%
Change in errors	2.4%	4.8%	1.3%
Change in omissions	1.5%	0.8%	1.6%
SUB TOTAL	18.2%	25.8%	12.6%
CONTRACT	81.8%	74.2%	87.4%
ADJUSTED TOTAL	100.0%	100.0%	100.0%

The PIPS contractor when compared with the other two:
1. Had the smallest change in schedule.
2. Finished the earliest in respect to the schedule.
3. Had the smallest change in scope (additional cost).
4. Had the smallest charge for errors and omissions.

The facility manager rated the contractor (Table 20-5). The user and Facility Management Program Director were very satisfied with the contractor's services.

Table 20-5: Project Manager Evaluation of Performance

No	Criteria	Unit	Score
1	Is the project currently running on schedule?	Y/N	Y
2	Is the project currently running on budget?	Y/N	Y
3	How many contractor change orders have been issued?	(#)	0
4	Please rate your overall satisfaction with the contractor.	(1 – 10)	9

Overview of the State of Utah PIPS Tests

There were four other major projects procured at the State of Utah, including:

1. Southern Utah University Project: (Budget: $17.3 Million) Construct a new 3 story building, composed of classrooms, a gymnasium with an elevated track, a central hall, and a competition size indoor swimming pool.
2. Gunnison Correctional Facility Project: (Budget: $9 Million) Construct a new 288 bed dormitory style correctional housing unit, a guard tower, a hazardous storage unit, a kitchen, and support building.
3. Richfield Youth Correctional Facility Project: (Budget: $3.5 Million) Construct a facility that includes administrative offices, a service wing with a kitchen, a detention wing, a gymnasium, a secured housing wing, a security yard, parking, and landscaping.
4. Bridgerland Applied Technology Center Project: (Budget: $3 Million) Renovation of an existing technology building at Bridgerland ATC.

The following are the overall results of the State of Utah implementations (Table 20-6).

Table 20-6: State of Utah Results

No	Criteria	Utah Results
1	Total number of projects procured	5
2	Awarded Cost	$80,506,376
3	Budget	$85,770,000
4	Percent Under Budget	7%
3	Users comparison of Low-Bid vs. Performance-Based Low-Bid: Performance-Based (10 is the max)	4:9
4	Percent satisfied with PBPS	90%
5	Percent of users that met higher performing contractors using PBPS	100%
6	Percent of users that procured a higher performing contractor using PBPS than previous methods of procurement	88%
7	Overall quality of construction that was procured using the Performance Based Systems.	9.2
8	Performance rating of the contractor/system your company procured.	9.9
9	Percent of users that would hire the contractor again	100%
10	Percent of users that would use the Performance Based Systems to procure another project	90%
11	Percent of projects that finished on time	80%
12	Percent of projects that finished within budget	80%
13	Number of contractor-caused change orders	0
14	Number of companies that were evaluated (PPI)	357

Lessons Learned

1. Despite the modifications, the PIPS system procured outstanding results on large projects.
2. The site superintendent and the project manager are key components in a large construction project.
3. The pre-award period is critical before the award of a contract.
4. A high performance contractor will fix a design, which is less than optimal.
5. High performing contractors minimize the risk and think in the best interest of the owner.
6. Contractors need to be educated on the differences between legal requirements and PIPS requirements.
7. The robustness of PIPS.
8. The importance of creating and educating a "core team."
9. Partnering contractors worked very well together (the system allowed for high performing subs to partner with high performing generals).
10. The management plan ratings can be skewed if the raters know the origin of the proposal. However, a trained PIPS administrator can catch any possible mistakes.
11. The raters of the management plan should sign a document that states they do not know the origin of the proposals and do not have a conflict of interest.
12. Users need to be educated more on the system and on the theory. The users should minimize decision-making and control.

13. The designers are not minimizing the risk of non-performance. In the Gunnison Project, the user stated that the biggest problem was the Architect. The user stated the contractor could have added $200,000-$300,000 to cover unforeseen events. Ultimately, this project didn't finish on time or within budget.

14. An information interface, which is posted on the Internet, is required which quickly identifies participants who are not passing information. Information stops the bureaucratic process of pointing fingers when something goes wrong.

Value Based Selection Process

Richard Byfield was a visionary who brought innovation to a very conservative State of Utah. The author commends him on his integrity, vision, and accomplishments in the delivery of construction. Without his trust in the process, PIPS may not have been implemented in the State. After the five projects were run, contractors and DFCM modified PIPS and called it the Value Based Selection (VBS) process. The major changes were:

1. Deleted the critical subcontractors past performance.
2. Minimized the number of references from 40 to 10, and only required verification of 3-5 references.
3. Replaced the nonbiased artificial intelligent prioritization tool with a subjective decision of a review panel who saw the past performance information, the risk assessment management plan, interview scores and the bid price.
4. Did not use the risk minimization factor of the number of references.
5. Did not use the rating on the latest performed project to modify the future rating by 25%.
6. Did not use the pre-award phase (technically this was not a change, since they did not use this in their initial tests).

The modifications made the process more subjective, more difficult for high performance contractors to differentiate, and harder to justify. Over time, the author predicted that they would return to the design-bid-build low-bid award. This was based on the hypothesis that if decisions are made with subjective bias, performance information becomes less important and price becomes more important. This prediction is being fulfilled as three years later, in the December 2003 DFCM Building Board Meeting, the policy is being forwarded to not use VBS in design-bid-build projects (Utah State Building Board Minutes 2003). In the other delivery systems (design-build and construction management at risk), where subjectivity can be used in the awards, VBS will be continued.

Comments by the State of Utah Participants

The following are comments made by various people that were involved with the PBPS projects:

"...Ten to twelve months have been cut off of our completion schedule. Our students will have access to the facility one full year sooner. The bids did not go over estimation, leaving equipment money for this project intact...Bridgerland has enjoyed the greatest and most rapid successes that we have ever experienced..." – Richard Maughan (Superintendent, Bridgerland ATC)

"...The contractor took full responsibility for the project and made it run very smoothly...there were certain instances that the contractor went beyond their 'responsibility' by proposing solutions to problems that arose during the process of the project..." – Lyle Knudsen (Program Director, State of Utah DFCM)

"...In my twenty years of project management experience I have never had a better experience or outcome to a project (Southern Utah University Project)..." – Frank McMenimen (Program Director, State of Utah DFCM)

"...When an owner chooses a contractor on the sole basis of cost, the General Contractors in turn have no option but to use any and every low subcontractor bid that comes across the fax machine. Therefore the contractor's main focus on the project will be the cost. When this method is used, the quality and schedule will become secondary issues at best..." – Dennis Forbush (Project Manager, Hogan & Associates Construction)

"...The results of PBPS have given us the best construction results in ten years..." – Richard Byfield (Director, State of Utah DFCM)

Conclusion

Richard Byfield was personally responsible for bringing PIPS to deliver large construction projects. Even though the State of Utah may not have been able to sustain the innovation and see the vision of "outsourcing" construction, his efforts led to successful efforts in the State of Hawaii, the Dallas Independent School District, the Denver Hospital, and current efforts with the US Coast Guard, the Federal Aviation Administration, and Harvard University. Like his peers Gordon Matsuoka, Steve Miwa, Chris Kinimaka, Miguel Ramos, Ron Campbell, Marcos Costilla, and Charlie Serikawa, his visionary efforts led to the following conclusions:

1. PIPS can work on large and complex general construction projects.
2. 4 out of 5 projects were completed on time and within budget. The overall cost of the projects was approximately $5 Million below the estimated budget.
3. The State of Utah received a much higher level of quality (PIPS scored a 9 and Low-Bid scored a 4). The users also rated the contractors that they procured a 9.9 out of 10.
4. The State of Utah had difficulty grasping the concepts of IMT. They began making decisions and trying to alter the system without understanding the theoretical impacts they would make.

The PIPS process worked at the State of Utah using a less developed, constrained process. Since these tests PIPS has been improved using the following:

1. Data collection process refined to be done by contractors.
2. Criteria minimized to eight criteria for all contractors.
3. Pre-award phase has become the most critical. Clients are instructed that if this phase is not run, there is risk.
4. Explanation of the designer and contractor functions has become very clear. The designer is always responsible for design.
5. General contractors are given the average ratings of the specialty contractors.

Chapter 20 Review

1. What was the biggest difference in the PIPS tests in the State of Utah?
2. Why was this modification allowed?
3. What is the most important criteria in the selection of the best performer on a large construction project?
4. What did performance cost?

References

Kashiwagi, D. & Byfield R. (2002). State of Utah Performance Information Procurement System Tests. *ASCE: Journal of Construction Engineering and Management,* 128 [4], pp: 338-347.

Kashiwagi, D. & Byfield, R. (2002) Testing of Minimization of Subjectivity in 'Best Value' in Procurement by Using Artificial Intelligence Systems in State of Utah Procurement. *ASCE: Journal of Construction Engineering and Management,* 128 [6], 496-502.

Utah State Building Board Minutes. (2003, December 3). Salt Lake City Utah. Committee Room 129.

21
State of Hawaii Case Study

Introduction

The State of Hawaii had been plagued by poor construction, specifically poor roofing quality. In 1997, a very visionary leader in construction, Gordon Matsuoka, and a very perceptive deputy, Steve Miwa, were introduced to PIPS. Gordon and Steve were Type A individuals, who wanted to use their experience to help the State of Hawaii take a huge step forward in increasing the value of construction and the quality of life of those affected by the construction. They were ahead of their time, and definitely out of step with the political machinery that was running the State of Hawaii. Their vision was to:

1. Streamline the delivery of construction.
2. Minimize the management overhead.
3. Optimize the construction delivery process by going cradle to grave.
4. Minimize the inefficiencies and problems of the low-bid awards by going to the performance based PIPS.
5. Increase the value of construction.

The PIPS process was implemented in 1998, and by 2002, 96 roofs had been procured using this method. Matsuoka and Miwa found another visionary project manager Chris Kinimaka, and a very capable architect, Gaylyn Nakatsuka, to implement the process. It is important to note that over the four years, PIPS was modified to minimize management work, decision-making, and risk. Over the four years, the following results were documented (State of Hawaii PIPS Advisory Committee 2002):

1. Out of 96 PIPS re-roofing projects; leaks were reported on two roofs. One leak was a flashing leak, which was quickly repaired by the contractor. The other leak was a leak through a mechanical fan. There are no current leaks on the 96 roofs.
2. Contractors received an average post project rating of 9.6 (maximum of 10) on roof performance by facility users.
3. No specifications were required on any of the retrofit projects. Design costs were reduced from 11% to 2.5%.
4. Roof inspections were minimized to the start and end of construction.
5. Enforceable roof warranties increased from two years to a range of 10 to 20 years.
6. Project management was minimized by 80%.

7. The cost of the installed roofing systems was 5% below the budget and 3% below the cost of the low-bid roofing.
8. The performance based roofing construction was twice as fast as the low-bid construction.
9. The projects had very few change orders (including scope changes), and fewer punch list items (which were immediately handled by the contractors).

This group of projects led to the following results:

1. Minimized design, and minimized construction management and inspection.
2. The highest performance of roofing the schools and manufacturer's representatives had seen.
3. High customer satisfaction.
4. Fast and efficient construction.
5. No roof maintenance was required on the new roofs.

A contractor, who had performance issues, protested the PIPS process. The protest went through an administrative hearing. Although the hearing officer penalized the State of Hawaii for not stopping a construction project that was under protest (miscommunication between workers), the hearing concluded that PIPS:

1. Met the requirements of the State procurement law.
2. PIPS did not favor anyone (the contractor was unable to prove that the system was unfair).
3. Subjective performance information can be used to determine best value.

Matsuoka and Miwa understood that to deliver best value, the entire delivery process must be made efficient. This is a "win-win" only when all parties in the delivery process are efficient and maximize their profit or efficiency. A 'win-win" exists when the owner receives best value, and the performing contractor maximizes their profit. Matsuoka and Miwa ran the most efficient construction delivery process the author had seen.

Both Matsuoka and Miwa (M&M) realized that efficiency is only achieved when management and other overhead functions are minimized. Outsourcing is efficient because, by definition, outsourcing requires no management and direction. This is difficult to understand because so many companies outsource and then manage the outsourced function. However, outsourcing is when a company gives another company the complete responsibility to perform a function where they do not have the technical expertise and efficiency.

In the outsourcing of roofing construction, the State of Hawaii gave the contractors and manufacturers a requirement to waterproof the roof of the building, but did not direct the contractor on how to do the waterproofing. In the roofing application, the delivery of roofing construction resembles a design-build process. A design-build process is a process where the owner hires one entity (a joint venture composed of a contractor and designer) that will design and build the project. It minimizes the functions of the user's project management, design, construction management, and inspection. Deductively, the only reason to manage the outsourced function is when the outsourced function does not meet the expectation of the owner. Companies who can perform will know what their performance is and will be able to provide the performance without management from their buyer.

PIPS has the following features, which forced efficiency, motivated performance, and minimized management and direction:

1. There was no directed technical design solution on waterproofing, painting, and roofing work. The designer identified the current condition of the roof and any special requirements.
2. Past performance of every contractor and manufacturer was documented. The documented performance numbers of the manufacturer and the contractor directly impacted the competitiveness of the contractor. For example, a roofing manufacturer's system that had a performance barcode of 10 years proven performance, 95% customer satisfaction, and 98% roofs not leaking was more competitive than a manufacturer's system that has the following performance barcode: 3 years proven performance, 90% customer satisfaction and 80% roofs not leaking. Unlike most pre-qualifying procurement systems, where roofing contractors are either considered as qualifying or not qualifying, each manufacturer and contractor was forced to compete based on their actual performance numbers and price.
3. The performance on the current project impacted both the manufacturer and contractor's future performance numbers by 25%. If a contractor's past performance showed a leaking roof, the contractor and the manufacturer become noncompetitive for future work. This created a true partnership between the contractor and manufacturer.
4. The perceived value of each contractor's roofing warranty was considered in the selection (see Chapter 13).
5. To compete, the contractors were required to identify the risk to the owner in terms of cost, time, risk of leaking, their method of minimizing the risk, and how they would add value to the roof. This proposal was rated and became a major factor in the selection.
6. The installation time of the roof affected the contractor's competitiveness.
7. The relative price of the roofing system also affected competitiveness.

The contractors were no longer bidding to install roofing materials. They were bidding to waterproof the building. They competed based on performance and price. Performance was being measured in terms of success of waterproofing, customer satisfaction, not having change orders, and speed of installation.

PIPS allowed the State of Hawaii to outsource construction, relying on the identification of a high performing contractor rather than the management of a poor performing contractor. PIPS was embraced by the building users, the project manager, the majority of contractors who participated, and industry organizations who were interested in improving construction performance. However, there were others who were not as comfortable with PIPS due to the following:

1. Certain manufacturers and contractors were hesitant to accept responsibility for performance. Manufacturers with non-performing systems (or systems that did not support the contractors to perform) were not selected by the high performing contractors.
2. High performing systems have an advantage over unproven systems. Contractors were motivated to select the best performing manufacturer's products. Contractors were also selecting manufacturers based on their support in terms of technical knowledge and promptness.
3. The system is not price based. The low-bidder was not assured the award.
4. Non-efficient functions are minimized. The efficiency of the process minimizes functions (engineering, design, and sales order taking) that were heretofore perceived as "critical."
5. Change. The PIPS changes the functions of the delivery process.

The discomfort with change and accountability resulted in accusations of high costs and technical incompetence. This resulted in an internal audit by the State of Hawaii to identify the true value of the roofing procured through the PIPS process. The two options being compared were the standard design-bid-build (low-bid), and the performance based design-build process (PIPS).

The State of Hawaii used the hypothesis that the PIPS process was less costly and provided higher performance for procuring the retrofitting of roofing systems. Based on this hypothesis, the State broke up the analysis into two parts, delivery cost and performance. If the cost of the performance based construction was higher, than a comparison of the value of both processes would be analyzed. Due to the lack of "total information," when decisions have to be made in the analysis, the decisions will be made on the conservative side (in favor that PIPS is not more economical than the low-bid).

Transaction Cost Analysis

The objective of the analysis is to identify the relative first costs of PIPS delivered construction in relation to the standard design-bid-build (low-bid) delivered construction. The methodology to be used is the transaction cost analysis of the two processes that procure construction. The transaction cost analysis will cover the relative cost of the owner's (State of Hawaii) delivery processes. The traditional drawbacks of doing transaction costs analysis in construction include (Hughes 2002):

1. The lack of full information of all costs.
2. The number of related functions that cannot be completely quantified.

3. The uniqueness of every construction project requiring different levels of each function.
4. Difference in quality of the end product.

Transaction cost analysis has been used for two different purposes: first, to identify which costs are related to the delivery of construction (Hughes 2002), and secondly to assist in identifying more efficient and economical processes (Leffler 2003). Unlike Leffler's study which used hypothetical data, this transaction cost analysis uses actual cost data with conservative assumptions, to compare the two processes, which are run by the same organization for a specific type of construction (roofing) (Chang and Ivie 2001).

Since the same organization did two processes, and the type of construction is the same, the only critical functions would be the functions that resulted in a difference in cost. The objective is to identify if the cost of PIPS is more than the design-bid-build process costs.

The analysis first identified the major user functions or costs involved in the two delivery systems. They include:

1. Planning and programming.
2. Design and procurement.
3. Bidding and award.
4. User project / construction management and inspection.
5. Construction.
6. Rework: nonperformance (lack of quality).

The State of Hawaii identified no differential in the cost of planning, programming, bidding, and award phases between the two processes. The remaining four functions were then analyzed for differential.

The design costs were taken from the records of the State. It was costing the State 11% of the project cost to create roofing designs (selection of materials, means, and methods). It was costing 2.5% for designers to identify the requirement for PIPS. The procurement functions were the same.

To identify the project management, construction management, and inspection costs for the traditional process, the State took the delivered construction costs for the last three years, and divided them by the overhead costs. The State then used the most efficient rate, 2.65%. The State then assumed that the overhead or management costs for all projects was about the same.

The State then estimated how much of the management effort was minimized by PIPS in the delivering of the projects. The State took the 2.65% management rate, multiplied it by 0.2 (minimized work by 80%), and then divided the result by 1/3 (because the project managers could perform from 5 to 10 times the number of projects as the project managers who were managing under the design-bid-build process). The division by 3 was a conservative number (range of reduction by 2 to 5). The resulting management/inspection cost of PIPS was identified as .4%.

The State then identified the difference in construction costs of the low bid and the PIPS projects. The State identified 100 low-bid projects, and 96 PIPS projects from 1998 to 2002. All projects were being budgeted with a standard estimate based on previous low-bid awards. The low-bid roofs were 13% below the budget. However, upon closer analysis, it was identified that three of the roofing projects had large cost deviations between the budget and the awarded price. This usually signifies a mistake in budgeting. When the three roofs were taken out of the sample, the average cost was 8.4% below the budget. Another factor that skewed the average price of roofing was the changing of some roofing budgets for added insulation. Ten of the low-bid roofs were insulated roofs, which had increased budgets. Without the impact of the budget changes and errors, the average cost of the low-bid roofing systems was 2.3% below the budget. These two factors, inaccurate budgets and the insulated roof budget increases, were taken out to compare the prices for the same type of roof jobs.

In the design-bid-build process, a specification is used to direct the contractor in exactly what to do, how to do it, and when to do it. Huge differentiations should come only when the contractor is using another procedure. Therefore, it is rather easy to identify when the budget is wrong (30-50% difference between the budget and the low-bid). The insulated roofs were taken out from both the low-bid and the PIPS projects due to the inconsistency of the budgets for these projects.

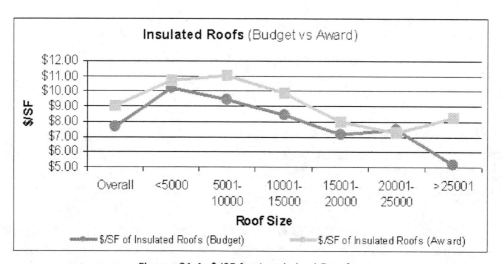

Figure 21.1: $/SF for Insulated Roofs

The average cost of the PIPS projects was 7% over the budget. However, upon closer analysis, 36 of the roofs were insulated roofs. Upon checking with the programmers, the roofs were not budgeted for the installation of insulation. After plotting the costs against the budgets (Table 21-1), it was identified that the PIPS insulated roofing project costs were consistently above the budgets by an increment of 18%. This identification caused the budgets for low-bid procured roof to increase in 2002 (due to the protest of PIPS on the basis of costs, no roofing projects were procured using PIPS in 2002). The average cost of PIPS delivered roofs without insulation was 5.6% below the budget.

Table 21-1: State of Hawaii Construction Costs

Construction Costs	PIPS	LB
Audit Report Costs on all projects	7.0%	-13.0%
Average costs without projects with poor budget estimates		-8.4%
Projects without insulated roofs and poor budgets	-5.6%	-2.3%

The last cost is the cost of quality or cost of nonperformance (Crosby 1980). The State analyzed three projects done within the last three years. The first project, Kalanimoku Building, was a waterproofing project that was designed by the State and awarded to the lowest bidder. The project cost $575,000. After the contractor finished the project, the leaking continued. The State had to hire another contractor based on performance to temporarily stop the leaking.

The second project was the State of Hawaii capitol roof, which after being re-roofed, continued to leak. The estimated cost of fixing the leaks was $350,000. The State continued to do temporary repairs on the building.

The third project was re-roofed in 2001 (the UH Activity Center roof). The roof had been installed five years earlier and leaked from its inception. The State was unable to get the general contractor or the roofing contractor to fix the problem because no engineer could identify the source of the leaks. The owner re-bid the project under the PIPS process for a cost of $400,000. The project was completed on time, without any change orders, and the leaking was stopped.

There were many other low-bid projects that resulted in nonperformance. The low-bid process was assessed a conservative .5% cost of nonperformance. The PIPS by definition has no cost of nonperformance, because the contractors are paid to perform, not install construction materials. This definition is supported by the fact that none of the PIPS projects over four years were leaking.

Table 21-2 shows the results of the transaction cost analysis. The PIPS delivery costs were 14% better or more economical than the low-bid process. The transaction costs analysis is comparing first costs and not life cycle costs. If the performance of the two processes is compared, it is easy to identify the PIPS process as the better value process (Table 21-3). PIPS has documented higher customer satisfaction, longer maintenance free performance, faster delivery of performing products, and no leaking roofs.

Table 21-2: Transaction Cost Analysis

NO	ITEM	PIPS	Low Bid
1	Design Cost	2.50%	11.00%
2	Project Management Cost	0.40%	1.90%
3	Construction Cost	-5.60%	-2.30%
4	Cost of Quality	0.00%	0.50%
	Total	-2.70%	11.10%

Savings due to PIPS   13.80%

Table 21-3: Performance Results of PIPS and Low Bid

No	Criteria	Results
1	Percent of DOE users that would rather use PIPS over Low-Bid	100%
2	Percent of users that would use the PIPS contractor again	100%
3	Performance rating of PIPS (10 is maximum)	8.1
4	Performance rating of Low-Bid (10 is maximum)	5.6
5	Average PIPS post project contractor rating (10 is maximum)	9.6
6	Percent increase in delivery schedule of PIPS compared to Low-Bid	35%
7	Average PIPS ensured warranty	10-25 years
8	Average Low-Bid enforceable warranty	2 years
9	Percent of PIPS project completed on time	98%
10	Average PIPS production rate per day ($/day)	$4,500
11	Average Low Bid production rate per day ($/day)	$2,500
12	Number of PIPS projects (with leaking roofs) repaired by the owner	0

Other Projects

The State of Hawaii ran other types of projects using PIPS including mechanical renovation, electrical, painting, waterproofing, and classroom renovation. Due to the lack of resources and a tremendous influx of construction work (the government was trying to stimulate a very bad post 9/11 economy in Hawaii), Matsuoka modified PIPS and used it to procure millions of dollars worth of construction renovation. Due to the lack of trained PIPS personnel, PIPS was not embraced by all. However, the construction results from using the modified PIPS were as good as anything the State had seen.

Lessons Learned

There were some lessons learned in the State of Hawaii.

1. PIPS was modified to minimize the number of performance criteria to 10 for all contractors except roofing contractors.
2. Instead of the government sending out the surveys, the contractors would be responsible for sending out their surveys and having the references send the surveys back to the procurement person.
3. The DIM would be used to generate the relative performance information and prioritization. The procurement person would then select the best value. 95 out of 100 times, the procurement person would pick the highest prioritized contractor.
4. PIPS cannot be used by those who are not educated in the process, theory, and practice. Education is the most important element in assisting construction professionals to use PIPS.
5. The implementation of PIPS should be done slowly.
6. One of the most important functions in the PIPS process is to keep the performance information updated and accurate. The information worker described in Chapter 11 is a critical function.
7. The risk from PIPS is political and not construction related. PIPS concepts are based on correct principles and successful business practices. The political risk is from individuals who are not ready for the change to become very efficient.

The author, Matsuoka, Miwa, Kinimaka, and Nakatsuka learned some valuable concepts that will be used by future PIPS users.

Conclusions and Recommendations

The State of Hawaii case study comparing the transaction costs of PIPS versus the traditional low-bid process leads to the following preliminary conclusions:

1. Roofing can be procured more economically by procuring with performance-based procurement rather than the traditional design-bid-build process.
2. Retrofit roofing can be procured more economically by procuring the system solution with the best-documented performance instead of using an expert's design.
3. This case study suggests that the difference in the construction first cost has less impact than other component costs in the delivery of roofing systems.
4. The value brought by performance-based procurement far exceeds the value of low bid awards.
5. This case study suggests the value of high performance does not cost more. The results identify performers that can make a profit while bringing owners a better value.

6. This case study suggests that the practice of awarding retrofit roofing projects to the lowest bidder is more expensive and does not bring value to the user.

Matsuoka and Miwa had proven that the delivery of renovation work could be outsourced by using a best value design-build approach. Unknown to both of them at the time, the results they achieved would have an impact on those to follow (Dallas Independent School District, the Federal Aviation Administration, Harvard University, and the US Coast Guard). Their efforts had resulted in a significant discovery: best value construction has the same or lower first costs as the low bid, minimum standard construction. This was the first time that the inefficiency of the low-bid system had become so apparent.

As with all visionaries who fly with the eagles, they were not understood by the slower moving bureaucrats. As a new governor and comptroller took over the State of Hawaii, they returned to the design-bid-build, low-bid, environment. However, the efforts of Matsuoka and Miwa will take their place with the Demings of the world. Their efforts became the greatest impetus for the proliferation of PIPS.

The conclusions are that the traditional design-bid-build process is inefficient, offers relatively poor value, and costs building owners more in terms of first cost. It is only because of the complexity of the construction process, and the lack of information that allows the current inefficient construction processes to continue. The research performed confirms the concept that the traditional delivery process, which does not use performance information to differentiate but uses management and control to deliver a commodity, may be the number one reason for construction nonperformance.

Chapter 21 Review

1. Why would low bid prices differ greatly from the client's engineering estimate?
2. Why would the prices in a performance based bid differ from the engineer's estimate?
3. Which had a lower first cost, the performance based or the low bid?
4. Which had a greater performance, the low bid or the performance based?
5. Why would the State's engineers not like the PIPS process?
6. How did the clients respond to the PIPS process?
7. How did the contractors react to the PIPS process?
8. How much rework was there using PIPS?

References

Chang, C.Y. & Ive, G. (2001). A comparison of two ways of applying a transaction cost approach: The case of construction procurement routes. *Bartlett Research Papers*, pp. 13, 41.

Crosby, P. B. (1980). *Quality is Free, The Art of Making Quality Certain*. New York: Penguin Group.

Hughes, W. (2002). Developing a system for assessing the costs associated with different procurement routes in the construction industry. Uwakweh, B. & Minkarah, I. (Eds)., *CIB 2002 10th International Symposium*, 9-10 September 2002, Cincinnati, OH, Vol. 2, pp. 826-840.

Kashiwagi, D. & Byfield, R. (2002). Testing of Minimization of Subjectivity in 'Best Value' in Procurement by Using Artificial Intelligence Systems in State of Utah Procurement. *ASCE: Journal of Construction Engineering and Management*, 128 [6], pp. 496-502.

Leffler, K. (2003). Transaction Cost Approach. Retrieved April 30, 2003, from http://faculty.washington.edu/~krumme/readings/transaction_cost.html

State of Hawaii PIPS Advisory Committee. (2002). Report for Senate Concurrent Resolution No. 39 Requesting a Review of the Performance Information Procurement System (PIPS).

Attachments

Attachment 21.1: DAGS Audit Report
Attachment 21.2: DAGS Administrative Hearing's Report

REPORT FOR
SENATE CONCURRENT RESOLUTION NO. 39
REQUESTING A REVIEW OF THE
PERFORMANCE INFORMATION PROCUREMENT SYSTEM (PIPS)

PREPARED BY THE
PIPS ADVISORY COMMITTEE

NOVEMBER 2002

PART I – EXECUTIVE SUMMARY

A. Purpose

S.C.R. No. 39, S.D. 1, requested the Department of Accounting and General Services (DAGS) to form an advisory committee to make recommendations to improve the PIPS system. The resolution required the committee be comprised of construction industry employer organizations, construction employee organizations, and other interested construction industry organizations as approved by the Comptroller, and requested a report to identify the following:

1. If PIPS resulted in cost savings.
2. If PIPS resulted in greater accountability.
3. If construction projects were equitably distributed among contractors.
4. If PIPS resulted in a lower number of change orders.
5. If PIPS resulted in higher quality (including timeliness) as compared to alternate forms of outsourcing State construction projects.

B. PIPS Advisory Committee

In June 2002, the Comptroller appointed 12 representatives of various construction industry organizations to the PIPS Advisory Committee to review and make recommendations to improve PIPS (Appendix B).

C. Independent Auditor

The Comptroller hired an independent auditor, KPMG LLP, to conduct an unbiased review of PIPS. The auditor researched, reviewed, and reported on PIPS and low-bid projects completed by DAGS. Based on the findings of the audit, the advisory committee produced this report on the review of the PIPS system.

D. Background - Why PIPS?

Prior to 1999, DAGS Public Works Division (PWD) received numerous complaints on the quality of the completed construction projects and poor coordination of the projects during construction, especially in re-roofing and painting. Roofs were poorly constructed, contractors were slow in correcting punch list items, response to warranty work was slow or non-existent, and there was no accountability between the designers and the roofing contractors. Painting was in an even more critical situation. Even with tight specifications and detailed plans, the quality of work was so bad that DAGS Central Services Division (CSD) assumed repainting work on Oahu with their in-house staff.

It was in search of a process to correct these problems that PWD was introduced to PIPS.

E. Summary of Conclusions

1. PIPS resulted in 3% savings of overall project costs, which includes reduced design, project management, and maintenance costs.
2. PIPS resulted in greater contractor accountability. For example, immediate responses to trouble calls, no leaking roofs, no outstanding issues on completed projects, good

communication with customers, contractors are motivated to obtain and continue training, fewer punch list items, and fewer change orders.

3. PIPS projects were not as widely distributed as the low-bid projects. Recommended modifications will make PIPS more equitably distributed.
4. PIPS resulted in a lower number of change orders.
5. PIPS has given higher quality construction. PIPS is the only best value process with documented results over a period of time. Other forms of outsourcing State construction projects do not have documentation of higher quality, timeliness and distribution.

F. PIPS Modifications

PIPS is a dynamic system. The staff and performing contractors are always striving to improve the system. The following changes have been proposed to improve the value to the State and increase the opportunity and distribution of projects to contractors:

1. Reduce and standardize the rating criteria from an average of forty-seven (47) items down to ten (10) items, except for roofing. (Retain two additional roof performance criteria for roofing.)
2. Allow the contractors to send out the surveys to the owners, and the owners send it back to the State. This would allow contractors to ensure that their references got the survey.
3. Initiate continuous registration.
4. Establish a price override mechanism. (Award to the second best proposal if the cost difference between the best and second best exceeds a percentage established for each project in the range of 15% to 20%.)
5. Award the project to the low-bidder if all bids exceed the project budget by over 20%. If additional funds are justified to award the project, we should consider the lowest bid without consideration for past performance. This allows contractors with little or no past performance the opportunity to compete on price alone. Although this brings risk, the low bidder must still pass technical review and will be rated on the completion of the project.
6. Publicize PIPS formula and sample calculations.
7. Provide a one-week interim period between cost proposal due dates and management plan submittal dates.
8. Post project budgets immediately after closing of cost proposal receipt deadline, provided at least one responsive and responsible cost proposal is within budget. If no proposals are within budget, the budget will not be posted. This will allow contractors the opportunity to determine whether or not they want to proceed with the mandatory management plan submittal one week later.

G. Recommendations

It is recommended that:

1. PIPS be used as an alternative means to procure construction and not used to replace the low-bid process. Those who would rather participate in the low-bid system, should keep bidding on the low-bid projects (majority of projects.)
2. The PIPS modifications discussed in the previous section be implemented to minimize large differentials in award price and increase the opportunity and distribution of work.
3. The performance delivered by all procurement processes should be well documented in a timely manner.
4. User agencies should have the prerogative to select the PIPS process.

5. The PIPS modifications proposed in the previous section be adopted and analyzed after more procurements are run.

PART II – ANALYSIS

This comparison of PIPS and low-bid is based primarily on the roofing projects since the PIPS roofing program is in its fourth year, has the largest number of completed projects and includes participants who have been involved with the PIPS program from its inception.

A. Cost of the PIPS

A comparison is being made of the entire delivery system (Appendix G, Table G1). The costs were derived in the following manner:

1. Design costs. These come from PWD records. The design costs are based on a percentage of the project cost for roofing.
2. "In-house" Project Management costs. This was derived from PWD records on the total construction project expenditure and the staff personnel expenditure, resulting in a management cost in percentage of the project expenditure (Appendix G, Table G2.)

    For 2002, PWD delivered a higher amount of construction, resulting in a management cost of .0265 or 2.65%. The conservative assumption is that the cost before and after construction contract award is 30% / 70% due to the planning function being less than a third of PWD functions. Based on the University's case study with roofing and painting, 80% of the remaining 70% of the function is deleted for PIPS projects .

    The PWD inspectors and engineers are also spending less time on PIPS projects, but it is harder to document due to the number of personnel involved and the mix of projects each personnel is covering. It was also noted that one project manager could manage all the roofing and painting contracts. A conservative estimate is the project manager can handle up to 3 times the number of projects compared to the traditional process. The management of design and inspection of construction is minimized. The PIPS "in-house" PM costs is therefore .4% of the total project costs.

3. Construction Costs. The PIPS construction costs is based on all the PIPS projects (100 vs the 34 in the independent audit.) The low bid costs came from the audit numbers (34 roofs), which was 13% under budget. The construction costs for the PIPS projects (based on 78 roofs with no insulation) is 5.6% below the budget (Appendix G, Table G3). The budgets for projects with insulation are listed in Appendix F, Table F8, which show that the budgets were relatively accurate for non-insulation projects and inaccurate for insulated projects.
4. Costs of Quality. The cost of quality is substantial when what is procured does not work. The cost of quality is the cost of what the State has to pay when the low-bid project does not perform. A couple of examples are:

    a. The University of Hawaii Stan Sheriff Center, which leaked from the day it was constructed. The cost to repair the leak was $401,675.
    b. The State of Hawaii Capitol roof, which also leaked from the day it was built. The roof was repaired numerous times but still leaked. After the State Capitol was last re-

roofed, gaps between the original roof construction and wall, which allowed water to penetrate below the roofing membrane, were discovered.

c. The refusal of the coating manufacturer to warranty the roof coating for Ali'iolani Hale building.

d. The waterproofing of the Kalanimoku Building, which did not stop the leaking. The original cost of the waterproofing of the Kalanimoku Building was $589K (with an interim repair finally done with a PIPS contractor for $20K on the completed section of the project and an additional $338K for redesigned work remainder of the project.)

e. Another couple of examples of a designer specifying a roof construction and not knowing the performance results are the Hamilton Library roof and the State of Hawaii Convention Center walking deck roof. In both cases, the general contractors are liable to repair the systems, however, the repaired system is never as good as a performing system (and the warranty will only be for the minimum amount of time).

f. High risk projects are ideal for PIPS, but the major advantage can only be quantified as "the problem has been fixed." The only reason risk exists, is a lack of performance information and insufficient funds to do the project. Using the 80/20 rule, it is these projects which consume the "in-house" project manager's time. It is also the reason for customers being dissatisfied with PWD work. The cost of quality for the low-bid procurements is listed at .5% of the project costs.

5. Total Costs. The costs for low-bid is 3.07% higher than the costs for PIPS (Appendix G, Table G1.)

In conclusion, PIPS resulted in roofs that were 3.07 percent less expensive for systems that were over 5 times more value (last longer, maintenance is less, contractors and manufacturers respond versus the low-bid roofs where the State responds to repairs over two years old.) Additionally there are no costs for nonperformance on over 100 roofing installations over the last four years (i.e. the State has not paid for any maintenance costs.)

B. Accountability of Contractors

The KPMG audit (Appendix D) reported that there were less punch list items on PIPS projects than on the low-bid projects. In addition, the following information was not covered in the scope of the audit:

1. PIPS roofing contractors responded immediately to three reports of leaking PIPS roofs. Two of the problems were non-roof related, and the third was fixed immediately by the contractor.

2. There are no leaking PIPS roofs (oldest being four years old) and no anticipation of any leaking in the near future. CSD has not had to respond to any leaks.

3. Painting contractors have done outstanding work without specifications. Out of 33 painting projects, there are no outstanding issues. Many of the painting jobs had minimum inspection during construction. When unforeseen problems occurred, the contractors worked with the State to come up with logical solutions at no cost to the State.

4. PIPS contractors have fixed unforeseen conditions without promise of reimbursement by the State. Notice is given to the inspector, fixes are made, and unforeseen conditions change order is turned in when the project is complete. (In many cases, contractors have not asked for extra payment.)

5. Contractors have gone ahead on their own risk without any directive from the State to perform work during windows of opportunity to assist the State.
6. Performance has been so good in terms of the contractors being accountable, that two schools have given a party/luaus for the contractors, principals have requested PIPS roofs, and inspection is minimized on PIPS roofs (Appendix N).
7. When the University of Hawaii ran PIPS for painting jobs, the painting contractors requested the local training group to either provide a quality control person, or train the contractors to quality control their own work. Ironically, all the contractors had been previously trained. However, under the low-bid environment, training and craftsperson skilled work is not a requirement, and therefore the training had no impact. PIPS makes the contractors liable, puts them at risk, motivates and encourages the use of training .

C. Distribution of Work

An analysis of the roofing projects compared low-bid awards with PIPS awards, as follows:

1. The low-bid roofing awards of 96 projects from 1998-2002 were awarded to 33 contractors with the top five contractors being awarded 50% of the work (20%, 8%, 7%, 7%, 7%).
2. The PIPS roofing projects were awarded to 8 contractors with the top five being awarded 96% of the projects (32%, 24%, 17%, 16%, 7%).

These numbers seem to show that PIPS distributed work to fewer contractors. However, when a more detailed analysis was done on the entire sample of roofing awards, only seven roofing contractors received at least one or more jobs a year under the low-bid system (Table C1 and C2), and five roofing contractors were getting repeated work under the PIPS system. When these numbers are compared, the two processes are fairly similar in their distribution of work.

Regardless of these results, modifications to the PIPS process (see Part I above, PIPS Modifications) will make the PIPS results even more similar to the low-bid distribution requirements. It should also be noted that PIPS is relatively new, and contractors and manufacturers need to be educated on the importance of performance, and liability for nonperformance.

D. Change Orders

All change orders on the 100 completed PIPS projects were for unforeseen or scope changes for the benefit of the State. There were no change orders due to design error or omission. Based on the KPMG review (Appendix D) of compiled data, there was, on average, fewer change orders associated with PIPS than low-bid projects.

E. Higher Quality

PIPS has given performance (i.e., higher quality construction and better communication with customers) without increasing cost. PIPS has given a superior product at a reasonable cost, reduced the overall delivery cost of construction, distributed the work among performers, required the low-bidders to perform, and motivated the contractors to improve. PIPS is the only best value process with documented results over a period of time.

PIPS is unique for several reasons:

1. It forces the contractor to identify their performance before bidding.
2. It uses past performance as a key component for the award.
3. It rates the contractor at the end of the project, which affects the contractor's future competitive nature.
4. It compares subjective performance factors (contractor met quality expectations, was considerate, did not impact operations, communicated with the user), objective observation factors (on-time and within budget), and performance numbers (number of years of roof performance, number of leaking roofs) simultaneously, without the subjective translation into numbers that have less meaning. The non-performing contractor cannot depend on a State decision maker making a subjective decision to allow nonperformance for any reason.
5. It forces competition among alternatives with different approaches to the problem, maximizing the use of State funds.

G. Conclusions and Recommendations

PWD has been criticized for a lack of performance (timely, within cost, and satisfying the customer.) It is this perceived lack of performance, not their financial management (3% overhead) that is being criticized. The issue is performance. PWD recognized the significance of performance and implemented PIPS to improve performance results.

The PIPS procurements so far have provided an increase in quality without an increase in expense (overall costs have actually been 3% lower than similar low-bid projects). However, the PIPS information environment created change and opposition because it forced all functions (contracting, design, and management) to self-analyze their performance and productivity. Change causes consternation. Therefore, DAGS has committed to provide education on PIPS to its personnel and the construction industry since education can increase understanding and acceptance,

Some of the industry (designers, PWD project managers, and contractors who prefer the low bid award) involved with the delivery of construction have voiced opposition to PWD's use of PIPS. However, the customers (State of Hawaii Executive Branch Departments) have voiced tremendous appreciation of the quality work. Accordingly, PWD will continue to use PIPS as an alternative procurement method because PWD is a servicing agency to the customers. Customers dictate performance, not the components that deliver construction.

It is important to note the difference between a construction delivery system and a procurement selection process. PIPS is a selection process that is information based. It can be used with different delivery processes. Accordingly, it is recommended that:

1. PIPS be used to procure construction as an alternative delivery mechanism and not used to replace the low-bid process. Those who would rather participate in the low-bid system, should keep bidding on the low-bid projects (majority of projects.)
2. The PIPS modifications discussed in Part I be implemented to minimize large differentials in award price and increase the opportunity and distribution of work.
3. The performance delivered by the processes should be well documented in a timely manner.
4. State agencies should have the prerogative to select the PIPS selection process.
5. The PIPS modifications proposed in Part I be adopted, and analyzed after more procurements are run.

PART III – RESULTS AND DISCUSSIONS OF THE KPMG AUDIT

A. Audit Results

The audit performed by KPMG, LLP (KPMG) (Appendix D) produced the following results (Appendix E):

1. Low-bid project awards (construction) were consistently under the budgeted amounts.
2. PIPS project awards (construction), with the exception of air conditioning projects, were higher than budgeted figures.
3. PIPS projects had fewer change orders.
4. PIPS projects had fewer punch list items, which tended to be resolved by relevant deadlines.
5. PIPS projects were not as widely distributed as the low-bid projects.
6. PIPS projects resulted in a lower number of change orders.
7. There was no information on other delivery systems with regard to quality, timeliness, and distribution of work.

B. Discussion of Audit Results

A discussion of the KPMG audit results is provided in Appendix E.

APPENDIX C
ANALYSIS OF PIPS PROJECTS

APPENDIX C
ANALYSIS OF PIPS PROJECTS

Table C1: Analysis of All PIPS Mechanical Projects

MECHANICAL ANALYSIS	AVERAGE
Total Number of Projects Awarded	15
Overall Estimated Budget	$ 2,492,000
Total Overall Cost	$ 2,718,835
Percent +/- Overall Budget	8.3%
Number of Different Contractors Awarded Jobs	3
Projects That Were Awarded to Lowest Bidder	60%
Number of Project Completed On Time	100%
Number of Change Orders	0
Average Post Project Rating	9.8

Table C2: Analysis of All PIPS Painting Projects

PAINTING ANALYSIS	AVERAGE
Total Number of Projects Awarded	33
Overall Estimated Budget	$ 1,470,038
Total Overall Cost	$ 1,537,672
Percent +/- Overall Budget	4.4%
Number of Different Contractors Awarded Jobs	11
Projects That Were Awarded to Lowest Bidder	39%
Number of Project Completed On Time	100%
Number of Change Orders	0
Average Post Project Rating	9.7

Table C3: Analysis of All PIPS Roofing Projects

ROOFING ANALYSIS	AVERAGE
Total Number of Projects Awarded	100
Overall Estimated Budget	$ 8,816,252
Total Overall Cost	$ 9,174,684
Percent +/- Overall Budget (All Roofs)	+4.1 %
Percent +/- Overall Budget (78 Non Insulated Roofs Only)	-5.6 %
Number of Different Contractors Awarded Jobs	8
Projects That Were Awarded to Lowest Bidder	22%
Number of Project Completed On Time	98%
Number of Change Orders	0
Average Post Project Rating	9.6

APPENDIX E: DAGS ANALYSIS OF KPMG AUDIT RESULTS

1. The independent audit was performed by KPMG on a limited sample of projects completed between May 1, 1998 through June 30, 2002. The KPMG audit compared 50 projects from PIPS, and 50 projects from the low-bid process (roofing 34 each, painting 9 each, and mechanical 3 each, and repair 4 each.) DAGS' in-house staff reviewed the results of the audit and its limited sampling to verify the validity of the results by comparing it to data from the entire sample of PIPS projects (completed between May 1, 1998 through June 30, 2002).

2. The in-house staff review of the representative population samples of projects revealed the following:

3. The sample amounts of projects for the air conditioning and repair projects were insufficient (3 projects each and only 2 PIPS and 2 low bid projects had complete information on them).

4. The construction costs of the PIPS air conditioning projects were 2% higher than the low-bid projects, but required much less design effort (one designer did all ten PIPS projects.)

5. The PIPS Mechanical project results are listed in Table E1. The projects were professionally done, were well under the total budget, and were highly coordinated such that the facility users showered praise on the PIPS process. However, the mechanical contractors did not fully understand the process resulting in several contractors taking a "wait and see" attitude, which was the same problem in other areas that did not have a large sample of projects.

6. The low-bid repair projects were 17% below the budget, and the PIPS analysis included only two PIPS repair projects (only two projects had complete data) that were 7% over the budget (Table E2).

One of the PIPS repair projects in the sample had a high risk problem which the low-bid process would not have solved. This project began as a low-bid roofing job, but no bids were received. The project was reissued under PIPS, and through the cooperative partnering environment inherent in PIPS, PWD discovered that water infiltration problems far exceeded the scope of roofing work. The entire building envelope (roof, parapet and exterior walls) needed to be repaired and waterproofed in order to address all the leaks and provide full material and labor warranties. In addition, since the building was listed on the State Historic Register, many considerations had to be made to address the aesthetic value of the finished product. However, despite the complete change and growth in scope, all changes were not reflected in the "official" budget reported in the PWD database. This oversight alone skews the cost results for the overall sampling within this category.

The results of the painting projects are not comparable because there was only one low-bid Oahu project, which was actually a play court resurfacing and striping project (previously all the painting work on Oahu was done "in-house" by CSD due to the very poor and unacceptable performance of the low-bid awarded projects.)

It was not until PIPS was introduced, that CSD was persuaded to allow contractors to bid painting projects on Oahu. The PIPS results were surprising to CSD as the test included side-by-side comparisons of CSD work and the industry work.

7. The painting industry work was superior in prep work and detailing, and the industry contractors were fast, professional, and flexible in handling unforeseen problems. The results on the DAGS PIPS painting projects are included in Appendix E. The results of the University of Hawaii PIPS painting projects are included in Appendix L.

8. Conclusions on PIPS cannot be drawn from the mechanical, repair, or painting projects for the reasons mentioned above.

9. The roofing projects offer the best study of the performance of PIPS based on:
    a. Longevity of the program - 4 years
    b. Education of the industry
    c. Large number of PIPS and low-bid projects - 34 in the independent audit and 100 PIPS and low-bid projects over the last four years.

Accordingly, the analysis and conclusions on the performance of PIPS is based on the roofing projects, which has the largest sample of completed projects and whose participants have been involved with the program for the longest period of time.

Table E1: Analysis of PIPS vs. Low Bid Roofing Projects (from KPMG Audit)

	ROOFING	
	PIPS	**LOW BID**
Total Number of Projects	34	34
Average Contract Award	$ 108,484	$ 94,143
Average Budget	$ 101,387	$ 113,754
Percent Over Budget	7%	-17%
Average Number of Change Orders	0.2	0.7
Total Number of Change Orders	7	24
Average Cost of Change Order	$ 1,906	$ 2,308
Average Contract Duration	24	38
Average Actual Duration	22	36
Average Number of Punch List Items	0.6	2.3

Table E2: Analysis of PIPS vs. Low Bid AC, Painting, and Repair Projects (from KPMG Audit)

	AIR CONDITIONING		PAINTING		REPAIR	
	PIPS	**LOW BID**	**PIPS**	**LOW BID**	**PIPS**	**LOW BID**
Total Number of Projects	3	3	9	9	4	4
Average Contract Award	$ 200,573	$ 156,780	$ 85,772	$ 60,541	$ 92,261	$ 269,975
Average Budget	$ 228,650	$ 181,439	$ 71,600	$ 79,076	$ 86,000	$ 326,000
Percent Over Budget	-12%	-14%	20%	-23%	7%	-17%
Average Number of Change Orders	1.0	1.7	0.0	0.0	0.0	1.0
Total Number of Change Orders	3	5	0	0.0	0	4
Average Cost of Change Order	$ 7,973	$ 4,650	$ 0	0	$ 0	$ 1,061
Average Contract Duration	49	59	19	26	30	46
Average Actual Duration	49	60	16	26	48	46
Average Number of Punch List Items	5.0	17.7	1.2	1	1.3	6.0

APPENDIX F
ANALYSIS OF ROOFING PROGRAM

PIPS Roofing Conclusions

The following are conclusions based on the tables and discussions in this appendix:

1. 100% of DOE users surveyed would rather use the PIPS process over the low bid process (Table F6).
2. 100% of the users would use the PIPS contractor again (Table F6).
3. Performance rating by customers of PIPS vs. low-bid: 8.1 : 5.6 (Table F3)
4. PIPS average performance rating: 9.61 (9.86 when deleting the lowest performer)
5. PIPS cost is 6% under budget (after adjusting for insulated roofs) (Table E3).
6. There were 5 contractors that received 4 or more roofing jobs in the last four years using PIPS. This is similar to the low-bid process that resulted in 7 contractors that received 4 or more roofing jobs in the last four years (Table F2).
7. PIPS projects finished approximately 35% faster (Table D1).

Introduction

The roofing projects are the only sample large enough to be considered representative based on (the painting projects in the audit were not comparable because the majority of low-bid projects were on the outer islands.):

1. Education of contractors.
2. Time of program.
3. Number of projects.
4. Similarity of the projects (The majority of the projects on the same island Oahu).

Procured Performance

The PIPS purchased product was an ensured 10 – 25 year roof with an enforceable warranty. The low-bid awards resulted in a 2-year enforceable warranted roof. (After the 2-year period, DAGS/CS would repair the low-bid roofs due to the difficulty in getting the contractor and manufacturer to repair the roof.) The PIPS product is at least 5 times as valuable as the low-bid product when considering enforceable warranty period and customer satisfaction. Three types of surveys were done on the PIPS projects. An end of the project rating to upgrade their performance line, a survey asking the owners to compare PIPS vs low-bid, and a contractor generated form to ask customers how much they appreciated the PIPS procured contractor services. The following were the results:

1. The average post project rating on PIPS projects was 9.6.
2. PIPS contractors improved their performance numbers from 9.3 to 9.6. When one of the lower performing contractors is removed, the numbers went from 9.4 to 9.7.
3. 98% of the roofs were completed on time.

4. Comparing PIPS vs low-bid: On a scale of 1-10, 10 being the best, respondents rated PIPS 8.1 and rated low-bid 5.6 (Table F3)
5. DOE users who used PIPS said they would choose PIPS over low bid 100% of the time (Table F6).
6. PIPS contractors produced approximately two times as much work as low-bid contractors ($4.5K/day vs 2.5K/day: audit numbers).
7. Customers (DOE) were so happy with the PIPS projects, two schools threw a party and a luau for the contractor.
8. Over the four-year period of PIPS (2 years over the 2 year enforceable warranty period of the low-bid roofs), CS had not had to repair any roof leak.

Budgets

Budgets were analyzed based on available information. The result is that the budgets did not consider insulation since there was an average cost differential of $1.42. Based on this information, some of the budgets are inaccurate and are not a good comparison of PIPS vs the low bid. Of the 100 PIPS roofing projects:

1. 35 were over 20% of the budget.
2. Based on the insulation, 36 of the budgets were incorrect.
3. Deleting these projects, the awarded cost was 5.6% below the budget.

Accountability

When issues arose on roofs, the manufacturers and contractors took charge and solved the problem without technical expertise, management, or monitoring by the State. This happened at Ewa Beach Library roof and Pearl City Library roof.

At Ewa Beach Community School Library, the manufacturer sent sub-optimal material, and the contractor approached the State and informed them that he did not want to install the bad material in the best interest of the State. The contractor ordered new material, however, the construction schedule was affected because the construction was supposed to be done within the Christmas break of two weeks. After receiving a new shipment of material, the contractor worked on weekends and after-hours so they would not impede the operations at the school. The customer gave the contractor 10 ratings.

At Pearl City Public Library, the contractor removed the existing waterproofing membrane and found that none of the roof drains had collars. A quick call to suppliers revealed that the proper fasteners were not available in Hawaii. Accordingly, the contractor air shipped the proper fasteners and finished the roof before submitting a change order request. The contractor did not wait for the approval and execution of a change order, which would have delayed the project, because his primary concern was to complete the project on time. The contractor knew how critical the schedule to complete the work was for the DOE Library Services.

Table F1: Analysis of PWD Low-Bid Roofing Awards (1998-2001)

Contractor	1998	1999	2000	2001	2002	TOTAL
Contractor 1	1	14	2	2	0	19
Contractor 2	0	4	1	3	0	8
Contractor 3	0	4	3	0	0	7
Contractor 4	2	1	1	3	0	7
Contractor 5	0	4	2	0	1	7
Contractor 6	0	2	1	1	0	4
Contractor 7	0	2	1	1	0	4
Contractor 8	3	0	0	0	0	3
Contractor 9	1	0	2	0	0	3
Contractor 10	0	3	0	0	0	3
Contractor 11	0	2	1	0	0	3
Contractor 12	0	0	0	3	0	3
Contractor 13	0	0	0	2	0	2
Contractor 14	0	1	0	1	0	2
Contractor 15	0	0	2	0	0	2
Contractor 16	0	2	0	0	0	2
Contractor 17	0	0	1	0	0	1
Contractor 18	0	0	1	0	0	1
Contractor 19	0	0	0	1	0	1
Contractor 20	0	1	0	0	0	1
Contractor 21	0	1	0	0	0	1
Contractor 22	0	0	0	1	0	1
Contractor 23	0	1	0	0	0	1
Contractor 24	0	1	0	0	0	1
Contractor 25	0	1	0	0	0	1
Contractor 26	0	0	1	0	0	1
Contractor 27	0	0	1	0	0	1
Contractor 28	0	0	0	1	0	1
Contractor 29	0	1	0	0	0	1
Contractor 30	0	1	0	0	0	1
Contractor 31	0	1	0	0	0	1
Contractor 32	0	0	1	0	0	1
Contractor 33	1	0	0	0	0	1
	8	47	21	19	1	96

Table F2: Distribution of PWD Low-Bid Roofing Awards (1998-2001)

Number of Contractors that received 1 projects	17
Number of Contractors that received 2 projects	4
Number of Contractors that received 3 projects	5
Number of Contractors that received more than 4 projects	7

33

Table F3: Facility User Evaluation of PIPS (Based on 20 evaluations)[1]

NO	CRITERIA	AVERAGE*
1	Overall results of PIPS	8.11
2	Overall results of the Low-bid process	5.61
3	Ability of PIPS to encourage the industry to take responsibility for quality construction.	8.71
4	Ability of PIPS to allow the contractors to improve the quality of construction.	8.55
5	Ability of PIPS to allow PWD to be more effective in meeting user's construction needs.	8.47
6	Ability of PIPS to allow the contractors to provide a quality product.	8.22
7	Ability of PIPS to allow contractors to improve performance.	7.88
8	Facility users that would choose PIPS over Low-bid.	19 out of 20

* Based on a scale of 1-10, with 10 being the best.

Table F4: Contractor Evaluation of PIPS (Based on 6 evaluations)[2]

NO	CRITERIA	AVERAGE
1	Contractors that made a fair profit using PIPS.	6
2	Contractors that would participate with PIPS again.	6
3	Contractors that preferred PIPS over Low-bid.	6
4	Contractors that increased their performance under PIPS.	6
5	Contractors that reached a high level of performance using PIPS	6
6	Contractors that reached a high level of performance using Low-bid	0

Table F5: Inspector Evaluation of PIPS Projects (Based on 20 evaluations)[3]

NO	CRITERIA	YES	NO	NO RESPONSE
1	Have you been involved with PIPS?	17	3	0
2	Have you seen PIPS contractors work?	14	4	2
3	Was it better?	4	1	15
4	Were you satisfied with the work you saw?	17	0	3
5	Was it less of a hassle to get PIPS contractors to do what was supposed to be done (low-bid vs. PIPS jobs)?	18	0	2
6	Are PIPS contractors more willing to perform?	17	1	2
7	Is there a difference between the same contractor's performance on low-bid vs. PIPS jobs?	11	4	5
8	Is PIPS less work for staff?	18	1	1
9	If PIPS did save time, was there other work you could accomplish with the saved time?	12	0	8

[1] Kenny, 2001.
[2] Kenny, 2001.
[3] Kenny, 2001.

Table F6: Customer Evaluation (Based on 55 DOE projects done by 3 contractors)

NO	CRITERIA	AVERAGE
1	Jobs started on time	53
2	Jobs completed on time	49
3	Contractor was responsive before the job	55
4	Contractor was responsive during the job	53
5	Job sites that were kept clean	53
6	All the work specified was completed	55
7	Contractor did everything they agreed to do	55
8	Clients that were pleased with the quality of work	53
9	Contractors workers were courteous	53
10	Contractors workers were professional	53
11	Customers that would consider using the contractor again	55
12a	Customers that thought the contractors performance was poor	0
12c	Customers that thought the contractors performance was excellent	55
13	Customers that prefer PIPS over the Low Bid System	55

Table F7: PIPS Roofing Results Based on Square Feet

	Overall	<5000	5001-10000	10001-15000	15001-20000	20001-25000	>25001
Total Number of Roofs	96	10	40	24	7	8	7
Total Area (SF)	1,135,025	34,386	311,259	277,396	121,685	176,800	213,499
Total Award ($)	$8,899,766	$343,912	$2,800,363	$2,332,235	$799,159	$1,152,048	$1,472,049
Estimated Budget ($)	$8,360,252	$344,742	$2,653,620	$2,246,900	$749,010	$1,138,990	$1,226,990
Award ($/SF)	$7.84	$10.00	$9.00	$8.41	$6.57	$6.52	$6.89
Budget ($/SF)	$7.37	$10.03	$8.53	$8.10	$6.16	$6.44	$5.75

Table F8: PIPS Roofing Comparison of Insulated vs. Non Insulated Roofs

	Overall	<5000	5001-10000	10001-15000	15001-20000	20001-25000	>25001
Number of Non-Insulated Roofs	60	6	27	16	2	5	4
Number of Insulated Roofs	36	4	13	8	5	3	3
$/SF of Non-Insulated Roofs (Budget)	$7.16	$9.84	$8.09	$7.94	$3.69	$5.78	$6.21
$/SF of Non-Insulated Roofs (Award)	$6.99	$9.31	$8.05	$7.65	$3.08	$6.00	$5.82
$/SF of Insulated Roofs (Budget)	$7.67	$10.22	$9.46	$8.42	$7.18	$7.48	$5.16
$/SF of Insulated Roofs (Award)	$9.09	$10.73	$11.04	$9.89	$8.02	$7.31	$8.25
Difference in Budgets	$0.51	$0.39	$1.37	$0.49	$3.49	$1.71	-$1.05
Difference in Awards	$2.10	$1.42	$2.98	$2.25	$4.95	$1.31	$2.43

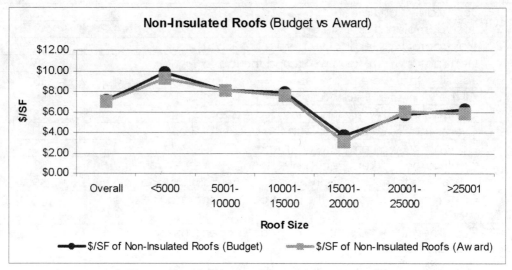

Figure F1: Analysis of Non Insulated Roofs

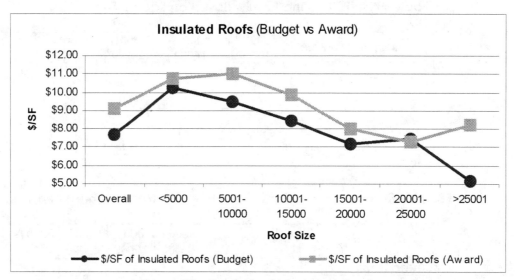

Figure F2: Analysis of Insulated Roofs

APPENDIX G
ECONOMIC ANALYSIS OF PIPS vs. DESIGN-BID-BUILD DELIVERY SYSTEM

TABLE G1: Comparison of Delivery Costs for Roofing Construction

NO	ITEM	PIPS	LB
1	Design Cost (percent of project cost)	2.50%	11.00%
2	Project Management Costs (percent of project costs)	0.39%	1.86%
3	Construction Costs (percent under budget)	-5.6%	-13.0%
4	Cost of Quality	0.00%	0.50%

Total Costs	-2.71%	0.36%
Savings due to PIPS process	3.07%	

Sources:
  Design Costs: PWD
  PM Costs: See Table G2
  Construction Costs: See Table G3
  Cost of Quality: conservative estimate based on failed
  projects, total amount of construction and 80/20 rule

TABLE G2: Identification of Project Manager Costs

Year	Project Expenditures	Payroll Expenditures	Overhead Costs
1999	$181,994,317	$6,488,038	3.56%
2000	$189,735,430	$6,089,599	3.21%
2001	$187,221,387	$6,071,320	3.24%
2002	$195,021,532	$5,172,543	2.65%

Amount of work saved by PIPS (.0265* .7*.8)   1.49%
  (80% of construction management and 70% of total delivery cost)

Amount of work done by PIPS   1.17%
  (normal amount of work (.0265) - work saved (.0149)

Work accomplished by PIPS project manager is 3
times higher   **0.39%**
  (divide cost of PIPS by 3)

TABLE G3: Construction Costs

COSTS	PIPS	LB
Audit report	7.0%	-13.0%
Audit projects (in-house analysis of numbers)	7.0%	-17.2%
Audit projects (minus 3 projects listed on page 3)	7.0%	-8.4%
Audit projects (minus 10 insulated roofs)		-2.3%
All PIPS roofing projects	4.1%	
All PIPS projects (minus 36 insulated projects)	-5.6%	

APPENDIX L
CASE STUDIES

University of Hawaii PIPS Case Study

The University of Hawaii implemented the PIPS process on over 35 projects. An analysis of these projects shows that they came in 14% under budget, and 100% (of the complete projects) have finished on time and within the award cost (Table L1).

The following is taken from a document issued by Charlie Serikawa (the University of Hawaii PIPS administrator):

"I'd like to take this opportunity to express my thanks for introducing and educating me in the use of the Performance Information Procurement System (PIPS). In all my years of construction experience, both in the private and the public sector, I have never been more impressed with a procurement process such as the process provided by PIPS. The system promotes a partnering "win-win" scenario between the owner and the contractor that require minimum project management resulting in "on time", "on budget" and "outstanding quality construction". It reduces procurement time, it reduces risk to the owner and consultants, and it recognizes who the experts in construction are and allows the contractors to perform to the best of their abilities. It is a system founded on the basic human principles of honesty, trust and integrity.

I must admit that when I was asked to head the implementation of the PIPS Program at the University of Hawaii, I was very skeptical and believed that this type of procurement system would not work in a public institution. Fortunately, I was wrong. After attending several seminars three features of the system stood out in my mind — the system transfers the risks of construction from the owner to the contractor by relying on the contractor's construction expertise (minimizes control by the owner/consultant), the system has a self-policing effect (post performance rating that affect the contractor's future chances to obtain more work) and the system provides a "best value" product. In addition, the process, via artificial intelligence uses information (past performance, management plan, interview, and price) to select the contractor in lieu of using price as the only criteria. By using this method of selection, the owner greatly reduces his risk and has a reasonable chance of predicting the outcome of the project. The selection process virtually eliminates any construction surprises, namely contractor generated change orders.

At the University of Hawaii sixteen projects have been awarded using this process (one re-flooring of two Gyms; four re-roofing; and eleven exterior painting of buildings on campus). All but two have been completed with outstanding results. The University has experienced no significant increase in job cost; in fact, all but five projects were awarded at costs well below the respective estimated project budgets. Consequently the cumulative cost of all the projects was well within the total budget for all the projects. More importantly, there were no contractor generated change orders, all jobs were completed on or before contract completion date and quality was never compromised. I believe this process has brought back the "pride in construction" as evidenced when I observed that the contractors constantly strived to improve — scheduling, workmanship, communications, and cooperation. From this experience I have concluded that this process results in a quality product without any cost increase. A definite owner-contractor "win-win" scenario

PIPS is the only procurement process in existence today that when used by a Public Agency, provides that agency with a certain confidence that the services procured will be completed in accordance to the requirements set forth. The PIPS process is fair, equitable and appeals to a contractor who understands his responsibilities and obligations." - Charles Y. Serikawa, PIPS Program Administrator - University of Hawaii at Manoa

STATE OF HAWAII CASE STUDY

TABLE L1: Overall Results of the University of Hawaii PIPS Implementation

CRITERIA	OVERALL RESULTS
Total Number of Projects Procured	35
Overall Estimated Budget	$ 7,061,500
Total Award Cost	$ 6,085,787
Percent Over/Under Budget	-14%
Percent of Jobs Completed Within Awarded Cost	100%
Percent of Jobs Completed On Time	100%
Average Post Project Rating	9.8

TABLE L2: Results of the University of Hawaii PIPS Painting Projects

CRITERIA	PAINTING AVERAGE
Total Number of Projects Completed	9
Overall Estimated Budget	$ 2,310,000
Total Award Cost	$ 1,658,192
Percent Over/Under Budget	-28%
Total Size (SF)	991,221
Number of Different Contractors Awarded Jobs	6
Projects That Were Awarded to Top Prioritized Contractor	8
Projects That Were Awarded to Lowest Bidder	8
Percent of Jobs Completed Within Budget	100%
Percent of Jobs Completed On Time	100%
Percent of Jobs Completed Ahead Of Time	89%
Percent of Projects Where Contractor Performed Additional Work at No Charge	56%
Average Post Project Rating	9.8

Waterproofing the Courthouse Projects

The projects were:
1. Kauikeaouli Hale - waterproofing of the walking deck, roof sections, and parapet walls; and miscellaneous interior repairs
2. Kapuaiwa Building – waterproofing exterior walls and parapet/balusters, reroof, and repair interior water-damaged walls.

The understanding of the bidding contractors was clear. The projects were risky, if you cannot deliver, the contractor and manufacturer would be saddled with the risk. Both projects had leaking problems in different parts of the facility, and the user requested the leaking be fixed. Both courthouses were also aged, making the waterproofing prep work more difficult. PWD required the manufacturers to warranty the work. PWD received joint and several warranties from the contractor and manufacturer on both projects. The original budgets were set without a clear understanding of the scope of work. The same contractor who won these contracts, was called by the State of Hawaii to repair the State Capitol roof, after reroofing had failed to fix the leaking. The same contractor was called to the Kalanimoku building to also repair the leaks after the low-bid award contractor could not fix the leaking as specified and directed by the owner. This waterproofing contractor has also had a high performance track record of waterproofing FAA facilities that were leaking.

APPENDIX N
LETTERS OF SUPPORT

The following are comments from various DOE end users of PIPS roofing projects:

1. *"I highly recommend this company. Their job performance was more than sufficient. The crew were hard working men, very professional quality work. They started getting things moving as soon as they arrived, stayed after their time to make sure things were safe before leaving. This company (Tory's Roofing) is the best that I've seen that does terrific work. Having the PIPS Program is the best thing that ever happened. This was my second time that I had this company provide us with their quality work. Because I was very pleased we made a luaus for them. Thank you." Gail Greene, Custodian III - Kahaluu Elementary School – Building C Reroof*

2. *"Commendable job. Hard working and committed to providing quality construction needed for roofing projects. Project supervisor kept abreast with every detail. PIPS provided the opportunity for this quality roofing company to be offered the job." Helene Tom, Principal - Kahaluu Elementary School – Building C Reroof*

3. *"Communication and quality of workmanship was exemplary. Job started on time and ended well before timeline. Crew was polite, courteous and kept office staff informed on a daily basis, reviewing work details and timelines. Work areas were clean, classrooms were well respected and kept in good condition, and several areas were redesigned for our benefit (re-positioning of solar panels off the roof-tops and on separate support beams). After the job, the areas were remediated, and returned to their original condition. Overall performance was excellent...During the same time, two other "non performance based" jobs were being started. Once job finished later, and the second is yet to be completed. Neither "non performance based" project had the complexity of this re-roofing project.." David Hanaike (Vice Principal) - Nuuanu Elementary School – Buildings C, G & H Reroof*

4. *"All schools need the PIPS program because it helps the school and the contractor with quality of work. Also, low bid on our football field is still a nightmare." Willard Gouveia, Head Custodian - Roosevelt High School – Building G Reroof*

5. *"I prefer the PIPS program. Contractors do excellent and professional job. Low bid with only one-year warranty is not worth the time. There was an incident in 2001, roofing company cam and did not repair any vents. It sill leaks." Theola DeCosta - Laie Elementary School – Building B Reroof*

6. *"I prefer the PIPS program because it makes companies do better work and are more pleasant to work with. Contractor was very nice and kept area clean. Kept all equipment*

covered to avoid damage. They also were willing to do repairs and replace grass."
Daryllynn Jaralloa (Head Custodian) - Kalihi Uka Elementary School – Buildings B Reroof

7. *"I would prefer PIPS over Low Bid. Adjustments to work order were easier. Low bid contractor looked for the shorted path, not necessarily what is best for the school." Bruce Naguwa (Principal) - Kipapa Elementary School – Buildings I Reroof*

8. *"Responsive to our need to have job completed on time. PIPS results in providing superior product and service at a fair cost. Low bid process may save money in short term but may not have provided reliable service, on time completion and quality product." J. Vannatta VP - Highlands Intermediate School – Buildings I Reroof*

9. *"Prefer PIPS program over low bid system because of a better quality and has a better warranty." Alex Ubiadas, Head Custodian - Jefferson Elem school – Reroof buildings C & M*

10. *"They informed the office each day of their plan for the following day. Before leaving the work site each day, they cleaned thoroughly." They were so professional and their work was excellent. Charlotte White, Principal - Kahaluu Elementary, Building B - Reroof*

11. *"I really appreciate the PIPS program over the low bid system, working with the contractor to provide the best service possible, was a gratifying experience. We were able to work out problems on the spot and make adjustments where needed. When we needed an answer to a problem, the contractor worked with the school to come up with the best results. The conversation went two ways not the contractor making all the decisions." Bruce Naguwa, Principal - Kipapa Elementary, Building K - Reroof*

Attachment 21.2: DAGS Administrative Hearings Report

OFFICE OF ADMINISTRATIVE HEARINGS
DEPARTMENT OF COMMERCE AND CONSUMER AFFAIRS
STATE OF HAWAII

In the Matter of HI-TEC ROOFING SERVICES, INC., vs. DEPARTMENT OF ACCOUNTING AND GENERAL SERVICES, STATE OF HAWAII, Respondent.	PCH 2002-1 Petitioner, HEARINGS OFFICER'S FINDINGS OF FACT, CONCLUSIONS OF LAW, AND DECISION

HEARINGS OFFICER'S FINDINGS OF FACT,
CONCLUSIONS OF LAW, AND DECISION

I.   INTRODUCTION

On January 30, 2002, Hi-Tec Roofing Services, Inc. (Petitioner) filed a Request for Hearing to contest the January 23, 2002, denial of five protests which it had filed with the State Procurement Office and the Department of Accounting and General Services (Respondent). On February 1, 2002, a Notice of Hearing and Prehearing Conference was filed by the Office of Administrative Hearings, Department of Commerce and Consumer Affairs. The prehearing conference was set for February 8, 2002, and the Hearing was set for February 14, 2002.

On February 8, 2002, the Respondent filed a response to the petition and the prehearing conference was also held on that date, with the Petitioner represented by Matt A. Tsukazaki, Esq. and with the Respondent represented by Patricia T. Ohara, Esq. It was somewhat helpful in promoting an exchange of information, and discussing procedural issues - particularly as to the

Petitioner's need to obtain further documentation relating to the allegations in the petition. At that time it was agreed that the hearing would commence as scheduled on February 14, 2002, but its initial focus would be on the production of documents pursuant to various subpoenas issued on behalf of the Petitioner.

On February 11, 2002, the Respondent filed a motion for a protective order to quash the subpoenas, and that motion was heard on February 14, 2002. The motion was granted in part and denied in part, and thereafter the hearing was set to continue on February 26, 2002. However, since the production of documents was not fully resolved at the time of the February 28, 2002 proceedings7 an order was issued on that date regarding further proceedings (including the production of documents and the filing of exhibits), and a new date of April 9, 2002, was set for a continuation of the hearing.

On April 4, 2002, the Respondent filed a Motion to Dismiss, and on April 8, 2002, the Petitioner filed a memorandum in opposition to that motion, On April 9, 2002, the hearing resumed4 with consideration first being given to the Respondent's Motion to Dismiss. The motion was denied on the basis that there appeared to be material, factual questions that precluded summary disposition of the matter at that time. The substantive hearing then proceeded with respect to the allegations in the petition, and continued on April 10-12, 17-19, 23, 24, 26, and 30, 2002, as welt as on May 1, 3, 7-9, 14-16, and 22, 2002.1 Throughout the parties' presentations on each of those dates Mr. Isukazaki continued to represent the Petitioner and Ms. Ohara continued to represent the Respondent.

At the close of the Petitioners case in chief the Respondent made an oral motion for a directed verdict on substantially the same grounds upon which it had earlier presented its motion to dismiss the proceedings. The motion was denied on the basis that there still appeared to be material, factual questions that precluded summary disposition of the matter. The Respondent then proceeded to present its case in chief, which was followed by a short rebuttal by the Petitioner. At the conclusion of the hearing the parties made their closing arguments and the matter was taken under consideration.

The undersigned Hearings Officer, having considered the evidence and arguments presented during the course of the hearing in light of the entire record in this matter, hereby renders the following findings of fact, conclusions on law, and decision. The findings of fact have been presented in a generally chronological format, while the conclusions of law have been presented in a more topical sequence. It should also be noted that even though the focus of the hearing was on the Petitioners allegations about specific projects, it became obvious that any effort to understand them would require addressing limited elements of the Respondent's unique procurement program with which the projects were inextricably linked. At the same time, numerous portions of the Petitioners presentation were oriented toward a general critique of the Respondent's procurement program. While they were of peripheral relevance and perhaps worthy of consideration in other forums — they had only limited applicability in this case, or were oriented toward details which, while supportive of larger factual determinations, did not warrant repetition herein.

II. FINDINGS OF FACT

---

4 The extended length of, and frequent divergences in, the presentation of this case appear to be due in large part to the absence of provisions in the Hawaii Public Procurement code and/or In its regulations providing for mandatory discovery procedures to be used by parties *prior* lo a hearing. The lack of such prehearing mechanisms for expediting what is fundamentally a jury-waived civil trial constitutes a significant procedural deficiency that adversely affects all participants and warrants a modification of the existing law in this respect.

The Requests for Proposals and the Protests

1. During the month of September 2001 the Respondent, by its chief procurement officer, issued 3 separate Requests for Proposals (RFPs) for design and build reroofing projects covering maintenance and repair work to be performed at:

   a) The Honolulu and Windward School Districts - Aikahi Elementary School, Kalaheo High School, and Kuhio Elementary School, (advertised September 26, 2001),
   b) The Department of Health - Kinau Hale (advertised October 8, 2001), and
   c) The Central School District - Wahiawa Elementary School (advertised November14, 2001).

2. By a letter dated October 2, 2001, the Petitioner, by its attorney, submitted a protest regarding the RFP for Aikahi Elementary School, Kalaheo High School, and Kuhio Elementary School to the Respondent. By a similar letter dated October 12, 2001, the Petitioner also submitted a protest regarding the RFP for Kinau Hale to the Respondent.

3. During the month of October 2001 the Respondent, by its chief procurement officer, issued two separate RFPs for design and build reroofing projects covering maintenance and repair work to be performed at:

   a) the Department of Agriculture and Conservation's Buildings C & D (advertised November 2, 2001), and
   b) the Leeward, Central and Honolulu School Districts —Nanakuli High/Intermediate School, Aiea Intermediate School, Kipapa Elementary School, and Lincoln Elementary School (advertised October 16, 2001)

4. By a letter dated October 22, 2001, the Petitioner, by its attorney, submitted a protest regarding the RFP for Nanakuli High/Intermediate School, Aiea Intermediate School, Kipapa Elementary School, and Lincoln Elementary School to the Respondent. Except for its date, however, the first page of this October 22, 2001, letter was exactly the same as the first page of the Petitioners October 2, 2001 letter. Furthermore, this October 22, 2001, letter stated that it was "a protest of the three procurements" and its list of them began with the names of the same three procurements that it had protested in the October 2, 2001, letter. Only by an examination of the continuation of the list (on the second page) would the addition of four more procurements become apparent and would the contextual difference between these two superficially similar letters become distinguished.

5. On October 30, 2001, the Petitioners attorney sent a follow-up letter to the Respondent noting that it had not received any reply to its letter of October 2, 2001, protesting the Aikahi, Kalaheo, and Kuhio projects, and requesting information on the status of those projects. The Respondent, however, did not reply to this request.

6. By a letter dated November 7, 2001, the Petitioner, by its attorney, submitted a protest regarding the RFP for the Department of Agriculture and Conservation's Buildings C & D. By a similar letter dated November 19, 2001, the Petitioner also submitted a protest regarding the RFP for the Wahiawa Elementary School.

7. On November 7, 2001, the Petitioner's attorney also sent two follow-up letters to the Respondent noting that it had not received any reply to its letters of October 12, 2001, *and* October 22, 2001, protesting the Kinau Hale, Aikahi, Kalaheo, Kuhio, Nanakuli, Aiea, Kipapa,

and Lincoln projects. The Respondent, however, did not reply to these letters.[5]

8. Each of the Petitioners five protest Fetters were routed by the Respondent through its. Public Works Division Administrator who perfunctorily forwarded them to the Chief of its Staff Services Branch for attention and the preparation of a reply. Each of the Petitioner's protest Fetters had concluded with the following one sentence paragraph:

   As you know, Haw. Rev. Stat. Section 1030-701 and Haw. Admin. Rules Section 3-126-5 prohibit taking any further action on the solicitation or award of the contracts until this timely protest has been settled.

9. Approximately 16 weeks after the Petitioner's first protest and 10 weeks after its last protest, the Respondent replied to all five protests by a single letter dated January 23, 2002.[6] The Respondents letter stated that "DAGS initially concluded that all of these protests should be denied because they are untimely under Hawaii Revised Statutes § 103D-701 (a), ... and so would be denied.

   However, notwithstanding the initial decision to deny the protests, upon consideration of the entire circumstances surrounding this matter, DAGS has concluded that it will be canceling all of the above-captioned projects, because to do so would be in the best interests of the State. Therefore, we consider these protests to now be moot, and the issues contained in the protests will not be addressed.

10. By a reply letter dated January 25, 2002, the Petitioner contested the Respondent's initial conclusion that the protests should be denied as untimely, and asked for the basis of the Respondent's anticipated cancellation of the protested projects. The Petitioners letter also reiterated a demand that the Respondent correct purported errors in its performance rating.

11. By a second letter dated January 28, 2002, the Petitioner stated that it had learned that the Respondent had allowed certain of the reroofing projects under protest to go forward after it had received the protests, despite their supposedly having been stayed by the protests. The letter sought an explanation of how this was allowed to happen, raised allegations of procurement fraud, and asked that the appropriate authorities be informed of the situation.

12. On January 30, 2002, the Petitioner filed a Request for Nearing with the Department of Commerce and Consumer Affairs asserting that the Petitioner was aggrieved by the Respondent's January 23, 2002, letter "denying the October 2, 12, 22, November 7, and 19, 20011 Notices of Protestor The Request for Hearing also stated that "The protests were based on DAGS' failure to correct Protestor's performance ratings, which it learned about within a 5-day period before the filing of the initial October 2, 2001, protest."

The Development of the PIPS — RFP Approach

---

[5] Unfortunately, neither the code nor its regulations specify any time limitations within which a government agency must provide a response to a person's protest, or even provide an acknowledgment that the protest has been received and that the effected project has been stayed.

[6] This letter has been referred to, and treated, by the parties as constituting the Respondent's 'denial" of the Petitioner's protests despite its actual language being less than specific on this point. After setting out an opinion that the protests should be denied (future tense) it went on to state, however, that the projects would be cancelled (future tense again) and as a result concluded that the protests need not be further addressed.

13. The RFPs for each of the projects protested by the Petitioner were issued by the Respondent under a Performance Information Procurement System (PIPS) program that had recently been adopted by the Respondent The PIPS program was a proprietary, research based initiative centered on an information measurement and management theory developed by Arizona State University (ASU) under the auspices of Dean Kashiwagi, Director, Performance Based Studies Research Group, at the College of Engineering and Applied Sciences.

14. In early 1998 Gordon Matsuoka, the Respondent's Public Works Division Administrator, and Stephen Miwa, the Chief of the Staff Services Branch for the Public Works Division, attended a PIPS orientation presented by! Mr. Kashiwagi at Honolulu International Airport. Shortly thereafter, Mr. Matsuoka unilaterally decided that the Respondent would adopt the PIPS program for certain types of public works projects and instructed Mr. Miwa to gather additional information about it.

15. The Respondent's rationale for adopting PIPS as an alternative to the low-bid system was to better define the responsibility of contractors and manufacturers on projects by requiring them to "partner' on the submission of proposals. Although only contractors actually submitted proposals, a key element in the PIPS program was the requirement that the contractors - and the manufacturers whose products they intended to use - obtain a "performance rating" in order for the contractors to participate in the competition for projects. The performance ratings also became critical factors in the subsequent evaluation of any proposals that contractors submitted in response to an RFP.

16. In May of 1998 Mr. Matsuoka arid Mr. Miwa received individualized explanations of the PIPS program from Mr. Kashiwagi at the Department of Accounting and General Services ("DAGS") building in Honolulu. At about the same time, the Respondent contacted various entities within the roofing industry to discuss the PIPS program, and held a meeting with them to get early feedback on initiating such a program. The Respondent also reached an informal, cooperative understanding with Mr. Kashiwagi whereby his group at ASU would (without a contract or compensation) help gather and compile data on contractors and manufacturers in order to establish their performance ratings.

17. In late 1998, without any written analysis/determination of replacing the existing low-bid system with the proposed PIPS program, Mr. Matsuoka decided to implement PIPS on an ad hoc basis for a limited number of RFPs for design and build reroofing projects. This was done with the knowledge and cooperation of Mr. Kashiwagi, but without any contractual agreement with ASU permitting the Respondent to use the program. The implementation involved gathering and using contractors' and manufacturers' performance ratings in ranking the proposals that contractors submitted for specific projects.

18. The intention of the Respondent was to reevaluate contractors' and manufacturers' performance ratings on a regular basis by including updated evaluations of their performance on subsequent public works projects. The base rating was to be weighted at 75% and the subsequent rating was to be weighted at 25% to obtain the new rating. The reevaluations were done by the Respondent on a "time-available" basis, however, and were not always available for application to outstanding RFPs.

19. The initial compilation of performance ratings began with a request to contractors and manufacturers for a self-selected listing of their past jobs (public or private) as a basis for gathering data about their performance. This was followed by an inspection and/or written inquiries about topics such as the quality of their work and the merit of their warranties. No written guidelines were used in performing evaluations, but as a general rule graders were

instructed that projects which came in on time, on budget, and met owner expectations should be rated at 10, while those that did not should receive lower ratings.

20. The overall collection of data and the calculation of performance ratings were initially performed for the Respondent by Mr. Kashiwagi's group at ASU. In late 1999 or early 2000, however, the Respondent assumed these functions for rating roofing contractors and manufacturers after receiving complaints focusing on conflict of interest and manipulation of figures. The collection of data and the calculation of performance ratings for other types of public works projects such as general engineering or construction, painting, and electrical remained with Mr. Kashiwagi's group at ASU.

21. The contractor performance ratings consisted of multiple categories within three main sections: the application profile, the performance profile, and the customer evaluation profile. Each of these sections contained between 9 and 17 categories designed to reflect objective and subjective data for rating the contractor. Not all categories were rated on a scale of ten - many required input requiring other entries (e.g. the amount of square footage installed, the types of decking involved, the percentage of leaks, and the number of days to respond to emergencies). In some cases, however, raters did not provide ratings for certain categories, and in other cases their entries appeared to be inconsistent with the underlying factual data.

22. In or about mid-2000 the Respondent adopted a "15% Rule" as a result of criticism from certain contractors who felt that raters might be expressing an unfavorable bias in their ratings. This rule was supposed to be applied by combining all scores for a category except for the lowest one, calculating the average for the remaining scores, and determining whether the lowest score was within 15% of that average. Then, the lowest score was disregarded if it was not within 15% of the average, or else it was included with the other scores and a new average was calculated. This rule, however, was not applied consistently which caused mathematical errors in various ratings - and these errors were frequently compounded by subsequent calculations.

The Formalization and Application of PIPS

23. On October 26, 2000, the Respondent executed a non-transferable, non-exclusive, three-year contract with ASU (in the form of a licensing agreement) that provided the Respondent with the right to use the PIPS program in return for annual payments of $25,000. Also, at or about the same time, the Respondent negotiated a related contract with ASU (in the form of services/training agreement) for an annual term in return for a payment of $75,000. Neither agreement provided any express or implied warranty by ASU on any matter regarding the PIPS program or its fitness for any particular purpose.

24. At or about this same time the Respondent established a small working group within DADS to coordinate the administration of the PIPS program and to report directly to Mr. Matsuoka. This group consisted of Mr. Miwa as PIPS Administrator, Christine Kinimaka as PIPS Manager, and Gaylyn Nakatsuka as PIFS Projects Coordinator.[7] The PIPS group monitored the program's projects from start to finish - both within DADS (where multiple branches could be involved at different stages of the program) and as a liaison between DAGS and outside participants.

25. Although Mr. Miwa was the titular head of the PIPS group, and although the members were located in separate offices within the DAGS building, direct communication and interaction

---

[7] At a considerably later date David Dupont was added to this group as a staff assistant for data management.

took place between all members on, a frequent and relatively unstructured basis. One or more members would usually meet daily to discuss the' status of projects, protests, and similar events. This, team approach with a flat organizational setup existed because each member tended to have specialized functions, with no single member having a complete knowledge of .the total PIPS program. This interactive team approach also extended, to a lesser degree, to the members' contacts with Mr. Matsuoka.

The Suspended RFPs for Protested Projects

26. The September 2001 RFPs for reroofing projects at Aikahi Elementary School, Kalaheo High School, Kuhio Elementary School, the Department of Health's Kinau Hale, and Wahiawa Elementary School, as well as the October 2001 RFP for reroofing at the Department of Agriculture and Conservation's Buildings C & D were, for the most part, suspended shortly after the Respondent received the Petitioner's protests of these projects. The Respondent subsequently treated these RFPs/projects as at least being postponed if not cancelled.

27. On October 9, 2001, the Respondent (through its retained architectural consultant) issued a notice that, as a result of the protests, the pre-proposal walk-throughs at Aikahi, Kalaheo, and Kuhio schools that had been set earlier in the year for October 10, 2001, were cancelled.

28. On October 19, 2001, the Respondent issued Addendum No. 1 to the RFP for the Department of Health's Kinau Hale stating that the project had been postponed until further notice.

29. On October 24, 2001, the Respondent issued Addendum No. 1 (dated October 19, 2001) to the RFP for the Aikahi Elementary School, Kalaheo High School, and Kuhio Elementary School projects, stating that the projects had been postponed until further notice.

30. On November 23, 2001, the Respondent issued Addendum No. I to the RFP for the Department of Agriculture and Conservation's Buildings C & D stating that the project had been postponed and that the scheduled submittal of proposals had been cancelled. On this same date the Respondent also issued a similar addendum to the RFP for the Wahiawa Elementary School project.

The RFP for Nanakuli, Aiea, Kipapa & Lincoln

31. Although the October 2001 REP for reroofing projects at the Nanakuli, Aiea, Kipapa, and Lincoln schools were also PIPS design and build projects, they progressed in a markedly different manner from the other protested projects. Therefore, in examining them it is worth noting that the REP included language that:

The projects will be awarded and done using the Performance Information Procurement System (PIPS) technology developed by Arizona State University. Under this method, the bidder will propose which roofing or waterproofing system or systems it will use, unless specifically restricted in the Project Scope, and guarantee the performance of the system or systems for a stated warranty period during which it will make all necessary repairs and touch-ups. The Criteria Weighting is included in the Proposal as "Appendix B" of the Proposal.

32. The REP's "Appendix 6" entitled Weighting Criteria consisted of three sections designated as Overall Criteria, Roofing Contractor Criteria, and Roofing/Waterproofing Manufacturer

Criteria. The weighting criteria were selected by an informally appointed evaluation committee drawn from DADS, the user agency, and consultants that assembled the criteria. Each section of the Weighting Criteria had multiple subcategories with weights ranging from 0 to 10,000 - although the measured units consisted of different elements (e.g. %, sq. ft., years, points, #s, days, and scales). The two subcategory criteria with the greatest assigned weights were 1) the roofing manufacturer warranty period, and 2) the contractor's management plan - both of which, had a weight of 10,000.[8]

33. The RFP required that contractors intending to submit proposals had previously registered for, and attended, a PIPS registry meeting and a PIPS training session; had provided the Respondent with performance information for evaluative purposes; and had attended the mandatory pre-bid meeting and the site walk-through scheduled for October 26, 2001. The RFP also required that sealed proposals were to be submitted not later than 2:00 p.m. on November 20, 2001, and contractors were allowed to submit one or more alternative proposals for each project by separate Supplemental Proposal Forms.

34. At or about the time the Respondent received the Petitioner's October 22, 2001, letter protesting the RFP for these four projects it was routinely routed through Mr. Matsuoka to Mr. Miwa. Normally, Mr. Miwa would have then forwarded it to Ms. Kinimaka who would have made a copy for Ms. Nakatsuka. Either Mr. Miwa or Ms. Kinimaka would have then reminded Ms. Nakatsuka to stop all work on the project. The standard PIPS practice also included discussing the status of such matters with Mr. Matsucka and the Respondent's assigned Deputy Attorney General in preparation for drafting a reply. In light of the confusing similarity of the October 2, 2001, and October 22, 2001, protest letters, however, Mr. Miwa failed to recognize the October 22, 2001, letter as a separate protest and did not forward it to Ms. Kinimaka for normal handling.

35. The Respondent did understand that an appropriate response to any protest included stopping further work on the protested project, unless the chief procurement officer (i.e. the DAGS' Comptroller) made a written determination that proceeding was necessary to protect substantial State interests and that all parties involved in the RFP process were to be notified of the stay. The chief procurement officer did not make any such written determination at anytime, but on Friday, October 26, 2001, the Respondent held a pre-bid meeting and conducted an on-site walk through with the contractors that were considering submitting proposals for the four projects.

36. Then, on November 9, 2001, the Respondent continued post-protest activities by issuing an Addendum No. 1 to the existing RFP that modified the "Description of Work", and on or about November 20, 2001, the Respondent accepted and began tabulating the proposals and. supplemental proposals that had been submitted by contractors seeking awards. At this point it appeared that Mr. Miwa was still under the impression that the Petitioner's October 22. 2001 letter did not reflect a separate protest from the Petitioner's October 2, 2001 letter and thus had failed to separately address its contents, to forward it to Ms. Kinimaka for appropriate action, or to inform Mr. Matsuoka that it required his attention.

37. In late November and December of 2001 the Respondent's review of the proposals involved stripping the contractors' management plans from their proposals for separate review by the evaluation committee. The overall assessment included making (sometimes incorrect) determinations on whether warranties contained exclusions for which deductions

---

[8] Six of the other 74 subcategory criteria had an assigned weight of 5,000, and each of the remaining subcategory criteria had weights of 2,000 or less.

were required by the RFP. The overall assessment also focused on the subjective breakdown between performance and price factors, as well as on input data for the "model (displaced ideal) formula" (relative distance x information factor x weight factor = minimum distance) seemingly familiar only to Ms. Kinimaka (who inputted the data) and understood only by Mr. Kashiwagi (who originated the mathematics).

38. Nevertheless, the data and calculations that were used in the overall evaluative steps for the assessment of each of these four projects did not reflect any errors in the Petitioner's own performance rating nor any other errors that were significant enough to have changed the ranking of the contractors that submitted proposals.[9] Ms. Kinimaka did meet with Alan Meier, the Petitioner's President/Secretary on multiple occasions to address his general concerns about the PIPS program, but the Petitioners questions were not specifically about errors in, or corrections to, its performance line.

39. The Respondent's "Method of Award" involved examining the three top rated proposals for each project - without regard to price - to see if the top rated proposal was within budget The contractor submitting the proposal was then invited to a pre-award meeting to discuss any desired changes to the scope of the work or other RFP requirements and any desired changes to the contractor's proposal. There was then a discussion to confirm whether or not the contractor would be willing to accept an award.[10]

If an agreement could not be reached at this stage, the procedure would be repeated for the next highest rated proposal (which could actually have been submitted by the same contractor).[11]

40. In December of 2001 the Respondent held pre-award meetings with the contractors who had been initially selected for the Nanakuli (Commercial Roofing), Aiea (Certified Construction), Kipapa (Tory's Roofing), and Lincoln (Commercial Roofing) projects, and on or about December 13, 2001, Ms. Nakatsuka prepared the Respondent's internal recommendations for awards on these projects. The recommendations, however, did not necessarily reflect the Respondent's first ranked choice for a particular project since — after the discussions at the pre-award meetings — contractors had the option of declining to accept a potential award.

41. Later in December of 2001, the Respondent held pre-construction meetings with the selected contractors in an effort to arrange for most of the work at the schools to be accomplished during the time of the students' Christmas vacation. During the latter part of 2001, Mr. Miwa and/or Ms. Kinimaka, as well as Ms. Nakatsuka, had also met with various contractors and manufacturers' representatives who were, or had been, participating in these or other PIPS projects. The contractors and manufacturers' representatives were

---

[9] Of the ten projects that had been protested by the Petitioner, the only project for which the Petitioner had actually submitted a proposal was the Lincoln project. This was due, in part, by the Petitioner's belief that its protests would have stayed all activity on the RFP and thus precluded the need to submit proposals.

[10] If there was a change in the scope of the work desired by either party it could be negotiated, but the RFP would not be reopened for the resubmission of new proposals on the new scope of work by other contractors.

[11] If none of the contractors submitting the top three proposals agreed to accept an award, or if none of the top three proposals were within budget, then other rules for selecting another proposal would go into effect.

generally supportive of the Respondent's PIPS program and were concerned about what negative impact the Petitioner's protests might have on the specific projects that had been protested as well as on the overall status of the program.

42. Once the internal recommendations for awards were approved in later December, the manner of proceeding set out in the RFP was for the Respondent to issue a letter of award to the selected contractor, followed by the contractor providing notice of its acceptance. This was to be followed by the Respondent's issuance of a notice to proceed to the contractor and, at or about the same time, the execution of a written contract (that included both a performance bond and a payment bond). These timely requirements were not followed with respect to the Aiea, Kipapa and Lincoln projects - but in their absence the Respondent allowed the contractors to proceed with work "at their own risk."

43. The Nanakuli. project was not scheduled for work until the summer of 2002, and although the Respondent continued with limited preparatory activities after the date of the Petitioner's protest, no activity took place with respect to that project after the Respondent had prepared its mid-December recommendation for an award.

44. During December of 2001 Ms. Kinimaka and Ms. Nakatsuka exercised minimal monitoring of the Aiea, Kipapa, and Lincoln projects, with routine communications between the Respondent and the contractors being handled by the inspection branch (and later the contracts branch) of the Respondent's Public Works Division. The PIPS group, however, continued with its usual practice of holding meetings and discussions about projects, protests, and other related events. Mr. Miwa, Ms. Kinimaka and Ms. Nakatsuka were aware that work was underway at these- projects, but may have still been unaware that the projects had been protested.

45. The construction activities at the Aiea, Kipapa, and Lincoln projects went forward despite the Respondent's lack of compliance with the basic, required pre-construction documentation, including the notification (and acceptance) of awards, the issuance of notices to proceed, and the execution of contracts (including bonding) for the actual reroofing work.

46. In late December of 2001 the Respondent prepared a memorandum to the State Procurement Office recommending cancellation of the projects for Wahiawa Elementary School, the Department of Agriculture Buildings C & 0, Aikahi Elementary School, Kalaheo Elementary School, and Kuhio Elementary School.[12] The memorandum in its final form was dated December 26, 2001, and was addressed from Glenn M. Okimdto, the State Comptroller, to Aaron Fujioka, the Administrator of the State Procurement Office. The preparation of such a memorandum was unusual since the procurement office was not a participant in the Respondent's PIPS program, was not a part of nor mentioned in the RFPs, and was not otherwise involved in the protest process. The memorandum's recommendation was neither approved, nor disapproved by Mr. Fujioka.

The Post-Completion Paperwork

47. In early January 2002, Mr. Miwa worked on the preparation of another unusual memorandum from the Respondent to the State Procurement Officer. Its purpose was to provide background information on the status of all of the Petitioner's protests and to request approval to cancel the protested projects as an alternative to opposing them in

---

[12] The RFP for Nanakuli, Aiea, Kipapa, and Lincoln was noticeably not mentioned in this draft (which also did not mention the RFP for Kinau Hale).

anticipated administrative proceedings. The memorandum in its final form was dated January 9, 2002, and was addressed from Glenn M. Okimoto, the State Comptroller, to Aaron Fujioka, the Administrator of the State Procurement Office.

48. In this memorandum the Respondent specifically requested approval to cancel each of the ten projects that had been protested by the Petitioner in accordance with the provisions of Hawaii Revised Statutes (HRS) § 1030-308 and Hawaii Administrative Rules (HAR) § 3-1 22-96.[13] The memorandum stated that all of the projects involved RFPs solicited under the P1PS program and that all of the protests had been made by the Petitioner. The memorandum also stated that: "Because of the protests, there has been no action on these projects since the receipt of the protests."

49. The memorandum also stated that all of the projects (except Kinau Hale and the Department of Agriculture buildings) involved reroofing projects at public schools, and that the Respondent believed "it is imperative to proceed with these projects because the maintenance of the roofs involved is critical to the health and safety of the students and faculty." The memorandum went on to say that the Respondent believed the proceedings anticipated to accompany any administrative resolution of the protests would be counterproductive to this end and commented that:

However, in order to complete these projects and in light of the Governor's order to stimulate the economy and complete as many school repair projects as possible, we were considering resoliciting these projects under the authority of Act 5, Third Special Session, 2001, which increases the small purchase limit to $250,000. These projects would then be solicited as small purchases.

50. On January 10, 2002, Mr. Fujioka signed this memorandum approving the Respondent's request to cancel all the RFPs for the ten protested projects and routed it back to the Respondent. Nevertheless, at the time Mr. Fujioka gave his approval to cancel these projects, post-protest activity on four of them (Nanakuli, Aiea, Kipapa, and Lincoln) had already taken place from November of 2001 into January of 2002, and the actual work on three of them (Aiea, Kipapa, and Lincoln) had been completed - after the receipt of the Petitioners protests but prior to the date of the memorandum.

51. The approved memorandum was later transmitted through channels to the PIPS unit where Mr. Miwa gave it to Ms. Kinimaka who passed it along to Ms. Nakatsuka. This was the first time it was seen by Ms. Nakatsuka, who was surprised by its contents since she had been unaware of the protests although she had been aware that construction had gone forward on the Aiea, Kipapa, and Lincoln projects. She expressed her surprise to Ms. Kinimaka, as well as to Mr. Miwa - Who commented that although he had not specifically stayed the projects, he thought they had been stayed as a consequence of PIPS' standard operating procedures.

52. Mr. Miwa, Ms. Kinimaka, and Ms. Nakatsuka then talked about how to handle the situation, and contacted their assigned Deputy Attorney General for guidance. Mr. Miwa also informed Mr. Matsuoka that the situation reflected violations of the procurement law, and held additional meetings/discussions to further assess the problem. At this point Mr. Miwa did

---

[13] This memorandum has been referred to and treated by the parties as constituting the Respondent's "cancellation" of the protested projects. Nevertheless, its actual language demonstrates that it was prepared and approved as a request for authorization to cancel the projects rather than constituting a cancellation.

tell Ms. Nakatsuka to stop any work on the projects, but she reminded him that final inspections had already been carried out on January 17, 2002, for the Aiea and Lincoln projects. Ms. Nakatsuka was able to notify the inspection branch to stop the final inspection for the Kipapa project which had been scheduled for January 18, 2002, but the PIPS members did not otherwise directly inform contractors — or other branches of DAGS - that all activity on the protested projects was to stop.

53. On January 15, 2002, three days before the planned final inspection date for the Kipapa project, the Respondent sent an informational letter to the Principal of the Kipapa Elementary School stating that construction on the project would be initiated shortly, that a pre-construction conference would be scheduled, and that if the contractor were to appear with the intention of starting work before the necessary arrangements were made, the contractor should be referred to the Respondent's inspection branch.

54. On the same date (January 15, 2002), however, the Respondent issued a notice of award letter to the contractor for that project - authorizing the contractor to begin work on December 26, 2001 and setting a project completion date of January 18, 2002. And, on January 16, 2002, the Respondent executed a contract for the performance of the already completed work at Kipapa - which had previously been scheduled for a final inspection on January 18, 2002. The final inspection for the Kipapa project was subsequently rescheduled for January 30, 2002.

55. Since the final inspection for the Lincoln project had resulted in a punch list of minor work to be done and/or corrected, the contractor had been given until January 31, 2002, to take care of these deficiencies. Nevertheless, on January 24, 2002, the Respondent issued an (Advanced) Project Acceptance Notice stating that "This is to serve notice that your performance of the contract[14] for the project listed above is hereby accepted as of the date noted." The notice made further reference to the "contract documents" and other documents for closing the contract. Thereafter, the project was reinspected by the Respondent on February 1, 2002 - and accepted as satisfactory.

56. Similarly, on January 31, 2002, the Respondent issued an (Advanced) Project Acceptance Notice for the Aiea project stating that "This is to serve notice that your performance of the contract[15] for the project listed above is hereby accepted as of the date noted." The notice also made further reference to the "contract documents" and other documents for dosing the contract

57 On March 14, 2002, the Respondent issued a memorandum from Mr. Okimoto to Mr. Fujioka entitled: "Report on Procurement Violation, Request for Affirmation of Contracts, and Approval of Corrective Actions projects]." The memorandum presented the Respondent's explanation that these three completed projects had been allowed to go forward because of inadvertent miscommunications, and requested after-the-fact payment approval for them. On March 18, 2002, Mr. Fujioka approved the request, and on March 27, 2002 the Respondent approved full payment (less a $1,000 retention amount) to the contractor for the Kipapa project.

---

[14] As noted above, no contract had actually been executed between the contractor and the Respondent for the Lincoln proiect.

[15] As noted above, no contract had actually been executed between the contractor and the Respondent for the Aiea project.

58. It is unclear what, if any, final payments have been made for the Aiea and Lincoln projects, but by separate memoranda dated March 21, 2002, the Respondent resubmitted its prior, internal recommendations for awards (adjusted for allowances in calculation discrepancies or breakout costs) for the Aiea and Lincoln projects, as well as for the Nanakuli project. Each of these recommendations was approved on the following day.

III.   CONCLUSIONS OF LAW

The Petitioner's request for an administrative hearing raised allegations that the Respondent had 1) based its performance rating on subjective data which was improperly inputted/calculated, 2) failed to provide a factual basis/analysis of its "in the best interests of the State" determination[16], 3) refused requests to correct mistakes in the performance ratings of itself and others, and 4) acted in bad faith during its handling of the protests. n subsequent pleadings/proceedings the Petitioner also alleged that the Respondent had generally violated the procurement code by using the PIPS program as the basis for issuing its RFPs for the protested projects.

These allegations have been evaluated in light of the requirement of the Hawaii Public Procurement Code ("Code") (HRS Chapter 1030) as set out in HRS § 1030-709(c) that a petitioner has the burden of proof to establish its allegations by a preponderance of the evidence. They have also been examined with a view toward the legislative goal of clarifying, enhancing, and simplifying procurements, as well as the requirement in HRS § 1030-101 that "All parties involved in the negotiation, performance, or administration of state contracts shall act in good faith." At the same time, the solicitation/contract/construction process for public works projects is a complicated process under even the best of circumstances, and in a time of economic downturn it is also a process which has seen both legislative adjustments in an effort to spur the economy and agency modifications in an effort to enhance program effectiveness. The focus of this proceeding was on the allegations raised by the petition and not on conducting an overall inquiry into the merit or legality of DAGS using a PIPS program for public works projects.

The Data Collection/Application for Performance Ratings

The preponderance of the evidence did show that a number of the weighting criteria which the Respondent used in developing performance ratings were inherently subjective in nature, but the fact that they involved human estimates of work quality did not. render them inappropriate or inapplicable. Not all of the measured categories lent themselves to a strict application of impersonal mechanical formulas. In addition, it was not factually established that the Petitioners own performance rating was improperly inputted or miscalculated - or that the errors which were subsequently discovered. in the performance ratings of others would have altered the rank of any of the contractors in regard to the protested projects.

In considering any deliberate actions by the Respondent to manipulate the collection of data or to improperly adjust calculations, the best that could be said is that the Respondent attempted to minimize collection errors; the use of its 15% rule and the rounding of numbers were not unreasonable; and the PIPS complex mathematical formulas were not shown to be improperly applied. Much of the frequently contradictory and contentious testimony in this

---

[16] In the absence of clarification by the Petitioner, this reference appeared to be in relation to the Respondent's use of the phrase in its January 23, 2002 "denial" letter as the basis for its proposed cancellation of the protested projects.

regard consisted of a "he said, she said, they said" type of presentation, which left no preponderance of the evidence in favor of either party.[17] Furthermore, although various contractors and manufacturers were, at one point, concerned with the potential for bias in their performance ratings, the possibility or suspicion of wrongdoing falls short of the factual evidence necessary to conclude that a violation of law has actually occurred.

The Respondent's "Best Interests of the State" Determination

Although the Respondent used the phrase "in the best interests of the State" in its January 23, 2002, "denial" letter without providing a factual basis/analysis of this determination in that letter, it is by no means clear that the Respondent was required to do so. The provisions of HRS § 1030-308, which address the cancellation of invitations for bids or requests for proposals, provides that:

An invitation for bids, a request for proposals, or other solicitation may be cancelled, or any or all bids or proposals may be rejected in whole or in part as may be specified In the solicitation, when it is in the best interests of the governmental body which issued the invitation, request, or other solicitation, in accordance with rules adopted by the policy board. The reasons therefore shall be made part of the contract file.

This provision is restated in substantially the same language in the rules adopted by the policy board. It is expanded somewhat, however, by HAR § 3-122-95(b) (Cancellation of solicitations and rejection of offers) which requires that:

> (b) The reasons for the cancellation or rejection shall:
>   (1)   Include but not be limited to cogent and compelling reasons why the cancellation of the solicitation or rejection .of the offer is in the purchasing agency's best interest; and
>   (2)   Be made part of the contract file.

The reasons for the Respondent's action in this respect, while not specified in. the January 23, 2002, "denial" letter, were clearly set out in its January 9, 2002, memorandum from the State Comptroller to the Administrator of the State Procurement Office. That memorandum requested approval to cancel all of the protested projects (as an alternative- to opposing them) because of what was, anticipated to be prolonged administrative proceedings. The memorandum also stated that most of the projects involved reroofing projects at public schools, and that it was important 'to pursue an alternative approach to the projects because maintenance of the roofs was critical to the health and safety of the students and faculty. This memorandum (although inaccurate in other respects) was retained as a file document within the Respondent's records.

The Correction of Mistakes in Performance Ratings

As noted in the above discussion regarding Data Collection/Application, the facts presented during the hearing revealed that there were instances where errors had been committed by the Respondent in the collection and/or inputting of data for the contractor and manufacturer

---

[17] Unfortunately, the inherent complexity of the PIPS mathematical formulas made it equally difficult to tell if they were properly applied, but the burden of proving otherwise rested with the Petitioner.

performance ratings. The Respondent's actions to correct such errors in past ratings, as well as the lack of impact they had in the ranking of contractors' proposals, have also been addressed above. Next, to the extent that the Petitioner is seeking a prospective order requiring the Respondent to correct past or possibly future errors that might impact on future RFPs, it does not appear that (while the Respondent should take all reasonable steps to minimize errors) such an order would be relevant to the past mistakes as asserted in this matter.

The PIPS Program within the Procurement Code

The Petitioner also alleged that the use of competitive seated proposals, in lieu of competitive sealed bids, was not allowed under the Hawaii Public Procurement Code. The provisions contained in Part III of the Code (Source Selection and Contract Formation) make it clear that, as specified in HRS § 1030-301, "Unless otherwise authorized by law, all contracts shall be awarded by competitive sealed bidding pursuant to section 1030-302 ..." This requirement is restated in HRS § 1030-302 which specifies that competitive sealed bidding is the required method of awarding contracts - except as provided in FIRS § I 03D-301. The exceptions within HRS § 1030-301, do allow the use of competitive sealed proposals but only in a manner consistent with HRS § I 03D-303[18] which specifies that:

> (a) Competitive sealed proposals may be utilized to procure goods) services, or construction which are either not practicable or *not* advantageous to the State to procure by competitive sealed bidding. Competitive sealed proposals may also be utilized when the head of a purchasing agency determines in writing that the use of competitive sealed bidding is either not practicable or not advantageous to the State.

On one hand, the evidence did not show that the use of competitive sealed bids was impractical or disadvantageous to the State. Establishing such a determination involves more than the presentation of after-the-fact, conflicting testimony offered at a subsequent administrative hearing. Similarly, there was no showing that a written determination had been made by the head of the purchasing agency that the use of competitive sealed bids was not practicable or not advantageous, as would be re4uired for making an exception under HAR § 3-122-43(b) and/or HAR § 3-122-45(b).

On the other hand, however, HAP § 3-122-45(a) provides an additional exception for such determinations by stating, in relevant part, that pursuant to subsection 103D-303 (a), HRS, the procurement policy board may approve a list of specified types of goods, services, or construction that may be procured by competitive sealed proposals without a determination by the head of the purchasing agency. This list, as provided in Exhibit A, entitled "Procurements Approved for Competitive Sealed Proposals" dated 06121/99, attached at the end of this chapter shall be reviewed biennially.

As one of its four categories of exceptions, the listing provided in Exhibit A includes "design and build public works projects." Accordingly, since the type of the protested projects was included in the approved list of exceptions, the Respondent's use of RFPs for competitive sealed proposals was an acceptable practice within the scope of the procurement laws.[19]

---

[18] Other exceptions set out in HRS §.103D-301 (professional services procurement, small purchases procurement, sole source procurement, and emergency procurement) are inapplicable herein.

[19] Other purported violations that were raised in closing arguments were not directly applicable to resolving the allegations raised in the petition and, while presenting interesting peripheral observations, were not deemed sufficiently relevant to warrant additional discussion.

Next, in examining the conduct of the Respondent after *receiving the protests*, the preponderance of the evidence established that 1) the Respondent knew or should have known about all ten of the protests, but 2) nevertheless engaged in significant and continuous activities on at least four of them over a period of many weeks after receiving the Petitioner's protests — and without any written determination by the chief procurement officer that it was necessary to do so to protect the State's substantial interests. It is noteworthy in this respect that subsection (f) of HRS § 103D-701 states that:

> In the event of a timely protest under subsection (a), no further action shall be taken on the solicitation or the award of the contract until the chief procurement officer makes a written determination that the award of the contract without delay is necessary to protect substantial interests of the State.

The major instances in which the Respondent violated this section have been highlighted in the findings of fact and need not be repeated here. It is sufficient to say that — especially with regard to the completed Aiea, Kipapa, and Lincoln projects — the Respondent acted in complete disregard of HRS § 1030-701 (f) and its conduct represented clear violations of both the RFP and the procurement law.

Whether the conduct of the Respondent in processing payment documents for the completed projects was also a violation of HRS § 1030-701(f) is less clear, since the statute appears directed toward imposing a stay on the performance of any work toward the construction/completion of a project rather than toward staying payments to a contractor for completed work not shown to have been done fraudulently or in bad faith.

The Question of Bad Faith by the Respondent

In viewing the entirety of the particulars surrounding the Respondent's handling of the RFPs *after receiving the Petitioner's protests*, the obvious focus is on its handling of the Nanakuli, Alea, Kipapa, and Lincoln projects. Of these, its handling of the Nanakuli project is the least offensive — but probably only for the reason that construction work was not planned until the summer of 2002. As a result, although some additional planning took place in violation of HRS § 1030-701(f) it was minimal in comparison to the work done on the three other projects.

Even giving the Respondent the benefit of understandable confusion between the Petitioner's October 2, 2001 letter and its superficially similar October 22, 2001 letter, and even considering the Respondent's lack of attention to preparing a punctual response to the Petitioner's protests or its follow-up requests, one must conclude that the Respondent eventually became aware that it had been proceeding on projects that should have been stayed. Precisely when this occurred is unclear, but the preponderance of the evidence showed that there was never a time when the PIPS group did not know that the Aiea, Kipapa, and Lincoln projects were going forward. Thus, the focus of the query becomes when they actually knew (rather than when they should have known) that the projects had been protested.

It is indeed possible that Mr. Miwa carefully read the second page of the Petitioner's October 22, 2001 letter and thus actually knew the extended content of that protest shortly after that date. It is equally possible that in scanning the first page he mistakenly concluded that its content was the same as the October 2, 2001 letter and paid it no more heed. The probability is that even though Mr. Miwa - and all of PIPS -unquestionably had known that work activities had never ceased on these projects, his actual awareness that the projects had been protested may not have occurred until late December of 2001 or early January of 2002. And, since he was the conduit through which such information was passed on to other PIPS members (and, in turn, from them to other parts of DAGS and/or contractors) this information may have been unknown to them prior to that time.

Nevertheless, Mr. Miwa must have realized that work was in progress on the projects *despite the Petitioner's protests* by the time he began preparing his draft of the January 9, 2002, "cancellation" memorandum from the Respondent to the State Procurement Office. This chronology would be consistent with the absence of any mention of the Nanakuli, Aiea, Kipapa, and Lincoln projects in the earlier December 2001 draft memorandum. It would also be consistent with Mr. Miwa's rather confusing statement to the PIPS members in the middle of January 2002 that he thought the projects had been stayed under PIPS standard operating procedures despite his having taken no personal action to stay them nor to coordinate a stay with Ms. Kinimaka or Ms. Nakatsuka.

Accordingly, from October 2, 2001 until early January of 2002, the most fitting characterization for the Respondent's conduct in this regard would likely include descriptive adjectives such as inattentive, incompetent, or indifferent. By comparison, however, many of the Respondent's subsequent activities — including factual misrepresentations in its January 9, 2002 memorandum to the State Procurement Officer, after-the-fact creation and issuance of award letters and contracts, and scheduling/conducting final inspections — strongly connoted that they were done by the Respondent intentionally, knowingly, and in bad faith.

The Selection of Available Remedies -

In its Request for Hearing the Petitioner sought the following relief: 1) a stay of projects that had not been completed by DAGS; 2) a termination of any contracts issued for those projects; 3) a holding that any contracts for those projects were null and void; 4) an order that DAGS correct the performance rating of the -Petitioner and other companies; 5) a finding that DAGS and certain employees acted in bad faith[20], and 6) an award of attorney's fees and costs.

A reasonable starting point in evaluating the Petitioner's requested relief would be to look at the legislative purpose behind the enactment of the Code, Its relevant history, as stated in Senate Standing Committee Report No. S8-93, 1993 Senate Journal, page 39, reveals that:

> The purpose of this bill is to revise, strengthen, and clarify Hawaii's laws governing procurement of goods and services and construction of public works. Specifically, the bill establishes a new comprehensive code that will:
>
> (1) Provide for fair and equitable treatment of all persons dealing with the procurement system;
>
> (2) Foster broad-based competition among vendors while ensuring accountability, fiscal responsibility, and efficiency in the procurement process; and

---

[20] This request for a finding (rather than a request for relief) has been addressed in the findings of fact.

(3) Increase public confidence in the integrity of the system.

Nevertheless, the legal and contractual remedies set out in Fart VII of the Code appear to severely restrict the application of just remedies, since they tend to assume misconduct by contractors rather than by government agencies, and inaccurately reflect certain realities inherent in the procurement process.

The provisions applicable to remedies after awards are contained in HRS § 103D~707[21], which reads as follows:

Remedies after an award. If after an award it is determined that a solicitation or award of a contract is in violation of law, then:

(1) If the person awarded the contract has not acted fraudulently or in bad faith:

(A) The contract may be ratified and affirmed, provided that doing so is in the best interests of the State;[22] or

(B) The contract may be terminated and the person awarded the contract shall be compensated for the actual expenses reasonably incurred under the contract, plus a reasonable profit, prior to the termination;

(2) If the person awarded the contract has acted fraudulently or in bad faith:

(A) The contract may be declared null and void; or
(B) The contract may be ratified and affirmed if the action is in the test interests of the State, without prejudice to the State's rights to such damages as may be appropriate.

In determining what relief would be appropriate for this particular matter it is worth noting that the Petitioner's main focus was the allegation that "its performance -rating under the PIPS program was incorrect (i.e., determined based on subjective evidence and improperly inputed and calculated)..." Its underlying protests at the agency level were also based "on DAGS' failure to correct Protestor's performance ratings..."[23] This allegation was not established by the evidence, however, and neither was the Petitioner's broader allegation that the Respondent should not have used the P1PS program for the protested projects. Finally, the Petitioner did not establish that it should have been selected for the Lincoln project (the only one for which it

---

[21] It would be theoretically possible to apply the "remedies prior to an award" set out in HRS § 1030-706 since no actual letters of award appear to have been issued, but the pre-award remedies provide no better offerings and are impractical in light of the Respondent leapfrogging the award stage for these projects.

[22] Determinations made by an administrative hearings officer as to "the best interests of the State" under either HRS § 1030-706 or 1030-707 are to be distinguished from determinations made by a chief procurement officer or the head of a purchasing agency as to "the best interests of the State" under HAR § 3-122-21 (a)(6).

[23] Petitioner's Request for Hearing, filed January 30, 2002, Statement of Violations and Protests, page 3.

submitted a proposal), and it is entirely speculative whether the Petitioner would/should have been selected for the Aiea and Kipapa projects if it had submitted proposals for them.

In view of the above factual findings and legal conclusions the most realistic relief compatible with the law would not appear to include a further stay of projects that had not been worked on by the Respondent nor an order that the Respondent correct the performance rating of the Petitioner and others. Nevertheless, it would appear to include termination of any post-performance contracts issued for the Aiea, Kipapa, and Lincoln projects as having been entered in violation of the law, thereby making them null and void. The ratification or affirmation - of contracts under such circumstances cannot reasonably be argued to be in the best interests of the State given the legislative purposes for the enactment of the Code. In reaching this position, consideration has also been given to the (regulatory) provisions of HAR § 3-126-38(a)(4) as well as the (statutory) provisions of HRS §~ 1030-705 to 1 03D~707 as reflected in *Carl, Id.* at 448 et seq.; despite their apparent design to address contractor, rather than government, misconduct.

In making the determination whether ratification of the contract is in the best interests of the State, the following factors are among those considered:

(A) The costs to the State in terminating and resoliciting;
(B) The possibility of returning goods delivered under the contract and thus decreasing the costs of termination;
(C) The progress made toward performing the whole contract; and
(D) The possibility of obtaining a more advantageous contract by resoliciting.

Carl, Id. at 446, citing HAR § 3-126-38(a)(4). These factors, however, are generally inapplicable in light of the nature of the work involved, the Respondent's overall conduct, and the currently completed status of the projects. In addition, while a narrow application of these factors could arguably lead to a ratification of the contracts, as being in the (technically favorable — yet unlawfully procured) best interest of the Respondent, a more meaningful interpretation/conclusion would be that termination is the preferred remedy. The Respondent's unlawful conduct should not be validated as to do so would neither be in keeping with the stated intention of the Legislature, nor truly be in the best interests of the *State*.

Nevertheless, since there was no finding that the contractors which were allowed to proceed with work on the projects had acted fraudulently or in bad faith, the provisions of HRS § 103D-707(1)(B) would entitle them to their actual expenses and a reasonable profit for their performances on the projects. This constitutes, of course, substantially the same result as a ratification or affirmation of the unlawful contracts — and illustrates the futility of applying the Code's limited remedies to instances where the violations are committed by a government agency.[24]

Finally, despite statutory language, which- would appear to preclude it, the Petitioner's

---

[24] The lack of realistic sanctions to punish governmental misconduct and/or compensate persons exposing such misconduct through the administrative process is another area where amendments to the Code appear to be sorely needed. The present set of remedies leaves little room to enhance or even enforce the Code's stated purpose of strengthening and clarifying Hawaii's laws governing procurements as well as enhancing public confidence in that system.

additional request for an award of attorney's fees and costs may present a legitimate issue for consideration in this forum. As originally adopted in 1993, the Code did not include a provision for such an order, but in addressing this issue in *Carl Corporation vs. State Dept of Educ.*, 85 Haw. 431 (1997) the Hawaii Supreme Court held that a successful protestor at the administrative hearings level was, under circumstances showing it should have been awarded a project, entitled to recover its bid preparation costs - and under circumstances showing bad faith on the part of the government agency, entitled to recover its attorney's fees, The *Carl* decision differs from the present matter in that the Petitioner herein did not show that it should have been awarded the project '(Lincoln Elementary School) for which it had submitted a proposal, but the *Carl* decision reflects substantially similar circumstances with respect to the bad faith conduct of the Respondent.

In essence, the court held that the Code did not specifically preclude an award of attorney's fees, and that under certain factual circumstances its purposes could be fatally undermined if a successful protester were required to bear the fees it had incurred in pursuing relief.

> Although the Code does not expressly authorize the award of attorney's fees under the circumstances of the instant case, interpreting MRS § 103D-704 to preclude such an award renders the Code incapable of furthering the purposes and policies that required its enactment

Carl, Id. at 460. After discussing 1) the lack of legislative contemplation on a governmental agency's bad-faith violation of the code, 2) the very limited civil enforcement mechanisms in the code, and 3) the resulting disincentives for an agency to comply with the code's procedural requirements, the court concluded that:

> ...we hold that a protester is entitled to recover its attorney's fees incurred in prosecuting its protest if: *(1)* the protector has proven that the solicitation was in violation of the Code; (2) the contract was awarded in violation of HRS § 103D-701 (9); and (3) the award of the contract was in bad faith.

Carl, Id. at 460.

The 1999 Legislature subsequently passed an amendment to MRS § 1030-7Q7[25] that added the words "other than attorney's fees" in describing the types of relief available to a person whose contract had been terminated despite no showing of fraud or bad faith on its part. While this is significant where it is factually applicable, it is limited to the provisions of that statute, and is of questionable relevance under the facts seen in both the *Carl* decision and the present matter. Furthermore, the Legislature did not amend. any portion of HRS § 103D-704 which the court had relied on for its determination that such an award was not only appropriate, but almost mandated, under such circumstances.[26] Thus, an award of attorney's fees would appear to be allowed by the court in the resolution of petitions at the administrative hearings level.

---

[25] The 1999 Legislature also passed an amendment slightly modifying the language in HRS **§** 1030.701(g), which arguably strengthened its language precluding an award of attorney's fees in the resolution of *protests* **at** *the* agency *review level* (prior to the commencement of an administrative proceeding).

[26] Not to be entirely overlooked, however, was a very well reasoned dissenting opinion in Carl written by Justices Ramil and Nakayama that reached a different conclusion.

IV. DECISION

Accordingly, it is hereby ordered that, in accordance with the above findings of fact and conclusions of law, the contracts for the Aiea, Kipapa, and Lincoln projects are terminated (although the contractors are entitled to their actual expenses and a reasonable profit for their performances), and the Petitioner is awarded its reasonable attorney's fees incurred in pursuing this matter.

DATED: Honolulu, Hawaii JUN **282002**

RICHARD A MARSHALL
Administrative Hearings Officer
Department of Commerce and Consumer Affairs

Hi-TEC Roofing Services, Inc.
PCH-2001 -2

22

University of Hawaii Case Study

Introduction

In 1998, the State of Hawaii's Department of Accounting and General Services (DAGS) implemented the Performance Information Procurement System (PIPS). DAGS immediately began noticing a difference in attitude from the contractors who were bidding the projects. As the projects were completed, the State observed significant improvements in performance, which were unlike anything that DAGS had seen before. The results of the four-year implementation of PIPS were:

1. PIPS resulted in 3% savings of overall project costs.
2. PIPS resulted in greater contractor accountability.
3. PIPS resulted in a lower number of change orders.
4. PIPS provided the State with higher quality construction.

The University of Hawaii (UH), like most other agencies, awarded projects based on the lowest cost. This had been the accepted method of ensuring that the University was receiving quality work at an affordably low cost. However, the marginal performance was requiring a high level of owner management. Projects were not completed on time, not on budget, and were not meeting quality expectations.

In 2000, Allan AhSan (Director of Facilities at the UH) implemented PIPS after recognizing the increase in construction performance that the State of Hawaii had received using the PIPS process. UH also wanted to know if PIPS could do the following:

1. Increase the quality of work.
2. Complete the projects on time, within budget, and with no contractor-cost change orders.
3. Shift risk from the UH to the contractors (that were performing the work).
4. Provide justified documentation on using best-value procurement to select a contractor / system.
5. Minimize management, regulations, qualifications, user specifications, and inspections.
6. Optimize the University's project management personnel. The UH wanted to see if it could become more efficient by doing more construction work with fewer project managers (or by increasing the number of projects each project manager could successfully manage).

What made the implementation at the UH successful was the identification of Charlie Serikawa as the PIPS project manager. Charlie was the visionary at the UH. He was searching for a process to ensure the best interest of the UH. He had many years of experience working as a project manager for a performance oriented general contractor, and was searching for a solution that would minimize the tremendous amount of management, control, and decision making of the UH engineering and construction management staff. He quickly fell in step with the PIPS process, due to his logical understanding of the construction process. He was a leader, coordinator, and facilitator of successful construction projects. When the UH decided to discontinue PIPS, and all efforts failed to implement a process like PIPS, Charlie retired and is now working as a consultant.

Implementation of PIPS by UH

The UH ran PIPS in three different areas: painting, roofing, and gymnasium sports flooring. The UH PIPS project manager (Serikawa) noticed a positive change in contractor attitude soon after PIPS was implemented. The project manager strictly followed the three basic rules of the PIPS process, which are:

1. Minimize decision-making.
2. Minimize the amount of work performed by the UH project managers.
3. Minimize risk.

Painting Projects

No technical specifications were issued on eleven painting projects. The project manager's only requirement was the desired color coordination of the buildings. The award would go to the contractor who proposed the best value, longest warranty with a proven past performance, and could offer the work within the University's budget and time constraints. This was a complete shift in the manner in which painting projects had been previously awarded. The project manager stated the contractors would be responsible for identifying what they could install, the quality they could provide, and the cost it would take to do the entire project. Some contractors, who may have been inexperienced at identifying their performance, did not participate in this process. The remaining contractors competed based on price, past performance history, and their ability to identify and minimize potential risk.

The project manager did not make any decisions during the projects. The project manager told the contractors that the minimum level of quality they should provide should be the minimum level of quality they would require if someone were painting their own homes. Once the project was awarded, the contractors began asking the project manager to check their quality of work. The project manager refused, knowing that user inspection brings risk (the contractors should be quality controlling their own work). After repeated requests, the project manager finally gave-in and performed spot-checks during walk-throughs to assist the contractors. If there were problems, the contractor immediately responded without the assistance of the project manager.

Overall, the amount of management, inspection, control, and decision-making was minimized by 80%.

A couple of lesson were learned from the painting projects at the UH. The first was that the contractors requested quality control training from the union trainers. When the author was approached on the new training requirement, the author asked if they had previously received the training in their certification. The contractors had all been trained. However, when working in the low bid award environment, the training was not utilized, and the contractors did things their own way. When the performance based environment was implemented, the contractors now wanted to be retrained. This shows that when contractors are working in the low bid environment, training does not increase the quality of the work. The second lesson was that the project manager asked the contractors to add value to the owner's buildings by identifying work that could be done more economically by the contractor while they were painting the buildings. The project managers had more funding than the projects cost. However, the contractors explained that they were used to low bidding, and that they would have to be educated in how to add value and act in the owner's best interest. The contractors had been conditioned by the low bid environment of the UH to do work fast, cheap, and according to strict directions.

Results

The results of the UH projects were consistent with other PIPS projects. The projects were finished on time (90% of jobs ahead of time), within budget (had no change orders), and with very high quality. Table 22.1 summarizes the overall results of the UH-PIPS painting projects.

Table 22-1: University of Hawaii PIPS Painting Results

No	Criteria	Results
1	Total Number of Projects Awarded	11
2	Overall Estimated Budget	$ 2,310,000
3	Total Award Cost	$ 1,658,192
4	Percent Over/Under Budget	-28%
5	Number of Different Contractors Awarded Jobs	6
6	Percent of Jobs Completed Within Budget	100%
7	Percent of Jobs Completed On Time	100%
8	Percent of Jobs Completed Ahead Of Time	90%
9	Percent of Projects Where Contractor Performed Additional (No Charge)	56%
10	Average Post Project Rating (Maximum is 10)	9.8

Table 22-2 illustrates the overall comparison of the Low-Bid process compared to the PIPS process (as identified by the UH Project manager and awarded PIPS contractors). 100 percent of the individuals stated that they were satisfied with PIPS and that they would rather use PIPS over low-bid.

Table 22-3 illustrates the evaluation of factors relating to the movement from the low-bid process to the PIPS process. The table also illustrates the percent decrease of: change orders, punch list items, specifications, design work, user inspection, and user management when moving from the low-bid process to the PIPS process. The UH Project manager and four contractors (that were awarded a PIPS project) evaluated the PIPS system.

Tables 22-4 and 22-5 analyze the perception of the contractors and the UH project manager towards the comfort levels of the different parties involved with construction procurement. This includes the analysis of Industry Training Programs, Designers, Procurement Personnel, Lawyers, Engineers, and University Leaders with the PIPS process.

Table 22-2: Overall Comparison of the Low-Bid Process and the PIPS Process

No	Criteria	LB	PIPS
1	Ability to encourage contractors to perform high quality work.	2.3	9.7
2	Overall performance of contractors.	3.2	9.1
3	Overall quality of projects procured.	3.2	9.1
4	Overall satisfaction.	2.8	9.2

Table 22-3: Evaluation of Factors

No	Criteria	Contractor Ratings	UH Ratings
1	Percent decrease in cost generated change orders	83%	75%
2	Percent decrease in the number of punch list items	96%	75%
3	Percent decrease in the amount of detailed specifications	91%	75%
4	Percent decrease in the amount of design work	17%	75%
5	Percent decrease in user inspections	63%	80%
6	Percent decrease in the amount of user management	13%	80%

Table 22-4: Comfort Levels of the Industry

No	Criteria	UH Ratings	Contractor Ratings
1	Percent that felt that the PIPS process was a fair process	100%	100%
2	Percent that felt that the Low-Bid process was a fair process	100%	33%
3	Percent of individuals that would use PIPS rather than Low-Bid	100%	100%
4	Percent that felt that there was political pressure with the PIPS process	0%	25%
5	Percent that felt that there were legal pressures with the PIPS process	100%	25%

Table 22-5: Comfort Levels of the Industry

No	Criteria	UH Ratings	Contractor Ratings
1	Overall comfort level of the contractors involved with the PIPS process.	9.0	9.0
2	Comfort level of the industry training programs with the PIPS process.	8.0	7.5
3	Comfort level of the designers with the PIPS process.	9.0	6.7
4	Comfort level of the procurement personnel involved.	3.0	7.3
5	Comfort level of the lawyers involved with the PIPS process.	3.0	4.5
6	Comfort level of the facility engineers involved with the PIPS process.	5.0	9.3
7	Comfort level of the university leaders with the PIPS process.	5.0	8.0
8	Overall acceptability of the PIPS process	5.0	5.0

Charlie Serikawa had worked for the university for approximately 15 years, and had previous experience working for a general contractor for 15 years. He stated:

> *"In all my years of construction experience (both in the private and public sectors) I have never been more impressed with a procurement process such as the process provided by PIPS. The system promotes a partnering 'win-win' scenario between the owner and the contractor that requires minimum project management resulting in on time, on budget and outstanding quality construction."*

Charlie observed that the contractors involved were extremely comfortable with the PIPS process and felt that they would rather use the PIPS process than the low-bid process in future. This indicates that high performing contractors favored the system. Charlie noted that one contractor was not comfortable with PIPS. This contractor had received awards under the low bid system, but was not being awarded any PIPS projects. The contractor was not competitive when both performance and price were considered. In addition, Charlie observed that the procurement personnel, university lawyers, facility engineers and university leaders, were all uncomfortable with the PIPS process. This is not uncommon, since individuals are afraid of change.

Conclusion

By implementing the PIPS process based on performance and price, UH procured higher quality construction projects and minimized project management requirements. The test results support the hypothesis that the low-bid award process may be the reason for poor construction performance. The high performance can be related to the minimization of project management, inspection, and specifications, which are required under the traditional low-bid environment. These results validate the Construction Industry Structure model.

The UH project manager and the majority of contractors felt very comfortable with the PIPS process and stated that PIPS resulted in a substantial increase in overall performance. However, the procurement personnel were uncomfortable with the process due to the minimization of control and procurement functions. The University lawyers were uncomfortable due to a change in thinking and their inability to understand the concepts of performance information.

The University chose to return to the low bid environment and increase project management of construction. In the past year, they have tried to come up with another performance-based process, which attempts to duplicate the results of PIPS, but have not been successful. This resulted in the retirement of the project manager who was assisting the University in implementing PIPS or a substitute performance based process. His final statement was, *"I am convinced that PIPS is the only way to go, especially for a public institution."*

The lessons learned from the University of Hawaii test case include:

1. Change must be required by the owner. The procurement officer for the University of Hawaii did not want to release the control over the contractors. Even after seeing better results from less effort, the procurement officer resisted the change. The owner must have enough information of the process to override the procurement officer's resistance to change.
2. Initial education should include the owner's legal representative. After conversing with the lawyers, it was evident to the project manager and contractors that the lawyers did not understand the concepts of information and impact of minimum standards.
3. There must be a requirement by the owner to increase construction performance.

The author proposes that based on the results of the University of Hawaii test, poor construction performance may be a result of the current bureaucratic construction delivery process and not solely poor performing contractors. Owners must hold their representatives accountable. Owners must be educated. More understanding and direction by the University administration would have increased the opportunity to make the change to performance based contracting permanent.

Chapter 22 Review

1. What was the impact of PIPS at the University of Hawaii?
2. Who did not like the PIPS implementation at the UH? Why?
3. Why did the project manager not inspect the contractors?
4. Who performed the quality control of the contractors?
5. Were the contractors comfortable with the PIPS process?
6. What was the major reason for construction nonperformance on the UH campus?
7. What were the contractors' major requests after participating with PIPS?

References

State of Hawaii (SOH) PIPS Advisory Committee. (2002). Report for Senate Concurrent Resolution No. 39 Requesting a Review of the Performance Information Procurement System (PIPS).

Serikawa, C. (2002, June 28). Letter written to PBSRG. University of Hawaii at Manoa, Facilities Planning and Management Office, Manoa, HI, USA.

Serikawa, C. (2003, July 14). Email from Charlie Serikawa to Dean Kashiwagi. University of Hawaii at Manoa, Facilities Planning and Management Office, Manoa, HI, USA.

23
State of Georgia Case Study:

Introduction

The State of Georgia is considered (by the author) as one of the failures of the implementation of PIPS. The failure was not PIPS, but in the users understanding of the process. The failure was due to the lack of a mechanism that clearly defines the plan of action in case a project is over-designed and causes contractors to bid over the stated budget.

The Georgia State Financing and Investment Commission (GSFIC), tasked with the delivery of capital construction, had been analyzing methods of increasing the value of construction (Butler 2002). The State of Georgia was also interested in implementing different delivery mechanisms. In 1999, they tested the PIPS process to increase the value of construction. Two tests were conducted. The first procurement of construction was a $45M environmental technology building, and the second was a $7.8M occupational technology facility.

The State of Georgia was made aware of the results from both the states of Utah and Hawaii through presentations at the National Association of State Facility Administrators (NASFA). It is the perception of the author that the GSFIC personnel were looking for a process to select a high performance contractor. GSFIC would then use its traditional construction delivery methodology during the construction phase. PIPS is a process that covers the selection, procurement, construction, and the performance of the constructed facility. PIPS will not work if the client does not do all three phases.

The State of Georgia case studies resulted in the following conclusions:

1. Designers do not design to minimize risk. Even though third party cost estimators are utilized, the designers do not design to minimize risk.
2. High performance construction does not cost more.
3. Clients and construction professionals may not understand the value of what they are procuring.
4. Nonperforming construction may be caused by an inefficient delivery system.
5. The Quadrant I environment of regulation, mistrust, and owner direction causes havoc with the value of construction.
6. The information environment and PIPS identifies the best performing contractor. In the two test cases, there was only one logical choice for the project.

Project 1: Environmental Science and Technology (ES&T) Building (Georgia Institute of Technology)

The scope of this project was to construct an environmental research laboratory (approximately 287,000 SF) with facilities that included laboratories, classrooms, lecture theaters, offices, and administrative areas.

The PIPS process brought high performing contractors. There were three general contractors, five mechanical subcontractors, and seven electrical subcontractors who participated. A general contractor who withdrew from the project informed the owner that the list of mechanical and electrical contractors was one of the best pre-qualifications of mechanical and electrical contractors in the City of Atlanta that he had seen. When informed that they were not short-listed, but were the contractors who responded to the project, he was amazed. This is a result of PIPS. If the invitation is unrestrained, the highest performing contractors will respond.

Three general contractors submitted bid proposals for the project. The bids were $52.6M, 54.9M, and $56.2M. Since the original budget was $45M, the architect and the University BOR claimed the contractors had inflated their costs due to the "best value" process, and they wanted the project to be awarded through a traditional low-bid process.

The author was amazed that the bid results were so far off. The designer had an independent cost estimator verifying the costs. However, two factors convinced the author that something was drastically wrong:

1. A construction professional, with knowledge of a recent completed project (similar to the facility being bid), informed the author (before bids were submitted) that the bids would come in around $52M.
2. A comparison of two of the contractors' bids (the high bidder and the low bidder) with the designer's cost estimate showed three areas (general requirements, metals, and mechanical) was off by $8.5M and $7.5M. The mechanical section alone was off by $6.7M and $5.4M.

The author followed up with the construction professional and found out that he had arrived at the $52M by taking the finished cost of the facility that had recently been completed ($181/SF) and multiplied it by the area of the new facility (287,000 SF0).

The designer did not have an objective of risk minimization. Instead the designer and the University Board labeled the PIPS process as one which increased costs. However, the GFSIC project managers identified that they had been misled by the designer. The author encouraged them to award to the low bidder since the contractors had all been over budget. However, GFSIC felt that because the award process was not clearly defined (in the case that every bidder was over budget) it may be open to protest. They decided to redesign and award using the low bid award process.

The process had been open to value engineering by the general contractors and subcontractors. However, the majority of the VE concepts were disapproved by the designer. After the bids came in, and the differential was noted, GFSIC and the designer became very open to the VE concepts. The VE concepts were bought from the contractors and used to redesign $4.5M from the project.

The project was re-bid under the low-bid process, and the new proposals came in at $46.6M, $47.0M, $47.2M, $47.5M, and $48.0M. Even though all the proposals were still over budget, the project was awarded to the lowest bidder, which was still 3% over budget ($46.6M). Coincidentally, the general contractor who was awarded the project had the lowest past performance ratings (when compared to the generals from the first round). Out of the five rated mechanicals, the winning general contractor selected the lowest rated mechanical subcontractor. Their average performance rating was 8.2 (out of 10) in comparison with the average rating of the other mechanicals that had 9.1. The winning general contractor did not select an electrical that had documented past performance information.

After the conclusion of the project, the cost of using the low-bid process can be identified. The final construction cost was $48.8M, and the project was extended over 300 days. From past experiences on PIPS implementations, the performance-based contractor had the capability to finish the project in 660 days instead of 960 days (45% earlier). If the State of Georgia had awarded to the lowest cost performance based contractor ($52.6M), with the $4.5M reduction in scope, the award price would have been $48.1M for a performance-based contractor with the best-qualified subcontractors. PIPS results have shown that performers deliver on time, on budget, and do exceptional quality work. The cost of the low bid turned out to be over $1M higher and 300 days late.

A major task in this project was commissioning, which is usually done by experts. This was made obvious by the fact that the low bid contractor was at 90% complete and still took over a year before the user could use the facility. The Quadrant I environment is managed by construction professionals. The author proposes that the construction professionals should become designers, coordinators, and facilitators of construction, and not manage and direct low bid contractors.

If PBSRG did not have a reason to track and measure the performance, it would not have been in the best interest of the University, the designer, the contractor, or GSFIC to track the performance information. This conclusion matches the previous results at the states of Utah and Hawaii and later results at DISD and the University of Hawaii. The concept that highly qualified contractors are more expensive is unproven when considering first costs and time. The author proposes that when the costs of management, control, and inspection (that clients do on low bid contractors) are added, there is no comparison. Contractors who know what they are doing get it done faster and more efficiently. They also maximize their profit.

Two sources have since contacted GSFIC to request information about PIPS and have been told that PIPS inflates prices for quality work, is not efficient, and that GSFIC is not interested in PIPS. The author encourages high quality contractors and clients who are trying to efficiently deliver construction to contact pbsrg.com to get the complete information on this project.

Project 2: Occupational Technology Building (Savannah Technical Institute)

A second test project was conducted by GSFIC, an Occupational Technology Building at Savannah Technical Institute. This project consisted of constructing two new structures on the existing Savannah campus. The first building was approximately 45,000 SF and houses industrial laboratories, classrooms, offices, faculty offices, and support spaces. The second building houses the automotive services and body repair labs, paint spray facility classroom, and supporting spaces.

The concerns of the user were that the site was located in a rural area, which might limit the number of skilled subcontractors from Atlanta and also minimize the number of bidders. GSFIC's experience with the contractors from this area was not exceptional.

After the experience of the first test project, the designer was made aware of the importance of not over-designing the project. However, the proposals still came in over the $7.8M budget ($9.4M, $9.4M, $9.7M, and $10M). Once again the designers were not minimizing risk. The designers were trying to please the client. The State then asked the contractors to bid deductibles to see if any proposals would fall within budget. The deductibles reduced the bids by an average of $1.4M.

Table 23-1 shows the performance ratings of the contractors, which includes the past performance information (of all the generals and the subcontractors), and the current capability of each company (interviews and management plans). Each rating is from 1-10 with 10 being the best.

Table 23-2 shows the final best value selection process. The best value was identified by using linear relationships between performance and price. Since the performance to price ratio was 53%: 47%, the highest performer would get 53 points (for the performance factor) and the lowest cost contractor would get 47 points (for the cost factor). The model selected Contractor 1 as the best-valued contractor. Intuitively, someone would have selected the same contractor (based on the information in Table 23-1 and Table 23-2)

Contractor 2 had the lowest rating on the management plan, and interviews. This shows a relative lack of understanding of the project by both the contractor and their key personnel. Contractor 2 is also the low bidder. Contractor 1 had the best management plan rating, best project manager interview rating, and second best site superintendent interview rating. Contractor 1's price was approximately 1% more than the Contractor 2.

Table 23-1: Contractor Performance Ratings

NO	CRITERIA	Cont 1	Cont 2	Cont 3	Cont 4
1	Management Plan	7.9	4.1	7.0	6.3
2	Project Manager Interview	8.2	6.3	8.1	7.4
3	Site Superintendent Interview	8.1	6.7	8.1	7.2
4	General Contractor Past Performance Average	9.4	8.6	8.8	9.1
5	Plumbing Contractor Past Performance Average	9.6	8.9	8.9	9.6
6	Electrical Contractor Past Performance Average	8.9	8.9	8.9	8.9
7	Mechanical Contractor Past Performance Average	9.0	9.0	9.0	8.8
8	Roofing Contractor Past Performance Average	9.1	9.1	9.6	9.1
9	Project Manager Past Performance Average	9.5	9.1	8.5	8.6
10	Site Superintendent Past Performance Average	9.6	9.1	9	8.1
	Overall Average	8.92	7.97	8.6	8.31

The following conclusions could be made:

Table 23-2: Best Value Selection (Performance vs. Price)

Rank	Contractor	Total Points	Performance Score	Performance Points	Price	Price Points
1st	Contractor 1	99.6	0.05	53.0	$8,104,000	46.6
2nd	Contractor 3	56.5	0.23	11.4	$8,371,723	45.1
3rd	Contractor 4	50.9	0.39	6.8	$8,561,000	44.1
4th	Contractor 2	50.4	0.78	3.4	$8,033,645	47.0

Construction Management

GSFIC had instructed all the bidders that a performance-based contract would be awarded. They had instructed the contractors that they would have to set up an information system that would quickly transfer information and allow the contractor to take control of the project. However, once the construction was awarded, the state issued a standard low-bid contract to the contractor. When the contractor attempted to start the project, the designer would not allow the start unless a detailed schedule was approved. When the contractor attempted to service the client, the contractor was told that he did not have the authority to make changes in the best interest of the client. When the contractor tried to give the designer training on the information system, the designer did not show up. The contractor immediately turned back to the low bid behavior to protect themselves from the owner actions.

Amazingly, without PIPS, the contractor who would have been selected was a contractor who did not understand the project. Once again, performance did not cost more. The differential between the highest and lower performers was insignificant. The highest performing critical subcontractors were also very cost competitive.

The client or building user was asked to rate PIPS (Table 23-3a & b). They were under the impression that PIPS environment was being used to manage the project. He did not understand that the designer was using the low bid environment of management and control. This is shown by his comments on the low bid system. However, his rating of the contractor was 9 (out of 10) and his comment was (Burke 2003):

"The contractor Paul Akins, Inc. made all the difference in taking a flawed system (PIPS), and making this construction experience a good one. I would strongly recommend Paul Akins, Inc. for any construction project they bid on. They exhibit a strong team-mentality combined with a professional concern for quality. I would work gladly with Paul Akins, Inc. on any future project."   - Vick Burke, Savannah Tech

Table 23-3a: User Rating on PIPS and Low-Bid process (Burke)

No	Criteria	Unit	Rating
1	Rate your satisfaction with the performance-based system of contracting (PIPS)	(1-10)*	5
2	Which process would you rather use: Low-Bid or PIPS?	PIPS/LB	Low Bid
3	Rate the ability (of PIPS) to encourage contractors to reduce the amount of management and inspections	(1-10)*	4
4a	Rate the ability (of PIPS) to encourage users to reduce the amount of management and inspections	(1-10)*	1
4b	What was the percent decrease?	%	0%
5	Rate the ability (of PIPS) to encourage partnering	(1-10)*	5
6	Rate the ability (of PIPS) to reduce the number of punch list items	(1-10)*	1
6	Would you participate in another PIPS procurement?	Y/N	Y
7	Were you satisfied with PIPS?	Y/N	N
8	Rate your satisfaction with the low-bid system of contracting	(1-10)*	7
9	Rate the ability (of the low-bid process) to encourage contractors to perform high quality work	(1-10)*	7

Table 23-3b: User Rating on the Contractor

No	Criteria	Unit	Rating
1	Rate the contractors ability to use the PIPS process	(1-10)*	9
2	Rate the contractors ability to assist you in increasing quality	(1-10)*	9
3	Rate the contractors ability to manage the project cost (minimize change orders)	(1-10)*	8
4	Rate the contractors ability to maintain project schedule	(1-10)*	9
5	Rate the contractors overall quality of workmanship	(1-10)*	9
6	Rate the contractors professionalism and ability to manage	(1-10)*	10
7	Rate the contractors ability to close out the project (no punch list upon turnover, warranties, operating manuals, tax clearance, submitted promptly)	(1-10)*	8
8	Rate the contractors ability to communicate, explanation of risk, and documentation	(1-10)*	9
9	Rate the contractors ability to follow the users rules, regulations, and requirements (housekeeping, safety, etc...)	(1-10)*	10
10	Rate your overall satisfaction and your comfort level hiring the contractor again based on performance	(1-10)*	9

* 10 = Highest score or strongly agree, 1 = lowest score or strongly disagree

This was confirmed by the contractor's ratings (Table 23-4) as he rated the low bid system unsatisfactory, with no ability to motivate to encourage skilled craftspeople, training, quality work, and that the process does not assist in making a profit. The contractor gave PIPS high marks in satisfaction, helping the contractor perform high quality work, make more profit, minimize management and inspection, and encourages partnering. He would definitely participate in PIPS again, and was satisfied with the outcome. The contractor gave high marks to the inspectors, designer, and user's project manager, but lower marks on helping the contractor, utilizing the PIPS process effectively, and minimizing bureaucracy. The contractor also made the following comments (Futch 2003):

1. The end user wanted to use all aspects of PIPS, but the state of Georgia did not change the general conditions of the contract, we really did not have the opportunity to construct or manage the project according to the PIPS guidelines.
2. We were not allowed to pursue any VE items for credits, we were forced to do additional changes at no cost. (This is the only part of PIPS that the state heard.)
3. We could not make recommendations that would change the design etc.
4. The State only used PIPS to procure a Quality Contractor to build this project, the process (PIPS) ended at the signing of the contract.

Table 23-4: Contractor Rating on PIPS, Low-Bid, and the User

No	Criteria	Unit	Rating
1	Rate your satisfaction with the performance-based system of contracting (PIPS)	(1-10)*	9
2	Which process would you rather use: Low-Bid or PIPS?	Circle	PIPS
3	Rate the ability (of PIPS) to encourage contractors to reduce the amount of management and inspections	(1-10)*	10
4a	Rate the ability (of PIPS) to allow contractors to make higher profit margins than in low-bid.	(1-10)*	8
4b	What was the percent increase?	%	1.5%
5a	Rate the ability (of PIPS) to encourage users to reduce the amount of management and inspections	(1-10)*	8
5b	What was the percent decrease?	%	5%
6	Rate the ability (of PIPS) to encourage partnering	(1-10)*	7
7	Would you participate in another PIPS procurement?	Y/N	Y
8	Were you satisfied with PIPS?	Y/N	Y
9	Rate your satisfaction with the low-bid system of contracting	(1-10)*	4
10	Rate the ability (of the low-bid process) to encourage contractors to maintain skilled craftspeople?	(1-10)*	2
11	Rate the ability (of the low-bid process) to encourage contractors to maintain training programs	(1-10)*	2
12	Rate the ability (of the low-bid process0 to encourage contractors to perform high quality work	(1-10)*	2
13	Rate the ability (of the low-bid process) in making larger profit margins	(1-10)*	1

* 10 = Highest score or strongly agree, 1 = lowest score or strongly disagree

Table 23-5a: Project Manager Rating on PIPS, Low-Bid, and the Contractor

No	Criteria	Unit	Rating
1	Rate your satisfaction with the performance-based system of contracting (PIPS)	(1-10)*	6
2	Which process would you rather use: Low-Bid or PIPS?	Circle	PIPS
3	Rate the ability (of PIPS) to encourage contractors to perform high quality work	(1-10)*	6
4a	Rate the ability (of PIPS) to encourage users to reduce the amount of management and inspections	(1-10)*	2
4b	What was the percent decrease?	%	0%
5	Rate the ability (of PIPS) to encourage partnering	(1-10)*	7
6	Would you participate in another PIPS procurement?	Y/N	Y
7	Were you satisfied with PIPS?	Y/N	Y
8	Rate your satisfaction with the low-bid system of contracting	(1-10)*	6
9	Rate the ability (of the low-bid process) to encourage contractors to perform high quality work	(1-10)*	6

Table 23-5b: Project Manager Rating on PIPS, Low-Bid, and the Contractor

No	Criteria	Unit	Rating
1	Rate the contractors ability to use the PIPS process	(1-10)*	5
2	Rate the contractors ability to assist you in increasing quality	(1-10)*	5
3	Rate the contractors ability to manage the project cost (minimize change orders)	(1-10)*	6
4	Rate the contractors ability to maintain project schedule	(1-10)*	5
5	Rate the contractors overall quality of workmanship	(1-10)*	7
6	Rate the contractors professionalism and ability to manage	(1-10)*	7
7	Rate the contractors ability to close out the project (no punch list upon turnover, warranties, operating manuals, tax clearance, submitted promptly)	(1-10)*	2
8	Rate the contractors ability to communicate, explanation of risk, and documentation	(1-10)*	6
9	Rate the contractors ability to follow the users rules, regulations, and requirements (housekeeping, safety, etc...)	(1-10)*	7
10	Rate your overall satisfaction and your comfort level hiring the contractor again based on performance	(1-10)*	8

* 10 = Highest score or strongly agree, 1 = lowest score or strongly disagree

The GSFIC project manager ratings are shown in Table 23-5a and 23-5b. He annotates that (Tremer 2003):

"PIPS would be a lot more effective if the state were committed to the process. There are no coming PIPS packages for the State and the contractors know this. There is no incentive to perform under this model."

The author concludes the following:

1. The user was happy with the performing contractor.
2. The contractor was happy with the process but was not allowed to service the owner.

3. The GSFIC was unable to create a PIPS environment. GSFIC is not committed to the program and does not understand that their delivery system may be the source of nonperformance.
4. Designers are over-designing.
5. Performance does not cost more.

Comparison to Other Low-Bid Projects

A comparison of the results of the two PIPS projects was compared with 18 projects that are currently 90% complete (GSFIC website). Table 23-6 shows that even though PIPS was not properly implemented, PIPS may have the capability to increase construction performance (by the substantial savings of cost increases). When compared to a 0% increase in cost for PIPS projects and 0% cost increase, and 96% on time record, there is a potential for higher performance, lower costs, and maximized contractor profits.

Table 23-6: Analysis of PIPS projects and Low Bid projects in Georgia (best available data)

Criteria	Savannah Tech (PIPS)	Georgia Tech	Other Project Averages
Original Contract Sum	$8,299,157	$46,595,000	$8,380,387
Adjusted Cost	$8,429,198	$48,764,990	$9,085,770
Number of Change Orders	33	89	40
Original Time (Days)	425	660	485
Time Extension (Days)	146	338	120
Percent Increase in Time	34%	45%	25%
Percent Increase in Cost	1.6%	4.7%	8.4%

Conclusion

The State of Georgia construction projects gave a unique opportunity to:

1. Compare the cost of quality vs. the cost of low bid.
2. Compare low bid performance vs. the PIPS performance.
3. Compare the perception of the user or client, the contractor, and the project manager.

These conclusions are preliminary, but agree with previous results of PIPS in that PIPS selects high performers, and that performance does not cost more. The author concludes that the user's delivery system of management, control, and low price is one of the largest sources of nonperformance.

Chapter 23 Review

1. What is the cost of performance?
2. What is the impact of high performance contractors with vision on the price and delivery time of construction?
3. What are the sources of nonperformance construction?
4. Why does performing construction seem more expensive?
5. How did the PIPS project compare to the traditional design-bid-build in terms of change orders, time, and cost increases?
6. Why did the client on the PIPS project not like the PIPS process but love the contractor?
7. Was that predictable?
8. How was the PIPS project run in the State of Georgia?
9. By going with the low bid price on the Georgia Tech project, did the State save money? Did they save time?
10. Did the designer, project manager, and Georgia Tech minimize their risk?
11. Who created the risk in the State of Georgia's projects?
12. Who were they trying to force to minimize the risk that was created?
13. What was the major source of construction nonperformance in the State of Georgia?

References

Burke, V. (2003, April 22). Survey Evaluation Form. User Evaluation of Contractor, Low-Bid Process, and Performance-Based Process. Evaluation of Paul Akins, Inc. Savannah Tech.

Butler, J. (2002, March 18). Construction Quality Stinks, *Engineering News Record*, 248, 10: 99.

Futch, G. (2003, February 12). Survey Evaluation Form. Contractor Evaluation of Low-Bid Process, Performance-Based Process, and User. Paul S. Akins Company.

Triemer, A. (2003, May 27). Survey Evaluation Form. Project Manager Evalution of Contractor, Low-Bid Process, and Performance-Based Process. Evaluation of PIPS Process. GSFIC.

24

Dallas Independent School District
Case Study

Introduction

The Dallas Independent School District (DISD) is the tenth largest school district in the United States. They have been using the design-bid-build process (typically referred to as the low-bid award process) for construction procurement. The DISD roofing program was hampered by poor contractor performance, the lack of manufacturer support, the inability to attract contractors to bid their work, and the inability to get contractors who perform high quality work.

DISD was introduced to the Performance Information Procurement System (PIPS) in 2000. The visionary person at DISD was Miguel Ramos. Near the end of his career at DISD, he wanted to ensure that DISD got the best possible value for its money. He formed a performance team made up of Mike Brown, Mike Cekosky, and Mike Smith (M&M&M). This team would become instrumental in becoming a watchdog for performance at DISD. DISD ran PIPS on nine different roofing projects in 2001. DISD tested the PIPS process to see if it could meet the following objectives:

1. Increase competition and participation of contractors and manufacturers.
2. Increase the performance of the procured roofing systems.
3. Change the attitude of the contractors and manufacturers to be more service oriented.
4. Increase value without increasing construction costs.
5. Complete the projects on time, within budget, and with no contractor change orders.
6. Shift the risk of non-performance from the DISD to the roofing contractors.
7. Provide longer and/or better warranties.

DISD Implementation of PIPS

The scope of the work was to use the PIPS process to re-roof 9 school buildings. DISD used a two-step approach. The first phase was used to have contractors and manufacturers identify their past performance and assess the risk on the 9 roofs. DISD then short-listed the best five contractors. In the second phase, the five contractors competed based on the ability to identify and minimize risk (management plan), perceived warranty value, past performance of both the contractor and manufacturer, and MWBE requirements. The Displaced Ideal Model was used to prioritize the options. DISD awarded the projects using the following award rules:

1. The 9 roofs were prioritized.
2. No contractor could receive over 33% of the roof awards (by roof area), and no system could be used on over 60% of the roofs being considered. These guidelines were put in place to minimize the risk to DISD of not receiving the roofs on time and not being biased against any specific type of roof system.
3. The roofs were awarded if one contractors was within budget and met the above two requirements.
4. If not the roof was passed over, until all the roofs within budget were awarded. DISD then picked the highest eligible contractor within the remaining budget.

Results and Analysis

The impact of using performance information was that the roofing contractors and manufacturers started servicing previous roof installations for DISD on both warranty and non-warranty issues. The DISD maintenance supervisor noted that now all contractors wanted to fix their past roofing problems (Smith 2002, Cekosky 2002). The use of performance information assisted in increasing the level of service, even before the subject roofs were being bid.

The PIPS process attracted 11 manufacturers (increase from 3 that usually bid), and 21 contractors (increase from 3 that usually bid). The difference in the level of competition obtained between the low-bid process and the PIPS process is explained in Figure 24.1.

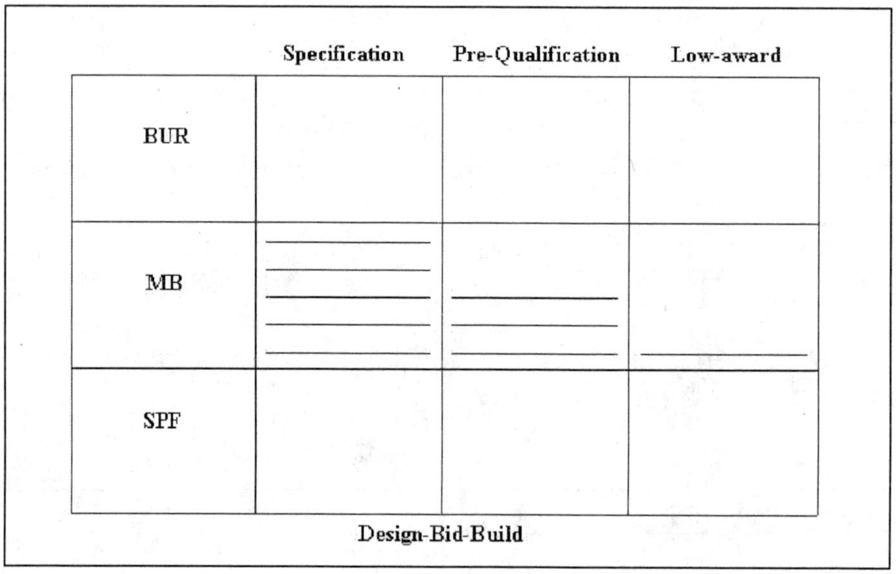

Figure 24.1: Impact of Low-Bid Specifications on Competition

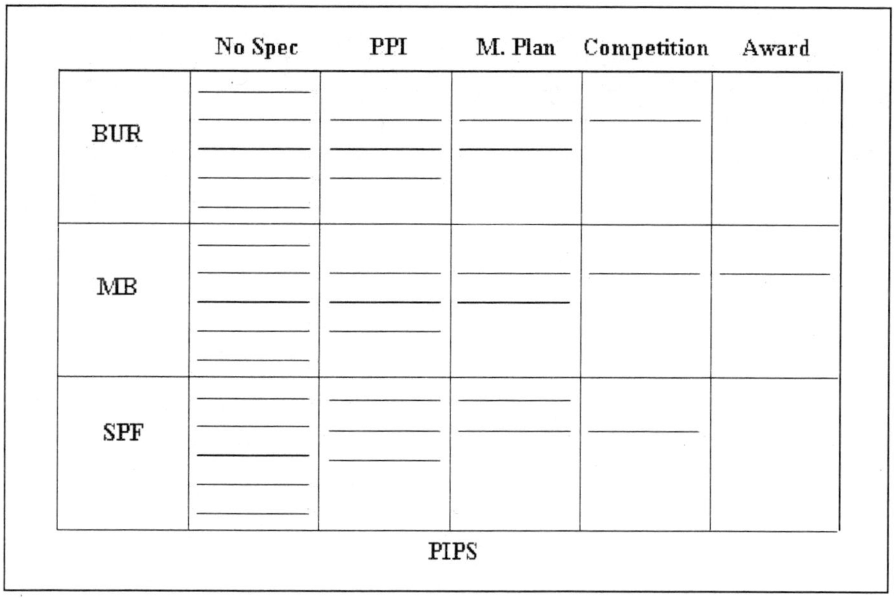

Figure 24.2: Impact of Competition Using PIPS

As shown in the figure, the specification of Modified Bitumen (MB) prevents contractors and manufacturers of other roofing systems to compete. The award is ultimately made based on the lowest price. In the PIPS process (Figure 24.2), no specifications were used except that the systems had to be a type that DISD could maintain (built up roof (BUR), modified bitumen (MB), and sprayed polyurethane foam (SPF)). The elimination of this specification assisted in increasing competition.

The first phase, pre-qualification, considered past performance of contractors and manufacturers, and their ability to identify and minimize risk. The process short-listed six bidders, which represented five different contractors (one contractor submitted two different systems).

Although allowed to submit a maximum of 40 references, the average number of references submitted was 10. The contractors and manufacturers were instructed only to turn in their best references to show the capability and potential of their systems. However, 22% of the contractors submitted references that were not satisfied. One manufacturer did not receive any of their requested references, penalizing the contractors working with that manufacturer. These preliminary results verify that contractors and manufacturers don't really know their own performance. The use of performance information causes a change in the way contractors and manufacturers look at the installation of roofing systems.

Table 24-1 below shows the award results of the DISD best value implementation. The Edison and Carver School awards are explained as an example. The results indicate that Edison was awarded to the highest ranked bidder, which was Contractor 17. Contractor 17 was the highest ranked proposal on the next project (Carver). However, if they were awarded this project they would have exceeded the 33% (by total square feet) rule. Therefore, Contractor 10, the next highest prioritized, was awarded the project.

Table 24-1: Award Results of the DISD Best-Value Implementation

School	1st	2nd	3rd	4th	5th	6th	Budget
Edison	CONT 17 $ 875,818	CONT 10 $ 1,084,712	CONT 27 $ 1,133,200	CONT 30 $1,017,998	CONT 32 $ 1,835,664		$ 1,153,634
Carver	CONT 17 $ 474,418	CONT 10 $ 428,540	CONT 27 $ 541,300	CONT 30 $ 545,820	CONT 32 $ 461,415	CONT 29 $ 560,000	$ 548,347
Madison	CONT 17 $ 575,799	CONT 10 $ 703,571	CONT 27 $ 589,300	CONT 30 $ 673,276	CONT 32 $ 936,517		$ 587,336
Johnston	CONT 6 $ 447,000	CONT 10 $ 654,378	CONT 17 $ 509,719	CONT 27 $ 635,000	CONT 30 $ 580,846	CONT 32 $ 790,663	$ 716,928
Donald	CONT 10 $ 187,054	CONT 17 $ 155,694	CONT 6 $ 178,000	CONT 30 $ 186,498	CONT 27 $ 244,700	CONT 32 $ 281,746	$ 175,576
Long	CONT 17 $ 425,281	CONT 10 $ 529,801	CONT 27 $ 501,500	CONT 30 $ 512,752	CONT 32 $ 875,750		$ 437,080
Foster	CONT 10 $ 352,770	CONT 17 $ 328,086	CONT 6 $ 368,500	CONT 30 $ 388,502	CONT 27 $ 595,900	CONT 32 $ 608,617	$ 434,444
Auburn	CONT 10 $ 406,531	CONT 17 $ 365,981	CONT 6 $ 533,000	CONT 30 $ 420,989	CONT 27 $ 487,700		$ 434,120
Macon	CONT 10 $ 366,445	CONT 17 $ 295,739	CONT 6 $ 334,200	CONT 27 $ 397,600	CONT 30 $ 353,588	CONT 32 $ 373,174	$ 336,892

*Shaded cells represent awarded contractor.

The award results show that:

1. Price is comparable: All roofs were awarded for 14% under the total budget (which was based on previous low-bid awards).
2. Proposed performance is very high: All bids included treatment of, not only the roof, but treatment of surrounding facia, parapets, walls, penetrations, and windows (unless directed by the DISD to not consider). All bids included the waterproofing of the buildings. This included coordination with the schools, minimization of any problems occurring during the reproofing, and the aesthetics of the project. It also included the design. All warranties were enforceable from 15-25 years.

During the construction of the roofing, the project engineer, roofing consultant, and roofing maintenance manager recognized the following:

1. Roofing contractors met with unknown, hidden conditions. In most cases, they took care of the problem without additional costs. This included repair of walls, repair of insulation, installation of new expansion joints, installation of new flashing, painting, removal of hardened tar, and the cleanup of water penetrating the building for one reason or another.

2. Roofing solutions that were previously unknown to DISD, including flashings, parapet treatments, and penetration treatments, were implemented.
3. Contractors who had not performed under the low bid process, were much more cooperative, perceptive to details, and provided quality work which was not commonly received under the low-bid system.

After the completion of the roofing projects, the project manager and maintenance manager were asked to compare the traditional design-bid-build process with PIPS.

The following can be noted based on their feedback:

1. PIPS results were rated a "10," and the design-bid-build was rated a "1" (10 being highest).
2. Both wanted to use the PIPS system again.
3. PIPS was rated a "9" to motivate high performance, design-bid-build was rated a "1" (10 being highest).
4. PIPS was rated a "9" to minimize management and inspection. The amount of reduction in management and inspection was estimated at 72.5%.
5. PIPS also rated an "8.5" to encourage partnering and reducing punch list items.

Conclusion

DISD achieved all their goals: High quality, high competition, and no increase in cost. The results of the test propose that the design-bid-build process may be the source of construction non-performance. The vision of Miguel Ramos was validated, and may move to other schools in the Dallas area. The DISD core group (Smith, Cekosky, and Brown) minimized quadrant I functions of control and management. The DISD case study validates the following concepts:

1. Performance does not cost more.
2. PIPS increases competition.
3. PIPS minimizes management and inspection.
4. Performing contractors and manufacturers know what they are doing.

Chapter 24 Review

1. What was the immediate impact on DISD of changing to a PIPS environment?
2. Did performance cost DISD more?
3. What were other effects of the PIPS implementation?

References

Cekosky, M. (2002, November 6). Letter written to PBSRG. Specialist III Facilities Planning, Dallas Independent School District, Dallas, TX, USA, 6 November 2002.

Kashiwagi, D.T. (2001). *PIPS/IMT Manual*. Performance Based Studies Research Group, Arizona State University: Tempe, AZ, USA.

Kashiwagi, D.T. & Mayo, R.E. (2001). Best Value Procurement in Construction Using Artificial Intelligence. *Journal of Construction Procurement*, 7 [2], pp. 42-59.

Kashiwagi, D.T. & Mayo, R.E. (2002). Case Study of Potential Impact of Subjective Decision Making on Construction Performance. *Journal of Construction Procurement*, 8 [2], pp. 101-116

Shearer, R. (2000, September). Hold Architects Accountable. *Engineering News Record (ENR)*, 245 [9], p. 83. New York: McGraw-Hill.

Smith, M. (2002, November 6). Letter written to PBSRG. Maintenance Supervisor, Dallas Independent School District, Dallas, TX, USA, 6 November 2002.

25

State of Washington Case Study:
How to Implement An Information Environment in the Low-Bid Quadrant

Introduction

Many government groups are constrained by the legal requirements of the low price award. The State of Washington is one of these owners. The State of Washington identified their environment with the following characteristics:

1. 20% of their contractors cause 80% of their nonperformance.
2. Although their construction quality could be better, 80% of the construction is on time, on budget, and meets expectations.
3. There is a perception that the State of Washington construction management services may not be optimized, but no one can quantify the area of inefficiency.
4. State of Washington project managers (PM) are managing some of the projects.

How to Implement Performance Information to Raise Performance in the Low-bid Environment

There are two ways to establish the Quadrant II environment in a low bid environment:

1. Procure a Job Order Contractor Services (JOC), and force the JOC contractor to run the JOC using PIPS.
2. Use the performance concepts to create a performance-based environment.

A JOC contractor can be procured usually by performance and price. The owner should make it a requirement that the JOC contractor use PIPS or another performance-based system with documented performance. The unit prices become the budget, and every contractor is forced to perform similar to Quadrant II.

The other option is to establish an environment using the performance concepts. Quadrant I is different from Quadrant II (performance based) because performance information cannot be considered to select, disqualify, or punish a contractor. There are only two ways to require performance:

1. Change the policy based on performance information to disqualify nonperformers.
2. Move to a performance based procurement system.

The Quadrant I environment is not performance-based because the owner is regulating and forcing the contractors to perform. Quadrant II is performance based because:

1. Quadrant II has performance information.
2. The contractors are forced to minimize risk and therefore, nonperformers who cannot minimize risk do not enter the environment.
3. The environment forces contractors to use performance information to self manage themselves. Non-performers can neither effectively collect nor use performance information to minimize risk.

Performance Information

The author proposes to take these concepts into the low bid environment. The problem with the low bid Quadrant I environment is the lack of performance information (which causes confusion). No one knows who is truly at fault. Everyone has a different perception. The client, the project manager, the contractor, the inspector, the manufacturer, and the facility manager all have different points of view. The source of the problem could be anyone. The perception is that because it is a low-bid environment no one cares. This could not be farther from the truth. Performance information should be kept in the low bid environment. It should be kept on all parties who have an impact on the construction performance.

If a project manager wants to increase performance in the low-bid environment, they must first find out who is the source of the nonperformance. To arbitrarily blame the contractor would not be wise. Every party is at risk and should keep performance numbers. The project manager should keep performance numbers on all contractors (on time, minimized change orders, and meeting quality expectations). The project manager is at risk only because the contractor is not performing. If the project manager can prove that this contractor is not performing because they have never performed, cannot perform, and will not perform in the near future, the project manager puts the policy maker at risk. The policy maker can change the policy and disqualify nonperformers, allow pre-qualification, or accept the poor performance and the fact that the project manager cannot change the contractor. In either case, the poor performance of the contractor no longer can be blamed on the project manager.

The above action will put the policy maker and the nonperforming contractor at risk. The policy maker must now explain to the client and others why they continue to allow poor performing construction. The policy maker will then change the policy to eliminate the contractor. This puts the contractor at risk. They must now change and perform. However, it may not be the contractor who is at fault. In a large number of the cases, PBSRG has identified the owner as the source of nonperformance. The contractor must therefore minimize their risk by keeping performance numbers on the client and anyone else who is preventing the contractor from performing. This number is a combination number that will measure time and money. Remember, quality is governed by standards in Quadrant I. The contractor will multiply time delays by the cost of the action. If the client, project manager, or inspector has a relatively large influence or risk number, the contractor can move the risk to that person.

The bottom line, every component at risk must keep performance information. The performance information will transform Quadrant I to a modified Quadrant I halfway, between I and II.

Minimization of Risk

In Quadrant II, any contractor who cannot identify, prioritize, and minimize risk, will not have a competitive chance to get the award. In Quadrant I, this ability to minimize risk must be forced. It cannot be forced before the bid award, as in Quadrant II. It must be applied after the award in a pre-construction review.

The designer will identify a pre-construction review phase where the contractor will be given an allotment. The contractor will then perform the same function as during the pre-award phase in Quadrant II. If the contractor comes up with too many cost increase change orders that seem unreasonable, the contractor will be paid the allotment, the contract will be terminated, and the project will be re-bid.
If the contractor does not identify any un-constructible or problem areas, the contractor will assume the risk. The task of the pre-construction review includes:

1. Destructive testing.
2. Coordination of drawings.
3. Identification of anything that cannot be constructed or made to perform.
4. This process forces the contractor to take responsibility for potential risk and makes it difficult for the contractor to later make claims.

Contractors who can do this function easily or who already do this, will have the advantage. Contractors, who cannot do the pre-construction review, will have to spend more resources to do the review. Also, they can no longer bid low, hoping to recoup their profit through change orders. The impact of the pre-construction review will result in an even playing field. This will stop the low bidding contractors who are inexperienced.

Contractors Manage Using Performance Information

The difference between contractors in Quadrant II and I is that in Quadrant II, the contractors:

1. Use performance information.
2. Measure their risk.
3. Plan ahead.
4. Minimize risk.

The contractors in Quadrant I must be forced to do the same functions. If they cannot, they should be identified as contractors who cannot manage their own construction, and be disqualified (for being a non-responsible bidder). The assumption is that if a contractor manages their project using performance information, they will perform. Therefore, the objective is to make the contractor manage themselves. The following will be done:

1. *The risk of nonperformance will be moved to the contractor.* The contractor should be forced to manage his or her own construction using performance information.
2. *The contractors will document their own performance* in terms of on time, on budget with any change order information, and meeting expectations in terms of quality. The contractors will document this in terms of risk.
3. *The amount of information passed to the owner will be minimized.* The information will be in terms of numbers and short bullet descriptions on a spreadsheet.
4. *Only the information at risk will be checked by the PM (20%).*
5. *PM will have a weekly report of performance* on both their PM function and the contractors. The information will be passed on a weekly basis by e-mail attachment. The attachment will be automatically sent to a directory, where a database will absorb the information. The information will then be processed in terms of risk.
6. *The project managers will check the projects at risk,* and verify correctness. The percentage of times the contractor does not submit information, or is incorrect with the information, will be annotated in the contractor's file.
7. *Contractors who do not manage their own projects will be disqualified* from future bidding. Management of projects will be defined as 90% accuracy and reporting at least 90% of the time.

This simple information process will provide updated non-technical performance and risk information in a compact format on a continuous basis with minimal effort from the PM function. It will also identify the PM function performance with the latest updated information. It will identify the contractors which are inexperienced and which require assistance in managing their projects. It will also generate a minimum requirement of management on the project (by use of performance information). The results of the implementation of the information system will test the hypothesis, that in an information environment, the performance of all functions will increase. It will also identify if the minimization of management will lead to an increase in construction and project management performance.

The project manager will have assistance in identifying which projects are at risk. A contractor response information system (CRIS) will receive the reports on spreadsheets from the contractors on a weekly basis. The database will prioritize the project manager's projects by risk (time, cost, expectation).

Conclusions

The concepts that make Quadrant II a performance-based quadrant can be applied in Quadrant I. The concepts are:

1. Collect performance information.
2. Force contractors to minimize risk.
3. Force contractors to manage their project using performance information.

The client's project manager should let the contractor document all risk. They should force the contractor to always carry their risk report, and they should use CRIS to identify which projects are at risk and manage them more closely.

Chapter 25 Review

1. What does this chapter assume is the largest source of construction nonperformance?
2. What is the performance information used for in the low bid environment?
3. Who keeps performance information in the low bid environment?
4. What are the two largest implementations of performance information in the low bid environment?
5. What are two impacts of the performance information in the low bid environment?

Attachments

Attachment 25.1: CRIS Instructions

Attachment 25.1: CRIS Instructions

Contractor Response Information System (CRIS)

Overview

For an information-based system to work in any environment there must be three components for the project manager: less work, less decision-making, and less risk. If the system does not posses all three factors, the system will not be sustainable over a long period. Based on this concept and on previous case studies (performed by PBSRG), research has shown that contractors who do not manage their projects and do not plan ahead to minimize risk have a higher risk of nonperformance. It is difficult to determine if a contractor is managing their work. PBSRG proposes if a contractor is managing their work, they are doing the following:

1. Documenting where they are in terms of schedule.
2. Identifying risk of nonperformance in terms of money, time, and expectations.
3. Documenting risk and change orders on a continuous basis.

When used in conjunction with the pre-construction review, the contractor is forced to do the above tasks. If they cannot do it, they will not be able to efficiently manage their projects, and someone else will be forced to manage them.

Rather than use past performance as a pre-qualification requirement, the PBSRG proposes identifying low-performing contractors by measuring their lack of ability to manage a project. To accomplish this, a construction interface system should be created with the following goals:

1. Force contractors to manage and accurately document their projects based on performance information on a continuous basis (weekly).
2. Be capable of identifying contractors who cannot manage their projects.
3. Be sustainable (must not create additional work for the user).
4. Be able to define the nonperforming contractor as non-responsible.
5. Be capable of identifying how less responsible contractors bring risk, and how they impact the overall performance of the DEAS.

Construction Interface

To make the system sustainable, the project manager and the performing contractors who manage their construction should minimize additional work. Since contractors must manage their own work, the system requirement will be for the contractors to send weekly status updates of their projects. The information will be contained in a spreadsheet program and then e-mailed once a week for the duration of the project. The information required (performance and risk information) will be information that a performing contractor already collects. The information collected in the weekly spreadsheet file should include:

1. Award information (project ID, original completion date, estimated budget, and award cost).
2. Current completion date.
3. Current overall project cost.
4. Number of change orders (approved and not yet approved) in terms of cost and time.
5. Number of scope changes and the total cost of the changes.
6. Potential risk items, including possible unforeseen conditions, schedule items, and public relations items.

Once this information is sent into the owner, a database program automatically compiles all of the contractor spreadsheets and analyses the information to generate the following reports:

1. An executive summary: This includes information such as total number of projects, total number of projects updated/not updated, total number of projects with low/high risk (to schedule, cost, and submission of the report), and total risk to DEA in terms of $ and time.
2. Prioritized projects with high risk: This includes project information such as percent behind schedule, percent over budget, percent of missing reports, cost of change orders, and days behind schedule.
3. Project manager summary: This includes information on the performance of each project manager such as the total number of projects being managed, total cost, risk percentages (cumulative risks on all projects they manage), change order costs, and total days behind schedule.
4. Contractor summary: This includes information on the performance of each contractor including the total number of projects awarded, total cost, risk percentages (cumulative risks on all projects), change order costs, and total days behind schedule. The risk percentages also indicated the percent of times the contractor did not submit a weekly report.

Figure 1 shows an example of how the system may work. The first step is for the contractors to e-mail their files to the project managers and to the database e-mail address. A program takes the report from the e-mail account, strips the data off the email, and sends the data to a database. The project manager reviews the projects at risk. If an inaccuracy is found, the project manager has the option to send an updated file to the database replacing the contractor's file. The PM is also required to identify the report as inaccurate. The information is uploaded into the database weekly. Final reports are then generated. This is one manner in which this process may work. There are other methods, such as creating an online website, which may also perform the same functions in a similar manner.

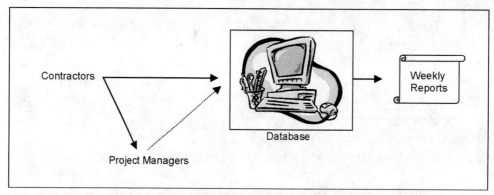

Figure 1: Steps Involved With the Contractor Interface System

From past experience, there are select groups of contractor that do not (or cannot) manage their projects. They do not document performance information, do not minimize risk, and do not think ahead. These are the contractors that the interface will identify as not responsible. Since these contractors do not manage their projects, they will have a difficult time quantifying the performance and risk information. PBSRG recommends that a responsible contractor be defined as one that manages their construction and documents the performance and risk information as part of their management. This is measured by the following:

1. Submitting their weekly project reports at least 90% of the time.
2. Submitting accurate information at least 90% of the time.

If a contractor cannot manage their project, they will be identified and be listed as not responsible. To reapply, they should be required to show the management capability on a similar scope of project by showing their log of spreadsheets with the reports throughout the project (90% of the time, 90% accurate). The owner should verify the information with the owner that they serviced. This document will go through how the CRIS database works.

Project Details

This button navigates to a screen providing information on various projects available in the database. Also, this screen can be used to enter details of a new project.

View / Add New Project

Projects can be viewed one at a time by using navigation tools at the bottom of the screen. *Find Record* button enables searching the desired project based on *Project ID*. Following are the steps to search a particular project:

1. Click the *Find Record* button.
2. In *Find What,* key in the project ID. In case the exact project ID is not available, select *any part of field* in the *Match* drop down.
3. Click *Find Next* button.
4. To search a project based on some other particular instead of project ID, place the cursor on that particular box and follow steps 1 through 3.

For adding a new project, blank form can be made available by clicking ▶* at the bottom of the screen. For maintaining data integrity, *ProjectID* and *Start Date* should are required at the minimum.

Note: *Project Completed* check box indicates whether the project is in progress or completed. By default, the project is in progress (*Project Completed* unchecked). On completion, *Project Completed* should be checked. Completed projects do not count in calculations for reports.

Import Current Data

Project data sent by contractors in MS-Excel files are stored in *Files* under *CRIS* folder. The data in these MS-Excel files can be imported into the CRIS database using the Import Data button on the main screen.

Importing current data into the database flushes out previous week's data. There is a built-in feature in the database to create back-ups of data from each week.

Note:

1. Importing data into the database typically takes a few minutes. "Data Successfully Imported" message indicates that data is now available in the database.

2. All the MS-Excel files received from Project Managers should be saved in Files folder. Please do not alter the contents of Data folder.

Import Data From Previous Weeks

This feature enables calling data from previous weeks. Note that whenever current week's data is imported into the database, data from previous week is flushed out and stored in a separate location. In case, old data needs to be recovered for reporting purpose, backed-up data can be imported into the database with the help of this feature.

A list of all dates corresponding to all previous data will be available in the *Backup Date* box. Selecting a particular date and clicking the Import button instantly imports data corresponding to that date. All reports will now be linked to this imported data.

Reports

All the management reports that we want to generate can be obtained by clicking on the reports button. Once you click on this button, you will reach a new menu as described in Figure 2.

Executive Summary

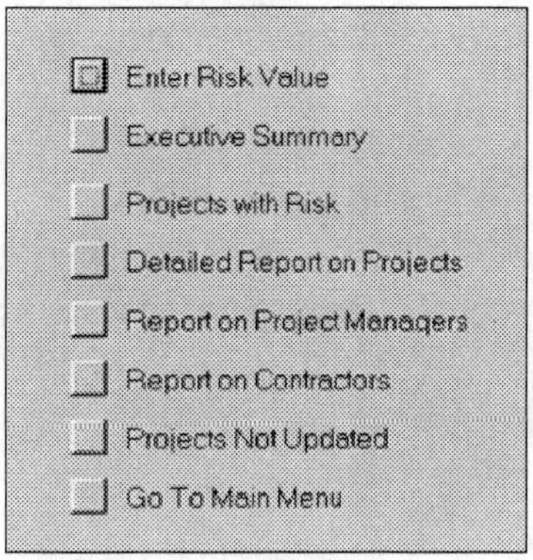

Figure 2: Menu

The Executive Summary gives an overview of total risks to various projects in progress.

If updates for some projects are not available at end of the prior week, *Projects without updates this week* indicates the number of such projects and the total award amount for these projects. Quantification of risk items would give a wrong picture of overall risks in absence of latest data. Hence, risk items are not indicated for projects without latest updates.

Risk is quantified for projects that have most current updates available. Based on level of risk, these projects are into following categories:

1. No risk
2. Risk to schedule only
3. Risk to cost only
4. Risk to reports only
5. Risk to schedule and reports
6. Risk to schedule and cost
7. Risk to cost and reports
8. Risk to schedule, cost and reports

Here, a project is considered to have risk associated with it if the risk is greater than or equal to risk value that we have entered.

Executive Summary		
Date 6/20/2003		Risk Value = 4 %
	Number of Projects	Award Amount (in thousands)
(a) Total Number of Current Projects	48	$21,556
(b) Projects Updated	35	$15,801
(c) Projects Not Updated	13	$5,755
(d) Projects With low risk	1	$101
(e) Projects with high risk	34	$15,699
- to schedule only	1	$201
- to cost only	1	$222
- to report only	5	$3,207
- to schedule and cost	1	$301
- to schedule and report	16	$9,117
- to cost and report	1	$501
- to schedule, cost and report	9	$2,150

Projects With Risk

This report provides a list of projects that have risk associated either to cost, schedule, reports or any combination these three. All these projects have risk greater than or equal to risk value that we have entered for at least one of cost, schedule or missing reports. Risk details on each project are available in *Detailed Report on Projects with Risk*.

Detailed Report on Projects with risk

This report details the risk % for the various projects. These are the projects for which prior-week update is available.

Detailed Report On Projects With Risk							
Date	6/20/2003					Risk Value =	4 %
Project ID	**Project**	**Risk% (+/-)**			**Days Ahead/Behind (+/-)**	**Change Orders**	
		Schedule	Cost	Missing Reports		($, thousands)	
100-120	Daniel School	33%	29%	94.1%	120 days	4	
100-110	Will Elementary	25%	36%	94.1%	92 days	5	
100-103	Elementary	36%	15%	0%	55 days	50	
100-102	Associated	40%	0%	0%	61 days	6	
100-107	Dept.	30%	3%	94.1%	110 days	50	
111-345	Daniel Webster Elementary	30%	2%	94.1%	110 days	50	
100-122	Rich Bldg	22%	9%	94.1%	82 days	23	
100-123	Sid Science Bldg	25%	4%	94.1%	92 days	25	
100-118	Communication Ctr	27%	-1%	94.1%	100 days	0	

Report on Project Managers and Contractors

This report provides status overview on projects managed by the various project managers. The list is arranged in descending order of total risk. The contractor report is identical to the project manager report.

Report On Project Managers

Date   6/20/2003   Risk Value =   4 %

Project Manager	Projects	Total Award Cost ($, thousands)	Risk% (+/-)			Days Ahead/Behind	Change Orders ($, thousands)
			Schedule	Cost	Missing Reports		
Kathy Welch	4	1,396	89 %	38 %	94.05 %	326 days	92
Angus McDonald	3	974	73 %	12 %	94.05 %	268 days	98
Mickey Hillock	2	665	36 %	38 %	94.05 %	131 days	55
Michael Hegman	4	3,088	63 %	8 %	94.05 %	229 days	173
Charles Addington	3	1,843	63 %	4 %	94.05 %	229 days	30
Steve Bostick	3	524	40 %	15 %	0.00 %	61 days	49

Projects without updates

This report provides a list of projects not updated at the end of prior week.

26
The Last Frontier

Conclusion

It took ten years to write this manual and run PIPS 380 times on $230M of construction. It will take only five more years to triple those numbers and locations. I could not have done this alone. It took:

1. Bill Badger, who allowed the author to go outside of the box and challenge the conventional processes in construction. His only rule was there are no rules.
2. Ron Campbell, who used PIPS to select contractors at United Airlines without specifications. He challenged the corporate engineers who were spending hundreds of thousands of dollars to do feasibility studies on writing better specifications.
3. Richard Byfield, who took the risk of using PIPS on the $53M Olympic Village Project.
4. Gordon Matsuoka, Steve Miwa, and Chris Kinimaka, who had great courage to run PIPS at the State of Hawaii in an environment of great political agendas.
5. Charlie Serikawa, who proved that PIPS could be more effective than the control and inspection efforts of the procurement and engineering staff at the University of Hawaii.
6. Mike Steele and Thom Tisthammer, who designed the Alpha program to make monumental changes in the sprayed polyurethane foam roof industry.
7. Miguel Ramos, who brought PIPS to the Dallas Independent School District to increase the value of construction that it deserved.
8. Ed Maxey and Mark Bollig, who went out on a limb to bring PIPS into the hospital arena by selecting designers.
9. Kevin Freese, Jamie Ho, Gaylyn Nakatsuka, Mike Smith, and Mike Cekosky, who shared the dream of bringing best value to the owner and maximizing the profit of the contractor.

The last frontier is the total optimization of the delivery of construction. It is to create a totally efficient process. The owner must get best value. The contractor must maximize their profit. The environment invariably will be information based. No optimization will occur without continuous improvement and measurement.

The worldwide marketplace is forcing the optimization of all functions. The delivery of construction is no different. As processes become more efficient they needs less management, control, and regulation, and becomes self-regulating. An optimized process is in an openly competitive marketplace. Due to the unlimited resources available worldwide, any constraint is artificially created. Those who see this future environment of efficiency are visionary. These are those that have tremendous experience, information, and understanding of the construction industry and the delivery of construction. These people have a commonality: they have the same vision, the same dream.

The Dream

The visionaries all have the same dream. We must become efficient to bring best value to the owners and maximize the contractors' profits. PIPS and IMT are new concepts with a familiar voice of logic. It is the personal commitment to excellence and adding value to others that will push those with the dream to bring change. The tools of change are PIPS and IMT.

IMT states that an efficient environment will have:

1. High performance.
2. Responsibility.
3. Minimized management.
4. High degrees of leadership.
5. Win-win.
6. Efficiency.
7. Quality control.
8. High value.
9. Predictability.
10. Continuous improvement.
11. Constant measurement.
12. Free competition.
13. Performance information.
14. Maximized profit.

PIPS may be ahead of its time. But as the competitive marketplace becomes more competitive, the demand for the visionary who can be an "information worker" will become greater. The competition will shine the light on every function, forcing everyone to identify what they do and how much value they bring. The future belongs to the visionary leaders and the performers. There will be very few middlemen. PIPS turns managers into leaders without all the leadership qualities that are born with leaders. The information system will hire the right people for the right job, requiring very little management and decision-making. The performers will all do their jobs as if they were following a great leader.

Reality is not magical. Great leaders perceive the reality around them. They have a natural gift to perceive. They constantly are focused on others, ensuring that everyone succeeds. They are great examples of patience, understanding, and success. PIPS brings the same results. Information workers who use PIPS will become as successful as great leaders. Leaders and information environments are synonymous. And because the majority have a difficult time understanding leadership and information work, those that do, are truly visionary.

Every visionary who applies PIPS will bring the future to us that much quicker. PBSRG will be the gathering place for visionaries. PBSRG will create a synergy between visionaries. PIPS is not only for the procurement of construction, it is the solution to any outsourcing or supply chain management problem. It is the method to outsource procurement itself. To control without controlling, to manage without managing, to react without reacting. This may have seemed impossible ten years ago, and may still seem impossible to many in construction management with 25 years experience, but it will become a reality in ten more years. Thanks to all those who have shared the dream, who have lived the dream, and who now know that their efforts have not been in vain and that their dream is alive.

Dean Kashiwagi